INTERTEXTUAL
PURSUITS

INTERTEXTUAL PURSUITS

Literary Mediations in Modern Spanish Narrative

Edited by

Jeanne P. Brownlow
and John W. Kronik

Lewisburg
Bucknell University Press
London: Associated University Presses

Associated University Presses
440 Forsgate Drive
Cranbury, NJ 08512

Associated University Presses
16 Barter Street
London WC1A 2AH, England

Associated University Presses
P.O. Box 338, Port Credit
Mississauga, Ontario
Canada L5G 4L8

The paper used in this publication meets the requirements
of the American National Standard for Permanence of Paper
for Printed Library Materials Z39.48–1984.

Library of Congress Cataloging-in-Publication Data

Intertextual pursuits : literary mediations in modern Spanish narrative / edited by Jeanne
P. Brownlow and John W. Kronik.
    p. cm.
Essays in honor of H. L. Boudreau.
Includes bibliographical references and index.
ISBN 0–8387–5370–1 (alk. paper)
    1. Spanish fiction—20th century—History and criticism. 2. Spanish fiction—20th century—Themes, motives. 3. Intertextuality. 4. Influence (Literary, artistic, etc.)
I. Brownlow, Jeanne P., 1937– . II. Kronik, John W. III. Boudreau. H. L. (Hal L.)
PQ6144.I58   1997
860.9'006—DC21   97–19958
                                                  CIP

PRINTED IN THE UNITED STATES OF AMERICA

To H. L. Boudreau

The authors and editors warmly dedicate this volume to a friend and colleague whose critical insight has left a permanent imprint on the discipline of Hispanic studies. Always in the vanguard of literary thought, he proclaimed the intertext before many of us knew the meaning of the word.

Contents

The Death and Life of Intertextuality:
An Introduction

A September 1994 issue of the *New York Times Magazine* quoted John Guillory's opinion that the "project of intertextuality—understanding relations between texts across time—has been more or less abandoned in the profession" (Begley 1994, 35). In other words, intertextuality is dead, and we need no longer be mindful of it. Like most opinions, Guillory's is based on one of the innumerable existing presuppositions about the nature of the project described: that intertextuality is linear and relational, that it requires immediate understanding, and that it in some sense animates or articulates the connective tissue between two participating texts in a transhistorical dialogue. The notion of intertextuality as a dialogue between texts has also fallen into disfavor with Gustavo Pérez Firmat, himself a notable contributor to the theoretical feast of commentaries on intertextuality. "Dialogue," he says, "is intersubjective not inter-textual. One cannot have dialogue when each of the interlocutors is limited to just one utterance, as is the case in intertextual relationships. The earlier text 'speaks'; the later text 'answers'"; but the earlier text in no sense addresses the later one, nor does the later text hear it, and so they cannot be said to be in dialogue with each other. According to Pérez Firmat, the dialogical metaphor, like many that are used to describe rhetorical phenomena, commits the sin of anthropomorphizing the text and thus demands "considerable cognitive leaps" on the part of the critic who would use it (Pérez Firmat 1990–91, 166).

In fact, the metaphorical maneuver that relates intertextual activity to dialogue in Pérez Firmat's literal sense of the word is not now, and probably never was, entirely appropriate. The analogy reflects an early attempt to distinguish intertextuality from the study of sources and influences that Julia Kristeva, persuaded by the gospel according to Mikhail Bakhtin, set out to discredit. What has been more recently perceived as intertextuality's nonlinear dynamics diminishes the dialogical metaphor's usefulness and allies it more nearly with today's computational models of the mind, which, as Sherry Turkle points out, "often embrace a postmodern aesthetic of complexity and decentering" (Turkle 1996, 149). In the age of the Internet and the World Wide Web, intertextuality comes into its own as a trope of privilege; its contemporary descriptive metaphor is the cybertext, the continuous fabric of cognition that absorbs both dialogue and dialectic. Revolutions in culture and technology not only affect perceptions of reality and the world but determinations about rhetoric and its uses. Just as chaos is no longer a tumultuous state or condition but a revision of order, so is intertextuality no longer a formalized contract between two distinguished and distinguishable parties but a wide-ranging instrument of relevance retrieval whose function is the accrual rather than the immediate exchange of knowledge.

It is now generally conceded that we are living in a network world. Modern Spain, its history, and its literary texts are inescapably caught up in that network, and the Hispanists who have contributed to this volume reiterate the age's epistemic metaphor over and over again. The most web-oriented among them are Robert Spires, who discovers a sphere of discourse that transcends the borders of the Iberian Peninsula and encompasses history, politics, religion, and science; Gonzalo Navajas, who alludes to complex webs of signification and identifies meaningful chains of significance; Maryellen Bieder, who finds ambiguity in the proliferation and incompatibility of texts; and Diane Urey, whose deconstructive orientation leads her to conclude that there is no beginning or end to the chain of intertextual connections in and around the work she discusses. Most of these practiced readers of Spanish narrative recognize, either explicitly or implicitly, that intertextuality in literature and culture is a defining component of textuality itself. Such recognition of textuality is an acknowledgment of endless and inexhaustible possibility.

The once visionary concept of textuality has become common currency in the postmodern era of literary criticism, so much so that it has been easy to forget what a cataclysmic paradigm shift this vision represented. Literary activities defined as intertextual rather than intentional, influential, or determinate depend on an acceptance of the absolute and infinite interconnectedness of things, conditions, and ideas. Particularly for poststructuralist and postsemiological theoreticians, the bewilderment of that infinitude is a permanent impediment to significant communication. For the structurally or semiologically minded, however, concrete intertexts can still be effectively isolated and examined, and they remain necessary resources for intelligent reading. Since intertextuality is based on a mind-expanding abstraction and on material particulars, it is almost unique in having at once the philosophical authority of a world view and the rhetorical autonomy of a master trope. That combination of attributes has secured for intertextuality a turf of its own and at the same time constitutes its most unresolvable contradiction.

One consequence of intertextuality's semitropic nature is its durable viability. Whether in fashion or out of it, intertextuality, like other abiding master tropes, is always an active agency in literature. It is always present in writing and always a force that drives the readerly act. As Michael Riffaterre has said, "we must recognize that what impels the reader to pursue the search for the intertext, to experience the intertextual drive, as it were, is . . . its being consistent with, or a variant of, the ubiquitous mechanism of tropes" (Riffaterre 1990, 77). Like all tropes, intertextuality experiences the dynamics of a life cycle, one stage of which is its lexicalization—that is, its gradual passing from a privileged place in the figural hierarchy to the dehierarchized realm of discourse. Having begun life as the offspring of a seismic paradigm shift, it has been equally affected by other, less obvious, cognitive modifications, movements inside and outside of literature that reflect changing perceptions of its usefulness. In a technological age, life is measured in terms of utility, and survival means keeping pace with perceptual change. Interest in computers, for example, has shifted from mechanics to communication, that is, from the computer itself to its expanding capabilities. One-time trend setters like Macintosh and IBM have been displaced by the more attractive agendas of Netscape, SimLife, and Virtual Reality. Computer language is in a state of constant reinvention; the search for sites takes precedence over the fabrication of systems.

The life cycle of intertextuality has taken an analogous turn, as the contents of the present volume demonstrate. With few exceptions, the contributors prefer seeking out intertextual sites to elaborating intertextual systems. Critical interest in intertextuality can be gauged in terms of four readjustments in thinking that have taken place over the last four and a half decades. The revisions began in the 1960s with the displacement of the anxieties of influence by the far vaster implications of textuality. Emphasis then shifted from conceptual intertextuality to its mechanics, from its mechanics to its applications, and from its applications to its potential range of relevance. The mechanical phase is by now universally distinguishable as the phase of vigorous theorizing that culminated in the 1970s and 1980s. All of the classic theories of intertextuality from that period have been well documented in a number of quarters—perhaps most methodically by Thaïs Morgan in her 1989 essay "The Space of Intertextuality" and by Michael Worton and Judith Still in their introduction to *Intertextuality: Theories and Practices*. As Morgan points out, theories of sources and influence, most eloquently expounded by T. S. Eliot and Northrop Frye, were effectively corrected by Harold Bloom, who redefined influence as tormented misreading and who systematized his theory of misreading rhetorically in terms of refurbished classical tropes (*clinamen, tessera, kenosis, askesis*, etc.). As Angel Loureiro observes in this volume, Bloom's theorizing is essentially psychological; he perceives intertextual relations entirely in terms of desires and defenses.

Although Bloom is perhaps the most readily recognized of intertextuality's principal architects, the work of several other ground breakers in the field should not go unmentioned. The theorists most aware of the cultural dimensions of intertextuality are the anthropologists (e.g., Claude Lévi-Strauss) and the linguists (Roman Jakobson and Ferdinand de Saussure). For these social philosophers, intertextuality is an organizable system of signs that emerge from archetypal aspects of society, both cultural and aesthetic, and from human manners of thinking and speaking. Accordingly, it is semiological in its functions and purport. Julia Kristeva is, of course, the coiner of "intertextuality" as a literary term, an intertextualizer of psychologies, ideologies, and philosophies and an early introducer of the work of Mikhail Bakhtin to the rest of the reading world. The dialogical model of relational intertextuality is ultimately attributable to Bakhtin, for whom dialogicality soon becomes polyphony, individual speech patterns become double-voicing and then heteroglossia, and patterns of human behavior become a polycultural and essentially parodic carnival of interconnections. Like the anthropologists and the linguists, Bakhtin places culture and literature in the same synchronic context and in so doing demonstrates his acceptance of the inclusive textuality paradigm.

Jacques Derrida's deconstruction of the synchronic intertextuality model is probably as well studied as is Bloom's reinterpretation of influence. For Derrida, the infinite proliferation of texts amounts to the infinite deferral of meaning, and so deconstruction becomes "an iconoclastic theory of the *necessary intertextuality of all discourse*" (Morgan 1985, 17). Roland Barthes, too, takes a deconstructive view of intertextual sign systems, drawing on mass culture to identify the semiology of the self as a cultural construct of infinitely compounded components. Gérard Genette and Michael Riffaterre are intertextuality's mechanics par excellence, the former a classifier of intertextual models and creator of hermeneutic typologies, the latter a believer in the capabilities of enlightened readers to intuit the idiolects and hypograms of poetry and thereby "produce" the texts that they are reading.

These and other trendsetters in the field of theoretical intertextuality—

Jonathan Culler, Michel Foucault, Umberto Eco, Linda Hutcheon—act as each others' interpretants and mediators, as each others' intertexts, even as they provide groundwork for subsequent theoretical refinements. Theirs are all revered names among literary theorizers of the twentieth century. Their interest is in the mechanics of a newly identified instrument, and what they have most abundantly generated are quests for deployment of the instrument they have created. Thus have the gradual shifts taken place from mechanics to applications and from applications to extended relevance. Genette's rigid taxonomies, for instance, in general and on a theoretical level intersect with Derrida's equally rigid indeterminacy and modify it, make it less daunting. The mere coexistence of the two disparate theoretical models makes possible the contemplation of a more welcoming intermediate space where the search for understanding remains possible. At the same time, particular Genettian categories have reinforced the dynamics that link literary theory to cybernetic simulation and interaction. Technology's creative misreading of Genette's "hypertext" is a case in point. In literary criticism, the concept of "hypertext" has cycled into lexicalization and relative disuse; in the field of computer informatics, "Hypertext" has revived Genette's taxonomical instrument through a kind of paronomasia or punning on the original term and in so doing has infinitely extended the instrument's communicative range. (See Shapiro and Shapiro 1988, 39, on the revivification of dead tropes through punning.)

As with H/hypertext, so, in different ways, with the vast reaches of intertextuality itself. The contributions to this collection abundantly demonstrate the interest that professional readers continue to show in expanding literature's range of communication through intertextual pursuits and, in at least one case, in adding to the bedrock mechanics of intertextual theory. During the past thirty years, the concept of intertextuality has accumulated an extensive bibliography and generated numerous edited volumes of criticism. This collection of essays is unique among those multitudes in its focus on the literature of modern Spain and in making criticism of Spanish texts and their extremely varied intertexts accessible to an English-speaking readership. The areas of intertextuality these essays address range as widely as textuality itself and embrace topics that are under immediate and sometimes polemical scrutiny in the global critical exchange.

Two of the contributors, Randolph Pope and Angel Loureiro, identify the disputed genre of autobiography as the environment for their intertextual investigations, selecting fictionally constructed selves as the texts under examination. Pope's approach to the intertextuality of autobiography postulates an autobiographical "I" that is not an inward-looking integral self remembered in tranquillity but a center of loneliness in a crowd of intertexts that family and social institutions circumscribe. For Pope, the mind itself is a text, and as both text and cognition it must learn that significance comes from a continual bringing together and reassessment of other texts, if it is to respond to the autobiographical imperative of bearing witness to a life that has been lived. This necessary convocation of texts is aleatory in its inclusiveness. In order to reveal the contemporary Spanish novelist Luis Goytisolo to the reader, Pope constructs a chain of analogous selves that takes in classical autobiographers and historians, Spaniards, Englishmen, Germans, and the autobiographer's own more famous brother Juan, whose previously published version of his family's story Luis more or less unconsciously sets out to modify. The modifications predictably lead to a proliferation of versions, the Derridean predicament sets in, and Luis is entrapped in an intertextual web only partly of his own creating. The master web-weaver in this instance is of course the critic Randolph Pope himself.

Loureiro concerns himself more with the implications of intertextuality for autobiography theory. His image is of autobiographers as apostates or exiles who try in vain to return to the homes they have left in search of their identities. The lives he addresses are those of two Spanish exiles, José Blanco White and Juan Goytisolo, the former a highly eccentric figure whose life spans the turn of the nineteenth century, the latter a living author and avid admirer and translator of his predecessor. Using excerpts from the autobiographical texts of both, Loureiro develops one writer's reading of the other into a feat of reincarnation, intertextuality in this case not being the random happenstance of reading but a psychic coincidence that makes the two writers virtually interchangeable in the later autobiographer's eyes. Intertextuality here is the agency of a temporary fusion of selves, a fusion brought about by a shared seme of deviation.

Other contributors to this collection are also concerned to expand the parameters of existing genres through the application of intertextual mechanics and the analysis of specific intertexts. Maryellen Bieder, Hazel Gold, and Debra Castillo address domestic fiction, the opera, and the middlebrow novel, respectively, as areas of intertextual discord in the fictions they consider. In a broad application of relational intertextuality, Bieder selects four novels by the formidable nineteenth-century woman writer and early feminist Emilia Pardo Bazán to illustrate that entire genres can be seen as intertexts that make some of the Spanish author's hitherto unappreciated novels both admirable and intelligible. Interestingly, intelligibility in Bieder's formulation comes from denying intertextual assumptions and accepting deliberately created intertextual anomalies.

While Bieder takes the textuality of genre as a given, Gold questions whether a genre can in fact serve as an intertext. Having ascertained the feasibility of treating genre as text, Gold attempts to determine the peculiar properties of the opera genre. Upon scrutiny, opera proves to be generically unstable and highly intertextualized, and it therefore becomes an emblem of the heterogeneous intertextual process—a potential *mise en abyme*. What then can be the contributions of that unstable genre and that heterogeneous process to the elemental fabric of realistic fiction? The test case that Gold selects is an oddly conceived novel by the nineteenth-century author Leopoldo Alas, more familiarly known as "Clarín." Clarín avoids the potential abyss of intertextual self-reflexivity by simply giving his novel over at certain points to its operatic subtext. In Gold's reading, Clarín's handling of the asymmetrical relations between genres proves to be not wholly realistic, modernist, or postmodern but expansively informational in its generic inclusiveness. Although it is unusual for a critic to celebrate an author's uniqueness in a context where an intertext is being specified, Gold in fact demonstrates Clarín's exceptional inventiveness in his novelistic experimentations with the opera genre.

Debra Castillo is less interested in genres as intertexts than in the production of genres by means of intertexts. She argues that the crossing of low fiction (the women's novel of romance) with high art (traditionally masculine canonical texts), two prominent intertextual loci, generates the middlebrow novel, a genre of vast popularity and limited intellectual pretensions. The submerged subtext that Castillo identifies is a cultural correlative of women's fiction and a widely recognized element in Francoist propaganda, the Falangist "Sección Femenina" or "Women's Section." Few academic readers of Spanish narrative would recognize Castillo's subject, Mercedes Salisachs, as an author of canonical stature, although she has written at least twenty-five books and is the winner of numerous Spanish literary awards. Fewer still will know how to read and think about the implications of Salisachs's apparently undemanding fictions. As Castillo explains, Salisachs's work is neither low enough to appeal to popular culture studies nor literary enough to be considered high art. Writing in the later years of the Francoist period and after the dictator's death, the composer of middlebrow novels finds herself in the historical middle as well, extending in a lesser mode such early and intellectually lofty projects as Carmen Laforet's *Nada* and empowering later highbrow versions of the woman's novel by such writers as Esther Tusquets, Ana María Moix, Montserrat Roig, and Mercé Rodoreda, all members of the acclaimed Catalan Women's Renaissance movement. Castillo thus looks backward to the pre-texts and forward to the post-texts as she explains the contrasting demands of authoritarian conduct codes and mass sociology on a Spanish woman writer of popular fictions.

The intertextual foundations of totalitarian mythmaking are more centrally the subject of David Herzberger's study of the relationship between Francoist historiography and postmodern Spanish fiction. The strong tradition that isolates the so-called reality of history from the fictiveness of fiction makes Herzberger's intertextual linking of the two discursive practices an unusual critical achievement. Herzberger's study works through the familiar tensions and ambiguities of intertextual defer- ral to suggest that in division there can be fusion. For Herzberger, Span- ish postmodern narrative is a powerfully dissident intertextual force in the face of Francoist historiography primarily because it discredits on the levels of language and genre rather than by disputing fact. Novelists like Gonzalo Torrente Ballester and Camilo José Cela do not contest the intertextual referentiality of the past; they simply write fictions that negate it. Consequently, there appears to be an unresolved dynamic between the naively referential and the radically nonreferential. Herzberger does not conclude with that irresolution, however. He instead postulates a split referentiality, nurtured by intertextuality, that admits language into the real world and serves as a catalyst for understanding.

Gonzalo Navajas similarly modifies the postmodern self-referential agenda by arguing that the ethical propensity of objective realism carries over into later, seemingly antirealistic modes. Navajas's study offers a useful overview of the intertextual reorientation of narrative and film since the decades immediately following the Spanish Civil War. He suggests a division of the contemporary period into two phases—mimetic (neorealistic) and intradialogic (postmodern). He further suggests that intertextuality might easily be seen as the instrument that could perhaps settle the referential debate between realism and modernism, were it not that intertextuality does not manage to free fiction entirely from external dependence. Ethics continues to be an integral dimension in fiction, even when its aim (apparently) ceases to be that of informing directly about the world. Navajas describes the effects of sociopolitical constraints on the intertextual project and draws provocative parallels between fiction and film in each of the two phases. The cinematographic work of Luis Buñuel, for instance, shows markedly postmodern tendencies as it passes from one phase to the next, through censorship and out of it. Yet Buñuel and directors like Carlos Saura and Víctor Erice remain powerfully indebted to a past that determines their ideological and artistic orientations. More recent filmmakers like Pedro Almodóvar are also intertextually determined by contemporary history as well as by the popular and the trivial elements that parody history even as they repossess it. Navajas's panoramic study encompasses many texts and a bitterly divisive historical period. In none of those texts does intertextuality become entirely divorced from immediate moral reference.

Robert Spires's essay on Luis Martín-Santos's definitively postmodern novel *Tiempo de silencio* ranges widely in a different way from Gonzalo Navajas's. The premise of Spires's critical project is the very unconstructedness of global discursivity. Basing his definition of discourse on Foucault's epistemic archeologies, Spires identifies the epistemological links that join the rhetorical practice to the philosophical abstraction and the philosophical abstraction to a scientific metaphor—field—that commonly suggests a significant commingling of concentration and dispersion. Inevitably, Spires takes Francoist propaganda as his intertextual jumping-off place. More specifically, he focuses on the activities of the powerful group called Opus Dei, a political and cultural phenomenon of Spain in the 1960s, the decade when *Tiempo de silencio* was written. Appointed by Franco to effect economic and moral reform in a country at last accepted into the larger European community, the Opus Dei both symbolizes and exalts the role of technology and science that Martín-Santos's novel so virulently condemns. Like all the Spanish artists of the period, Martín-Santos is denied the freedom to express his condemnation openly, so he devises a rhetoric for denouncing technology in terms too universal for immediate understanding. He calls into question syllogistic logic and systems of power and authority, thereby rhetorically demolishing much of the conceptual undergirding of modern Western thought. In describing this demolition project, Spires the critic rehierarchizes intertextuality in its new computational, semitechnological role, just as the writer Martín-Santos exploits the contrapuntal hierarchies of an ever-expanding intertextual discourse.

Taking as its metaphorical point of departure Kristeva's perception of a text as a mosaic of quotations, Diane Urey's essay goes on to develop an analogously expansive kaleidoscopic view, as it discovers numerous "extratexts" nested within one of Benito Pérez Galdós's most complexly narrated historical fictions. The "episodio nacional" *Gerona* tells the excruciating tale of one famous siege by evoking other sieges more excruciating still, signals its own hybridity of genre by allying itself to a variety of other genres, cultivates characters by analogy to their fictive and historical counterparts, and develops style and structure by evoking external and internal resonances. That is, the text of this single fiction

generates multiple sign systems that thread their way in and out of the
stories and discourses of Galdós's novels in a constant state of metamorphosis. Given the undisputed historicity of the 1809–10 siege of Gerona
and the subsequent disputed versions of the event, Urey's essay
inevitably questions history's capacity to rationalize the fictionality of
fiction and to validate the reality fiction purports to imitate. In Urey's
reading, the stuff of history provides fiction with endless intertexts—*is* in
fact an inescapable and never-ending intertext. Yet it at no time yields up
truth for the reader because, finally, history only teaches that readers are
historical and fictional intertexts themselves. In the absence of definitive
truths, however, the multilateral text delivers the unilateral message of a
deeply felt condemnation of war, a condemnation made more harrowing
by the constant duplicity of the novel's intertextual resonances. In the
area of moral valuation at least, the novelist's intertextual obfuscations
do not inhibit intersubjective communication between author and reader
but rather support and strengthen it. Urey's antireferential application of
intertextual mechanisms is therefore a negation that affirms, that identifies commonality as the flip side of difference.

Although she too takes a novel by Pérez Galdós as her model, Akiko
Tsuchiya is less interested in the text's intercommunicative dynamics
than in its aggressively authoritarian corporeality. The post-Foucauldian
perception of the body as a social and discursive construct descends
directly from the epistemological breakthrough in which textuality
renders all things and ideas intelligible in terms of one another. Tsuchiya
founds her argument on Foucault's expanded understanding of the
human body as a pathological and biological text, which is often the site
of institutional struggles for power. To the Foucauldian engagement with
body politics Tsuchiya adds the concerns of feminism for rescuing the
female body from an unwelcome but omnipresent male surveillance. She
observes that male awareness of the female body is central to Galdós's
fictions and that in them a relational system involving social institutions,
culture, and literature establishes a link between corporeality and textuality. In her Foucauldian reading of Galdós's *La desheredada*, Tsuchiya
does not argue for or against intertextuality, nor does she define it or
offer metaphors that articulate its workings. She simply puts it to practice, vigorously and unself-consciously, and in so doing demonstrates
intertextuality's continuing vitality as a facilitating critical instrument. In
Tsuchiya's hands, the notion of surveillance develops the full richness of
thematic interconnectedness. It moves freely among the domains of
perception, authoritarianism, voyeurism, and gaze (in its various senses
of male lust, possession, containment, and insecurity), and it culminates
in the self-scrutiny and ultimate self-repossession of the novel's belea-

guered heroine. Tsuchiya's study treats Isidora Rufete's body as a primary text that is being observed and modified in the light of many other texts—political, psychosocial, erotic, medical, and legal. The textual body thus mirrors the protagonist's own body, which becomes a cultural battlefield where bourgeois patriarchy and the protagonist's own imagination are in dramatic conflict.

Combining Cervantine techniques with the contemporary naturalism that underlies nineteenth-century realism, Pérez Galdós creates a female protagonist whose textual autonomy permits her to defy on her own terms the patronizing condemnation to which her male creator constantly subjects her. Female authors working in the early years of the twentieth century fight the same battle but, being of another age and not being characters in fiction, are denied the liberating autonomy that realistic characterization can provide. Roberta Johnson's essay addresses the divisive effects of twentieth-century modernism on the Spanish writing culture, a culture that drives male writers to devalue and supersede the practices of nineteenth-century realism but that binds women writers to representational forms of expression and to mediational rather than directly revisionist intertextualizing. In commenting on the work of four women authors of the modernist period, Johnson convincingly demonstrates that intertextual practices can indeed be gender specific and that female-gendered intertextuality in the early 1900s can be seen as symptomatic of an incipient feminist rebellion. Most appropriately, the archetypal Don Juan is the essay's intertextual focus, since the figure surfaces in various guises in novels by both men and women. Johnson's reading of the women's dilemma in characterizing the Don Juans in their novels is Bloomian in its attention to the oppressive burden of precursorship they face. Since their anxieties are thematic rather than aesthetic or formal, social rather than philosophical, the female novelists summon up the archetype almost exclusively through a secondary version, its contemporary (and male authored) variant, Ramón del Valle-Inclán's Marqués de Bradomín. Exuberantly ironized, unrealistically stylized, incorrigibly amoral, and constructed from numerous mirror images of himself, Bradomín is an immediately threatening contemporary literary figure and is therefore the mediator of choice for the female intertextual agenda. Fearing for their own survival in the face of a literary market increasingly dominated by the aesthetic artifices of modernism, the women writers deliberately set out to feminize, proletarianize, or domesticate Valle-Inclán's refurbishing of the classical Don Juan text. In so doing, they reclaim by common endeavor their subtext's original negative status.

In Johnson's essay, as in all of the essays so far summarized, and as in most of the historical accounts of intertextual procedures, the fact of the intertext itself, its nature and its existence, remains an undisputed and untheorized given. It falls to H. L. Boudreau to explore that theoretically uncharted territory. This volume's closing essay pushes through and beyond the problem of text-author relationships in search of a new vocabulary and a revitalized dynamic for the study of texts as autonomous cultural phenomena. Drawing his new lexicon from the fields of biology and genetics, Boudreau concerns himself with the contents of the collective mind of which the content of literature is but a small part. Instead of describing the invasion of literary texts by other texts, he follows the biologist Daniel Dennett in perceiving the human brain's invasion by culture. Instead of intertexts, Boudreau speaks of "memes," which partake of both genes and semes. Instead of dwelling on the fiction of mimesis, he expounds a new science of memology in which minimal units of culture are genetically (or memetically) linked and can either perpetuate or annihilate one another. Boudreau departs in this study from the exclusive scrutiny of Spanish texts and combines struc-turalism with sociobiology in the examination and tabulation of the elemental substances of which culture is made. That is to say, he takes the by now familiar theorizing that surrounds the concept of intertextual-ity into other spheres altogether, those of genetic replication and cultural evolution. In this way, he offers renewed evidence of intertextuality's own self-replicating properties.

That intertextuality is itself dynamically intertextual has already been suggested by the technological orientation of these introductory remarks. In intertextuality, as in the web-like nexus of the computer aesthetic, the continuous interactivity of site calling to site and the continuous regres-siveness of windows opening onto windows point to the mathematical abstraction that underlies this volume's literary project. In the mathemat-ical sphere, the paradoxes related to the concept of continuousness or continuity have given rise to many efforts of definition and have provoked the most cataclysmic rethinking of fundamental mathematical problems. Continuity has led mathematicians to ponder the problematics of the spaces between numbers, for instance, and the incommensurability of numbers like the square root of 2. As the mathematician Edward Rothstein points out, "Continuity, in both space and number, is a matter of coherence: it poses the challenge of matching mathematical thinking to everyday experience" (Rothstein 1995, 52). Ever since the seventeenth century, mathematicians have been devising metaphors that attempt to take up that challenge, to demonstrate that coherence. Calculus was invented as a means of grappling with the paradoxes of continuousness, and in Newton's formulation the methods of calculus depended on nothing more nor less than a rhetorical conceit (53). In the present episteme, textuality, along with any or all of its discriminating prefixes (inter-, hyper-, meta-, para-, hypo-), constitutes another of those metaphorizing (though not anthropomorphizing) conceits and is equally susceptible to practical survival and theoretical atrophy.

To speak of the survival or mortality of a literary practice, of its death or of its life, is to acknowledge the theoretical validity of the much impugned anthropomorphizing tendency and to recall into play the side-lined relationship of intersubjectivity. Are not precursorship, influence, self-reflexivity, and dialogue all intersubjective? Insofar as intertextuality is a conscious or unconscious element of an author's style and cosmic vision, it partakes of the modal and epistemological ubiquity of tropes. Insofar as intertextuality suggests a critical engagement on the part of the reader rather than a rhetorical device that a writer or speaker employs—like allegory or symbol, pleonasm or prosopopoeia—it can be said to die when it goes out of fashion, becomes clichéd, or falls into disuse or disrepute. In another essay, Boudreau observes that intertextuality has arrived at the discursive phase of its life cycle, has in fact been "replaced to a large degree by the word *discourse*" (Boudreau 1996, 23). This discursive phase is marked by a general disinclination on the parts of critics to use the term, an understandable reluctance to flog an apparently moribund horse. There is some evidence of that disinclination in several of the essays in this volume. Yet, just as with allegory writers continue to allegorize and readers continue to practice allegoresis on texts, so with intertextuality does the detection of transtextual mutations and transgressions remain a paramount adventure in the literary-critical enterprise. As all of the essays in this collection demonstrate, the professional critics who might wish to proclaim the death of the intertext are the same fascinated superreaders who keep intertextuality—or replication, or discourse, or continuity, or evolution, or the trope by any other name—alive.

J.P.B.
Mount Holyoke College
J.W.K.
Cornell University

Works Cited

Bakhtin, Mikhail. 1981. *The Dialogic Imagination: Four Essays*. Ed. Michael Holquist. Trans. Caryl Emerson and Michael Holquist. Austin: University of Texas Press.

———. 1984. *Rabelais and His World*. Trans. Hélène Iswolsky. Bloomington: Indiana University Press.

Barthes, Roland. 1977. *Roland Barthes by Roland Barthes*. Trans. Richard Howard. New York: Hill & Wang.

———. 1988. *Mythologies*. Trans. Annette Lavers. New York: Noonday Press.

Begley, Adam. 1994. "Colossus among Critics: Harold Bloom." *New York Times Magazine*, 25 September, pp. 32–35.

Bloom, Harold. 1973. *The Anxiety of Influence: A Theory of Poetry*. New York: Oxford University Press.

———. 1975. *A Map of Misreading*. New York: Oxford University Press.

Boudreau, H. L. 1996. "Rewriting Unamuno Rewriting Galdós." In *Self-Conscious Art: A Tribute to John W. Kronik*. Ed. Susan L. Fischer, 23–41. Lewisburg: Bucknell University Press.

Culler, Jonathan. 1976. "Presupposition and Intertextuality." *MLN* 91: 1380–96.

Derrida, Jacques. 1976. *Of Grammatology*. Trans. Gayatri Chakravorti Spivak. Baltimore: Johns Hopkins University Press.

———. 1978. "Structure, Sign, and Play in the Discourse of the Human Sciences." In *Writing and Difference*. Trans. Alan Bass, 278–93. Chicago: University of Chicago Press.

Eco, Umberto. 1979. *The Role of the Reader: Explorations in the Semiotics of Texts*. Bloomington: Indiana University Press.

Foucault, Michel. 1972. *The Archaeology of Knowledge*. Trans. A. M. Sheridan Smith. London: Tavistock.

———. 1977. *Language, Counter-Memory, Practice*. Ed. Donald F. Bouchard. Trans. Donald F. Bouchard and Sherry Simon. Ithaca, N.Y.: Cornell University Press.

Genette, Gérard. 1982. *Palimpsestes: La littérature au second degré*. Paris: Seuil.

Hutcheon, Linda. 1986. "Literary Borrowing . . . and Stealing: Plagiarism, Sources, Influences, and Intertexts." *English Studies in Canada* 12: 229–39.

Jakobson, Roman. 1968. "Poetry of Grammar and Grammar of Poetry." *Lingua* 21: 597–609.

Kristeva, Julia. 1967. "Bakhtine: Le mot, le dialogue et le roman." *Critique* 23: 438–65.

———. 1984. *Revolution in Poetic Language*. Trans. Margaret Waller. New York: Columbia University Press.

Lévi-Strauss, Claude. 1969. *The Raw and the Cooked: Introduction to a Science of Mythology*. Trans. John Weightman and Doreen Weightman. New York: Harper & Row.

Morgan, Thaïs. 1985. "Is There an Intertext in This Text? Literary and Interdisciplinary Approaches to Intertextuality." *The American Journal of Semiotics* 3: 1–40.

———. 1989. "The Space of Intertextuality." In *Intertextuality and Contemporary American Fiction*. Ed. Patrick O'Donnell and Robert Con Davis, 239–79. Baltimore: Johns Hopkins University Press.

Pérez Firmat, Gustavo. 1990–91. Review of *Transparent Simulacra: Spanish Fiction, 1902–1926*, by Robert Spires. *Siglo XX/20th Century* 8: 165–70.

Riffaterre, Michael. 1990. "Compulsory Reader Response: The Intertextual Drive." In *Intertextuality: Theories and Practices*. Ed. Michael Worton and Judith Still, 56–78. Manchester: Manchester University Press.

Rothstein, Edward. 1995. *Emblems of Mind: The Inner Life of Music and Mathematics*. New York: Random House.

Saussure, Ferdinand de. 1983. *Course in General Linguistics*. Ed. Charles Bally and Albert Sechehaye. Trans. Roy Harris. London: Duckworth.

Shapiro, Michael, and Marianne Shapiro. 1988. *Figuration in Verbal Art*. Princeton: Princeton University Press.

Turkle, Sherry. 1996. "Who Am We?" *Wired* 4.01: 148–52, 194, 196–99.

Worton, Michael, and Judith Still, eds. 1990. *Intertextuality: Theories and Practices*. Manchester: Manchester University Press.

Autobiographical Selves as "Transpersonal Beings": Gibbon, Kierkegaard, Goethe, and Luis Goytisolo among Others

RANDOLPH D. POPE

The I among Others

> [W]e should prolong all our passing moments, uncertain though they are, not perhaps by action . . . but at any rate by literary work. Since we are denied a long life, let us leave something to bear witness that at least we have lived.
>
> —Pliny 1969, 1:187[1]

The I never stands alone in an autobiography but is instead determined by a fragile and shifting series of complementary positions. The I of the autobiographical narrator points, however imperfectly, to the author as he or she writes and confronts the I of the character, who stands for the author in the remembered past, separated by the gap that writing recalls and tries to bridge. In each moment, the I appears surrounded by others: the child's I among parents and relatives, friends, and fleeting role models, placed within a family and in a school. The adolescent I suffers the discovery of a body, racked by desire, actively pursuing or fearfully pursued, always whispering in a language of its own that often bypasses the known, the authorized, and even the legal. The adult I seeks to establish itself in a profession and start a family, battling against rival suitors and discovering the limitations that make Fortune elusive. The narrator's first person invokes real or imagined readers, who will be the jury that examines his or her veracity and talent. The autobiographer also likes to appear surrounded by literary heroes, to establish a genealogy and to bask in the glow of their fame. He or she designs an identity within institutions and well-known spaces.

One Spanish autobiographer, Diego de Torres Villarroel, claims to have been born among books—his father owned a bookstore in the university city of Salamanca—and his life is framed by the library and the university. Another, José María Blanco White, is a man of the church, within its ranks or striving against it. Yet another, María Teresa León, finds fulfillment fighting for the Republican Army's cause. There is an odd quality to this process. Introspection discovers in the deepest self an I that can only be described by a scrupulous reconstruction of institutions that are anything but private: family, school, army, church, academy, and so on. Moreover, the self in writing must be expressed in words that are common to all speakers of a language—a humbling realization. The mind itself, constituted as a text (Lacan *dixit*), learns that meaning comes from a simultaneous convocating, shifting, and rejecting of other texts. The autobiographer shows traces of this insecurity. Is there anything more to this I than a slight and always threatened distinction from others similar to it? How can this I claim to be more than a place within shared institutions, a place someone else can easily fill? Is the I anything more than a function in a system of oppositions without positive terms, like the phonemes Saussure describes?

It is tempting to fall back on the authority of Foucault and de Man and to affirm that the disappearance of the individual from the realm of stable and independently existing entities is already a well-observed and established fact. Autobiography must be nothing more than an epitaph and its language funereal. Jail, hospital, school—and the categories that create them—generate prisoners, patients, students, as the psychiatric ward creates madmen and the autobiographical "machine" spouts autobiographers. Derrida contributes strategies that allow some critics to regard race, gender, nationality, social standing, signatures—deciding factors for autobiographers—merely as constructed oppositions useful to the powerful and the cunning. The title of Paul Julian Smith's admirable book *Representing the Other* could well be altered to *Representing the Self*, and his analysis of race and gender could be applied to the way in which autobiographers trace themselves.[2] Yet, if readers dislodge the autobiographical self from the testimony of a lived life, if they forget that after the collapse of the body and all that supports it at least the trace of a life can be left behind and can *matter* to other human beings, they miss by their clever and overprecise idealism the testimony the autobiography leaves: the I has lived, it has existed. That the effort to scramble through a maze of intertextual materials and to reduce the breadth and density of life to a thin thread of narrative can produce only a simulacrum of an individual I does not mean that the effort is destined to failure.

Architects also contend with materials and conditions that determine their work and may even seriously interfere with it. Most buildings are forgettable, but some attain a level of uniqueness that excites the imagination and makes citizens want to preserve them. Those few architects whose buildings are still admired and those few autobiographers—Teresa of Avila, Cellini, Alonso de Contreras, Torres Villarroel, Goethe, Rousseau—whose autobiographies scholars continue to study have followed Pliny's recommendation. They have left something that has made their lives memorable. They do not hand down mirrors with their images still lingering in them—there was never anything to be reflected, unless it was to be reflected about or upon—but rather instruments to conjure the convincing illusion of lives that matter. Students of architecture and readers of autobiographies learn not so much from the materials accumulated or the texts meshed together as from the subtle revelation of a way of proceeding, a manner of handling things, a perceived direction, and a set of preferences and dislikes that can be recognized as the faint traces of the individual. A series of choices reveals the now absent hand. As Goethe writes in his autobiography *Poetry and Truth*, "the perspicacious reader . . . is capable of reading between the lines what does not stand written, but is indicated" (Goethe 1949, 643). In what follows, the perspicacious reader will find a few examples of how the autobiographer's I negotiates the difficulties of living among others and yet leaves in the record of this anxious effort the compelling indication of a unique life.

The Most Important Intertext Is the One That Has Not Yet Been Written

> If a person possessed a letter that he knew or believed contained information about what he had to consider his life's happiness, but the characters were thin and faint and the handwriting almost illegible, then, presumably with anxiety and agitation, he would read it most passionately again and again and at one moment derive one meaning, at the next moment another, according to how he would explain everything by a word he believed that he had deciphered with certainty, but he would never progress beyond the same uncertainty with which he had begun.
>
> —Kierkegaard 1987, 190

Edward Gibbon (1737–94), who completed a monumental history of the decline and fall of the Roman Empire, was unable to finish his own autobiography. The prodigious erudition, daunting power of synthesis, and admirable style that make him still today one of the most admired English authors of all time proved insufficient to help him decide on a final version of his own life story. Seven different attempts are extant, some of them covering the same events in different renditions. Most notably, he describes three times the famous moment when he decided to write his best-known history:

[I]t was the view of Italy and Rome which determined the choice of the subject. In my Journal the place and moment of conception are recorded; the fifteenth of October, 1764, in the close of evening, as I sat musing in the Church of the Zoccolanti or Franciscan fryars, while they were singing Vespers in the Temple of Jupiter on the ruins of the Capitol. (Gibbon 1896, 270; Memoir C, written in January 1790)

I must not forget the day, the hour, the most interesting in my literary life. It was on the fifteenth of October, in the gloom of evening, as I sat musing on the Capitol, while the barefooted fryars were chanting their litanies in the temple of Jupiter, that I conceived the first thought of my history. (Gibbon 1896, 405–6; Memoir D, written 1790–91)

It was at Rome, on the fifteenth of October, 1764, as I sat musing amidst the ruins of the Capitol, while the barefooted fryars were singing Vespers in the Temple of Jupiter, that the idea of writing the decline and fall of the City first started to my mind. (Gibbon 1896, 302; Memoir E)[3]

The memory of the event is thinner and fainter than Gibbon would desire. In the first version, the view of Italy and Rome, a broad experience, determines his choice of subject. He was a young man in search of a topic and had considered a life of Sir Walter Raleigh, a history of the Swiss or of Florence, but he abandoned these ideas. He had studied Greek and Latin, had read the classics, and his father had authorized a trip to the Continent that would take him to Italy. During a ten-month stay in Lausanne, where he had lived earlier and still had many friends, he prepared his trip by reading extensively about ancient Rome. In October of 1764, his mind was busy with the hum of the numerous books and documents that he had read and reread, as was his practice. He affirms that during this period "Horace and Virgil, Juvenal and Ovid, were [his] assiduous companions" (Gibbon 1896, 209; Memoir B), and as he read "the Tuscan writers on the bank of the Arno . . . [his] conversation was with the dead rather than the living" (Gibbon 1896, 302; Memoir E).[4] His view of Italy was mediated by an intertextual network that seemed to him insufficient, inexact. He felt compelled to add his own text to all those, so as to quell the frenzy of inadequate descriptions and to render the object translucent. The clash between the Christian prayers and the pagan temple of Jupiter seemed emblematic of the rich complexity of the late Roman Empire that he wished to capture. Yet, when Gibbon remembers this significant moment in the first autobiographical version, he refers the reader to another text, his diaries: "In my Journal the place and moment of conception are recorded." Like the Virgin Mary when visited by Gabriel, Gibbon received the message of the vesper prayers from a pagan god who planted in him the seed of his great work. Unfortunately, the journal does not record the place or the time. Gibbon, like any dutiful historian, probably realized his error and in the second version excised any corroborative text. This version emerges from anxiety: "I must not forget the day, the hour, the most interesting in my literary life." Why does he appeal to himself not to forget, if the experience has not already receded behind a flutter of erudition and elegant syntax? And to the historian's unease when his grasp of the past becomes tenuous, Gibbon adds a new element: this event, which was probably fabricated retrospectively, is now the most interesting of his *literary* life. His life has become a text or, better, a series of texts that not even the impressive master can control. In the third version, the scene is sharper and Italy has been removed, leaving only Rome, the germinative concept, pushed to the end of the scene as a climax. What the historian demands—the removal of the reference to an invented document—allows the aesthete to reconsider and rewrite: Gibbon shifts his location from the Church of the Zoccolanti or Franciscan friars to the ruins of the Capitol, certainly a more dramatic spot but one evidently conjured for the occasion from a repertory of literary images.[5] This third version was the one his friend and protector Lord Sheffield selected for his own edition of Gibbon's autobiography, which he published in 1796 and which became the standard text.[6] Yet, as is now apparent, Sheffield was putting into circulation counterfeit images that had not satisfied Gibbon himself.

Gibbon had started his autobiographical project for his own amusement and because "the public is always curious to *know* the men who have left behind them any image of their minds" (Gibbon 1896, 104; Memoir B); but could he allow the public to *know* that he could not even remember what he had written or exactly where he was during the most interesting moment of his literary life? This was not the only problem of candor he encountered in trying to make public a more explicit image of his mind than the one he had already offered in *The Decline and Fall of the Roman Empire.* He came from a family of merchants who had been involved in a financial scandal of national proportions; he claimed aristocratic relatives he did not have; his life did not reach the heights his tutor had expected of him; and in his own personal life a moment of flawed choice haunted him. Gibbon converted to Catholicism while at Oxford and was promptly sent by his family to Switzerland in the hope that he would return to his previous faith, which he eventually did. In the process, he "ceased to be an Englishman" and fell in love with Suzanne Curchod.[7] His description of her is affectionate and admiring. She returned his love, and her family saw with pleasure "a connection which might raise their daughter above want and dependence." But Gibbon's parents frowned on this alliance and threatened to disinherit him. In a terse sentence, Gibbon recounts the outcome: "After a painful struggle I yielded to my fate; the remedies of absence and time were at length effectual, and my love subsided in friendship and esteem" (Gibbon 1896, 151–52; Memoir B).

This second event—a broken engagement—is closely related to the first—the call of genius. Gibbon, always an avid reader and prodigious scholar, postpones his love life for his literary life. He has been touched by concepts and must conceive a book, a text, that will be a testimony to his existence, a text among texts. In his library he had the works of Pliny the Younger, and he must have read the Latin author's invocation to create a literary work that would remind others of the author's life: "relinquamus aliquid, quo nos vixisse testemur" [let us leave something to bear witness that at least we have lived] (Pliny 1969, 1:186).[8] For Gibbon, the road to fame includes a complex move that combines the prudent acceptance of his father's will and the avoidance of a relationship that would have saddled him with a family.

Gibbon's is not an isolated case. Kierkegaard's (1813–55) broken engagement to Regina Olsen (1822–1904) is legendary, in part because of Kierkegaard's own obsessive description of the event in several of his works. In an essay called "Silhouettes," included in *Either/Or* and attributed there to the anonymous aesthete who is the putative author of almost half of that conflicted book, Kierkegaard describes the suffering of three abandoned women. The thrust of the essay is to illustrate that deep suffering cannot be properly drawn by art without becoming super-ficial. The sorrow caused by imagination and memory, by the theater of fantasy incessantly renewing pain, doubt, and hope in the inner recesses of the mind—the pain Regina must have felt—is indescribable and can only be known by direct experience. To illustrate his point, Kierkegaard reaches out to three other fictional texts and their suffering female characters: Marie Beaumarchais from Goethe's *Clavigo*, Donna Elvira from Mozart's *Don Giovanni*, and Margarete from Goethe's *Faust*. Kierkegaard dispatches Marie Beaumarchais with unusual swiftness: "Her story is brief: Clavigo became engaged to her; Clavigo left her. This information is enough for the person who is in the habit of observing the phenomena of life as one observes rarities in a curio cabinet; the shorter the better, the more one can manage to see" (Kierkegaard 1987, 177).

These sentences are particularly perverse, even though they are not spoken directly by the author but are mediated by his usual Cervantine layers of pseudonyms and characters. In this case they are attributed to the aesthete known only as A in the manuscript found by Victor Eremita. The comparison of his triptych of suffering women with rarities in a curio cabinet reveals the conflict between the cold passion of the collec- tor and the dread of the observer who fears that the objects of his contemplation may strike back at him. Kierkegaard does not mention that Clavigo is forced by Marie's brother to reconsider his broken engage- ment and decides to return to her, only to abandon her yet again. If anyone has ever understood the power of repetition, it is Kierkegaard; yet in this case he conveniently forgets. Goethe's play shows Clavigo struggling with his own writing: he is the editor of a newspaper that tries to bring fresh ideas to Spain, and he is well received in Madrid's intellec- tual and social circles. He wants to leave a mark, to write his indelible text. Playing on this ambition, his friend Carlos repeats to him time and again that an alliance with Marie will not help his career. Like Gibbon, Clavigo fears that his literary life will be sapped by the obligations of marriage. The existential choice between work and family, between glory and love, is played out in a conflict of texts. There is one text too many, the spoken promise, and one text endangered, the one still unwritten. This is a serious conflict because "[w]hat he [Clavigo, and also Gibbon] broke off was his solemn promise, not a frivolous affair or a mere social attachment" (Goethe 1988, 157).[9] Here is how his friend Carlos paints the future for Clavigo:

> [B]ehold the good fortune and greatness that await you. I won't depict your
> prospects in bright poetic colors; you can imagine them for yourself as they
> were present to your mind's eye in all their clarity before that French hothead
> confused you. But there too, Clavigo, you must be a true man and pursue
> your goal without looking right or left. Let your soul expand and be filled
> with the certainty that extraordinary men are extraordinary precisely because,
> among other reasons, their duties differ from those of ordinary men: he whose
> task it is to survey a great whole, to govern and preserve it, need not reproach
> himself if he neglects petty details and sacrifices trivial things to the welfare
> of the whole. (Goethe 1988, 178)

Carlos is proven wrong. Marie is not a petty detail or a trivial thing, and Clavigo dies over her coffin with his literary prospects unfulfilled. The play does not seem to take sides but rather to dramatize the fact that the desire to conceive a text can conflict with the desire for a family, a conflict more often voiced today by women than by men.

Goethe (1749–1832) was familiar with this conflict, and he wrote *Clavigo* while going through his own vocational crisis. He penned it in a week in May 1774, when he was twenty-four years old. Almost a year after composing *Clavigo*, he became engaged to Anne Elisabeth Schönemann (1758–1817), known then as Lili, and the relationship flourished, but Goethe's family was not welcoming. Goethe himself was tempted by the wider world of the court and the attractions of Italy. Marriage would have meant settling down in Frankfurt and exchanging poetry for a bureaucratic career—"the end of desire" (Boyle 1992, 199). Lili was sacrificed but not without the high cost of a lacerating memory. Many years later, Goethe confessed to a friend: "She was . . . the first woman whom I deeply and truly loved. And I can say also that she was the last. . . . I was never so near to my own proper happiness as in the period of that love for Lili. The obstacles that kept us apart were not really insuperable—and yet I lost her" (198).

Kierkegaard was repeating Goethe's and Gibbon's choice by yielding to the siren's song of fame, the passion of literature, the allure of texts, and the strong urge to join the intertextual network with a text of his own. For all of these writers the call of the unwritten text was more powerful than their need for the intelligent and graceful women who loved them: Regina Olsen, Lili, and Suzanne Curchod. Yet, when the men wrote the texts they wanted to write, they implicated the women as names in their intertextual projects. Regina, Lili, and Suzanne married other men and had families. Suzanne Curchod, for example, became the wife of Jacques Necker, the Genevan banker who was Louis XVI's finance minister, and she established a literary and political salon in Paris. Her daughter, Anne Louise Germaine Necker, is better known as Madame de Staël.[10]

The Intertextual Family

> One must always guard against contracting a life relationship by which one can become many.
> —Kierkegaard 1987, 297

In January 1992, the Spanish novelist Luis Goytisolo published *Estatua con palomas* [*Statue with Pigeons*], a hybrid text that teeters between autobiography and novel. The statue refers to the empty death mask or the public-square monument by which an illustrious person is institutionally remembered, frozen into one posture and place. The pigeons, domestic and peaceful birds that they are, promise nevertheless to alter the rigor of the fixed image with their restless flight and their haphazard gray droppings. Here again, as in the previously discussed cases of Gibbon, Kierkegaard, and Goethe, the I is not alone, and the monument is surrounded, threatened, and enlivened by others. The one, under scrutiny, becomes many.

The text of *Estatua con palomas* starts as a conventional narrative, with the news of an uncle's death. This falling of one branch of the family tree provides the narrator with the occasion to present a portrait of the Goytisolo genealogy and to locate himself within this immediate circle. Most Spanish readers would realize that the Goytisolo household is not ordinary but one with a recognized place in literature. Of four children, three boys and a sister, the three men are highly respected authors: José Agustín a poet, Juan and Luis mainly fiction writers and occasionally profound and challenging essayists. Both Juan and Luis have written extensively about their family before 1992, Luis in *Antagonía*—a series of four novels—and Juan in the first volume of his autobiography, *Coto vedado* [*Forbidden Territory*], and in many of his fictions. Why is this new version, this repetition, needed? The reader soon observes that the family portrait is a correction. According to the Luis who is the text's first narrator—not to be confused with the implied author Luis Goytisolo, who is a much more complex figure—José Agustín has failed to understand him and mismanaged the family's economic resources. Juan has misunderstood, even maligned, his grand-parents, his father, and his brothers, fueling his career by exploiting the family and presenting a distorted image of his early years. Luis has already become a character in his brothers' texts and needs to intervene in this intertextual power struggle with a text of his own.[11] To effect a change, he must grapple not only with the specious accounts of the family tree already in circulation but with the whole forest that surrounds his I. The family and society have formed the individual, but now that they have receded into the past, he recasts them as he wishes in a prolif-erating confusion of claims and counterclaims. Luis's autobiographical rebuttal is interfered with and blocked by other previous and divergent versions, the obstacle here being not a woman but two brothers, not a broken promise but published texts. How is one to stake a claim in already occupied territory; how to reclaim authority over one's own life?

Luis tries all the usual tricks: he states bluntly that he is more objec-tive, that José Agustín is frivolous, that Juan is an egocentric dandy. He makes the usual assertions that school had no influence on him, that he never fully believed in political parties, that he has always been ruggedly independent, bringing into his life with prescient and innovative flair the correct mixture of sex, writing, and action. By restricting the influential figures of his formative years to his immediate family, he distances himself from other institutions that could define him: school, university, political party, profession, social class, religion, marriage, and literary movement. A reader used to autobiographical strategies can anticipate all of these maneuvers. Something much more radical is needed to dislodge Luis from his brothers' prior texts, and he indeed finds the means to make that dislodgement happen.

In the fourth section of chapter 4, exactly at the center of the book (it has nine chapters and the fourth chapter seven sections), the narrator abruptly shifts from first- to third-person narration. The description focuses on someone at the beach in Ostia, Rome's port, who is meditating on the individual as a single grain of sand or a star in the vastness of the cosmos. The new voice also expresses a desire to attain the correct mixture of sex, writing, and action in the narration. From subsequent sporadic appearances of this same narrator and character, which have been skillfully interpolated into the first-person account of the Goytisolo family, readers discover that the action takes place in the second century A.D., during the very period of splendor and decadence that Gibbon so admirably recreated. The first Roman character to appear in the novel— the man on the beach—is Gayo Junio Cornelio Escipión, a relative of the African Scipio and therefore familiar with the higher echelons of power in the Roman Empire. Junio travels to Alexandria, reports on the activities of the Christian sect, and writes letters to his friend Fulvia. His story is remarkable for what it reveals about somebody else's story, that of his friend Basilio Rufo, a senator's son and a distinguished military leader. Rufo, usually a successful and respected person, is prey to sudden and irresistible surges of wild sexual desire during which he masturbates dogs, offers himself to slaves as a passive sexual partner, especially to Nubians, and rejoices in the contemplation of the sophisticated sexual acts of other companions in debauchery, acts that appear unorthodox even in the Roman Silver Age of Nero and Caligula. There is a highly plausible, although far from obvious, reason for this curious displacement of narrative focus. To identify Basilio Rufo, it is necessary to recall that in *Paisajes después de la batalla* [*Landscapes after the Battle*], a novel published in 1982 by Juan Goytisolo, a pseudoautobiographical character named juan goytisolo (without capital letters) lives at the same Paris address as the author's, in the rue Poissonnière, and among other scandalous acts masturbates dogs in parks and public squares. Juan Goytisolo's homosexuality, as well as his avowed preference for sexual partners of inferior social class and Arab origin, relates him clearly to Basilio Rufo and his liking for Nubian slaves. Through this displaced and nightmarish writing, Luis's history of his family denounces his brother

without mentioning him, a move that would have delighted Freud. Luis
even puts an end to the scandal by having Basilio Rufo assassinated. But
that is not the end of the story.

Among the friends of Junio Cornelio Escipión are Pliny the Younger
(c. 62–c. 113) and Tacitus (c. 56–c. 115). Pliny is known today as one of
the masters of the epistolary genre, and there are hundreds of letters
extant, among them eleven to Tacitus and many others in which he
informs the emperor Trajan about the activities of the Christians he
observed in his travels as a special envoy to Africa. In other letters, Pliny
speaks eloquently about his country houses, his friends, his family, and
his place in history. The descriptions of his villas, one near the port of
Ostia, the other in Umbria, are especially detailed and notable (book 2,
letter 17, and book 5, letter 6). Regarding his place in history, Pliny
writes to Tacitus (book 7, letter 33):

> I believe that your histories will be immortal; a prophecy which will surely
> prove correct. That is why (I frankly admit) I am anxious to appear in them.
> We are usually careful to see that none but the best artists shall portray our
> features, so why should we not want our deeds to be blessed by a writer like
> yourself to celebrate them? (Pliny 1969, 1:559)

House, family, friends, reputation: these are Luis Goytisolo's preoccupations also. A recurrent idea insinuates itself ever more explicitly into
Goytisolo's text: "en el fondo no hay más que una sola persona"
[ultimately there is only one person] (Goytisolo 1992, 170), or, more
pointedly, there are "seres transpersonales" [transpersonal beings] (245,
313, 345), who, because they have similar interests and capacities, walk
themselves into similar situations and resolve their problems in a similar
way. Both Pliny and Tacitus wrote under the reign of Trajan, who
brought an interlude of peace and legality after decades of dictatorship
and violence.[12] Luis Goytisolo writes in the democracy following Franco's regime, but the author of *Estatua con palomas* is not primarily interested in Pliny.

As the narration progresses, the reader discovers that the story of Junio
Escipión has been invented by Tacitus, who attempts, through a fiction in
which he becomes a character instead of history, to give a more exact
account of his contemporaries and of the period. In the pages referring to
the contemporary period, the narrator affirms in exactly the same way
that the writer Luis Goytisolo only *seems* to be writing autobiographical
texts, but in reality (in reality?) he writes fiction. Events and facts are
modified in the workshop of letters to provide a better and more precise
image of contemporary life than history ever could. To reinforce the

similarity, Tacitus—the character in Goytisolo's book—declares that the most productive period in his life was when he was exiled from Rome (Goytisolo 1992, 230). Almost immediately there follows a section in which Luis Goytisolo speaks of his confinement in the jail of Carabanchel in Madrid (239). By analogy, the figure of Basilio Rufo is to Juan what Tacitus is to Luis.

Tacitus's intricate and epigrammatic style, his fast-paced, abrupt sentences, are comparable to many pages by Luis Goytisolo. Furthermore, the Spanish writer claims that the sexual licentiousness in the Barcelona of Franco's last years is reminiscent of the moral breakdown Tacitus criticizes in imperial Rome. Tacitus wants for Rome what Luis Goytisolo wants for Spain, a difficult balance that would encourage freedom of individual expression while retaining enough modesty to allow society to function efficiently in tolerant diversity. Tacitus contributes to the new order by telling the story of his father-in-law, Agricola, the governor of Brittany and a civilization builder. He also describes the Germanic nation, a power threatening Rome from the outskirts of the empire, and he writes the history of the first-century emperors, especially the four who ruled in the year 69 (Galba, Otho, Vitellius, and Vespasian), when the government nearly collapsed. Tacitus thus defines the institutions that have shaped him: family, army, empire. These will be known through the centuries by his words, which the rulers for whom he has built lasting verbal monuments will try in vain to erase. But this is still not the end of the story, although it offers a satisfying resting point. Cornelius Tacitus and Luis Goytisolo are left enjoying their transpersonal selves and the power of their words to define the institutions that have produced them, as they draw them all into a textual network that they themselves define. There is one more turn of the screw; there are still the pigeons.

In the ninth and final chapter, readers learn that what has seemed to be Luis Goytisolo's eccentric autobiography is nothing other, at least in the narrative line, than the transcript of an interview with the "author" by one David, who appears to have been fathered by Luis Goytisolo but who has grown up unrecognized by him. The son confronts the novelist with an unsettling genre: the interview. In *Estatua con palomas,* Luis recalls three interviews, one with each Goytisolo brother, that were published next to one another. The comparison glaringly revealed the contradictions among them. In the interview, there is no longer one voice speaking its uncontested version of truth, as in the autobiography, but at least two voices, one of which is frequently distrustful and intrusive. The interviewer potentially represents all those others who can question an individual's conception of self by challenging the adequacy of the self-

image and the veracity of the stories that can be told about it. The interviewer, like Toto in the famous revelation of *The Wizard of Oz*, can pull
aside the curtain and reveal the unglamorous truth masked by autobiographical special effects.

The autobiographer's trajectory is deflationary and sobering. The
novelist and historian of his own time that Luis Goytisolo portrays in
most of *Estatua con palomas* becomes the subject of a humiliating interview in the final pages. From the monumentality of historical annals and
Tacitus's meticulous vigilance, readers are abruptly shifted to ephemeral
journalism and the improvisation of an interview conducted by a young
apprentice. An institution built in bronze becomes a disposable product
that is discarded at the end of the day. And there is more to this surprising ninth chapter.

In his actions and ideas, David differs significantly from his father, the
Goliath he sets out to deflate. David is a fast-paced, cosmopolitan executive. He believes film is the new narrative form to watch, and he pooh-
poohs Luis's humanism disrespectfully as "una gran trampa" [a great
falsification] that consists of regarding "tanto la Historia en su conjunto
como cualquiera de sus aspectos, las artes, las letras, la propia filosofía
como un todo coherente en pleno desarrollo, mientras . . . se [impone] la
evidencia de que no [hay] una pintura, una música, una literatura, sino
muchas, muchos sistemas de pensamiento y hasta muchas Historias" [all
of History as well as any of its aspects—arts, letters, even philosophy—
as a coherent whole in full development, while the evidence is clear that
there is no such thing as one painting, music, or literature but many,
many systems of thought, and even many Histories] (Goytisolo 1992,
325).

When there is no longer one history, how is it possible to pin down
one version of the family history? How to delineate the filiation that
establishes the link between Barcelona and Rome, between Luis and
Tacitus? How to record the many possible "inters" between sections,
nations, texts, and persons? In spite of conjuring up the authoritative
phantom of the greatest Roman historian of the empire, Luis is unable to
prove that his story is the authorized Goytisolo history. Like Gibbon, the
greatest British historian of the Roman Empire, Luis—the character—is
left trying to remember correctly that most important part of his literary
life, his self-creation in his own novels and the creation of his self in his
brother's autobiography. Taking a step back, though, the author Luis
Goytisolo, by collapsing history and autobiography into the thrill of
gossip, has effectively reduced all of these intersecting versions to a
blurry palimpsest, where readers can never progress beyond the same
uncertainty with which they began. Knowing that his I has unavoidably

become many, that he is trapped in an intertextual web, Goytisolo allows all the voices to clamor in his text, all equally groundless and equally creative. Strapped to the pillars of writing, his own, his brother's, to the writing of all the classics, he, like Samson, brings the temple down. From this radical gesture, from the pattern of the pigeons' flight as they flee the crumbling monument, a strong and memorable image arises, however faint and elusive, of the man Luis Goytisolo, who has lived among others, written among others, and left his entangled traces, following Pliny the Younger's advice: "Since we are denied a long life, let us leave something to bear witness that at least we have lived."

Notes

1. Pliny's entire letter to Caninius Rufus is moving and appropriate to the occasion of this essay, a collection of studies dedicated to H. L. Boudreau. In his letter, Pliny remembers Silius Italicus with admiration and offers a portrait of him that could apply today to the ideal of a scholar that Hal represents: "He ranked as one of our leading citizens without exercising influence [that is, abusing his power] or incurring ill-will . . . and so passed his days in cultured conversation whenever he could spare time from his writing. . . . He was a great connoisseur . . . he had quantities of books, statues and portrait busts, and these were more to him than possessions—they became objects of his devotion, particularly in the case of Virgil, whose birthday he celebrated with more solemnity than his own" (Pliny 1969, 2:183–85).

2. Smith affirms, for example: "the very fact that such signs of the self as the signature can be repeated reveals that the differentiation that enables identity to come into being also calls it into question" (Smith 1992, 19). It is not my wish to argue against these useful observations but to suggest that there is an even more subtle trace of the self, one that is less subject to repetition.

3. Bonnard (1944) discusses these three versions and ultimately considers them all a form of erasure or forgetfulness of Gibbon's thorough preparation in Lausanne for his choice of the topic of ancient Rome. For a good description of the successive drafts of the unfinished autobiography, see Pearson 1991.

4. This remark immediately precedes the famous lines where Gibbon describes deciding on the topic of ancient Rome for his future book.

5. Bonnard, in his excellent edition of Gibbon's *Memoirs of My Life*, compares the three versions and concludes: "Lord Sheffield's substitution of the last (E) version for the former ones was justified from a literary point of view. . . . But such an urge may have entailed some disregard for the actual facts. Where did G really sit musing on the fateful evening? The 'ruins of the Capitol', he had only seen in his imagination, for, in 1764, the Capitol was already what it now is. To what extent is the famous sentence fact, to what extent imagination?" (Gibbon 1966, 305).

6. Betty Radice, the editor of the Penguin edition of *Memoirs of My Life* (Gibbon 1984), today the most readily accessible edition of Gibbon's autobiography (or what passes for it), restores the first version without noting the awkwardness of the false reference to the journals.

7. Gibbon's declaration that he had ceased to be an Englishman should not be taken lightly. His travels and readings had recontextualized his self not only in space but also in language and time, making of him an adoptive citizen of Switzerland who preferred to speak French and who dreamed of Ancient Rome.

8. According to Bonnard, Gibbon had two editions of the younger Pliny's *Epistolae* in his library at Lausanne, as well as W. Melmoth's translation of 1770 (Gibbon 1966, 231). Pliny the Younger's *Epistolarum* is item 193 in Sotheby's *Catalogue of The Library of Edward Gibbon, Historian*, which lists some of the books he left in Lausanne (*Catalogue* 1934). These were sold at auction on Thursday, 20 December 1934. It may be of interest to Hispanists that item 50 is a Spanish edition of *Don Quijote*, printed in Madrid in 1782; item 80 is a Spanish edition of *La Araucana*, printed in Madrid in 1776; item 92 is [Inca] Garcilaso de la Vega's *Royal Commentaries of Peru* in an edition of 1688; and item 233 is Solís's *History of the Conquest of Mexico by the Spaniards* from 1738. To imagine Gibbon at work in his library surrounded by the 274 "lots" listed in this catalogue is to see a life among books, an intertextual life. To see his books sold and dispersed is to witness another trace of the individual vanish, reduced now to a spare listing in a slim pamphlet thirty-one pages long.

9. This line is delivered by Buenco, who represents integrity and good judgment.

10. It is ironic that Germaine Necker greatly disappointed her mother when she refused to marry William Pitt, a rising star in English politics and prime minister from 1783 to 1801 and again from 1804 to 1806. He does not seem to have been a great catch, preferring younger boys and alcohol to conversing with French intellectuals. See Claude Manceron's chatty *Age of the French Revolution*, where he quotes from Germaine's adolescent diary: "Why must that wretched England have provoked the stiffness and coldness of *maman*? Accursed isle, source of my present fears, source of my future remorse" (Manceron 1989, 163). Were these still the effects of Gibbon's broken promise?

11. Díaz-Migoyo offers an excellent description of the textual struggle between Juan and Luis Goytisolo (Díaz-Migoyo 1991, 61–62).

12. Pliny writes in letter 13 of book 9: "Once Domitian was killed I decided on reflection that this was a truly splendid opportunity for attacking the guilty, avenging the injured, and making myself known" (Pliny 1969, 2:99).

Works Cited

Blanco White, José. 1845. *The Life of the Rev. Joseph Blanco White, Written by Himself.* Ed. John Hamilton Thom. 3 vols. London: John Chapman.

Bonnard, Georges. 1944 . "L'importance du deuxième séjour de Gibbon à Lausanne dans la formation de l'historien." In *Mélanges d'histoire et de littérature offerts à Monsieur Charles Gillard*, 400–420. Lausanne: La Concorde.

Boyle, Nicholas. 1992. *Goethe: The Poet and the Age*. Vol. 1, *The Poetry of Desire*. Oxford: Oxford University Press.

Catalogue of The Library of Edward Gibbon, Historian. 1934. London: Sotheby.

Díaz-Migoyo, Gonzalo. 1991. "La ajena autobiografía de los hermanos Goytisolo." *Anthropos* 125: 61–62.

Gibbon, Edward. 1796. *Miscellaneous Works of Edward Gibbon, Esquire; with Memoirs of His Life and Writings, Composed by Himself, Illustrated from His Letters*. Ed. John Baker Holroyd, Lord Sheffield. 2 vols. London: Strahan and Cadell.

————. 1896. *The Autobiographies*. Ed. John Murray. London: John Murray.

————. 1966. *Memoirs of My Life*. Ed. Georges Bonnard. London: Nelson.

————. 1984. *Memoirs of My Life*. Ed. Betty Radice. London: Penguin.

Goethe, Johann Wolfgang von. 1949. *Poetry and Truth*. Trans. R. O. Moon. Washington, D.C.: Public Affairs Press.

————. 1988. *Clavigo. A Tragedy*. Trans. Robert M. Browning. In *Early Verse Drama and Prose Plays*. Ed. Cyrus Hamlin and Frank Ryder, 153–88. New York: Suhrkamp.

Goytisolo, Luis. 1992. *Estatua con palomas*. Barcelona: Destino.

Kierkegaard, Søren. 1987. *Either/Or*, part 1. Ed. and trans. Howard V. Hong and Edna H. Hong. Vol. 3, *Kierkegaard's Writings*. Princeton: Princeton University Press.

León, María Teresa. 1970. *Memoria de la melancolía*. Buenos Aires: Losada.

Manceron, Claude. 1989. *Age of the French Revolution*. Vol. 4, *Toward the Brink: 1785–1787*. New York: Simon & Schuster.

Pearson, John H. 1991. "Reading the Writing in the Drafts of Edward Gibbon's *Memoirs*." *Biography* 14: 222–42.

Pliny. 1969. *Letters and Panegyricus*. Ed. and trans. Betty Radice. 2 vols. Cambridge, Mass.: Harvard University Press.

Smith, Paul Julian. 1992. *Representing the Other: "Race," Text, and Gender in Spanish and Spanish American Narrative*. Oxford: Clarendon Press.

Torres Villarroel, Diego de. 1972. *Vida, ascendencia, nacimiento, crianza y aventuras*. Ed. Guy Mercadier. Madrid: Castalia.

Intertextual Lives:
Blanco White and Juan Goytisolo

ANGEL G. LOUREIRO

In their attempts to define the genre, theorists of autobiography have been forced to abandon an epistemological model—autobiography as reproduction of a life—in favor of the idea of autobiography as performative act—autobiography as the creation or re-creation of the self at the time of writing. This displacement of one model for another is already perceptible in George Gusdorf's pioneer article "Conditions and Limits of Autobiography." Published originally in French in 1956, this essay is considered the founding piece of contemporary autobiographical studies precisely because Gusdorf leaves behind the simple and naive representational model of autobiography as duplication of a life and replaces it with a productive model, a departure that is clearly discernible in the slogan that Gusdorf chooses for autobiography: "To create and in creating to be created" (Gusdorf 1980, 44).

Barrett J. Mandel (1980), in an article with the expressive title "Full of Life Now" (the "now" being the time when the autobiographer writes his/her life), and James Olney (1980b), in "Some Versions of Memory/ Some Versions of *Bios*," are two important critics who propose a productive or performative model of autobiography. They emphasize the present time of writing in their theories, while the proponents of representational autobiography favor the past time of the narrated life. Still, the privileging of the present and the viewing of autobiography as a life-producing act do not cause the first group of critics to abandon the idea that autobiography, in some manner, reproduces the past life. The impulse to preserve the past is evident in *Fictions in Autobiography*, where one of the most sophisticated critics of the genre, Paul John Eakin (1985), argues that just as the child first gains access to its identity when

it enters the symbolic realm of language (*pace* Lacan), so does autobiography mark a second access to identity, also through language, but now at
the moment of writing.[1] The temporal displacement towards the present
of writing does not preclude the belief that autobiography in some way
re-produces a life.[2] Feminist criticism of autobiography faces a similar
quandary, since its proponents are torn between the notion of autobiography as reproduction of experience and poststructuralist ideas about
language, identity, and writing that seem opposed to such a conception.
Caught between a politics of identity and an opposing ethics of writing
and reading, feminist criticism of autobiography is by nature, and against
all appearances, a conservative stance. Olney summarizes, with understandable hedging, autobiography's central dilemma: "In some tangled,
obscure, shifting, and ungraspable way . . . , [autobiography] is, or stands
in for, or memorializes, or replaces, or makes something else of someone's life" (Olney 1980a, 24).

In the approaches considered so far, which are essentially epistemological or ontological because they try to relate autobiography to a
substance of the writing subject, the crux of the problem rests with the
life and self-knowledge of that subject. The autobiographical act imposes
a responsibility that must remain unfulfilled, since the subject is never
able to explain his or her life fully. Autobiography might be best appre-
hended not as epistemological re-production but as an act that is at once
intertextual, rhetorical, and ethical. All autobiographies are actually
heterobiographies, that is, autobiographies of an other who can assume
different shapes and roles.[3]

Like any text, autobiography emanates primarily from other texts, not
from the life of its author. As one observer argues, "autobiography more
than any other genre has been linked with [the] idea of a founding subject," a notion that, in her opinion, has been dismantled by intertextuality
(Jefferson 1990, 127). The fundamental problem confronted by modern
autobiography is the dwindling of faith in individuality. Autobiography
has become a struggle about origins and self-determination. Constituted
by the intertexts that precede them, modern autobiographers must ignore
those tainted origins and convert the writing of their autobiographies into
a struggle to discover a self that is personal, unique, and original—but
without origins. Thus, Rousseau's proclamation at the beginning of his
Confessions (Rousseau 1973, 33) that what he is going to do has no
antecedents and can have no imitators soon ceases to be a radical novelty
because that aspiration will be the implicit goal of all modern autobiographers, the foundation of the faith in their uniqueness. That aspiration is
also the main source of the blindness that prevents them from seeing their
debt to the other. As Paul de Man suggests, autobiography is not a genre

but a figure of reading (de Man 1984, 70); not a writing, I would add, but always a reading or a counterreading of the stories already in circulation about the autobiographer. Above all, it is a reading of the self, which in modernity becomes an infinite hermeneusis, an endless seeking after that self. It might be said, therefore, that autobiographers are apostates who strive vainly to find the road back to the home they have to leave in order to find themselves.[4]

José Blanco White, born in Seville to parents of Irish origins (Blanco is the repetition of his surname in translation), is an apostate in the modern sense of a person who abandons a religious faith or a cause. He became a Catholic priest, but in 1810, during the War of Independence, after fathering an illegitimate child and after a period of religious doubts, "almost by accident, . . . the idea occurred to him of leaving Spain altogether for England." So states Martin Murphy (1989, 56), accurately basing his account on the explanations in Blanco's autobiography. In England, where he had connections with distinguished dignitaries like Lord Holland, he became an Anglican and later was appointed a fellow of Oxford's Oriel College. Unhappy with Anglican dogmatism, he committed a new apostasy by leaving the Church of England to become a Unitarian. From the time of his arrival in England until his death there in 1841, he dedicated himself almost obsessively to combating religious dogmatism, first in Catholicism and later in the Anglican Church, which he accused of a religious intolerance as pernicious as the papists'. The narratives, diaries, and letters that constitute his autobiography were written in English and were published posthumously in 1845 with the title *The Life of the Rev. Joseph Blanco White, Written by Himself*. Menéndez Pelayo, who condemns Blanco White to his pantheon of heterodoxies, writes of him that he "pasó sus trabajos [*sic*] e infelices días, como nave sin piloto en ruda tempestad, entre continuas apostasías y cambios de frente" [spent his laborious and unhappy days, like a rudderless ship in a rough storm, between continuous apostasies and changes of mind] (Menéndez Pelayo 1987, 791).[5]

Blanco White started his autobiography in Oxford in 1830. At the beginning, he structured it as a series of letters to a friend, Dr. Richard Whately, later Archbishop of Dublin, who encouraged Blanco to write his life. Blanco launched the project moved by "the necessity of leaving my friends in possession of every important fact relating to myself, in order that they may refute the calumnies and misrepresentations of my enemies, when I shall be no more" (Blanco White 1845, 1:1). Blanco's *Life* is framed, therefore, as an apostrophe, that is, addressed to Whaltey but really destined for a third party. At the same time, he makes use of the typical autobiographical form of the confession. As Foucault argues, the confession is a fundamental technique of individuation, one of the privileged forms for creating a discourse of truth about oneself that impels the subject to constitute itself as self-consciousness within a power relationship in which the interlocutor wields complete authority to punish or forgive (Foucault 1980, 58–62).

As I have already suggested, Blanco White's life is a crusade against all oppressive religious dogmas, and confession, in his view, is one of Catholicism's most damaging practices. Blanco's sharpest indictment of confession comes in his description of the spiritual exercises as a discipline whose goal is to make the penitents reach "that peculiar state of the mind, that devotional tenderness, which renders the mental faculties powerless, and reduces the moral being to the weakness of infancy" (Blanco White 1845, 1:47). Confession, Blanco writes, "is one of the most mischievous practices of the Romanist Church" because of its minute attention to every fault and because it confers on another total authority over the conscience of the confessed (1:43). It is noteworthy, however, that of the two main characteristics of confession, self-examination and confession to another, Blanco actually rejects only the latter, the submission of the self to the authority of the confessor. He sees confession as a practice that could have destroyed "the quick moral perception which God had naturally given to my mind. . . . Free, however, from that debasing practice, my conscience assumed the rule, and, independently of hopes and fears, it clearly blamed what was clearly wrong, and, as it were, learnt to act by virtue of its natural supremacy" (1:44).

Blanco's attack on Catholic spiritual exercises provides the key to a reading of his *Life* because his account opposes the passions to natural morality, authority to freedom, deviousness to rectitude. The exercises are themselves devious because their goal is accomplished by spiritual discipline, by submission to the persuasive powers of another, the confessor. To the falseness of rhetoric as persuasion Blanco opposes a kind of transparent and primordial language of the soul that allows his conscience to assume the authority to judge, because "a love of what is right, and an abhorrence of baseness, however sanctified by superstition, had been implanted in my soul" (1:44).

Spontaneous, natural, granted by God: this is a series of interchangeable metaphors that Blanco opposes to what is artificial, imposed by man, and evil. He conceives his life as an endless search for the original being that his Catholic education perverted and was about to destroy. In order to recover that lost essence—mythic or metaphorical—Blanco must become an apostate, must renounce his current condition, religious and political.[6] The same passions that are opposed to the natural and original state of the soul also hide the transparency of meaning in writing, and the reading of texts as well as of souls will consist of finding out what those passions conceal:

> Autobiographies are instructive, almost without exception, provided that the reader knows how to study mankind, for, even when the account is written under the influence of vanity or some other passion, it will afford opportunities of studying the workings of the heart and mind in a state of transient or settled moral disease. . . . [B]ut, as the prejudices and passions of the reader can scarcely ever be identical with those of the writer, there is the greatest probability that the delusions of the latter will generally be apparent to the former, merely from the circumstance that he is placed in a different position. (Blanco White 1845, 3:366–67)

In this passage, Blanco is commenting on the memoirs of the Quaker John Woolman, a book that Blanco praises because it "teaches us to *translate minds*, just as, by means of Grammars and Dictionaries, we become able to translate languages. For such moral translations as I recommend, we are sure to find the key in our own hearts and minds, provided they are not in bondage to any man. The *truth* is one; and the Source of it One, accessible to all rational beings" (3:370).

The natural, rational, and benevolent being is the final image, the master trope on which Blanco's autobiography rests, the image that gives formal structure to the work and generates its central themes as well. One might also say that the most important lesson this apostate imparts is the right to read himself according to the natural and universal codes that run counter to the univocal, evil-inspired, and oppressive tenets of the church. This apostate, however, will never find a way to return home because, by following the logic of the passions that he proposes, his reading will only be the first in an endless chain of readings that will correct one another. Hence, his initial intention of writing his autobiography to correct false future readings of his life becomes a useless gesture that will be able to stop neither that endless reading nor the misunderstanding that is its consequence. In order to counter the univocal reading of the church, Blanco at once unleashes and tries to contain the terror of that infinite reading.

At the beginning of his *Life*, Blanco refers to the reading of souls: "The rest had to study me; you [Whately] read me without preparation" (1:2). It seems difficult to find a good reader of souls. Blanco's theory of reading leads to the surprising conclusion that Menéndez Pelayo will be his ideal reader, since the Spanish philologist denounces Blanco's life as a perpetual error precisely because he let himself be blinded by his passions:

Toda creencia, todo capricho de la mente o del deseo se convirtió en él en pasión; y como su fantasía era tan móvil como arrebatado y violento su carácter, fue espejo lastimosísimo de la desorganización moral a que arrastra el predominio de las facultades imaginativas sueltas a todo galope en medio de una época turbulenta. (Menéndez Pelayo 1987, 790–91)

[Every belief, every fancy conceived by his mind or his desire became for him a passion; and since his fantasy was as voluble as his character, he was a singularly painful example of the kind of moral disorganization produced by the predominance of the imaginative faculties, set free to gallop in the midst of a tumultuous age.]

Menéndez Pelayo's accusation is nothing short of paradoxical, given that Blanco's central religious and philosophical ideas rest on a strong exaltation of reason and on an equally clear condemnation of the passions and the imagination. Blanco rejects God's external revelation—in the Gospels, for instance—and insists on the idea that God's true revelation takes place in the individual's interior realm: "I believe in the internal presence of God in the sanctuary of the Soul. . . . That Oracle is the source of every Truth, of every Virtue in Man" (Blanco White 1845, 3:29). That internal revelation is the foundation and the guarantee of the soul or the spirit, whose main attribute is reason, which regulates the real and works in opposition to the imagination, a "treacherous Faculty" "intimately allied" with the flesh, desire, and the passions (3:23, 92, 121–22).

This extreme rationalism is Blanco's final philosophy, and it is the one that allows him to reconcile his philosophical ideas with his Christian faith. It could be argued that such rationalism is present in Blanco almost from the beginning, as his early fascination with the works of the eighteenth-century Benedictine friar Benito Jerónimo Feijoo attests. Blanco is a full-fledged man of the Enlightenment, and his entire life is a struggle to find a religious faith—in his case, Unitarianism—that will agree with his rationalism. When Feijoo states in the "Prologue to the Reader" of his *Teatro crítico* that he is going to deal with all sorts of common errors, he adds that he will purposely leave aside any consideration of religious ideas (Feijoo 1968, 81). Completing Feijoo's work, Blanco takes up religion's errors almost exclusively.[7] Actually, it would be difficult to distinguish between the ideas Blanco owes to Feijoo and those that he takes from the intellectual ambiance of the late eighteenth century. Blanco's religious position is best defined as a form of deism, with emphasis on an extreme rationalism that harks back to the Stoics, a philosophical school highly influential during the eighteenth century (see Gay 1977). In tune with various manifestations of deism, Blanco condemns all aspects of religion that are irrational or that constitute expressions of passion: superstition, enthusiasm, intolerance, oppression.[8] Given Blanco's insistence on reason and his denunciation of passion, it is therefore surprising to find that Menéndez Pelayo portrays him as a victim of his passions and whims.[9]

Blanco finds a much more receptive reader in Juan Goytisolo, who, coincidentally, also expresses himself in terms of readers and readings:

[A] diferencia de los demás países de Europa occidental, en donde todo lector capaz de comprender y valorar lo que lee tiene acceso libre a las fuentes de la cultura nacional, el lector de lengua española recibe ésta a través de un filtro purificador destinado a retener toda la escoria susceptible de contaminar los muy puros raudales de la ortodoxia hispana. Separados de la obra de Blanco por el denso telón de silencio y oprobio de nuestros *zombis*, sus eventuales lectores no han podido arrancarle de la casilla en que lo encerrara el conocido celo apostólico del polígrafo montañés. Mazmorra o sepultura más bien, ¡y vaya una!—la de apóstata, renegado, abominable y antipatriota, que justificaría por sí sola la mortaja piadosa que lo cubre. (Goytisolo 1982, 4)

[As opposed to the other Western European countries, where any reader who is able to understand and evaluate what he/she reads has free access to the sources of his/her nation's culture, the Spanish reader receives his/her culture through a purifying filter meant to retain all the scum that could contaminate the very pure streams of Spanish orthodoxy. Separated from Blanco's work by the thick curtain of silence and contempt of our zombies, his chance readers have been unable to remove him from the box where he was imprisoned by Menéndez Pelayo's apostolic fervor. A dungeon or a grave, more likely, and what a grave!—that of the apostate, the renegade, the abominable antipatriot, the latter alone being enough to justify the pious shroud that envelops him.]

Ninety-four pages later, Goytisolo ends the introduction to his anthology of Blanco White by confessing: "Acabo ya y sólo ahora advierto que al hablar de Blanco White no he cesado de hablar de mí mismo" [I am about to finish, and only now do I realize that when I was speaking of Blanco White I was speaking of myself all the time] (98). This perceived interchangeability between the two writers leads us to the only place where we can determine its veracity: Goytisolo's own autobiography.[10]

Juan Goytisolo closes *En los reinos de taifa* [*Realms of Strife*], the second volume of an autobiography that began with *Coto vedado* [*Forbidden Territory*], by pointing to the immanent pitfalls of any autobiographical project: the temporal and spatial limitations of memory, the "infranqueable distancia del hecho a lo escrito, . . . las leyes y exigencias del texto narrativo" (Goytisolo 1986, 309) [unbridgeable distance between act and written word, . . . the laws and requirements of the narrative text] (Goytisolo 1990, 261). It could be observed initially that this statement appears at the end of the more than five hundred pages of his two-volume autobiography, in which he narrates with emphatic sincerity the painful vicissitudes of his pursuit of an authentic and pure inner domain. Contrary to appearances, however, the very statement that seems to question the viability of autobiography in fact reinforces a thoroughly idealistic conception of that genre, since the imperfect mimesis that Goytisolo deplores helps to create the strongest possible illusion of a reality so real that it is ineffable. This frustration concerning a language incapable of representing the most intimate human dimension affirms the opposite of what it seems to negate. Against the laws of art and against aesthetics, Goytisolo wants readers to believe that they should not doubt the extreme fidelity to the real, the intention of sincerity, and the moral rigor that guide him in his struggle to represent reality. The denial of the possibility of mimesis becomes the strongest possible mimesis, which grants unmediated access to the purity proper to the subject. The limited memory of the autobiographer stresses the plenitude of a lived life, but memory works as a synecdoche here, as a part that cannot contain the totality of space or time's flux. Yet, because it is synecdochic, incomplete memory allows the reader to catch a glimpse of the reality of such totalities: memory as impoverishment and deferral is the imperfect remembrance of plenitude. At this point, autobiography as reproduction of a life becomes a rhetorical enterprise, and the only way to restore the epistemological dimension is through an ethical gesture, which, in Goytisolo's case, is the promise of sincerity. Epistemology, rhetoric, and ethics are inseparable in autobiography.

Goytisolo conceives of his self in terms of agon, genealogy, death, and rebirth (see Loureiro 1991–92, 85–88).[11] Is there anything in Goytisolo that stands as the final figure for the self in the same way that in Blanco there is the natural, rational, and benevolent being? What are the rhetorical maneuvers by which the self constitutes itself as figure when it seeks to recreate a substance? In particular, Goytisolo shapes his self through a series of substitutive exchanges between exterior reality and his presumed interiority. Commenting self-reflexively on an old article of his about Spain's present and future situations, rereading himself in a manner similar to Blanco's, Goytisolo confesses his error of having taken his desires for reality. Goytisolo rereads his old essay, but he is actually reading himself. His past error, his false identification in that article of Spain with the Third World, reveals that the truth of the subject is the confusion of the subjective with the objective. That false identification permits his self to take the shape of absolute interiority: Goytisolo can make a mistake, but, in his opinion, one cannot doubt the reality and transparency of his "dolorosa sinceridad" (Goytisolo 1986, 64) [painful sincerity] (Goytisolo 1990, 54). The generating formula of Goytisolo's identity and self-knowledge could be "I err (with passion), therefore I exist."

At about the same time, referring to his apocalyptic vision of life and unconscious desire to solve problems in a suicidal act of self-immolation, he writes: "Aunque sincero, tu gesto era excesivo y escamoteaba teatralmente el debate contigo y con tu verdad" (Goytisolo 1986, 65) [Although sincere, your gesture was excessive and theatrically avoided the debate with yourself and with your own reality] (Goytisolo 1990, 55). To counter the precariousness and defects inherent in memory, Goytisolo accuses himself time and again of "insidiosa irracionalidad" [insidious irrationality], of "falta de una relación limpia contigo mismo" (Goytisolo 1986, 63) [lack of an unsullied relationship with yourself] (Goytisolo 1990, 53), of disagreement between his being and his image, of a "sigilosa conciencia de impostura" (Goytisolo 1986, 114) [furtive awareness of being an impostor] (Goytisolo 1990, 97). Nevertheless, excess and error, far from preventing access to self-constituting reflection, allow it: the self at odds with itself allows for the possibility of a perfect harmony of the self. In these examples, Goytisolo's self takes the contours of an empty space carved out by excess and error. This empty, specular image acquires full representational force in other cases:

Pero la lucidez retrospectiva con que te juzgas no vino entonces en tu socorro: por espacio de un tiempo odioso, vivirías irremediablemente a la sombra de tu Mr. Hyde.

Figuraciones, pesadillas, desdoblamientos: impresión de asistir impotente a los manejos y ardides de un personaje que asume tus apariencias, actúa en tu nombre, lleva tus documentos, estampa tu firma, vestido y calzado como tú, identificado contigo por tus vecinos, inquilino de tu propio apartamento. . . . Evocar sus oníricas, espectrales hazañas, ser su juez y memoria. . . . Escudriñar los recovecos de una esquizofrenia remota y percatarte con alivio de su ausencia definitiva. ¿Producto morboso de un ofuscamiento pasajero o ente real, expulsado a escobazos, en enérgica, saludable barrida? (Goytisolo 1986, 222–23)

[But the retrospective lucidity with which you now judge yourself did not then come to your aid: for a hateful length of time you would live irremediably in the shadow of your Mr. Hyde.

Suppositions, nightmares, a split existence: the impression that you were a powerless witness to the wiles and maneuvers of a character who looks like

q

you, acts in your name, carries your documents, writes your signature, wears
your clothes and shoes, is identified with you by the neighbors, the tenant in
your flat. . . . You evoke his oneiric, spectral exploits, are his judge and
memory. . . . You peer into the hidden corners of a distant schizophrenia and
observe with relief that he has gone for good. The morbid product of passing
mystification or a real being, swept away in a healthy, vigorous cleanup?]
(Goytisolo 1990, 188–89)

Schizophrenia, compensatory fantasies, Mr. Hyde, the informer
("malsín") are some of the names, some of the figures that carve out a
space where Goytisolo's self will shine in all its truth, once the ghosts
that occupy the space are ousted. Goytisolo imagines his self as the result
of a purification process that will give him access to a space of pure self-
affection. That personal space is already evident in the titles of the two
autobiographical volumes. Once he figures the self as a (metaphorical)
space occupied by an unwelcome and treacherous guest, it becomes
possible for "cualquier cartógrafo competente y honrado" (Goytisolo
1986, 216) [any honest, competent cartographer] (Goytisolo 1990, 183)
to trace out and expel the bogus double and vacate the space for new,
exemplary figures. Jean Genet is the principal model that Goytisolo
attempts to imitate and interiorize in this endeavor, the major figure in a
pantheon of models like Beckett, Cernuda, and Lezama Lima, who represent authenticity, critical passion, and moral knowledge. [12]
   It comes as no surprise to find a familiar name occupying a special
place among that group of worthy paradigms: "deslumbramiento,
apropiación de Blanco White. Inolvidable experiencia de traducirte al
traducirle, sin saber a la postre si existió en realidad o fue una remota
encarnación de ti mismo" (Goytisolo 1986, 81) [you . . . are dazzled by
and appropriate Blanco White. The unforgettable experience of translat-
ing yourself as you translate him, without in the end knowing if he really
existed or was a distant incarnation of yourself" (Goytisolo 1990, 69).
With Blanco White, the chain of figurative substitutions, of would-be
Goytisolos—Genet, Beckett, Cernuda, etc.—reaches the culmination of
the phantasmatic: Blanco White is not merely translated by Goytisolo but
is appropriated in an act of cannibalism, transformed into Goytisolo's
flesh, a re-incarnation. At this point, we cannot help mistrusting every
reader, especially when the reading proclaims the utmost fidelity and
offers itself as an exemplary *lectio*. Because Goytisolo's reading of
Blanco White is deeply and openly moral, the perfect coincidence that
makes the two writers interchangeable in Goytisolo's view is only
possible if Goytisolo identifies himself with Blanco's apostasy. All that
their apostasies have in common, however, is a deviation from a previous

state. Their destinations, the new states they claim to reach, could not be farther apart. Blanco's apostasy is a reaching back to his original, rational, and benevolent self, the one granted by a God who represents a deism close to natural religion, whereas God and religion are necessarily absent from Goytisolo's life, at least in its textual form. Goytisolo's reading of Blanco White is in fact the perfect negative of Menéndez Pelayo's, since one praises what the other condemns, and both engage in their readings from the height of their respective and opposite passions. Blanco White teaches mistrust of the type of reading that must be dispossessed of its passion in order to be truthful. Such dispossession can be accomplished only through another reading, through another *lectio*.

Harold Bloom has demonstrated persuasively that all readings are necessarily misreadings: "Influence . . . means that there are *no* texts, but only relationships *between* texts. These relationships depend upon a critical act, a misreading or misprision" (Bloom 1975, 3). After initially charting those relationships between texts in a strictly psychological mode as Oedipal struggles between the later writer and the precursor, and after reacting to Paul de Man's criticism (de Man 1983), Bloom expands his map of misprision so that it becomes "a charting through revisionary ratios, psychic defenses, rhetorical tropes, and imagistic groupings" (Bloom 1975, 55). By making Blanco a precursor, Goytisolo commits a misreading that necessarily ignores the differences that separate the two authors. Blanco's concerns are almost exclusively religious, and his focus is on finding a religion that agrees with his rational philosophy. Goytisolo defines his self through a complete rejection of religion, fatherland, genealogy, language, and conventional sexuality. Although Blanco participates actively in political debates concerning the government of Spain and the destiny of its American colonies, he eschews the radical rejection of the fatherland that is an integral part of Goytisolo's self-definition. Nor is there anything resembling sexual liberation in Blanco, who in his *Life* glosses over his affair with a woman in Madrid. Possibly in order not to hurt the son born of that illegitimate relationship, Blanco destroyed the pages devoted to that affair in *The Examination of Blanco by White concerning his religious notions*, an unpublished manuscript he wrote around 1818–19, in which he dealt with his youthful amorous inclinations (Murphy 1989, 107). Goytisolo is far from being a reincarnation of Blanco White, but he represents a stunning case of what Bloom calls *clinamen*, a corrective reading "which implies that the precursor went accurately up to a certain point, but then should have swerved" (Bloom 1973, 14). Pretending to be his mirror image, Goytisolo swerves from Blanco White and effects a *tessera*, completing him where he did not go far enough. By not holding back anything that refers

to his homosexual awakening, Goytisolo also accomplishes a process of
daemonization, a self-immersion in an abject "Counter-Sublime, in reaction to the precursor's Sublime" (Bloom 1973, 15).

The delusion that leads Goytisolo to see himself as a reincarnation of
Blanco White is grounded in the rhetorical figures of irony, synecdoche,
and hyperbole (Bloom 1975, 84; de Man 1983, 275). By conflating his
self and Blanco's, Goytisolo believes he is disclosing his inner self, but
he is actually confusing psychology with rhetoric, in the same way that in
de Man's view Bloom uses in *The Anxiety of Influence* "a naturalistic
language of desire, possession, and power," a language of "pathos" (de
Man 1983, 271), when in reality he is merely talking of rhetorical
relationships. De Man's question concerning autobiography is thus pertinent: "is the illusion of reference not a correlation of the structure of the
figure, that is to say no longer clearly and simply a referent at all but
something more akin to a fiction which then, however, in its own turn,
acquires a degree of referential productivity?" (de Man 1984, 69). Blanco
and Goytisolo confuse rhetoric with psychology when they construe their
lives as a process of purification and reencounter with a self, without
realizing that they are actually creating intertextual selves that borrow
their constitutional images from the texts of religion, politics, or contemporary psychology. But could it be otherwise? De Man's insistence on
privileging the linguistic moment at all costs seems to me as unsatisfying
as Bloom's obstinacy in *The Anxiety of Influence*, where he sees intertextual relationships exclusively in terms of pathos and desire. The solution
based on "the analogical principle that tropes and defenses are interchangeable," which he offers in *A Map of Misreading*, also falls short
because "analogy" is too vague an explanation. Is psychology merely
blind rhetoric? As long as we believe that such a thing as autobiography,
with all its limitations, exists, that certain authors write their lives and
certain readers read autobiographically, it is not possible to maintain that
autobiography is a purely linguistic maneuver. This is not to say that the
referential dimension in autobiography comes from the reality lived by
the author, a reality that presumably determines what is narrated in an
autobiographical text, and how. When he or she writes, the author is
actually always reading—and there is no better example of that than
Goytisolo's identification with Blanco White.[13] Autobiography is a
mode of reading, de Man argues. I would add that it is also an ethical act,
a necessary blindness that transforms rhetorical tropes into psychological
traits and thus permits certain texts to be called autobiographical.

The autobiographies of Blanco White and Goytisolo are marked by
deviation. Both autobiographies have speakers who apparently address
narratees but have someone else in mind, and both are at once laudatory

justifications of the writers' lives and attempts to correct misrepresentations that already circulate or will circulate about them. But, as Menéndez Pelayo attests, Blanco White is incapable of controlling the insidious
stories that others broadcast about him. Upon abandoning their conditions, the apostates embrace a wandering destiny, and their return home
is always deferred. Their autobiographies, like all writing, suffer a similar
fate, because the fate of the apostates, of their lives as writing, is the
endless wandering of reading. The self is always, and above all, simply a
misunderstanding. That is the final reading, the ultimate *lectio* of
apostasy.

Notes

1. Eakin elaborates his theories in chap. 4, "Self-Invention in Autobiography: The
Moment of Language" (Eakin 1985, 181–278).

2. In his latest book on the subject, *Touching the World: Reference in Autobiography*,
Eakin insists on the referential aspects of the genre, reacting against the proponents of autobiography as a pure textual construct without ties to reality. See especially his discussion of *Roland Barthes par Roland Barthes* (Eakin 1992, 4–23).

3. For a detailed exploration of autobiography as heterobiography and as apostrophe,
see Loureiro (1991–92). In his lucid analysis of Blanco White's *Life*, Fernández also
mentions Quintilian's definition of apostrophe, but he reaches different conclusions about
its use in autobiography (Fernández 1992, 21–22, 55).

4. "Apostate" is formed by the Greek prefix "apo," meaning "out of," "from," and
"histemi," meaning "to place," "to set," "to stand." Etymologically speaking, an apostate
is a runaway slave or, more generally, someone who escapes from his/her place, who
leaves his/her estate or state, a renegade.

5. All translations of Menéndez Pelayo are mine, as are the translations from Goytisolo's *Obra inglesa de D. José María Blanco White*. Quotations from Goytisolo's *Realms
of Strife* are from Peter Bush's translation.

6. It is not surprising that the genuine state he seeks to regain is associated with reading, since, throughout his autobiography, he pays special attention to books; it is even
more revealing that he writes a good part of his autobiography by transcribing and commenting on his old diaries. For Blanco's continuous rereading of his life, see Fernández
(1992, 66–67). It should be noted, however, that Blanco does not change substantially
once he becomes a Unitarian, and the reassessment of his life often emphasizes the extent
to which his current ideas were already present in the past.

7. I use "completing" in Harold Bloom's sense (1973, 14, 49–73). For Blanco's devotion to Feijoo, see Domergue (1983).

8. A good overview of the religious situation in eighteenth-century Spain can be found
in Sánchez-Blanco Parody (1991).

9. Blanco's philosophical ideas are inseparable from the construction of his self in his
autobiography. He sees his soul as God-granted, rational, and naturally moral—three
characteristics that are intrinsically tied together—but perverted by pernicious religious

influences. His *Life* narrates the expurgatory journey that presumably allows him to find his original soul anew.

10. For other readings of Blanco White's *Life*, besides Menéndez Pelayo's and Goytisolo's, see Murphy (1989, 194–204) and Fernández (1992, 72–86).

11. Fernández (1991) sees Goytisolo's autobiographical project as the creation of a new genealogy, as the replacement of "filiation" by "affiliation."

12. For Goytisolo and Genet, see Epps (1992); for the relationship between Goytisolo and Blanco White, see also Mercadier (1989).

13. Villanueva (1993) finds a way out of this problem by proposing that the rhetorical mode proper to autobiography is paradox.

Works Cited

Barthes, Roland. 1975. *Roland Barthes par Roland Barthes*. Paris: Seuil.

Blanco White, Joseph. 1845. *The Life of the Rev. Joseph Blanco White, Written by Himself*. Ed. John Hamilton Thom. 3 vols. London: John Chapman.

Bloom, Harold. 1973. *The Anxiety of Influence*. New York: Oxford University Press.

———. 1975. *A Map of Misreading*. New York: Oxford University Press.

De Man, Paul. 1983. "Review of Harold Bloom's *Anxiety of Influence*." In *Blindness and Insight: Essays in the Rhetoric of Contemporary Criticism*, 2d ed., 267–76. Minneapolis: University of Minnesota Press.

———. 1984. "Autobiography as De-Facement." In *The Rhetoric of Romanticism*, 67–81. New York: Columbia University Press.

Domergue, Lucienne. 1983. "Feijoo y Blanco White (Homenaje de un 'hereje' al Padre Maestro)." In *II Simposio sobre el Padre Feijoo y su siglo*, 333–48. Oviedo: Universidad de Oviedo.

Eakin, Paul John. 1985. *Fictions in Autobiography: Studies in the Art of Self-Invention*. Princeton: Princeton University Press.

———. 1992. *Touching the World: Reference in Autobiography*. Princeton: Princeton University Press.

Epps, Brad. 1992. "Thievish Subjectivity: Self-Writing in Jean Genet and Juan Goytisolo." *Revista de Estudios Hispánicos* 26: 163–81.

Feijoo, Benito Jerónimo. 1968. *Teatro crítico universal*. Ed. Agustín Millares Carlo. Vol. 1. Clásicos Castellanos, vol. 48. Madrid: Espasa-Calpe.

Fernández, James D. 1991. "La novela familiar del autobiógrafo: Juan Goytisolo." *Anthropos* 125: 54–60.

———. 1992. *Apology to Apostrophe: Autobiography and the Rhetoric of Self-Representation in Spain*. Durham: Duke University Press.

Foucault, Michel. 1980. *The History of Sexuality*. Trans. Robert Hurley. Vol. 1, *An Introduction*. New York: Vintage Books.

Gay, Peter. 1977. *The Rise of Modern Paganism*. Vol. 1 of *The Enlightenment: An Interpretation*. New York: Norton.

Goytisolo, Juan. 1985. *Coto vedado*. Barcelona: Seix Barral.

———. 1986. *En los reinos de taifa*. Barcelona: Seix Barral.

————. 1989. *Forbidden Territory: The Memoirs of Juan Goytisolo, 1931–1956*. Trans. Peter Bush. San Francisco: North Point Press.

————. 1990. *Realms of Strife: The Memoirs of Juan Goytisolo, 1957–1982*. Trans. Peter Bush. San Francisco: North Point Press.

————, ed. 1982. *Obra inglesa de D. José María Blanco White*. 3rd ed. Barcelona: Seix Barral.

Gusdorf, George. 1980. "Conditions and Limits of Autobiography." Trans. James Olney. In *Autobiography: Essays Theoretical and Critical*. Ed. James Olney, 28–48. Princeton: Princeton University Press.

Jefferson, Ann. 1990. "Autobiography as Intertext: Barthes, Sarraute, Robbe-Grillet." In *Intertextuality: Theories and Practices*. Ed. Michael Worton and Judith Still, 108–30. Manchester: Manchester University Press.

Loureiro, Angel G. 1991–92. "Autobiografía del otro (Rousseau, Torres Villarroel, Juan Goytisolo)." *Siglo XX/20th Century* 9: 71–94.

Mandel, Barrett J. 1980. "Full of Life Now." In *Autobiography: Essays Theoretical and Critical*. Ed. James Olney, 49–72. Princeton: Princeton University Press.

Menéndez Pelayo, Marcelino. 1987. *Historia de los heterodoxos españoles*. 4th ed. Vol. 2. Madrid: BAC.

Mercadier, Guy. 1989. "Juan Goytisolo et Blanco White: partage d'exil." In *Littérature et double culture/Literatura y doble cultura*. Ed. Geneviève Mouilland-Fraisse and José María Fernández Cardo, 209–23. Calaceite (Teruel): Associations Noésis.

Murphy, Martin. 1989. *Blanco White: Self-Banished Spaniard*. New Haven: Yale University Press.

Olney, James. 1980a. "Autobiography and the Cultural Moment: A Thematic, Historical, and Bibliographical Introduction." In *Autobiography: Essays Theoretical and Critical*. Ed. James Olney, 3–27. Princeton: Princeton University Press.

————. 1980b. "Some Versions of Memory/Some Versions of *Bios*: The Ontology of Autobiography." In *Autobiography: Essays Theoretical and Practical*. Ed. James Olney, 236–67. Princeton: Princeton University Press.

Rousseau, Jean-Jacques. 1973. *Confessions*. Vol. 1. Paris: Gallimard.

Sánchez-Blanco Parody, Francisco. 1991. *Europa y el pensamiento español del siglo XVIII*. Madrid: Alianza.

Villanueva, Darío. 1993. "Realidad y ficción: la paradoja de la autobiografía." In *Escritura autobiográfica. Actas del II Seminario Internacional del Instituto de Semiótica Literaria y Teatral*. Ed. José Romera et al., 15–31. Madrid: Visor Libros.

Intertextualizing Genre:
Ambiguity as Narrative Strategy
in Emilia Pardo Bazán

MARYELLEN BIEDER

The literature women write is not about "life," contends Nancy Miller, but about "the plots of literature itself, about the constraints . . . on rendering a female life in fiction." She concludes that "[t]he attack on female plots and plausibilities assumes that women writers cannot or will not obey the rules of fiction" (Miller 1988, 43–44). This judgment echoes exactly the objection that the acerbic nineteenth-century critic Leopoldo Alas raises in his critique of the novel *Insolación* [*Sunstroke*] by his contemporary, Emilia Pardo Bazán:

> el fondo poético de la realidad, que tanto resalta aun en los mayores horrores *naturalistas* de Zola (*románticos* para doña Emilia y otros), ese fondo que existe en el amor más depravado si lo ve un artista verdadero, no hay que buscarlo en la *historia amorosa* figurada por doña Emilia. (Alas 1890, 82)

> [the poetic foundation of reality, which is so strongly evident even in the greatest horrors committed by Zola's *naturalism* (*romanticism* to Emilia Pardo Bazán and others), that foundation which exists in the most depraved love when it is observed by a true artist, cannot be found in the *love story* depicted by Pardo Bazán.][1]

Not a naturalist novel in the tradition of Zola, not "poetic" in Alas's sense of the word, *Insolación* defies the critic's sense of genre boundaries and artistic imperatives. As a result, because the "sensual love" in Pardo Bazán's text lacks artistic transcendence, Alas labels it "escandaloso, en la rigorosa aceptación de la palabra" [scandalous, in the precise meaning of the word] (Alas 1890, 83). The scandal that rocks his literary sensibility is that of a woman author whose fiction does not conform to his genre expectations. The double violation of a woman writing, and writing scandalously at that, lies at the intersection of genre conventions and woman's writing. This conjunction of genre and the gender of authorship is the subject of this essay.[2]

The premise implicit in Miller's thesis is cogently formulated by Linda Hutcheon: "what language refers to—any language—is a textual-ized and contextualized referent." These texts and contexts constitute the "layers of intertextual reference" that resonate in word and structure. One effect produced by the multiplicity of intertexts is the "overdetermination of reference" (Hutcheon 1987, 171, 180, 182), the irreducible accrual of discordant texts and contexts. Among these proliferating referents, genre serves as a primary recourse for making sense of a text, for reducing and organizing its layered contexts. In works of narrative fiction, one of the layers of reference intertextualizes genre itself. As Alison Booth reminds us, the defining characteristic of the novel is "its special capacity to differ from itself by incorporating other genres." "Generic pressure," she continues, is applied "as much by readers as by authors" (Booth 1993, 1). In a more inflected formulation of this "generic pressure," H. L. Boudreau describes the function of genre in terms of intertextuality: "the formal requirements of genre," he writes, "are a powerful intertextual determinant in both the creative and the interpretive process" (Boudreau 1985, 35).

This study will consider genre as a "textualized and contextualized referent" in several of Emilia Pardo Bazán's novels that have produced widely divergent or negative critical responses. In the fictions of the only canonical woman author of late nineteenth- and early twentieth-century Spain, the multiplicity of genre intertexts and the confusion of genre boundaries produce an "overdetermination of reference" that manifests itself in unresolvable generic ambiguity. The multiple genre intertexts in these novels and the gendered expectations they arouse are therefore a frequent cause of misreading.

The recognition of intertexts grounds the act of reading. According to Gerald Prince's pithy formulation, intertextuality operates in "the relation(s) obtaining between any given text and other texts which it cites, rewrites, absorbs, prolongs, or generally transforms and in terms of which it is intelligible" (Prince 1987, 46). Hutcheon, however, shows greater flexibility in her conceptualization of intertextual relationships by indicating that intertextual reference may point either to a word or to an entire structure. This broader usage allows for the possibility that genres, rather than individual works, function as intertexts in Pardo Bazán's novels. Only in terms of these generic intertexts do her fictions become fully "intelligible."[3] The alternative to acknowledging this intertextual maneuver is to posit a "self-deceiving" author who fails to recognize the reader's inability to locate the text's implied author.[4]

A recent study of Pardo Bazán's fiction echoes Alas's disapproval of a century ago but from an opposing critical perspective. This modern feminist reading dismisses two of her novels as "justifiably forgotten" examples of the "social masochism" that upholds the ideal of feminine abnegation and domesticity (Charnon-Deutsch 1994, 65, 42; see also 77). And yet, as the critic acknowledges, Pardo Bazán is widely considered the most clearly feminist of Spain's nineteenth-century women writers and the one whose fictional females occasionally transgress the conventions of gendered space and action.[5] There can be no doubt that a radical divergence of opinion exists among critics about the generic identity of Pardo Bazán's novels. What is at stake is a question of reading, the reading of genre.

The four Pardo Bazán novels in which this essay will explore genre and its gender implications are *Insolación* (1889), *Una cristiana* [*A Christian Woman*], *La prueba* (1890–91) [*The Test*], and *Dulce dueño* (1911) [*Sweet Master*]. *Insolación* has been read—and frequently condemned—as, among other things, a naturalist experiment, a feminist manifesto, an immoral work, and a "frivolous" novel (Mayoral 1987, 14–24; Charnon-Deutsch 1994, 152). The paired *Una cristiana* and *La prueba* have received less critical attention, and neither garnered much praise at its first appearance or subsequently. Critics have labeled the two works as naturalistic, realistic, psychological, and hagiographic. Maurice Hemingway accuses Pardo Bazán of confusing "la religion de la souffrance" and the idea of sanctity with "her heroic presentation of the saint figure" (Hemingway 1983, 82). Her contemporary, Alas, took *Una cristiana* to task for failing to deliver on the promise, implicit in the title, of revealing the essence of "a Christian lady" as only a woman writer could: "creía que iba a ver, si no una sincera, patética, natural confidencia de la misma dama, cristiana también, que escribía, por lo menos algo que en reflejo me hablase *de una vez*, la primera, de las cosas hondas e importantes de que jamás ha hablado doña Emilia" [I thought I was going to see, if not a sincere, poignant, natural confession by the woman who was writing, herself a Christian woman, at least something that in a reflected image would speak to me *for once*—for the very first time—of the profound and important things of which Doña Emilia has never spoken] (Alas 1973, 84).

Alas's disappointment in these novels is grounded, as is his critique of *Insolación*, in the genre expectations aroused specifically by the author's gender. As a woman, he seems to say, Pardo Bazán should be depicting

the soul of woman in the manner of the sentimental fiction written by
other literary women. Compounding her failure to produce the promised
Christian woman is the flawed representation of the woman author
herself: "A doña Emilia se le ve lo naturalista, pero no se le ve lo
católico. . . . [S]e le ven muchas cosas, pero no se le ve la *cristiana* que
dice que tiene dentro" [One sees what is naturalist in Doña Emilia but not
what is Catholic. . . . One sees many things in her, but one does not see
the Christian woman that she claims to have inside her] (84). The novels,
in Alas's view, convey only what is exterior and observable, the female
body: "no nos dejó ver más que el cuerpo de su *heroína*, y ése por una
combinación de espejos no muy claros" [she only allowed us to see the
body of her *heroine*, and that only through a series of not very clear
mirrors] (82). Here, embedded in Alas's dismissive critique of the novels
lies the key to the confusion of genre: the combination of mirrors that
mediate the representation of the Christian woman. Contradicting Alas's
critique of the novels, Charnon-Deutsch maintains that in *La prueba*
Pardo Bazán "creates a powerful argument against change by showing
that a woman's home service can reap both material and spiritual bene-
fits" and that in so doing she negates her own public feminist voicing of
"complaints about the treatment of women." Consequently, Charnon-
Deutsch assigns the two novels to the genre she labels women's
"domestic fiction" (Charnon-Deutsch 1994, 73).

The last novel, *Dulce dueño*, is the most elusive of all. Its multiple
discourses range from aestheticism to mysticism and madness. Few
critics have taken a firm position on the novel's generic identity. Marina
Mayoral's reading highlights the mystical intertext, but she concludes
that the protagonist seems more fanatic or mentally unbalanced than truly
mystical (Mayoral 1989, 40). While Hemingway traces Pardo Bazán's
use of hagiography, he also takes an important step in recognizing the
intertext of decadentism (Hemingway 1983, 81, 88). Most recently,
Susan Kirkpatrick, in a brilliant reading of the novel, calls it "a suggestive interrogation of modernist representation of the feminine"
(Kirkpatrick, forthcoming).

In all four of these novels, the tension produced by the interweaving of
incompatible genre intertexts creates a confusion of genre boundaries
that thwarts closure and precludes a stable resolution. This confusion of
genres is inextricably tied to the use of unreliable narration and narrative
ambiguity.[6] Each novel has a first-person narrator who mitigates the
credibility of the authorial voice and who accounts in great part for the
resulting undecidability. In *Insolación* and *Dulce dueño,* a shift in the
narrative voice (at least one abrupt change in narrative technique is
common to many Pardo Bazán novels) creates an ambiguity that forces

the reader to rely on the patterning of familiar genres rather than on the authority of a stable narrative voice. The gender assumptions borne by the conflicting genre intertexts not only shape reader expectations but foreground genre and gender construction in a dialogue among the novels.

Insolación is the story of a young widow, Asís Taboada, who allows herself to be seduced into socially inappropriate behavior by an Andalusian Don Juan. Their relationship culminates in a night spent together in her apartment. Although the subject of marriage is introduced, the couple is not married at the end of the novel. It has surprised critics from Alas's time to the present that a sexual relationship outside the bonds of holy matrimony is neither punished by the plot nor transformed by it into something transcendent and nonphysical. This plotting of female sexuality violates both reader expectations for the nineteenth-century female author and the genre conventions within which women wrote. Such plotting of the woman is consonant with naturalism, however, as well as with the realist novels written by Pardo Bazán's male contemporaries. In fact, Pardo Bazán is the one Spanish woman who took an interest in Zola's naturalism and incorporated certain of his theories and techniques into her early novels.[7]

What begins in chapter 1 of *Insolación* as a traditional, third-person narrative subsequently narrows in chapters 2 through 8 to the inherent limitations of first-person narration.[8] In transmitting her own story, Asís raises the problem of narrative reliability by questioning her memory of events and the validity of her interpretation of them. She alternates between blaming her actions on the effects of her *insolación*—a naturalist reading—and accepting responsibility for those actions—as the heroine of sentimental fiction must. The return to a third-person narrative voice in chapter 9 abandons this confessional mode and allows for commentary on the character's own self-construction. At the same time, the use of indirect free style interjects ambiguity into the third-person narration, since it blurs the boundary between the character's language and that of the narrator. Since readers cannot rely entirely on Asís or fix the position from which the narrator speaks, they are forced to seek in genre their relationship to the text.

First-person narration returns in the epilogue, where it takes the form of an undramatized narrative voice that gives its maneuverings a more overt presence. The voice is that of an "engaging" narrator, to borrow Robyn Warhol's useful term, one who addresses the reader directly and "guides the narratee's sympathies" (qtd. in Lanser 1992, 91). This narrative strategy attempts to "balance 'masculine' assertiveness with 'feminine' concern for audience" or, as I would argue in the case of *Inso-*

lación, to recover the "feminine" gender for the narrator of a transgressive "masculine" plot. For the remainder of the epilogue, the first-person
narrative voice negotiates among contradictory positions, condemning
Asís for violating social practice and divine laws, invoking the sun's
deterministic effect on her actions, and accepting marriage as an appropriate social resolution ("expiation") for an already consummated relationship. The affair alone offers sufficient subject matter for a memoir or
novel of self-analysis, since "bien cabe suponer que en las fiebres
pasionales tiene algo de necesario y fatídico, cual en las otras fiebres la
calentura" [it is fitting to suppose that in fevers of passion temperature
plays a necessary and fateful role, as it does in other kinds of fevers]
(Pardo Bazán 1987, 170). The equation of passion with fever evokes the
naturalist mode with its representation of the human animal in terms of
physiological process. By proposing that Asís's social violations are
inevitable responses to natural stimuli, the equation exculpates her
passion rather than condemning her failure to adhere to social and moral
norms. The sentimental mode, in contrast, requires a resolution that
brings both parties into harmony with the social order. In a distancing
maneuver, the epilogue begins by evoking the sentimental mode's
language of excess. The references to marriage at the novel's end thus
satisfy the ideological imperatives of this second mode and replicate its
pattern of closure. However, few critics have recognized that marriage is
a plan first referred to by the narrator and later elaborated only through
character dialogue; finally it is neither an accomplished fact nor an
assured outcome. Pardo Bazán plays with the convention of marriage as
closure without imposing that closure on the novel.

The invocation of contradictory models overdetermines the novel's
ending: on the one hand, naturalistic fatalism causes human affairs to
follow the laws of nature; on the other, the sentimental paradigm places
the blame, and hence the need for expiation, on the woman. By not privileging one genre over others, by signaling multiple intertexts and
overdetermining the referents, Pardo Bazán undermines all attempts to
naturalize the text within a single genre through a stable reading. This
strategy allows her to sidestep both the rejection provoked by naturalist
determinism and the anachronistic stasis that characterizes the sentimental mode. As a result, Pardo Bazán opens up a space for herself by
playing off one set of genre imperatives against another, as she plays off
one set of readers against another. The resulting indeterminacy allows
her to write both within and against conventional forms.

A feminist reading of the novel as a woman's renegotiation of the
conventions of gender—as a female realist text—posits that the sexual
relationship between Asís and her lover can stand on its own terms.[9]

Pardo Bazán inscribes this alternative reading into her text through her manipulation of narrative technique. The violation of gender norms, the escape to spaces where social decorum and class distinctions are turned on their heads—carnivalized in Bakhtin's terms—structures the central action of *Insolación*. In this way Pardo Bazán represents the possibility of alternative gender practices and at the same time questions the rigid construction of gender in the genres that dominate the novelistic discourse of her day. [10]

The truly extraordinary move that Pardo Bazán makes in *Insolación* is to open up a space for female sexuality. To grasp the extent of this break with the conventions for representing woman in nineteenth-century fiction, one need only think of *La Regenta* (1884–85), in which Leopoldo Alas portrays the protagonist, with her unfulfilled sexual desire, as a hysterical woman. [11] Pardo Bazán, in contrast, introduces female sexual pleasure into her novel without regard for the woman's matrimonial status. Asís is as much the subject of desire as she is the object. As Alas complained and Asís herself recognizes, her lover is not idealized by the text and has no particular virtues except the virtue of being the object of her desire. The narrator expresses the obligatory condemnation of her action, but the novel as a whole does not denigrate the protagonist. The ambiguity of the ending leaves open the reader's response to Asís and allows the reader to determine whether she is the agent, the victim, or an exemplar of a hypocritical society. In some sense, Pardo Bazán confronts the rigid morality of fictional genres and social norms with the situational morality of cultural practice. The maneuverings of narrative technique and genre intertexts thus resist closure and forestall a unitary reading.

The title of Pardo Bazán's next novel, *Una cristiana*, has led readers from Alas's day onward to expect a protagonist who exemplifies the model of Christian womanhood. The title evokes the generic tradition of the sentimental or domestic novel that upholds the ideal of the woman as the "angel of the house" whose role is self-sacrifice (see Aldaraca 1991; Jagoe 1994, 13–41). In this novel, the wife appears to sacrifice herself for a physically and morally repulsive husband. In point of fact, however, the Christian woman, Carmiña Aldao, is not mentioned until chapter 4 of the novel and does not appear until chapter 8. Her own words first reach the reader in chapter 14, just beyond the midpoint of the text, when the narrator overhears her confession to a priest. As a sacrament, confession is a reliably veracious form of discourse in the sentimental novel, but in this instance the narrator does not hear the entire confession. The novel and its continuation, *La prueba*, present little of what Carmiña says hereafter until the close of the second volume.

In attempting to account for the ostensible discrepancy that the woman

who had just written *Insolación* could create two such conventional, not
to say reactionary, novels, critics tend to overlook Pardo Bazán's use of a
first-person male narrator in both texts. In contradiction to its title, *Una
cristiana* initially takes the form of a young man's coming-of-age
novel—a bildungsroman of an innocent abroad. The narrator, Salustio, is
a country boy from Galicia studying in the big city of Madrid, and his
story is that of an idealized, impossible first love. Indeed, the opening
third of *Una cristiana* records his character traits and individual experiences in the boarding house milieu of a university student. The object of
Salustio's infatuation appears first as a projection of his imagination and
is then seen through his gaze. The "not very clear mirrors," which
according to Alas distance the reader from the female protagonist, are the
novel's first-person narrator and the secondary male characters through
whose eyes Carmiña is seen. The novel is, in fact, Salustio's autobiography, although the narrative instance is not identified and the narrator's
distance from the events not specified until the end of the second volume.
One of the few critics to discuss the significance of the first-person voice
in these novels concludes that the narrator-writer shows "no greater
wisdom or hindsight" than his younger self, the narrator-protagonist
(Hemingway 1983, 71). This lack of mediating narrative authority
requires the reader to recognize the limitations that circumscribe the
narrator's voice and vision.

The two novels recount Salustio's infatuation with a young woman,
his future aunt, whom he perceives as the perfect Christian woman.
Gender is therefore crucial both to the telling of the story and to the story
itself. Salustio's perception of his uncle's intended is also mediated by
the eulogies of a mendicant friar. This character implants the equation of
Carmiña with the model Christian woman and delineates the boundaries
of that equation with his tales of the Moorish women he has observed in
North Africa. Thus the term *cristiana* functions initially as a mark of
contrast rather than as an inherent quality. The presence of the Christian
woman in the title and within the text makes the sentimental mode, with
its prescriptive code of womanhood and its ideal of domesticity, a major
intertext. The reader privileges this intertext because Salustio does, both
as narrator and as focalizer. But Salustio's response to unfamiliar figures
and worlds may be read as erroneous, superficial misreadings, as unre-
flective reactions to cultural stereotypes—the Christian woman, the
saintly friar, the miserly Jew—rather than to individual words and deeds.
All three types emerge as Salustio's constructions, and it is the
constructed nature of his reading of these characters that the novels foreground. As a result of the intervening first-person narration, the Christian
woman is present only as a male construct. The insistent use by the narra-

tor and other males of the diminutive form Carmiña—from Carmen—further deforms the representation of the female by inserting another level of mediation between the female character and the reader.

The title *Una cristiana* cues the constructedness of woman—her "difference" from the self-styled liberal, rational narrator—and the uncorroborated nature of Salustio's narrative. The key here is Salustio's misreading. He is unreliable not only because he contradicts himself but, I would argue, because he meets Prince's definition of unreliability—that is, that the character's "norms and behavior are not in accordance with the implied author's norms" (Prince 1987, 101). Salustio's dislike for his uncle's miserliness and physical characteristics is a case in point. This revulsion contests his initial recognition that his mother is as much a Jew as his uncle and that he shares their heritage. His rational self rejects the prejudice, but it dominates his emotional self, despite the financial support and protection his uncle provides. At the same time, he proffers a naturalistic justification by accounting for his dislike in terms of "instinctive antipathies" born of "hereditary concerns" (Pardo Bazán 1890, 31). His definition of himself in opposition to his uncle suggests that his aunt has become the object through which he enacts his difference from his Other and his desire to displace the Other through possession of the forbidden woman. The disputed female is less the object of desire than the site of this rivalry, since, according to René Girard's theory, the rival confers value on the loved one. Salustio's dislike masks an envy of his uncle's superior social and economic position and his acquisition of a desirable wife. This irrational response to his uncle helps establish Salustio's inherent unreliability as narrator; his irrationality also prepares for his hyperbolic interpretation of his aunt and serves to undermine reader acceptance of that interpretation. Moreover, Salustio's text calls attention to his mother's notorious narratorial unreliability, which serves as a mirroring device that forces the reader to recognize the inherent instability of the narrative act.

The model of observation and reporting to which Salustio adheres in his narration allies his text with the realist mode. As in realism, the act of observing people and places structures his text. Salustio from the beginning warns of his tendency to view people and events through a romantic filter, to rewrite what he sees with his imagination. This is especially true at the end of *Una cristiana* where this filtering tendency creates an ambiguous closure: "ni puedo jurar que éstas [realidades] hayan existido más que dentro del sujeto que las percibía en mi propia representación, para mí mismo la verdad suprema" [I cannot swear that these realities have existed anywhere except within the subject who perceived them in my own form, for me the supreme truth] (Pardo Bazán 1890, 187). The

play between romantic and realist or naturalist readings, between desire
and observation, creates the undecidability of the ending. To follow the
conventions of the sentimental or even the realist genre, the novel should
end with a declaration of passion, with passion requited, or with a kiss. Is
Salustio in his fevered state—a literal state here, rather than the
metaphorical fever of *Insolación*—imagining that Carmiña returns his
passion, or is he reporting what is actually happening? Once again, the
narrative refuses to favor one reading over the other and leaves the reader
straddling incompatible genres. The impassioned and transgressive final
embrace between aunt and nephew seems to foreshadow adultery, which
would push the text back into the realist-naturalist mode. However, the
feverish fantasy within which this embrace occurs destroys the verisimilitude of the closure and reinstates the memoir of male desire as the text's
genre identity.

The sequel, *La prueba*, puts Carmiña to the test as the ideal of
womanhood. In her solicitude for her husband, who is dying of leprosy
(represented here as hereditary in accordance with the naturalist thread
that links the two novels), she enacts the model of Christian abnegation.
Salustio is drawn to her as the embodiment of an inherited cultural
construct—the angel of the house—and regards her as the living
reenactment of the familiar Murillo painting of Saint Isabel. Since the
reader sees Carmiña only in terms of Salustio's archetypal constructions
of woman, the narrative grants her no interiority, no independent voice,
no existence outside of the marriage that defines her. The Spanish
woman, as Pardo Bazán remarked elsewhere, exists in a subordinate,
relative relationship to (male) society (Pardo Bazán 1972, 184).

A first-person narrator necessarily mediates access to other characters.
Nevertheless, Salustio's fellow student, Luis, offers the reader independent evidence for the possibility that the narrator's conclusions are
simply wrong and that his aunt is a perfectly contented spouse and his
uncle a generous and caring man. Through Luis's girlfriend Maud
Baldwin, the novel sets up the opposition between an English feminist, a
caricatured woman of the future, and Carmiña, the ideal woman of the
past, even though Luis is, in his own way, as unreliable as his friend
when it comes to representing women. In the character of Salustio, Pardo
Bazán ironically juxtaposes the self-styled modern man with the model
woman of an earlier era. Readers must sort through several layers of
narrative unreliability and competing intertexts of woman to forge readings of their own.

The resolution of *La prueba* weaves together the contradictory threads
of comic, naturalist, and sentimental plotting. A sudden plot reversal in
the final chapter offers comic relief and further increases the reader's

doubts about the preceding narrative. Luis, an opponent of marriage, announces his engagement, while Salustio loses his passionate interest in Carmiña as soon as his uncle dies. In a mirroring of the text, a true *mise en abyme*, Salustio reads to his friend the manuscript that is *Una cristiana* and *La prueba*. As the reader's textual double, Luis signals the manuscript's confusion of genres when he argues against including the "brutally naturalist descriptions" of the uncle's illness and recommends instead that Salustio maintain the hegemony of the sentimental plot by bringing his "drama of passion" to a close with the figure of Carmiña (Pardo Bazán 1891, 198). The irresolution of this ending is highlighted by the parallel denouement of another drama of passion, the elopement of a young neighbor woman with her sister's fiancé. This subplot's decisive action undercuts Salustio's inconclusive protestations of passion throughout the two volumes. The anticipated marriage closure does not materialize but is instead displaced onto two comic couplings. That Salustio's obsession with his aunt fades once she is free to remarry underscores her role as the disputed object in his struggle with his uncle rather than as the true subject of his passion. Having been a creation of Salustio's gaze, Carmiña recedes from the text as soon as that gaze is withdrawn.

In the novel's final modal reversal, Salustio abandons his romanticism and shifts to positivistic analysis: "Ignoro lo que siento. . . Necesito analizar mi espíritu" [I don't know what I feel. . . I need to analyze my soul] (Pardo Bazán 1891, 204). Into the mouth of his friend Luis, who is often the voice of pragmatic reason in the face of Salustio's romantic projections, the author puts a judgment that overtly disrupts the sentimental, exemplary reading of Carmiña as the ideal Christian wife: "Esta clase de mujeres tan santas, tan excelentes y admirables, no pueden hacernos felices a nosotros . . . y nuestra existencia a su lado sería un infierno" [This kind of saintly women, excellent and admirable in their own way, cannot make us happy . . . and our existence by their side would be hell] (200). With this pronouncement, Pardo Bazán has the comic foil, the man who marries a Protestant woman and upholds the institution of marriage, call into question the ideal that underlies the two volumes.

As the observer who focalizes Carmiña as the idealized Christian woman, Salustio formulates the enigma that lies at the heart of the two novels: Why does she marry his uncle, and is she happy in her marriage? In the final analysis, these are novels about marriage, about the kind of woman the Spanish male wants for a wife, and about the circumstances that lead a woman into marriage. The working-class woman who becomes a high-class mistress implicitly parallels Carmiña's situation in marriage, and the parallel suggests that each is in her own way a kept woman. The novels might even be considered a woman's representation of the conflict between the socioeconomic factors that limit women's options in life (Carmen has no money and no morally acceptable home of her own) and the choices exercised by successful professional males. In both volumes, Pardo Bazán toys with the marriage closure and with the reader's desire for the convention of marriage as a "happy ending" without enacting the convention. Her plotting frees Carmiña, as it does Asís in *Insolación*, from the constraints through which, in Booth's phrase, "genre and ideology conspire against the figure of the woman" (Booth 1993, 3–4). In fact, marriage as closure is rare in Pardo Bazán's novels.[12]

In *Una cristiana* and *La prueba,* woman is the product, not the purveyor, of the dominant gender ideology. It is men who want "a Christian woman," men as disparate as the romantic idealist Salustio, the worldly priest, and Carmen's perhaps crass husband. By handing the narration over to a male, and by showing the woman through his eyes, Pardo Bazán presents the consequence of this gender ideology. The ideal is one in which men invest; woman becomes, or seems to become, what men want her to be. The counterpoints to this ideal are the less-than-moral women these same men also want. Pardo Bazán does not endorse the sentimental genre's view of womanhood. Instead, she exposes it for what it is: a male construct. In this sense, *Una cristiana* can be read as a response, if not to *Insolación* itself, then to the critical reception the earlier novel received. If you men don't want a woman like Asís, who can make up her own mind and find pleasure in life, she seems to be saying, then take a good look at the woman you say you do want.

Pardo Bazán's last published novel, *Dulce dueño,* is the most curiously unconventional of all her experiments with narrative form, for it juxtaposes the most surprising genre intertexts. Asís may narrate the initial chapters of *Insolación* in her own voice, but in this novel a woman's voice narrates the major part. This mediating narrative presence, like Salustio's in the two previous novels, has passed virtually unrecognized by the few critics the novel has attracted. In *Dulce dueño,* a woman turns her gaze on herself, constructing her own femaleness, and at the same time turns the male—a series of mentors and suitors—into the object of her female gaze. This self-absorption, this pleasure in the body as the object of one's own gaze, links the author's final novel with the esthetes in the male-authored texts of Spanish modernism. These are the works that Pardo Bazán invokes and regenders.[13] The primary male intertext of the narrator as female aesthete is, as Kirkpatrick has convincingly argued, Huysmans's decadent Des Esseintes. In her protagonist,

Pardo Bazán regenders the decadent hero and retraces Des Esseintes's trajectory from sensuality to pessimism, doubt, and, perhaps, religious experience (see also Felski 1991).

The opening fifth of *Dulce dueño*, appropriately entitled "Escuchad" [Listen] (Pardo Bazán 1989a, 47), is a hagiographic account of the martyrdom of Saint Catherine of Alexandria. This text is read by its author, a priest, to several listeners, including the novel's protagonist. The reading of the priest's construction of the saint's life and a woman's response to that reading constitute a *mise en abyme* of the novel.[14] The opening enacts and, in the readers' responses, simultaneously resists the hagiographic genre, since hagiography proffers a model for reading the life of the novel's protagonist and at the same time questions that reading. In tracing the transformation of a modern Catherine or Catalina—contracted to Lina throughout the text—from the poverty of orphanhood to inherited riches, the remaining chapters of *Dulce dueño* intertextualize a conventional plot from the sentimental novel. As Lina's first-person story, however, the narrative assumes the shape of a search for the oxymoronic "sweet master" of her life and instates her in the role of the female hero of a quest narrative. In Lina's equation of "master" with husband, Pardo Bazán problematizes gender relations in marriage, as she does elsewhere, and once again raises and frustrates the expectation of a marriage closure.[15]

Given the structure of the novel, the first intertexts the reader seeks to activate are Saint Catherine's rejection of her suitors, her conversion to Christianity, and her subsequent martyrdom. Although the hagiographic text initially seems only tangentially related to Lina's story, its position at the opening of the novel suggests its function of interior duplication in which Saint Catherine's conversion serves as the model for an anticipated religious experience. It is also possible to trace a link between Catherine's choice of martyrdom and Lina's rejection of marriage, since each woman resists an undesired subjugation of the self. Lina's search in the last chapters of the novel for other experiences and contexts that give meaning to a woman's life can be seen to mirror the saint's rejection of the practices of her own culture. Catherine's trajectory resonates in Lina's public self-debasement as a sinner, in her saintly self-sacrifice for the distressed and diseased (recalling Salustio's Carmiña), in her possible escape into madness, and in her search for a mystical union.

The ending of the novel is more radically ambiguous and more starkly subversive than that of any of Pardo Bazán's previous works. It confronts the fact that the absence of the marriage closure writes off a woman's life and erases her from traditional storytelling. Lina, however, retains control of her narrative; it is her voice that still narrates from the madhouse, the enclosure to which her society consigns the woman who resists marriage and destroys her suitor. Since Lina is the narrator and her narrative bears no marks of insanity, her own words undermine society's verdict. It is, of course, difficult for the contemporary feminist critic not to read Lina's "madness" through the intertext of Sandra Gilbert and Susan Gubar's "madwoman in the attic," the repressed Other of nineteenth-century English and American women writers. Pardo Bazán seems to relegate the creative, desiring, and embodied woman—her only writing woman—to a similar "attic" of repression and enclosure.

The woman who, like the author, resists the prevailing gender constructs and the social barriers constricting the emergence of a female self finds herself condemned and isolated, but this same isolation is a source of inner strength and above all a catalyst for the liberation of language. From her confinement at the end of her trajectory, the narrator of *Dulce dueño* writes: "En este asilo, donde me recluyeron, escribo estos apuntes, que nadie verá, y sólo yo repaso, por gusto de convencerme de que estoy cuerda, sana de alma y de cuerpo, y que, por la voluntad de quien puede, soy lo que nunca había sido: feliz" [In this asylum where they have confined me, I am writing these notes, which no one will see, and which only I will read, for the pleasure of convincing myself that I am sane—sound in soul and body—and where, by the will of one who can do such things, I am what I had never been: happy] (Pardo Bazán 1989a, 286). The isolation and silence that Lina chooses to accept are of course reversed by the reader's penetration of her enclosure and her text. The manuscript Lina writes without envisioning a narratee is, ironically, the very text the reader holds. Understood in this way, the novel opens up the possibility for agreement with Lina's diagnosis of her own sanity, against the prevailing opinion that she is mad. Thus the narrative structure of *Dulce dueño,* like that of *La prueba,* ultimately displaces closure by doubling back on itself, but in this case the doubling underscores Lina's control of text and self through writing.

The language Lina acquires at the end is both written language and the mystical language of communication with her apostrophized "sweet master," a language already implicitly gendered as feminine. This closing intertextual echo of mysticism's apostrophic mode functions much the way the sentimental intertext does in the earlier novels: it imposes a reading of genre that privileges an institution—not the social contract of marriage but a divine marriage—that the Catholic reader will find difficult to challenge. At the end of her narrative, Lina's apostrophe implicitly invokes her earlier quest for a human "dulce dueño" and in so doing reinstates the absent referents of subordination and marriage: "¡Estaba tan bien a solas contigo, Dulce Dueño! Hágase en mí tu voluntad" [I was so content alone with you, Sweet Master! Thy will be done in me] (Pardo Bazán 1989a, 291). The only sanctioned (and sanctified) alternative to marriage is the church, and if Lina's communion is with God, then she is not mad but holy. The religious intertext offsets Lina's rejection of marriage and even her catalytic role in her suitor's death. The evocation of mystical union offers an alternative ending through which Pardo Bazán can mask her more daring narrative maneuvers and thereby silence reader resistance.

One of the most powerful moves that Pardo Bazán makes is to inscribe female sexuality into the discourses of her two female narrators. The recognition of sexuality, both male and female, is implicit in naturalism, with its representation of the body as physiological process rather than the site of spirituality (an opposition, as we have just seen, that Pardo Bazán continues to exploit in *Dulce dueño*). If in *Insolación* the author intertextualizes naturalism to give Asís a body and prepare an alternative explanation for her awakening sexual desire, in the later novel she plots a way for Lina to understand the body at once as esthetic construct and sexual function. In the chapter ironically titled "Intermedio lírico" [Lyrical interlude], Lina seeks knowledge of physical sexuality from a medical doctor: like all discourses of knowledge, the discourse of the body is the purview of men. Human sexuality is articulated solely as medical discourse—that metaphor of Zola's novelistic naturalism— which treats it in terms of disease, degeneration, and disfiguration (Pardo Bazán 1989a, 201–11). At this point, Lina has passed beyond female language into the language of science and the body, to which a woman has access only through pictorial representations. (Her later mystical experience, of course, reinstates woman's control of the language of the body.) Pardo Bazán in this way has given Lina access to what woman cannot know and the novelist cannot say in her novel. In this emphasis on the deviant and the degenerate, on the implications and outcomes of the marriage contract, the preoccupations of naturalism overlap with the modernist fascination with the margins. Both genre intertexts ground possible readings of Lina's later madness, and both oppose the alternate reading of a mystical sublimation.

The consideration of the play of genre intertexts in four of Pardo Bazán's novels demonstrates her strategy of offsetting the radical implications of her plotting by incorporating more conventional, familiar genre intertexts for the reader to naturalize. Fredric Jameson has elucidated the intertextual nature of the way readers construct meaning: "texts come before us as the always-already-read; we apprehend them through sedimented layers of previous interpretations, or—if the text is brand-new—through the sedimented reading habits and categories developed by those inherited interpretative traditions" (Jameson 1981, 9). Pardo Bazán incorporates an awareness of these "reading habits and categories" into her fiction. If naturalism, with its implicit recognition of female sexuality, is anathema to the reader, as it was to many on religious or aesthetic grounds, then the sentimental intertext offers a way to actualize novels like *Una cristiana* and *La prueba*. If a woman's control of her body and a knowledge of its sexuality are unacceptable to a reader, then *Dulce dueño* can be read as an updated hagiography. If female desire for aesthetic stimulation and pleasure in the self, with its rejection of human love, violates the social construction of the feminine, then Lina's invocation of disembodied divine love through mystical communion revalidates her femininity.[16]

Pardo Bazán radically destabilizes inherited patterns of gender construction in all the novels studied here, and perhaps in her other novels as well. Gender constructs lose their fixedness as her unresolved endings propose modes of closure different from those sanctioned by codified genres. The refusal to write marriage as the ending to a woman's story is a refusal to submit to the hegemony of marriage in fictional plotting. By suggesting that woman can signify in her own terms, and not simply through institutions that subordinate her to other gazes and lives, Pardo Bazán implies the necessity of rewriting woman. Left with the destabilization of gender and the displacement of marriage as the dominant sign of closure, readers attempt to orient themselves by identifying the familiar patterning of genre. They find instead the ambiguity of proliferating and incompatible intertexts. In the space of undecidability left by these competing genres, it is possible to read the novels as Pardo Bazán's reworkings of the "always-already-read" intertexts of naturalist determinism, sentimental idealization, and mystical sublimation.

Notes

1. All translations are mine.

2. I am using "genre" to designate the codes and conventions that constitute a mode of writing that both writer and reader recognize implicitly to be distinct from other modes, for example, the codes and conventions that distinguish the realist-naturalist novel from the sentimental or didactic novel.

3. Mary Lee Bretz (1989) takes up a similar line of inquiry by identifying the intertexts in another of the author's novels but overlooks the larger patterns of genre codes, signaled by the narrative itself, that work to shape the reader's response.

4. Marianna Torgovnick uses the term "self-deceiving" to identify a writer "whose ending indicates a failure of control over the message communicated to the reader, often exposing a gap 'between the real and implied author'" (qtd. in Booth 1993, 31 n. 28).

5. For an excellent feminist reading of the author's life and writings, see El Saffar 1993.

6. The best study to date on Pardo Bazán's narrative technique is Hemingway's. He discusses her deliberate use of ambiguity in *Insolación* but considers the ambiguity of *Una cristiana* and *La prueba* "unintended," while dismissing her use of narrative unreliability in the two novels as a "failure" (Hemingway 1983, 88, 85).

7. Pardo Bazán so effectively appropriated a male-gendered narrative voice in her "naturalistic novels" that her canonical status essentially rests on these works alone. For a reconsideration of voicing in her novels, see Bieder 1987 and 1990.

8. At the end of the first chapter of *Insolación,* the narrator unexpectedly engages the reader directly for the first time with the caveat: "aunque, señores, [el caso] admita bien pocos paliativos" [although, ladies and gentlemen, the situation allowed for very few excuses] (Pardo Bazán 1987, 48).

9. Ruth Schmidt's insightful article (1974) was the first feminist reading of the novel.

10. The scene in Pardo Bazán's *La Tribuna* [*The Female Tribune*] in which the female protagonist dresses as a man and dances without restraint is a prime example of the transgression of gender boundaries, a *mise en abyme* of the novel's gender plotting. The title of the chapter, "El carnaval de las cigarreras" [The women cigarette workers' Mardi Gras], anticipates Bakhtin's concept of carnivalization with its inverted hierarchies in a world turned upside down.

11. The plotting of female sexuality in *Insolación* intertextualizes Juan Valera's novel *Pepita Jiménez* (1874), in which another young widow consummates her relationship with a former seminary student before their marriage. Valera has Pepita emerge from the bedroom a repentant temptress who apologizes for having seduced her suitor. Pardo Bazán, in contrast, silences the encounter between Asís and Pacheco following Asís's decisive "Quédate" [Stay] (Pardo Bazán 1987, 170), as she also silences the moment when the two characters discuss marriage. The culminations of both the naturalist and the moral dimensions of *Insolación* are thus absent from the text. Pardo Bazán refuses either to condone or to condemn Asís's desire and instead retains an ambiguously configured space for female sexuality. Mayoral also discusses *Pepita Jiménez* in relation to *Insolación* (Mayoral 1987, 34).

12. Pardo Bazán entices her readers to desire a marriage closure but does not fulfill this expectation in novels as diverse as *La Tribuna*, *La madre naturaleza* [*Mother Nature*] (1887), and *Insolación*. In contrast, she enacts a surprise marriage closure in *Memorias de un solterón* [*Memoirs of a Bachelor*] (1896) in counterpoint to the novel's dominant gender intertexts of the feminist woman and the sybaritic man.

13. Writing about Anglo-American modernism, Gilbert and Gubar contend not only that modernism is "differently inflected for male and female writers" but that both women and men are seeking to come to terms with "an ongoing battle of the sexes that was set in motion by the late-nineteenth-century rise of feminism and the fall of Victorian concepts of 'femininity'" (Gilbert and Gubar 1988, xii). For further discussion of a woman author's regendering of Spanish (male) modernist texts, see Bieder 1996.

14. This mirroring reflects the effect that Pardo Bazán introduces at the end of *La prueba*, where Salustio discusses the text he has written with Luis. In *Dulce dueño,* it is a woman, the narrator Lina, who voices her response to the male construct of the Christian woman. Lina then reworks that text in her own construction of self.

15. In *Dulce dueño,* Pardo Bazán retains the "contradiction between love and quest in plots dealing with women" that Rachel DuPlessis identifies in nineteenth-century English

and American novels. DuPlessis concludes that "[i]t is the project of twentieth-century women writers to solve the contradiction" between these plots and to construct a resolution that offers "a different set of choices" (DuPlessis 1985, 3–4). Pardo Bazán merges tradition and innovation in her resolution by invoking the intertexts of mysticism and writing that ultimately displace the love and quest plots.

16. Kirkpatrick identifies a "double vision" of spirituality and feminism in *Dulce dueño*'s conclusion (Kirkpatrick forthcoming).

Works Cited

Alas, Leopoldo. 1884–85. *La Regenta*. 2 vols. Barcelona: Daniel Cortezo.

———. 1890. "Emilia Pardo Bazán y sus últimas obras." In *Museum (Mi revista)* 51–88. Folletos literarios, no. 7. Madrid: Fernando Fe.

———. 1973. *Obra olvidada: artículos de crítica*. Ed. Antonio Ramos-Gascón. Madrid: Júcar.

Aldaraca, Bridget A. 1991. *El ángel del hogar: Galdós and the Ideology of Domesticity in Spain*. North Carolina Studies in the Romance Languages and Literatures, no. 239. Chapel Hill: University of North Carolina.

Bakhtin, Mikhail. 1984. *Rabelais and His World*. Trans. Hélène Iswolsky. Bloomington: Indiana University Press.

Bieder, Maryellen. 1987. "The Female Voice: Gender and Genre in *La madre naturaleza*." *Anales Galdosianos* 22: 103–16.

———. 1990. "Between Gender and Genre: Emilia Pardo Bazán and *Los pazos de Ulloa*." In *In the Feminine Mode: Essays on Hispanic Women Writers*. Ed. Noël M. Valis and Carol Maier, 131–45. Lewisburg: Bucknell University Press.

———. 1996. "Self-Reflexive Fiction and the Discourses of Gender in Carmen de Burgos." In *Self-Conscious Art: A Tribute to John W. Kronik*. Ed. Susan L. Fischer, 71–87. Lewisburg: Bucknell University Press.

Booth, Alison, ed. 1993. *Famous Last Words: Changes in Gender and Narrative Closure*. Charlottesville: University Press of Virginia.

Boudreau, H. L. 1985. "Antonio Machado's 'A un olmo seco': The Critical Use and Abuse of Biography." In *Studies in Honor of Sumner M. Greenfield*. Ed. H. L. Boudreau and Luis T. González-del-Valle, 33–47. Lincoln, Neb.: Society of Spanish and Spanish-American Studies.

Bretz, Mary Lee. 1989. "Text and Intertext in Emilia Pardo Bazán's *Memorias de un solterón*." *Symposium* 43: 83–93.

Charnon-Deutsch, Lou. 1994. *Narratives of Desire: Nineteenth-Century Spanish Fiction by Women*. University Park: Pennsylvania State University Press.

DuPlessis, Rachel Blau. 1985. *Writing Beyond the Ending: Narrative Strategies of Twentieth-Century Women Writers*. Bloomington: Indiana University Press.

El Saffar, Ruth. 1993. "Emilia Pardo Bazán." In *Spanish Women Writers: A Bio-Bibliographical Sourcebook*. Ed. Linda Gould Levine et al., 378–88. Westport, Conn.: Greenwood Press.

Felski, Rita. 1991. "The Counterdiscourse of the Feminine in Three Texts by Wilde, Huysmans, and Sacher-Masoch." *PMLA* 106: 1094–105.

Gilbert, Sandra M., and Susan Gubar. 1979. *The Madwoman in the Attic: The Woman Writer and the Nineteenth-Century Literary Imagination*. New Haven: Yale University Press.

———. 1988. *The War of the Words*. Vol. 1 of *No Man's Land: The Place of the Woman Writer in the Twentieth Century*. New Haven: Yale University Press.

Girard, René. 1966. *Deceit, Desire, and the Novel: Self and Other in Literary Structure*. Trans. Yvonne Freccero. Baltimore: Johns Hopkins University Press.

Hemingway, Maurice. 1983. *Emilia Pardo Bazán: The Making of a Novelist*. Cambridge: Cambridge University Press.

Hutcheon, Linda. 1987. "History and/as Intertext." In *Future Indicative: Literary Theory and Canadian Literature*. Ed. John Moss, 169–84. Ottawa: University of Ottawa Press.

Jagoe, Catherine. 1994. "Woman's Mission as Domestic Angel." In *Ambiguous Angels: Gender in the Novels of Galdós*, 13–41. Berkeley: University of California Press.

Jameson, Fredric. 1981. *The Political Unconscious: Narrative as a Socially Symbolic Art*. Ithaca, N.Y.: Cornell University Press.

Kirkpatrick, Susan. Forthcoming. "Gender and Modernist Discourse: Emilia Pardo Bazán's *Dulce dueño*." *Hispanic Issues*.

Lanser, Susan S. 1992. *Fictions of Authority: Women Writers and Narrative Voice*. Ithaca, N.Y.: Cornell University Press.

Mayoral, Marina. 1987. "Estudio introductorio a *Insolación*." In *Insolación*, by Emilia Pardo Bazán, 9–38. 3rd ed. Madrid: Espasa-Calpe.

———. 1989. "Introducción." In *Dulce dueño*, by Emilia Pardo Bazán, 7–44. Madrid: Castalia/Instituto de la Mujer.

Miller, Nancy K. 1988. "Emphasis Added: Plots and Plausibilities in Women's Fiction." In *Subject to Change: Reading Feminist Writing*, 25–46. New York: Columbia University Press.

Pardo Bazán, Emilia. [1890]. *Una cristiana*. Vol. 18 of *Obras completas*. Madrid, n.p.

———. [1891]. *La prueba*. Vol. 22 of *Obras completas*. Madrid, n.p.

———. [1896]. *Memorias de un solterón*. Vol. 14 of *Obras completas*. Madrid, n.p.

———. 1972. *La vida contemporánea (1896–1915)*. Ed. Carmen Bravo-Villasante. Madrid: Novelas y Cuentos.

———. 1987. *Insolación*. Ed. Marina Mayoral. 3rd ed. Colección Austral. Madrid: Espasa-Calpe.

———. 1989a. *Dulce dueño*. Ed. Marina Mayoral. Biblioteca de Escritoras, no. 3. Madrid: Castalia/Instituto de la Mujer.

———. 1989b. *La Tribuna*. Ed. Benito Varela Jácome. Madrid: Cátedra.

Prince, Gerald. 1987. *Dictionary of Narratology*. Lincoln: University of Nebraska Press.

Schmidt, Ruth A. 1974. "A Woman's Place in the Sun: Feminism in *Insolación*." *Revista de Estudios Hispánicos* 8: 69–81.

Valera, Juan. 1955. *Pepita Jiménez*. 10th ed. Madrid: Biblioteca Nueva.

Warhol, Robyn. 1986. "Toward a Theory of the Engaging Narrator: Earnest Interventions in Gaskell, Stowe, and Elliot." *PMLA* 101: 811–18.

The Novelist at the Opera:
Genre and Intertextuality in *Su único hijo*

An opera composer may be vexed
By later umbrage taken at his text

—W. H. Auden, "Metalogue to *The Magic Flute*"

Overture

Intertextuality, since its introduction by Julia Kristeva into modern critical parlance and its subsequent popularization, has proved to be a surprisingly malleable concept to which varying and sometimes mutually incompatible definitions have been assigned.[1] In the hands of some theorists, it designates a sophisticated means for uncovering the presence of other voices, discourses, and linguistic patterns (phrases, tropes, figures, and such) that antedate or coexist with the text under examination. In these cases, the intertext refers to a specific precursor text or texts that can be traced, stylistically and/or thematically, through the later text into which it has been incorporated, regardless of whether that incorporation has been achieved under the sign of homage or of parody (Riffaterre 1978, 136–37; Genette 1982, 91–92). At the opposite extreme, some readers contend that intertextuality is not based on direct correspondences between framing and framed texts but is, rather, a manifestation of the indivisible and fluid network, authorless and multidirectional, that is textuality itself; individual source texts can therefore never be identified or recovered intact (Barthes 1979; Derrida 1979).[2] Many others have positioned themselves along the parade route of this debate, inventing more precise vocabularies to describe the parameters of the intertextual relationship (Genette 1979, 1982; Dällenbach 1976; Jenny

76

1982), uncovering the logical inferences that are the underpinnings of these assumptions (Culler 1976), or chronicling and enlarging the history of the debate itself (Angenot 1983; Morgan 1985). As proof, one need only turn to the proliferating examples of literature on the subject: bibliographies (Bruce 1983; Hebel 1989), special issues of journals (*Texte* 2 [1983]; *Poétique* 27 [1976]), and collections of critical essays (Worton and Still 1990). Amid the growing cacophony, one writer has even decreed that "the project of intertextuality—understanding relations between texts across time—has been more or less abandoned in the [academic] profession."[3]

Rumors surrounding the supposed death of intertextuality as a subject of continuing concern to literary theorists are undoubtedly exaggerated, as the present collection of essays bears witness. Still, a sea change is underway. The current emphasis on situating literature within a larger political frame has sensitized many critics to view intertextuality as a writing and reading machine whose engine is fueled by a number of context-driven factors, including ideology, culture, and history. This view has, for such readers, eroded the validity of studies that concentrate on the transactions of intertextuality exclusively at the level of form, that is, on the repetition and transformation of verbal structures and sequences that intertextuality typically entails. This approach to intertextuality often elicits among cultural critics the same objections as have been raised in connection with the structuralist-dominated field of narratology: that it reduces the features and interactions of texts to a series of synchronic, semiotic processes whose very circularity effectively (but fallaciously) insulates them from contact with an extraliterary referent.[4]

Unfortunately, the issuing of an either-or ultimatum is painfully constricting for critics and theorists. Surely it ought to be possible to link the structuralist-influenced notion of a poetics, or system, of literature with the insights of discourse theory and the premises of cultural criticism. After all, the operation of intertextual systems at the level of form is a manifestation—sometimes highly visible, other times oblique—of underlying relationships of social power, politics, and tastemaking. My examination of operatic intertextuality in *Su único hijo* (1891) [*His Only Son*] by Leopoldo Alas (Clarín) ought perhaps to be evaluated in this light: as a case that tests the feasibility of combining structural concerns (in this instance, genre categories) with cultural history in the attempt to understand the place occupied by this alternately sensuous and philosophical novel in the complex intellectual landscape of Spain's *fin de siglo*.

In the novelistic universe of *Su único hijo*, opera represents both a genre and a cultural artifact. Because of the ways in which these two functions of opera intersect, Alas's novel becomes an exploration of possible literary responses to the growing sense of crisis that afflicts Spanish writers and thinkers at the turn of the century. Opera in this novel destabilizes narrative; it variously opposes music to silence, music to noise, and music to words, thereby raising serious questions regarding the viability of traditional novelistic form and the linguistic medium in which it is decanted. At the same time, the presence of an operatic intertext sets up other oppositions—between high culture and popular culture, national and foreign cultural production, romanticism and modernity— that indicate the intensity of Clarín's grappling with the miasma that characterizes late-nineteenth-century Spain. *Su único hijo* reaches the public during a decade afflicted with colonial unrest, imminent and ultimately unsuccessful foreign military involvement, unequal rates of regional industrialization and economic growth, and a notoriously corrupt Restoration politics based on *caciquismo* and oligarchy, all of which contribute to the eventual discrediting of the Spanish national image as projected on home soil and in the foreign arena. During this same decade, Spain also suffers less tangible but equally consequential privations in the intellectual sphere: for instance, the lack of a vigorous philosophical tradition and the loss of spiritual values, to name those most frequently eulogized by observers of the contemporary scene.

As witness to this state of political, social, and religious decay, Clarín can be seen in his essays and fiction of the 1890s to be searching for alternative modes of expression that will best give vent to the longing for an "espíritu nuevo" [new spirit].[5] *Su único hijo*'s incursions into the sphere of opera and its veneration of the voice suggest modifications of the novel form that diverge from the standard practices of naturalism and documentary realism. Yet Clarín never entirely resolves the discrepancies that an operatically modeled novel introduces. True to his dual reputation as a satirical, often fiercely combative literary critic and political commentator and as a cultivator of fiction in the lyric-elegiac vein (*Doña Berta, La Regenta*, "¡Adiós, Cordera!," among other works), Clarín in *Su único hijo* embodies a contradictory logic in which the novel simultaneously mocks what it values most and appears to denigrate its own vehicle of expression. Approached from the demystifying perspective of rationalism and the positivist emphasis on the real, the novel's protagonist, Bonifacio Reyes, is chided for his belatedly romantic sentimentality and idealism. Nonetheless, the contamination of the novel by the operatic genre suggests a movement away from realism toward a nonmimetic form that is expressionistic and deeply nostalgic for an impossible liberation from language and writing.

In arguing that the opera constitutes a significant intertext for Clarín's novel, I am adopting a position located somewhere between Riffaterre's and Genette's unitary view of textual ascendancy and the plurigenetic approach typified by Barthes, Kristeva, and Derrida. The complex narrative dynamics of *Su único hijo* are set into motion by the novel's relationship to an operatic intertext. Yet this intertext is one among many others and is, moreover, itself a compound that embraces disparate texts, authors, and artistic media. Thus, although Alas's very title alludes to lines of genealogical descent, it cannot be argued that one single text or author serves as the intertext that deploys the novel's signifying systems or that, once identified, such an intertext can, or will, stabilize interpretation for readers. The genealogical metaphor sets up an undeniable paradox, since paternity looms large in *Su único hijo* and has been the founding trope for much of the criticism devoted to Alas's novel.[6] Moreover, ever since Harold Bloom argued his vision of literature as a titanic struggle whereby sons assert their originality only by misreading their strong poetic fathers, concerns over legitimacy, priority, and precursorship have tended to cloud discussions of intertextual relations. Certainly in Alas's bourgeois society, overtly preoccupied with issues of property and inheritance, such anxious perceptions belonging to the psychoanalytical realm are understandably reinforced by economic and legal concerns as well.

Nonetheless, there is clearly no one father for Alas's novel but rather an extended network of literary aunts, uncles, and cousins, a veritable family of intertexts that presides over the creation of *Su único hijo* in much the same way that the portrait gallery of Valcárcel ancestors dominates the living quarters that Emma shares with her husband.[7] Valis has already shown the existence of a broad Flaubertian connection to *Su único hijo*. In her words, "Clarinian revision of Flaubert (whether *Madame Bovary* or *Bouvard et Pécuchet*) then becomes a form of correction and that correction a rebellious son's delicate and discreet act of homage to the (other) father of his text" (Valis 1989, 865).[8] Other readings have pointed out links between *Su único hijo* and the literature of *fin-de-siècle* symbolism, the Gospels, the Old Testament, the *Odyssey* and epic literature, and Clarín's own short stories (Valis 1981; Little and Schraibman 1978; Bandera 1969; Richmond 1978). Opera provides yet another key intertext for Clarín's story, and readers can come to understand the uniqueness of this novel within Clarín's literary production by focusing not on any single opera but on the operatic genre itself.

Act I

Unlike the author's only other full-length narrative, the two-volume
La Regenta (1884–85), *Su único hijo* is a brief work, by turns satirical
and meditative, that follows the story of the weak-willed copy clerk
Bonifacio Reyes and his imperious wife Emma Valcárcel. Secretary to
Don Diego de Valcárcel, Bonis, ever the romantic dreamer, passively
agrees to marry his employer's daughter. Shortly after the wedding,
however, Emma's ardent pursuit of the copy clerk turns to indifference,
and she abandons their marriage bed to devote herself full-time to
worshipping her ancestors and nursing a series of real and imagined
illnesses. Ignored by his wife and insulted by Juan Nepomuceno, the
administrator of Emma's estate, Bonis finds solace in music, playing the
flute and attending performances given by a traveling opera company
that has come to town. His friendship with the singers and their impre-
sario Mochi quickly deepens; soon he becomes the lover of Serafina
Gorgheggi, the soprano, and begins covering her and Mochi's expenses
out of his wife's pocketbook. The novel details the ensuing confusions
and role reversals that occur as the binary oppositions structuring the
story are systematically broken down: art mingles with commerce,
maternal love with erotic desire, spirituality with carnality, traditionally
feminine attributes with male-encoded comportment. Bonis is inherently
repelled by the admixtures born of "aquel amontonamiento *social* en que
vivían cómicos, alemanes y gente de su casa, su Emma, el tío, él mismo"
(Alas 1979, 229) [that social promiscuity in which the players, the
Germans and the people of the household, his Emma, the uncle and he
himself lived] (Alas 1981, 177), yet seems incapable of extricating
himself from the carnivalesque disorder that reigns in his household.[9]
Not to be outdone by her husband, Emma insinuates herself into the good
graces of the baritone Minghetti. Shortly thereafter comes the stunning
news of Emma's unanticipated pregnancy, whose dubious legitimacy the
reader is left to ponder in the absence of any conclusive textual evidence.
The novel's unresolved ending has been interpreted as tragic, burlesque,
or unrepentantly cynical: alone among his friends and family, Bonis
unquestioningly defends the legitimate paternity of his newborn son in
the face of mounting but unproven innuendo regarding his wife's
infidelity.[10]

In the course of relating the story, the narrator describes Bonis's
artistic tastes, which run to polkas and the scores of Italian operas that he
borrows and transcribes. He also alludes to the traveling company's
repertory, making frequent reference to operas by Verdi, Rossini, Bellini,

and others.[11] On occasion, the protagonist compares his life to the plots of familiar operatic works. His wife's jealousy reminds him of *Otello* (although the roles of the Moor and Desdemona are gender-reversed here), while the threat of the catastrophic revelation of his trysts with Serafina immediately suggests to him an analogy with the principals of *Norma*. Despite such allusions, the reader soon finds that the correspondences between *Su único hijo* and these individual works are surprisingly limited. What *Su único hijo* has in common with *Nabucco*, *Semiramide*, or *La Straniera*, for instance, rarely extends beyond their mutual preoccupation with the themes of passion, treachery, and vengeance or the existence of situational similarities at the level of plot. Not even the final scene of the novel can be traced with any exactitude to Verdi. During the infant Antonio's baptism in church, the scorned Serafina points to the organist (the baritone Minghetti) as the implied father of the child borne by Emma, at the very moment that the former is playing an air from *La Traviata*. While Verdi's work does raise the themes of adultery and the fallen woman, the details of Violetta's and Alfredo's story do not coincide with Bonifacio's. We are forced to agree with Sánchez Siscort when she states: "Los paralelismos que hay entre el argumento de las óperas y el de *Su único hijo* son mínimos" [The parallels between the plot of the operas and *Su único hijo* are minimal] (Sánchez Siscort 1987, 125).[12]

In fact, the operatic intertext of *Su único hijo* is simultaneously singular and plural, defined and yet elastic—in short, a genre or entire class of works that share a number of attributes, including subject matter, form, affective qualities, and so on.[13] Not coincidentally, the concept of genre is in itself intertextual, since the response of particular texts to generic paradigms—whether that response is one of adherence, discontinuity, or transformation—can only be determined relationally, that is, in reference to other historical texts. This inevitable intertextuality of genre is well noted by Todorov when, in his discussion of fantastic literature, he remarks that no work can be completely individualized or bear no relation to the past (Todorov 1975, 7). But can a genre properly function as an intertext? An affirmative answer can be posited if we take into account three crucial factors: a genre's dual identity as both program and text; the near impossibility of distinguishing in practice between generic codes and their realization in individual texts; and the relevance of genre signals to the reader's interpretive activity.

A genre is not just a set of rules, however flexible, governing the texts that fall under its rubrics; it is also constituted as a text unto itself. As Rosmarin indicates, a genre "is not, as is commonly thought, a class but, rather, a classifying statement. It is therefore itself a text. It is writing about writing" (Rosmarin 1985, 46), a notion that Pérez Firmat seconds:

"A genre is a text, or . . . a text of texts, and as such possesses a discursive existence apart from that of the works it brings together" (Pérez Firmat 1979, 278). Thus, a possible intertextual relationship between a text and a genre is by no means precluded, the genre being viewed as another, increasingly complex, discursive structure. Moreover, although texts (structures) and genres (codes) in theory occupy two distinct levels, somewhat akin to the relationship of *parole* to *langue*, practically speaking they often coalesce. For this reason, "genre archetypes, however abstract, still constitute textual structures"; conversely, reference to a text unavoidably refers as well to characteristics and meanings contained in the codes of the genre to which it belongs (Jenny 1982, 42). Not least of all, genre can operate as an intertext in that an intertext presupposes an act of interpretation while genre provides varieties of knowledge that enable the reader's interpretive response. As one critic puts it: "What is relevant to textual interpretation is not, in itself, the identification of a particular intertextual source but the more general discursive structure (genre, discursive formation, ideology) to which it belongs" (Frow 1990, 46). Seen in this light, the postulation of a genre as an intertext is feasible and, indeed, justified; it allows readers to connect literary systems to one another and to the extratextual social world and to evaluate the pressures each exerts.

An examination of several of the most salient generic properties of opera reveals the significance of this intertext to the structure of *Su único hijo* and to Clarín's shifting concept of the novel. Most notable among opera's attributes are its hybrid form, its antiillusionistic presentation, its collaborative mode of creation, and its unself-conscious recognition of its status as art. Opera is a composite entity, a melding of forms that cuts across the boundaries of several arts and the differing media they employ. It combines a musical score, a written text, movement, and visual effects, including set designs, costumes, and stage lighting. Not unlike drama, it may be published in book form and so read but is only fully realized in performance; moreover, that realization will vary from night to night and from one production to another.

Opera lays little claim to realistic effects but is instead grounded in melodrama and exaggeration. Notwithstanding efforts to portray psychological verisimilitude or a *mise en scène* that painstakingly reconstructs a past era, rarely in an operatic work does one find an accurate depiction of the characters' society, even in the so-called *verismo* opera of the nineteenth century as practiced by Leoncavallo, Mascagni, Puccini, Bizet, and Verdi.[14] Other stock features of operatic composition—characters who unaccountably burst into song to tell their tales, the distended nature of narrative time (it takes longer to sing than to speak the story), the formulaic or ceremonial character of certain scenes, typically rigid divisions between recitatives and arias—similarly work against the creation of a seamless illusion of life casually captured and registered. The mimetic potential of opera is further eroded by the apparent dictatorship of music over the libretto; while there is a verbal text, it is frequently unintelligible (a result of the combined effects of legato, the use of a foreign language, and singing in the most extreme, that is, soprano, register) and, in any event, is subordinated to the role of the voice. Finally, but of no less importance, opera is a product of collaboration. Its creative fathers include the composer and the librettist, whose efforts are supported and brought to fruition by the director, set designer, conductor, and singers. Considering the fact of opera's multiple parentage, its relationship with such other genres as classical tragedy, epic, allegory, and romance, and its assimilation and reworking of other materials (librettos based on preexisting works, performances whose interpretations refer to prior ones), opera becomes emblematic of the intertextual process in all its heterogeneous multiplicity.

By placing Bonifacio's soulful encounter with operatic music and his adventures with the members of the itinerant company of singers at the heart of *Su único hijo*, Clarín raises a number of questions regarding the shape and generic identity of the novel. Protest as Bonifacio may that his household has become a site of "confusiones abominables" (Alas 1979, 226), the novel in which he figures is itself a laboratory in which the author experiments by combining different generic reagents. Three years before the publication of *Su único hijo*, Clarín had written in *Mis plagios. Un discurso de Núñez de Arce* that "en toda idea de la novela se comprende la amplitud del género y su libertad, que la hacen apta para expresar la mayor variedad posible de objetos con las formas también más varias y con intensidad que bien puede calificarse de indefinida, ya que no infinita" [included in any notion of the novel are its amplitude and freedom as a genre, which make it appropriate for expressing the greatest possible variety of objects with the most varied forms as well and with an intensity that could well be described as indeterminate, if not infinite] (Alas 1888, 87). In *Su único hijo,* Alas not only allows the realist novel greater latitude by recasting aspects of its form and composition in line with the principles of opera, he also underscores the instability at the very core of literary realism. For, by alluding to an intertext such as opera, which is itself highly intertextualized, novels like *Su único hijo* are plunged headlong into a hall of mirrors, proposing to speak of the outside world but instead addressing only other texts. As we shall see, Clarín instinctively recoils from this possibility, with the result that his second novel is an oddly shaped one, as virtually all critics have noted, perhaps not quite an "abominable confusion" but at the very least an uneasy amalgam of styles, narrative tone, and generic features (Gramberg 1978, 204–6).

Act II

Where, concretely, are the points at which Alas's novel is overtaken by its operatic intertext? *Su único hijo* takes place over the course of two or so years in a nameless provincial capital during a similarly unspecified decade (1850s? 1860s?) when romanticism in the arts is already passé. This imprecise chronology and vague use of interior and exterior locations, coming unexpectedly from the author of the microscopically detailed *La Regenta*, may be related to the mythic handling of time and space that characterizes many of the operas that Clarín's copy clerk glorifies. Then again, in the same way that an aria, as locus of hyperbolic passion and ritualized action, interrupts the course of operatic recitative, so too in Clarín's novel the narrative is punctuated by a number of "operatic moments" that coincide not just with emotional climaxes but also with turning points in the story: the toast Bonifacio makes in the Café de la Oliva, which is received with bravos and applause by the opera company; his angry confrontation with Juan Nepomuceno over the administration of household finances; the conjugal seduction scene in which Emma assumes Serafina's identity; the musical reenactment of the Annunciation and Bonis's response to impending fatherhood; his tearful farewell to Serafina and her professional companions; the finale during which the protagonist steadfastly proclaims his faith in the legitimate birth of the infant Antonio Diego Sebastián Reyes y Valcárcel.[15]

Beneath these gestures toward the external structuring of opera, however, lies the more complex issue of the unresolved tension between music and speech that fills the pages of *Su único hijo*. The debate has long raged among opera scholars and cognoscenti (and was even thematized by Richard Strauss in his *Capriccio*) over whether primacy should be granted to an opera's score or its libretto. *Prima le parole* or *prima la musica*? The pendulum has swung back and forth a number of times since the seventeenth century; Monteverdi, Gluck, Verdi, Wagner, and Berg all believed that music should be subordinated to a poetic or dramatic principle, while Berlioz and Rossini viewed the text as merely a prop for music's intrinsic expressivity.[16] Particularly in the afterglow of romanticism's exaltation of the pure lyric impulse, the imitative aspect of words in opera is pushed aside in favor of music's nonreferentiality. Galdós, for instance, was certainly typical of many nineteenth-century critics and operagoers in affirming, as he does in his review of Tomás Bretón's *Los amantes de Teruel*, that music "es lo esencial en una ópera" [is what is essential in an opera] (Pérez Galdós 1923, 179).

It becomes immediately clear that in *Su único hijo* not only has Bonifacio Reyes idealized opera as the highest of all art forms, one in whose seemingly limitless expressive capacity aesthetic and religious value are commingled in the "temple of art," but also that his experience of opera, focused as it is on the performative dimension, is purely vocal, never verbal. Language (and with it, mimesis) has been erased as the other half of opera's twofold nature, and music takes over as the sole bearer of and access to signification: "Era que la música le ayudaba a entender, a penetrar el significado hondo de las cosas" (Alas 1979, 317) [The music helped him to understand everything even more clearly, to penetrate the deep significance of things] (Alas 1981, 251). Although Clarín's protagonist earns his living copying words in a beautiful hand, those words have devolved into empty husks, simple graphemes; and his confession to Serafina—"yo no sé hablar" [I don't know how to speak well]—is more than just a lover's apology for his lack of rhetorical skills during courtship. The successful manipulation of language is beyond him; although he may feel like the hero of a novel, he knows he can never aspire to be a novelist by merely reproducing words on a page. More often than not, words register in his consciousness solely as a sort of sonic disturbance.

As a man who, like his father before him, prizes silence above all, Bonis finds life with Emma unbearable because it consists of unending acoustic persecution. All the Valcárcels are characterized by their "palabra tarda" [slow speech] and "voz ronca" [harsh voice] (Alas 1979, 15; translation modified), and Bonis's wife, with her "voz chillona, estridente" [screeching, strident voice] (24; translation modified), is no exception. Her stinging criticisms are indeed agonizing to her husband, but only because they disturb his peace: "lo que le daba mayor tormento en las injustas lucubraciones bilioso-nerviosas de su mujer, era el ruido" (Alas 1979, 27) [Regarding his wife's unjust and nervous inventions, what pained him most was the noise] (Alas 1981, 19). Even a slap in the face would be preferable: "más quería un cachete, si a mano viene, que una chillería; el ruido lo último de todo" (Alas 1979, 109) [he even preferred her blows, perhaps, to her screams. Noise was by far the most painful torture] (Alas, 1981, 83). Small wonder, then, that Reyes flees his house and takes refuge first in the widow Cascos's store, with its balm of "lazy silence and tender memories" of romanticism, and later in the theater, where Serafina Gorgheggi's silvery soprano floods his being.

The opera signifies many things for Bonifacio: spectacle, exalted

emotion, beauty—in sum, a superior mode of existence whose ultimate
condensation is found in the female voice. Serafina is the human voice
incarnate; as Emma observes, "parecía que aun hablando cantaba" [even
when she spoke she seemed to be singing] (Alas 1979, 195; translation
modified). While la Gorgheggi's intimate charms are not lost on her
provincial swain, the latter does not fetishize her body but rather her
"instrument," which, with its unctuous sonority ("cualidad pastosa"),
evokes erotic and maternal feelings in him simultaneously. Lost in Serafina's singing of a hymn to the Virgin, Bonifacio is overcome first by a
sexual *frisson* and then by a mystical transport in which he hears that he
will sire a legitimate son, "un hijo suyo y de la *voz*" (Alas 1979, 200) [a
son he shared with the "voice"] (Alas 1981, 152). Quite apart from its
musical merits, Serafina's voice is both a siren song luring him with the
promise of passionate gratification and an angelic lullaby that promises a
return to a vanished paradise of childhood memories, a recovery of lost
origins he will later search for in his natal city, Raíces: "su voz de usted
no es como las demás voces; . . . debe de ser lo que yo llamo voz de
madre, voz que me arrulla, que me consuela, que me da esperanza, que
me anima, que me habla de mis recuerdos de la cuna. . . . Yo siempre he
sido muy aficionado a los recuerdos, a los más lejanos, a los de niño"
(Alas 1979, 63–64) [your voice is not like other voices . . . (it) must be
what I call a mother's tone, a tone which lulls me, consoles me, gives me
hope, encourages me, speaks to me of my memories of the cradle! . . . I
have always been very fond of my memories, of the most distant—those
of my childhood] (Alas 1981, 45). The elusive nature of the desire that
Serafina arouses in Bonifacio, emblematized by the fleeting nature of the
vocal object itself, effectively transforms her into a cipher of the knowledge that he seeks, "lo que seremos por dentro, por dentro del todo"
[what it is that we are inside, deep down] (139; translation modified). In
the words of Michel Poizat:

> Elusive and inaccessible, evanescent or nonexistent, the cause of desire, the
> locus of lack, and the nullification of lack, locus of jouissance both infinite
> and impossible, alluring and forbidden, death-ridden and deadly, trans-sensi-
> cal and trans-sexual, heavenly voice or hellish cry, angel or demon, The
> Voice and The Woman come together in these tightly woven fantasies. . . .
> For only the alchemy of music allows the voice to be purged of the meaning
> it usually conveys. (Poizat 1992, 156)[17]

But there is a price to be paid for such pleasure as the diva affords, and
that price is the sacrifice of the signifying process itself. The unintelligi-
bility of what Serafina sings is not only a function of her performing in a

foreign tongue and at the highest possible pitch. Since melodic continuity and operatic vocalise necessarily destroy the intervals of silence that allow us to distinguish between verbal signifiers, the *jouissance* Reyes experiences in hearing Serafina's voice can only be earned at the expense of speech. [18] As the voice verges on the cry, opera shrugs off any remaining pretense of being an art that fosters social integration and instead propounds a transgressive stance toward "the law of the word" founded in individual gratification (Poizat 1992, 43, 165).

At this precise point, the sway that the operatic intertext exercises over *Su único hijo* begins to diminish in intensity. Clarín as an author is deeply influenced by Krausist thought and its philosophy of harmonic rationalism as the root of social organization. He is therefore disinclined to advocate a paradise built on egotistical impulses or to allow that Serafina's voice, whose angelic purity is contaminated with the baser motives of sex, greed, and deceit, can ever lead to the quasi-religious transcendence Bonis seeks. The interrogation of the operatic intertext begins with the realization that the sublime emotions evoked by opera, while standing in positive contrast to the prosaic character of most realist and naturalist fiction, too often verge on inauthenticity and melodramatic overstatement. Yet an even bigger dilemma remains: how is the author to reconcile the ideal of pure voice (that is, nonsignification) with a literary form such as the novel, so closely intertwined with the concept of representation? Alas may indeed be searching for new novelistic formulas, but, as Beser notes, he never goes so far as to repudiate entirely the dominant realist aesthetic (Beser 1968, 332). If opera dramatizes the notion that "human beings can suffer from their status as speaking subjects, and they can find an ecstatic pleasure in seeking to forget or deny their fundamental attachment to language" (Poizat 1992, x), what are the consequences of this linguistic detachment within the novel, which can only sever its ties with language at the cost of its own destruction? The surest sign that Alas is loath to follow the operatic imperative to its ultimate conclusion is the novelistic fate assigned to Serafina in the final chapter: "¡He perdido la voz! Sí; perdida por completo" (Alas 1979, 320) [I have lost my voice! Yes, lost it completely] (Alas 1981, 253). Despite music's predominance through the agency of voice, opera cannot exist, generically speaking, without a libretto and the latter's concern, however minimal, for the referential mode. As Lindenberger reminds us, "opera has proved an ambivalent example for those theorists who, ever since Romanticism, have celebrated music for its freedom from the mimetic concerns characteristic of other arts such as literature and painting" (Lindenberger 1984, 128). *Su único hijo*, like its operatic intertext, cannot completely liberate itself from textual and representational concerns. In fact, the novel concludes not with a song or with Minghetti's playing of a few bars of *La Traviata* but with words: Bonifacio's newfound mastery of speech in the affirmation of his son's paternity.

Act III

As much as the intercalation of opera scenes in Alas's novel suggests an expansion of the boundaries of novelistic discourse, the intertext of *Su único hijo* is not restricted to the exploration of a crisis in literary form. On the contrary, the role of opera as cultural production allows Alas to expose the plight of a national discourse in disarray at the close of the century. The details of the local theatrical scene provided by the author (for example, the penury and tribulations of the touring opera company, the repertoire of works they perform, their audience's response) would all have been recognizable to readers and thus afford Clarín an opportunity to use the operatic intertext as a sounding board for issues affecting the national psyche. Here, too, the prevailing tone is one of ambivalence. On the one hand, opera's inquiry into "la misteriosa relación de la música con lo suprasensible" (Alas 1979, 197) [the mysterious relationship between music and the metaphysical] (Alas 1981, 150) deservedly earns a place for it among the paths to the new spiritualism (Rivkin 1987). But on the other hand, the predominance of foreign models and the popularity of opera as an art form that looks to the past rather than the present bespeak a crisis of identity that is as much political as it is aesthetic.

Through its intertext, *Su único hijo* engages with the debate over Spanish national opera (or the lack thereof), which was rekindled during the waning years of the nineteenth century. Although musicologists such as Peña y Goñi mounted an ardent defense of the *zarzuela* as an authentic element of Spain's cultural patrimony, the fact remains that the monopoly of Spanish theaters by Italian works and vocal techniques went virtually unchallenged. Peña y Goñi minces no words: "Felipe V . . . abrió las puertas a la invasión italiana, que hoy todavía se enseñorea de nuestra patria. . . . El arte italiano la asaltó, fue creciendo y rodeándola como una inmensa serpiente, y hoy yace todavía bajo la presión fatal del monstruo, aplastada, jadeante, víctima de la asfixia" [Philip V . . . opened the doors to the Italian invasion, which today is still master over our nation. . . . Italian art assaulted her, growing and surrounding her like some immense serpent, and today she still lies beneath the monster's deadly weight, crushed and panting, a victim of suffocation] (Peña y Goñi 1967, 32–33). The tone of *Su único hijo* is more ironic than apocalyptic, yet the colonization of the town's cultural life by musical creations imported from the rest of Europe is nonetheless viewed with a wary eye.

Almost all the operas performed by Mochi's company belong to the Italianate *opera seria* tradition (see n. 11). Moreover, Mochi himself is really Cayetano Domínguez, a Spaniard pretending to be an Italian who has convinced Serafina (an Englishwoman) to carry on a similar masquerade. They correctly calculate the cachet that accompanies a foreign pedigree; Bonifacio plays right into their hands, since his admiration for the artists is increased tenfold when he learns they have come from abroad. The portrait Clarín offers could not be clearer or more discouraging. While the German industrialist Körner and Juan Nepomuceno discuss the "general Spanish decadence" and the possibility of a rebirth of national theater (Alas 1979, 184), the townspeople are happily attending Italian opera and substituting French cuisine and table manners for the classic *puchero*. If it is true, as Valis (1989) has suggested, that one copies the thing one lacks, then Bonifacio and his fellow citizens are not simply imitating bourgeois patronage of the arts or the supposed refinement that characterizes devotees of high culture; they are compensating for a frayed (or absent) ideology promoting contemporary artistic and intellectual autonomy in Spain.

Reflecting on the interconnections of musical and political history, W. H. Auden wrote that "the golden age of opera, from Mozart to Verdi, coincided with the golden age of liberal humanism, of unquestioning belief in freedom and progress" (Auden 1969, 360). It is surely no coincidence that this precise span in operatic history—from *Don Giovanni* to *La Traviata*—is reproduced in *Su único hijo*. Intuiting most operagoers' resistance to change, Mochi and his singers devise a traditional program that will satisfy their public, and Bonifacio happily casts his gaze backward in appreciation. But these operatic pieces are performed in a degraded state, sung by has-been tenors and third-rate sopranos before a passive audience. The alternately exalted and parodic treatments of these operas in Clarín's narrative indicate the breakdown of the systems of belief in which they were grounded, for the myths of liberalism and progress come under increasingly critical scrutiny at century's end. Bonifacio's notion of history, meanwhile, remains as hopelessly mythic as that of his beloved romantic opera. He would suppress from his memoirs, on aesthetic grounds, all details of the physical abuse he suffers at his wife's hands. Instead, he recasts Emma's jealousy in terms of the struggle for national independence, musing: "Moriría al pie del cañón, a los pies de su tiple, sobre los escombros de su pasión, de su Zaragoza" (Alas 1979, 83) [He would die at the base of the cannon, at the feet of his soprano, (upon) the rubble of his passion—his own Saragossa] (Alas,

1981, 62). Needless to say, 1891 is not 1808; epic has become mock-epic. When held up to contemporary history, the operatic universe and its exaltation of fictionalized past glories make the deficiencies of the present seem all the more glaring. Bonis surely speaks for his author when he shakes himself out of his reverie, saying "No disparatemos" [Let's not talk nonsense] (Alas 1979, 83; translation modified).

Coda

The asymmetry of the intertextual relations between genres in *Su único hijo* makes for a fascinating novel. While Alas does not restrict his purview to the flesh-and-bone materiality of realist fiction, neither does he embrace without reservation a new literary and intellectual sensibility in which the referential narrative function is wholly abandoned in favor of an interiorized vision, sensorially fragmented, of spiritual and philosophical incertitude. Situated somewhere along the fault line between these two tendencies, his novel keeps company with a number of fundamental, transitional texts that adopt a policy of generic inclusionism (Galdós's experiments with the incorporation of dramatic form in the novel immediately come to mind). *Su único hijo* is, nonetheless, unique in drawing upon the opera—both its form and its social history—as a means of (partially) dislodging the representational mode and criticizing the bourgeois society that fetishizes it.[19]

In her exposition of the concept of intertextuality, Kristeva builds upon several notions first advanced in the work of Mikhail Bakhtin: dialogism, double-voicing, pluridiscursivity, and polyphony. This latter term, of course, is drawn from the musical sphere, and it would not be amiss to note parallels between opera and the particular kind of contentiously multiperspectival narrative that Dostoevsky exemplifies for Bakhtin (Lindenberger 1984, 91–95). The play of voices in *Su único hijo* is by turns harmonious and conflictive but is certainly not unknown in the Spanish novel at the approach of the twentieth century. Recent readers have illustrated how many texts, including Clarín's, pose stubborn questions about the shape and boundaries of novelistic discourse. Considered in this context, the generic intertextuality of *Su único hijo* should not be considered as striking a discordant note. It is part of a chorus that only grows louder with the approach of modernity.

Notes

1. The earliest uses of the word "intertextuality" are in Kristeva's essay on Bakhtin and in her *Sēmeiōtikē*. For an overview of the diverse and often conflictive ways in which intertextuality has been applied as a critical trope, see Angenot 1983.

2. A classic statement of this position is to be found in Barthes's "From Work to Text": "Every text, being itself the intertext of another text, belongs to the intertextual, which must not be confused with a text's origins: to search for the 'sources of' and 'influence upon' a work is to satisfy the myth of filiation. The quotations from which a text is constructed are anonymous, irrecoverable, and yet *already read*: they are quotations without quotation marks" (Barthes 1979, 77). Similarly, for Derrida the entire field of writing, shot through by the "instituted trace," may be considered intertextual: "a 'text' . . . is henceforth no longer a finished corpus of writing, some content enclosed in a book or its margins, but a differential network, a fabric of traces referring endlessly to something other than itself, to other differential traces" (Derrida 1979, 84).

3. This statement, attributed to John Guillory, is quoted by Begley in his 1994 profile of Harold Bloom (35).

4. Chatman is moved to ask "whether a narratology which views narrative as an immanent object containing its own strategy of context . . . has, in fact, failed" (Chatman 1990, 310). In discussions of intertextuality, the same question might be asked, for instance, of Riffaterre, who insists that texts always contain idiosyncratic features ("ungrammaticalities") whose presence in effect guides readers to the discovery of an intertext (Riffaterre 1978, 4–6). Thus, even when Riffaterre places a work within its contemporary context, historical considerations tend to be eclipsed by a generalized theory of reading according to which every text already contains the clues and signals necessary for the proper decoding of its significance: "the very core of the literary experience is that perceiving mode known as intertextuality. The text refers not to objects outside of itself, but to an intertext. The words of the text signify not by referring to things, but by presupposing other texts" (Riffaterre 1981, 228).

5. Lissorgues maintains that, in the evolution of Alas's philosphical and religious thought, the years 1890–1901 correspond to a period of disorientation in which the author's previous "hegemonic aspiration" has given way to "sentiments of frustration" (Lissorgues 1983, 369). During these same years, Alas's critical thinking on the novel, that is, his response to the crisis of narrative spreading across Europe at the turn of the century, is likewise viewed as a moment of indecision (Beser 1968, 300); he is sympathetic to calls for a new formula for writing novels but, other than alluding to possible examples (Paul Bourget, the Russian novel), does not arrive at a general definition of what such a formula might look like. As Beser notes, Clarín's critical vocabulary becomes markedly unstable after 1890 as he refers somewhat vaguely to such new currents as the "psychological novel," the "poetic novel," "the novel of sentiment," and the "novela novelesca" or "novelistic novel" (330–35).

6. For studies that focus entirely or in large part on the issue of Bonifacio Reyes's paternity, see Bandera 1969, Baquero Goyanes 1956, Little and Schraibman 1978, and Montes Huidobro 1972, as well as Richmond's introduction to her edition of the novel (Alas 1979).

7. The familial metaphor, frequently employed in discussions of intertextuality, also resurfaces in the terminology applied to explain the nature of literary genres. For a study

of the principal metaphors of genre—as families, biological species, social institutions, and speech acts—see Fishelov 1993, especially chap. 3, "Literary Genres as Families" (53–83).

8. Valis concludes: "Like Bonifacio's son, Clarín's novel has two fathers" (Valis 1989, 865). Given the illogic of this calculation in terms of biological paternity, why stop at only two?

9. All references to *Su único hijo* are taken from Carolyn Richmond's edition (Alas 1979). For translations into English, unless otherwise noted, I have relied on Julie Jones's *His Only Son* (Alas 1981). Where only one reference is given, it is to the Spanish original. Other translations are my own.

10. Bauer views the ambiguity of Clarín's ending, its "desafiador hibridismo" [challenging hybridism], as another index of the novel's incipient modernity (Bauer 1986, 69).

11. The operas that figure in the protagonist's or the narrator's discourse are the following: Mozart, *Don Giovanni* (1787); Donizetti, *Lucrezia Borgia* (1833); Bellini, *La Straniera* (1829), *La Sonnambula* (1831), and *Norma* (1831); Rossini, *Il Barbiere di Siviglia* (1816), *Semiramide* (1823), and *Otello* (1833); Verdi, *Nabucco* (1842), *Attila* (1846), and *La Traviata* (1853); Meyerbeer, *Il Crociato in Egitto* (1824); Gounod, *Faust* (1859); Arrieta, *La conquista de Granada* (1850). This last opera is the only one by a Spaniard. The majority of works cited are of Italian manufacture, and most had their premieres between 1823 and 1853, coinciding with the apogee of the romantic movement.

12. Oddly, Sánchez Siscort concludes that the use of operatic references in *Su único hijo* is merely erudite window dressing on the author's part: "El repertorio operístico que 'Clarín' expone en *Su único hijo* es bastante extenso y no viene justificado totalmente por la acción . . . más parece alarde de conocimientos del autor y una manera de demostrar su interés por el género" [The operatic repertoire mentioned by Clarín in *Su único hijo* is quite extensive and not entirely justified by the action . . . rather it seems to be a show of the author's knowledge and a way of demonstrating his interest in the genre] (Sánchez Siscort 1987, 124). In her attempt to equate the structure of *Su único hijo* with that of a sonata, she fails to consider operatic form or its distinctive generic features and relegates the role of opera in the novel to a supercilious display of Clarín's cultural savvy.

13. Here I find myself in disagreement with Barthes when he asserts that "l'intertexte ne reconnaît aucune division de genres" [the intertext does not recognize any division among genres] (Barthes 1971, 101).

14. Conrad vigorously denounces the "realistic intimidation of opera," that is, the *verismo* tradition in which dramatic implausibility is made to masquerade as psychological realism: "Verismo is conceived in bad faith because, ashamed of the artifice of opera, it is driven to rely on characters who are themselves artists and can therefore be counted on to behave unrealistically in the line of their trade: opera singers, actresses, clowns, poets or painters, composers and their music-masters, celebrated toreadors. For all their boast of verisimilitude, these works represent a new aestheticism. They are art about art" (Conrad 1977, 138). Shrader rebuts this view, insisting that *verismo* has less to do with naturalism of setting or plot than with psychological realism and the way that sentient motives are musically expressed, without relying on conventions, in a "new type of musical continuum unmarred by artificial or unnatural division" (Shrader 1983, 155). That Conrad sees the novel as opera's counterpart while Shrader sees the drama as the literary analogue to opera is one of the key issues at the root of their debate.

15. Valis discusses a number of scenes distinguished by their operatic (i.e., melodramatic) quality, in which the "farrago of cheap emotionalism and sentimentality" of the characters' behavior stands in contrast to a highly ironic authorial perspective (Valis 1981, 116–24). However, not all such operatic moments in the novel are played for laughs.

16. This polemic has been tackled anew, with no easier resolution, in recent interdisciplinary studies informed by the critical idioms of deconstruction and cultural studies. Levin, in his introduction to *Opera through Other Eyes*, vigorously disagrees with those who consider opera exempt from reading, with all the instabilities reading entails; to ignore the operatic text and concentrate solely on the music is "a nostalgic trip to the imaginary, a vacation from language and the insights of contemporary language-based accounts of textual meaning" (Levin 1994, 7). A similar position is adopted by Groos and Parker (1988) in their collection of essays devoted to (re)reading libretti. However, an essay by Paul Robinson, also included in their volume, argues contrarily: "Because the meaning of opera is at bottom musical—because its essential argument is posed in musical language—any interpretation of opera derived exclusively, or even primarily, from the libretto is likely to result in a misreading." On a more conciliatory note, Robinson agrees that, although "the words in opera sometimes count for little, they never count for nothing"; even if unintelligible, they are symbols of opera's "human subjectivity," an "expression of will" (Robinson 1988, 328, 345).

17. Poizat's Lacanian analysis of the female voice in opera is of special interest in light of Serafina's alternation between seraphic and demonic behavior. Bonis perceives clearly the difference between the soprano in repose and the woman in the throes of sexual passion. In the latter instance, Serafina "asustaba con sus gritos" [startled him with her cries] and speaks with "una voz ronca, gutural" [a harsh, guttural voice]. When her erotic frenzy is spent, however, she becomes another woman altogether: "Entonces *la diabla* se convertía en la mujer de la voz de *madre*, y las lágrimas de voluptuosidad de Bonis dejaban la corriente a otras de enternecimiento anafrodítico; se le llenaba el espíritu de recuerdos de la niñez, de nostalgias del regazo materno" [Then Serafina, no longer a sensual witch, became a woman with a mother's voice; Bonis's tears of voluptuosity gave way, and he was moved to a tenderness freed of sexual desire; his soul was filled with memories of childhood and nostalgia for his mother's lap] (Alas 1979, 91–92; translation modified).

18. Poizat notes that, overall, French opera is driven by the primacy of language, whereas Italian opera obeys a more purely lyrical principle (Poizat 1992, 58). It is surely no coincidence that *Su único hijo* is fixated almost exclusively on nineteenth-century Italian opera, which once again underlines a resistance to language.

19. Probably no other Spanish novel shows such an interest in the opera, except perhaps Alarcón's melodramatic piece of juvenilia *El final de Norma* (1861) (Valis 1981, 115 n. 16). Operatic references are frequent in Galdós's *Miau* and Clarín's *La Regenta*, for instance, but are not fundamental to the structure of either of these works (see Richmond 1987). There exists an ample corpus of works in European literature in which narrative reflects upon operatic discourse (see Lindenberger 1984, chap. 4, "Opera in Novels," 145–96).

Works Cited

Alas, Leopoldo. 1888. *Mis plagios. Un discurso de Núñez de Arce. Folletos literarios,* no. 4. Madrid: Fernando Fe.

———. 1979. *Su único hijo.* Ed. Carolyn Richmond. Madrid: Espasa-Calpe.

———. 1981. *His Only Son.* Trans. Julie Jones. Baton Rouge: Louisiana State University Press.

Angenot, Marc. 1983. "'L'Intertextualité': enquête sur l'émergence et la diffusion d'un champ notionnel." *Revue des Sciences Humaines* 189: 121–35.

Auden, W. H. 1960. "Metalogue to *The Magic Flute.*" In *Homage to Clio,* 70–73. London: Faber and Faber.

———. 1969. "Some Reflections on Music and Opera." In *The Essence of Opera.* Ed. Ulrich Weisstein, 354–60. New York: Norton.

Bandera, Cesáreo. 1969. "La sombra de Bonifacio Reyes en *Su único hijo.*" *Bulletin of Hispanic Studies* 46: 201–25.

Baquero Goyanes, Mariano. 1956. "Una novela de Clarín: *Su único hijo.*" In *Prosistas españoles contemporáneos,* 33–125. Madrid: Rialp.

Barthes, Roland. 1971. "Réponses." *Tel Quel* 47: 89–107.

———. 1979. "From Work to Text." In *Textual Strategies: Perspectives in Post-Structuralist Criticism.* Ed. Josué V. Harari, 73–81. Ithaca, N.Y.: Cornell University Press.

Bauer, Beth Wietelmann. 1986. "*Su único hijo:* la conclusión imposible." *Revista de Estudios Hispánicos* 20: 67–79.

Begley, Adam. 1994. "Harold Bloom: Colossus among Critics." *New York Times Magazine,* 25 September, pp. 32–35.

Beser, Sergio. 1968. *Leopoldo Alas, crítico literario.* Madrid: Gredos.

Bloom, Harold. 1973. *The Anxiety of Influence: A Theory of Poetry.* Oxford: Oxford University Press.

Bruce, Don. 1983. "Bibliographie annotée: écrits sur l'intertextualité." *Texte* 2: 217–58.

Chatman, Seymour. 1990. "What Can We Learn from Contextualist Narratology?" *Poetics Today* 11: 209–28.

Conrad, Peter. 1977. *Romantic Opera and Literary Form.* Berkeley: University of California Press.

Culler, Jonathan. 1976. "Presupposition and Intertextuality." *MLN* 91: 1380–96.

Dällenbach, Lucien. 1976. "Intertexte et autotexte." *Poétique* 27: 282–96.

Derrida, Jacques. 1979. "Living On/Border Lines." Trans. James Hulbert. In *Deconstruction and Criticism.* Ed. Harold Bloom et al., 75–176. New York: Seabury (Continuum).

Fishelov, David. 1993. *Metaphors of Genre: The Role of Analogies in Genre Theory.* University Park: Pennsylvania State University Press.

Frow, John. 1990. "Intertextuality and Ontology." In *Intertextuality: Theories and Practice.* Ed. Michael Worton and Judith Still, 45–55. Manchester: Manchester University Press.

Genette, Gérard. 1979. *Introduction à l'architexte.* Paris: Seuil.

———. 1982. *Palimpsestes: la littérature au second degré.* Paris: Seuil.

Gramberg, Eduard J. 1978. *"Su único hijo*, novela incomprendida de Leopoldo Alas." In *Leopoldo Alas "Clarín."* Ed. José María Martínez Cachero, 204–11. Madrid: Taurus.

Groos, Arthur, and Roger Parker, eds. 1988. *Reading Opera.* Princeton: Princeton University Press.

Hebel, Udo J., ed. 1989. *Intertextuality, Allusion, and Quotation: An International Bibliography of Critical Studies.* Westport, Conn.: Greenwood Press.

Jenny, Laurent. 1982. "The Strategy of Form." In *French Literary Theory Today.* Ed. Tzvetan Todorov. Trans. R. Carter, 34–63. Cambridge: Cambridge University Press.

Kristeva, Julia. 1967. "Bakhtine: le mot, le dialogue et le roman." *Critique* 239: 438–65.

———. 1969. *Sēmeiōtikē: recherches pour une sémanalyse.* Paris: Seuil.

Levin, David J., ed. 1994. *Opera through Other Eyes.* Stanford: Stanford University Press.

Lindenberger, Herbert. 1984. *Opera: The Extravagant Art.* Ithaca, N.Y.: Cornell University Press.

Lissorgues, Yvan. 1983. *La Pensée philosophique et religieuse de Leopoldo Alas (Clarín): 1875–1901.* Paris: CNRS.

Little, William, and Joseph Schraibman. 1978. "Notas sobre el motivo de la paternidad en *Su único hijo* de 'Clarín.'" *Boletín del Instituto de Estudios Asturianos* 93–94: 21–29.

Montes Huidobro, Matías. 1972. *"Su único hijo*: sinfónico avatar de Clarín." *Archivum* 22: 149–209.

Morgan, Thaïs E. 1985. "Is There an Intertext in This Text?: Literary and Interdisciplinary Approaches to Intertextuality." *American Journal of Semiotics* 3: 1–40.

Peña y Goñi, Antonio. 1967. *España, desde la ópera a la zarzuela.* Ed. Eduardo Rincón. Madrid: Alianza.

Pérez Firmat, Gustavo. 1979. "The Novel as Genres." *Genre* 12: 269–92.

Pérez Galdós, Benito. 1923. "Los amantes de Teruel." In *Obras inéditas.* Ed. Alberto Ghiraldo, 2: 175–80. Madrid: Renacimiento.

Poizat, Michel. 1992. *The Angel's Cry: Beyond the Pleasure Principle in Opera.* Trans. Arthur Denner. Ithaca, N.Y.: Cornell University Press.

Richmond, Carolyn. 1978. "La ópera como enlace entre dos obras de Clarín: 'Amor è furbo' y *Su único hijo.*" *Insula* 377: 3.

———. 1987. "Experiencias operáticas en *La Regenta: Il barbiere di Siviglia* y el *Fausto.*" In *Hitos y mitos de "La Regenta,"* 108–19. Oviedo: Caja de Ahorros de Asturias.

Riffaterre, Michael. 1978. *Semiotics of Poetry.* Bloomington: Indiana University Press.

———. 1981. "Interpretation and Undecidability." *New Literary History* 12: 227–42.

Rivkin, Laura. 1987. "El ideal musical de Clarín." In *Hitos y mitos de "La Regenta,"* 68–75. Oviedo: Caja de Ahorros de Asturias.

Robinson, Paul. 1988. "A Deconstructive Postscript: Reading Libretti and Misreading Opera." In *Reading Opera.* Ed. Arthur Groos and Roger Parker, 328–46. Princeton: Princeton University Press.

Rosmarin, Adena. 1985. *The Power of Genre.* Minneapolis: University of Minnesota Press.

Sánchez Siscort, Monserrat. 1987. "La música en *Su único hijo.*" In *Hitos y mitos de "La Regenta,"* 120–26. Oviedo: Caja de Ahorros de Asturias.

Shrader, Steven W. 1983. "Realism in Late Nineteenth-Century Opera: A Comparative View." Ph.D. diss., Northwestern University.

Todorov, Tzvetan. 1975. *The Fantastic: A Structural Approach to a Literary Genre.* Trans. Richard Howard. Ithaca, N.Y.: Cornell University Press.

Valis, Noël M. 1981. *The Decadent Vision in Leopoldo Alas.* Baton Rouge: Louisiana State University Press.

———. 1989. "*Su único hijo* and the Perfect Copy." *PMLA* 104: 856–67.

Worton, Michael, and Judith Still, eds. 1990. *Intertextuality: Theories and Practices.* Manchester: Manchester University Press.

Mercedes Salisachs, Ideal Womanhood, and the Middlebrow Novel

DEBRA A. CASTILLO

For Spaniards of this century, the Civil War provides the semantic axis around which social meanings have been organized and transmitted. The particulars of this process of organization and transmission are far from straightforward, however, for despite government efforts to control the production of meaning, to shape and direct understanding of social and sexual relations, there has clearly been a disjunction between the official image of Spain and the people's experience of everyday life. The Civil War in general serves as Mercedes Salisachs's historical subtext, but its particular effect in her work is felt through the overwhelming background presence of the Falangist "Sección Femenina" or "women's section" and its precursor arbiters of feminine behavior, the conduct books that specified the characteristics of the ideal woman for earlier generations of Spaniards. The women's section no longer enjoys the prestige or wide, official acceptance it had during the Franco period. Nevertheless, its influence has permeated Spanish society to the degree that virtually everyone recognizes the ideal of womanhood it proposes, and current women's magazines and advice columns continue its mission of preparing young women to catch and retain a man, to keep a beautiful house, and to prepare tasty meals. The Falangist socialization process still provides the grounding against which a Spanish practice of liberation must define itself and serves as one of the principal intertexts for Salisachs's fictional and nonfictional work.

With the description of "la escuela internacional femenina" [the international women's school] in her interesting and lamentably understudied collection of "estampas casi históricas" [semihistorical vignettes], *Adán-helicóptero*, Salisachs already serves up a ferocious parody of the women's section. Under the less-than-benign tutelage of the school's only teacher, Juana la Loca, young girls are taught what it means to be a woman. Juana's lesson has six basic points; each point is entitled "el hombre" [the man] because "en definitiva eso es lo único que cuenta para las mujeres" [definitively that is all that counts for women] (Salisachs 1957, 125; all translations are mine), and each point discusses some facet of the woman's subordination to her enemy, the man (father, lover, husband). Juana's advice is forceful, given in the imperative style of precepts or commandments that must be obeyed:

> Debéis reservar vuestro amor para los hombres que os hagan la vida imposible. (114)
>
> [You must reserve your love for men who will make your life impossible.]

> Cuanto más sufráis, más femeninas seréis. (116)
>
> [The more you suffer, the more womanly you will be.]

> Una madre ha de poder llegar, si conviene, a la santidad. (117)
>
> [A mother has to reach saintliness, if at all possible.]

> Escribid poco. Las mujeres escritoras pertenecen a la especia de mamíferas amputadas. (124)
>
> [Write little. Women writers belong to the species of amputated mammals.]

There is, for especially qualified students, an additional, elective course on "la incultura" [unculture], presumably to help society women learn to dislike Bach, to misunderstand modern art, to become ignorant about politics, and to appreciate fashion news and "historias del siglo romántico" [stories from the romantic century] (58).

Salisachs follows her vignette on the "escuela internacional femenina" with an equally pointed one describing the "escuela internacional masculina" along the parallel but sharply contrasting lines of this injunction to male students: "Prohibir a la mujer que os hable de los niños. Prohibirle que os hable del servicio. Prohibirle que os hable de la casa, de los amigos, de la situación internacional. . . . Prohibirle a la mujer que hable" [Prohibit your wife from talking about the children. Prohibit her from talking about servants. Prohibit her from talking about the house, about friends, about the international situation. Prohibit your wife from talking] (130). The implications of this satire are obvious enough. Living, breathing girls are turned into what Salisachs calls "cardboard children" in another of her books (*Derribos* [*Demolitions*] 1981, 67), and little boys are reshaped as monsters.

Mercedes Salisachs always felt the need to write, despite the pressures and discouragements of the Falangist society of her youth. In her more recent autobiographical sketches in *Derribos,* she reflects on the diffi-culty of embarking on her chosen career in the absence of support or role models: "La ignorancia era la gran enemiga de aquella vocación extraña que a veces pugnaba por abrirse paso. También lo era el hecho de ser mujer. Las mujeres no escribían. Las mujeres eran seres distintos que jamás firmaban libros. Era desalentador saber eso" [Ignorance was the great enemy of that strange vocation that at times fought to break into the open. So too was the fact of being a woman. Women did not write. Women were different beings who never signed books. It was discourag-ing to learn that] (Salisachs 1981, 97). The breakthrough for her is the discovery, in her hated convent school classroom, of Cecilia Böhl de Faber, better known by her pseudonym, Fernán Caballero. The young Mercedes, aptly tearing through the nun's moralizing half-recognition of the nineteenth-century novelist's talent, concludes: "No fue sólo aquella lección la que aprendí a partir de aquel momento. Fueron todas" [It was not just that day's lesson that I learned in that moment. It was all the lessons] (99).

Since that epiphanic moment, Salisachs has gone on to write at least twenty-five books, mostly novels, several of them translated into other languages. She has won numerous literary prizes, including the Premio Ciudad de Barcelona (1956, for *Una mujer llega al pueblo* [*A Woman Arrives in Town*]), the Premio Planeta (1975, for *La gangrena*), and, in an astounding 1983 sweep, the Premio Hucha de Oro (for *Feliz navidad, señor Ballesteros* [*Merry Christmas, Mr. Ballesteros*]), the Premio Ateneo de Sevilla (for *El volumen de la ausencia* [*The Volume of Absence*]), and the Premio Sara Navarro (for *Sea breve, por favor* [*Be Brief, Please*]). Not surprisingly, she has been a finalist for many more awards, and her works are perennial bestsellers in Spain.

Despite this public recognition, Salisachs's achievements are almost universally downplayed by those few critics who have looked at her work, who tend to see her as that dreaded and pitiful monster, the woman writer, with all that gender's typical limitations in terms of fictional output. In his famous survey of the contemporary Spanish scene, Juan Luis Alborg calls one of Salisachs's books "demasiado 'fácil' para ser un libro importante" [too "easy" to be an important book] (Alborg 1962, 388). He finds that another "arrastraba ya de por sí un lastre de cosas manidas y sentimentales. . . . se le desmaya en vulgaridades" [was already dragging along a millstone of sentimental tripe. . . . it fades away in commonplaces]; still another is "difícil de tragar" [hard to swallow]; and a third one "se diluye en una inacabable rueda de personajillos" [is diluted by an interminable wheel of minor characters] (390, 399, 402).[1] Aparicio López, whose work is interesting mostly as a measure of its time and place—"todos estamos comprometidos con nuestro tiempo," he reminds us, "y el que no lo está es que ha renunciado a ser *hombre*" [we are all committed to our own time, and he who is not has renounced his manhood] (Aparicio López 1979, 191; my emphasis)—generally repeats Alborg's judgments, frequently without crediting his predecessor, and when he adds a note (presumably) of his own harvest, it is generally of a vacuous but clearly antifeminine sort: to wit, in reference to the characters in *La gangrena*, "Todas iguales, y todas distintas. Todas, al fin, mujeres" [All alike, and all different. All, finally, women] (200).

The particularly vituperative tone of these male critics in addressing an overwhelmingly popular series of books by a female novelist demands consideration. Salisachs implicitly thumbs her nose at such critics in *El volumen de la ausencia* by her choice of a woman's novel format, while she directly and ferociously attacks the male-dominated critical establishment in her novel's internal reference to the pathetic noncareer of an aspiring male writer who apes the style of the typical avant-garde man's novel. At the same time, the high art novel serves as one of this book's two major intertextual reference systems. The first and most important of these is Salisachs's direct homage to her predecessor, Carmen Laforet, whose novel *Nada* [*Nothing*], winner of the 1944 Nadal Prize, is cited in numerous obvious references and rewritings in *El volumen de la ausencia* (1983).

The formulaic novel geared towards a female audience serves as the second major intertextual referent for Salisachs's work. The romance novel, or "la novela rosa," is a frequent literary correlative of the Falangist women's section, since it shares with the social movement a profound, if covert, conservative ideology and a severely limited social agenda. The "novela rosa" does not challenge the sorts of conventional assumptions about male-female relations that Salisachs outlines in her satire; rather, it manipulates those assumptions in the service of a fantasy gratification that asserts the power of love to create a psychological space for a woman's victory over a man. The victory, however, is an evanescent one, since it is limited to the single instant of the man's declaration of his love, and it can only endure for the reader in the formulaic repetition of the paradigmatic moment.

In blending these intertextual referents to high and low fiction, *El volumen de la ausencia* figures as a model of a middlebrow, "círculo de lectores" [readers' club] type of book, both profound and accessible, voluminous and absent, as its title implies. It falls somewhere between popular fiction and high literature and is especially interesting because it sits uneasily on the boundary lines between these two quite different modes of discourse. Since large numbers of people with the money and the leisure to afford and read books are clearly enjoying middlebrow works such as those by Salisachs, the problem for the critic is how to read and think about them.

It is my contention that Salisachs's novel, and other middlebrow novels like it, offers a particular challenge to the critic because it is constructed around two major intertextual nodes—high art and low fiction—and this intersection of cultural forms works for a vast audience of readers precisely because of these contradictory elements. Salisachs has cannily tapped into an audience that reads widely but without high cultural pretensions; her readers are proud of their love for serious books, do not need to be told who Cervantes or Laforet are, but they are not required by these works to have to know anything terribly specific or technical about them. As Janice Radway notes, and as a reading of the scant critical material on Salisachs confirms, critics tend "to dismiss the middle range as products of a fundamental insufficiency, therefore as the result of a certain incompetence." This conclusion, as Radway reminds us, is based on a presumed understanding of "a single set of criteria against which all works are measured, and thus [an insistence] that there is only one appropriate way to read" (Radway 1988, 518). In Radway's judgment, the critical dismissal of middlebrow works has everything to do with the system of values against which these works are judged as failures. More appropriate, she argues, would be to examine these works "as ways of writing rather than Literature, ways of reading rather than texts," since, for middlebrow readers, "books play a quite different role in their lives and serve other purposes than they do for people who make their living producing, analyzing, and distinguishing among cultural products" (519). While critics can and do write about almost anything these days, we seem to focus on the high and low ends of the cultural scale—precisely the two poles evoked and blurred in the middlebrow novel. In this respect, middlebrow fiction poses a kind of problem that does not occur when one considers either Laforet or Corín Tellado. *El volumen de la ausencia* is not low enough to appeal to popular culture studies or to receive a semiotic treatment, nor is it literary enough to be judged by the standards of high art (witness Alborg's objections). Like popular culture, this novel is a form of entertainment, but it is entertainment for at least moderately educated people who are aware that television and series romances are not art.

Feminist cultural critics have identified still another reason why the critical establishment is wary of middlebrow texts, a reason based on a long-standing and now much discussed discomfort with a perceived

feminization of literature that coincides with a feminization of reading.[2]
When both the hierarchy of literary values and the privileged mode of
critical discourse favor "masculine" referents, it is no suprise that critics
like Alborg and Aparicio López evince acute dislike of any feminizing
features—qualities that have to be all the more carefully guarded against
because of the age-old suspicion that reading books is an effeminate (or
feminizing) activity. The battle of the books between classical, masculine
works and vernacular, feminine fictions has been refought on differing
intellectual planes for hundreds of years as, curiously, an obsession of a
masculinist literary establishment. David Simpson's concise formulation
makes the point on a theoretical level:

> The feminization of literature was not, of course, uncontested. Wordsworth's
> famous outcries against popular novels and plays and high modernism's
> reaffirmation of sheer difficulty and massive intellectuality are just two
> instances of a masculinizing reaction. But the struggle has always occurred
> from within an already feminized general construction of the literary mode.
> Literary criticism, as an appendix or companion to literature, has experienced
> the same struggles. Its attempted diversions into theory have often been ges-
> tures of remasculinization, and have been resisted by an establishment whose
> lexicon is dominantly feminized: intuition, exceptionality, sympathy, empa-
> thy, lived experience, and so forth. (Simpson 1994, 62–63)

Simpson points to the complicated and invariably, if often unconsciously,
gendered relation of the critic to the text, even in terms of the theoretical
model he or she manipulates. Thus, the qualities of high art, as intimated
by Alborg and Aparicio López, would include such masculinizing
elements as a spare style and an intellectualizing or reflective mode of
expression, while they explicitly reject such feminizing counterparts as
lushness and appeal to sensation. The middlebrow woman's novel, in
pointing in both directions at the same time, is particularly resistant to a
remasculinizing intent and particularly threatening to the high-art value
system. As Jennifer Wicke reminds us, "on a methodological level, this is
to suggest the intimate relationship between 'high art' and its conditions
of production, and its shadow partner, the mass communication form that
constitutes its matrix" (Wicke 1988, 1). Wicke is exactly right in this
observation, the more so because her use of the term "matrix" hints at the
shadowy, feminized underpinnings of an overtly masculinizing structure.
By playing off competing value systems in an intertextual, overdeter-
mined, and theatricalized setting, the middlebrow novel also reminds us
of the masculinizing nature of the assumption that there is but a single
system of values.

In her book *Inventing High and Low*, Stephanie Sieburth brings this discussion specifically into the Spanish setting. While she does not address the middlebrow novel per se, she looks closely at the interrelationship of literature and social change in the context of the vexed—and often vexing—imbrication of mass fiction and high-art novels. As Sieburth points out, nineteenth-century Spain made a significant shift toward a more urbanized society, although still in a tardy manner and to a lesser degree than other European nations. The consequent growth of the working class, the increasing literacy and leisure of the bourgeois woman who looked to the popular press for cultural tips, and the greater freedom of the press following the death of Fernando VII all contributed to the rise of the novel targeted precisely, if somewhat duplicitously, at that upwardly mobile woman. This awareness of the woman reader is paradoxically tied to a concern for monitoring women's bodies and to a deep-seated conviction that women who show a tendency to stray from the time-honored model of the traditional housewife are also in some complicated way undermining the soul of the nation.

There is, thus, in nineteenth-century Spain, as in France and England, a delightfully quaint tradition of novelists trashing their (women) readers for reading serial novels exactly like the one they are at that very moment holding in their hands. In Spain, however, this polemic against the woman reader is tied to an uneasy sense on both the author's and the reader's parts that Spain itself is a weak or feminized (effeminate?) country when compared to the more potent, hence masculine, rival nations. Sieburth says it this way: "The kinds of dreams nursed by the protagonists who devour mass culture seem to flourish in unevenly modern countries, which see themselves as inferior to America or Europe and compensate with delusions of grandeur" (Sieburth 1994, 12). The move is strange and revealing. These writers and readers are particularly sensitive about the material conditions that allow for their own success; the great unwashed working class is, of course, an implicitly masculine threat, and one with the power to destabilize the scarcely established middle class. Likewise, the decaying upper class—the source of all that solid, masculine high art—seems distressingly effete. What can a writer manage to do to make a living and preserve good family values? How does a middle-class reader maintain her upwardly mobile trajectory?

For Sieburth, nineteenth-century writers like Benito Pérez Galdós establish a tradition carried on into this century in their very different ways by Juan Goytisolo and Carmen Martín Gaite. Pérez Galdós's solution to the immanent feminization of Spain is to invite his mass-culture-reading, middle-class female audience members to "immasculate" themselves (to borrow Judith Fetterley's term[3]) as a positive social and political gesture—that is, to identify with masculinizing values and social

forms and to maintain their feminine purity. Pérez Galdós does this by
showing his bad female protagonists as indiscriminate, frivolous, or
immoral readers of second-rate mass-culture fiction, the evil effects of
which have serious repercussions on the national social fabric. Men who
read or write novels in this world are similarly morally unsound. By the
same token, Pérez Galdós's morally superior fiction must establish its
distance from its own audience and its own publishing conditions so that
good women will resist the temptation to read serial novels like his.

Martín Gaite is the author whom Sieburth uses to represent a resolution of this impasse. In *El cuarto de atrás* [*The Back Room*], Martín
Gaite explores the liberating qualities of "low" fiction, and it is the
popular art form that triggers the novel. Popular texts also serve as the
medium by which memory is shaped, since the novelist salutes both the
pre-Franco, romantic novels of her protagonist's youth and the Franco
propaganda fiction of her adolescence and adulthood. Likewise, Martín
Gaite points out the transgressive subtexts in popular music, where, for
example, Conchita Piquer's bitter laments stand out against the sappy
sweet lyrics of popular boleros. Martín Gaite focuses on the ephemeral,
the ordinary, and the female, and in doing so creates a third term that
demonstrates the falsity of the artificial dialectic prominent in the texts of
the male authors Sieburth studies, a middle ground—if not a middlebrow
novel—for deconstructing the high/low dichotomy.

While Martín Gaite plays off her high-art novel against a low-culture
backdrop, Salisachs more nearly approaches profound intertextuality in
her use of themes and images from popular women's fiction. With a
readership of over 20 million women and more than 200 million dollars
in sales per year (Christian-Smith 1990, 12), the romance market not
only epitomizes "low" culture, it is, as the biggest paperback-sales sector
in the world, coming close to epitomizing book reading in general. Corín
Tellado, the undisputed queen of series romance in the Hispanic world,
is, according to Cabrera Infante's unattributed quotation, "el escritor
español más leído de todos los tiempos" [the most read Spanish writer of
all times], with her formula fiction based on a series of invariable
features that the Cuban writer roguishly identifies as follows: "La víctima
que termina por amar a su verdugo. El incesto. El fetichismo. El maso-
quismo como prueba de amor. El sadismo que engendra frigidez que
engendra amor que engendra celos que engendra sadismo" [The victim
who ends up falling in love with her executioner. Incest. Fetishism.
Masochism as a proof of love. Sadism that begets frigidity that begets
love that begets jealousy that begets sadism] (Cabrera Infante 1975, 39,
45). Cabrera Infante is right in identifying these themes—or their toned-
down versions—as constants in the formula romance, and many of them

appear in Salisachs's novel as well. Certainly, the narrative of the formula romance is not about happiness achieved but about happiness frustrated or deferred, and it would not be an exaggeration to say, paradoxically, that romance narrative is premised on lack (of happiness, of love, of the right man): in essence, a variation on a sadomasochistic theme. Once the woman receives acknowledgment of her man's love, the narrative ends with what could be called "the death of love." This inevitable conjunction of reciprocated love at the novel's conclusion leads to speculation on the proximity of death and marriage as the two traditional forms of narrative closure, but that would be another project.

Mercedes Salisachs's own disillusionment with the Spanish woman's condition does not necessarily lead her characters to a change in perception about the inevitable romance-novel trajectory, and much less to concrete action. Her typical protagonist, though betrayed and morally abandoned in her marriage, cannot generalize her experience to other human relationships. Quite the contrary, she places herself in the situation of being deceived again and again. Ida Sierra, the protagonist of *El volumen de la ausencia*, in a sad, funny, poignant, and true move, puts herself into precisely the same predicament with her lover as with her husband by handing herself over completely to his whims: "Mi casa era ya aquella casa tuya, Juan. Y mi único deseo, llegar a ella. Unirme a ti. Saberme totalmente tuya" [My house was already that house of yours, Juan. My only desire, to reach it. To unite with you. To know myself totally yours] (Salisachs 1983, 151). Ida is partly the victim of an over-rich diet of romantic novels in which union with the beloved is bliss unimaginable. She is also the victim of a definition of woman that does not question the division of representable space into married and unmarried, material and imaginative, empowered and (almost) dead. Nancy Armstrong writes:

> If the marketplace driven by male labor came to be imagined as a centrifugal force that broke up the vertical chains organizing an earlier notion of society . . ., then the household's dynamic was conceived as a centripetal one. The household simultaneously recentered the scattered community at myriad points to form the nuclear family, a social organization with a mother rather than a father as its center. The very fact of its interlocking symmetries suggests that the doubled social world was clearly a myth before it was put into practice. (Armstrong 1987, 136)

Ida, in her faithfulness to this hoary myth, repeats with her lover the dream of the household economy she has been unable to practice with her husband; and at this point, Ida, like the myth, is practically gone, as her punning name suggests. She has just been diagnosed with a fatal disease and has perhaps four months to live.

Ida does not question the values of her society in any profound way, yet Salisachs's novel suggests that society itself is in the process of rethinking its most basic rules for sexual relationships. What seems to be the plot—Ida's plot—turns out to be of secondary interest to the author's implicit plot, which conspires to teach a salutary lesson to a specific audience. The novel concerns itself covertly with the constraints of, and dissatisfactions with, a storytelling tradition that dictates that the woman's novel can only be some variant of a domestic drama and that the woman novelist's characteristic quality is her emotiveness. *El volumen de la ausencia* has a melodramatic plot line that tries at the same time to take itself seriously and to suggest a parody/pastiche of the limitations of melodrama. Ultimately, however, the novel questions its own need for the narrative controls and restrictions imposed by a melodramatic/romantic plot line. That need is all the more suspect because the subtext of the formulaic appeal to restriction and control typical of the "woman's book" is just too suspiciously similar to the social value that would contain women in the domestic space.

Noncoincidentally, the feminist reader-writer picks up the story where the romance writer leaves off. Many of the high-art variations on the woman's novel by women who constitute the Catalan Women's Renaissance group—writers like Tusquets, Moix, Roig, and Rodoreda— concern themselves with inevitable, postmarital disillusionments as women learn that love is not, after all, enough to empower them in social terms. Among the works written by women in modern Spain, however, Carmen Laforet's *Nada* (1945) is the one most specifically and clearly incorporated into the intertextual universe of Salisachs's novel. Laforet's novel retains the status of an ur-text capturing the dissonance between the official image of Spain and the people's experience of everyday life. In balancing *El volumen de la ausencia* against *Nada*, Salisachs is in some sense contributing to Laforet's project, weighing nothingness against absence, as it were. This modern rewriting of a prior text is borne out in Salisachs's many intertextual allusions to *Nada*: most obviously, Barcelona and the Calle de Aribau are the setting of both novels, and Laforet's protagonist, Andrea, appears in a less attractive guise in Salisachs's work. Then too, Salisachs's protagonist, like her predecessor, is characterized by her abstraction from quotidian reality. As Laforet's Andrea says, in terms equally appropriate to Salisachs's Ida, "Unos seres nacen para vivir, otros para trabajar, otros para mirar la vida. Yo tenía un pequeño y ruin papel de espectadora" [Some people are born to live, others to work, others to observe life. I had the small and insignificant role of spectator] (Laforet 1980, 224).

Laforet's celebrated novel begins and ends in a vacuum. Andrea's unexpected arrival on a train—"no me esperaba nadie" [no one was waiting for me] (11)—leads, after almost three hundred pages, to an equally unaccompanied, though enigmatic, departure: "no me llevaba nada. Al menos, así creía yo entonces" [I took nothing with me. Or so I thought at the time] (294). Andrea's tremendous sense of alienation from her surroundings in Barcelona is played out in the context of desperate poverty and small-minded squalor. At the same time, and perhaps as a consequence of postwar deprivations, the woman's romance looms large as a touchstone while the romantic myth of a contented domesticity seems ever more fraudulent. Andrea continually references the stories of the women of the Calle de Aribau apartment to frustrated dreams of a romantic, happy ending. Andrea herself fiercely resists such willful reinscriptions of memory in the form of a banal romance but cannot help being fascinated by the gothic tales Gloria tells her: "te voy a contar una historia, mi historia, Andrea, para que veas que es como una novela de verdad" [I am going to tell you a story, my story, Andrea, so you can see that it is like a real novel] (48). Andrea comments at one point that "toda la historia de Angustias resultaba como una novela del siglo pasado" [Angustias's whole story turned out like a novel from the last century] (108). Román comes closer to expressing the open-ended quality of Laforet's text when he warns the protagonist: "no te forjes novelas: ni nuestras discusiones ni nuestros gritos tienen causa, ni conducen a un fin" [don't go building novels: neither our discussions nor our screams have any cause, nor do they lead to any conclusion] (38); yet, he too phrases his warning in relation to the expectations of a melodramatic plot structure. Laforet's novel and Salisachs's both take into account a similar awareness of the effects of popular culture on literary form; both are transcoded for a double reading of the key presence/absence in their texts. Wallace Stevens, in his famous poem "The Snow Man," captures this conjunction of illusion and substance: "For the listener who listens in the snow / And, nothing himself, beholds / Nothing that is not there and the nothing that is" (Stevens 1972, 54). "Nothing" becomes a substantive essence in all of these works and reflects back on the intertextual building of fiction upon other fictions.

While on a first level Salisachs's book may be read as a frivolous soap opera, on a second level, like many other contemporary women's novels with which it could be compared, it offers an ideological statement about the deadening life of the typical housewife and her futile efforts to escape societally imposed constrictions. The frequent comparisons of Ida's life to that of a fish in a tank, just floating along meaninglessly, point up that

statement. Equally significant is the author's tic of beginning sentences
with the word "nada," as in "Nada en esa pecera tiene sentido" [Nothing
in this fishtank makes sense] (Salisachs 1983, 11) or "Nada era
soportable" [Nothing was bearable] (190). With these repetitions,
Salisachs cannily codes her text for two different, if ultimately coexten-
sive, ways of describing textual productivity and for two modes of
mapping integration into the social system. One involves the romance
plot's tight restriction of the woman into a recognizably domestic sphere;
the other suggests a nebulous dissatisfaction with the woman's typical
role; one hints at a high-art use of metaphor through abstract intellectualizing; the other reminds the reader of high art's conditions of production
through repeated and unsubtle reference to Laforet's key term. If
Salisachs does not resolve the tensions, she at least suggests forms of plot
resolution that allow for social recognition of these forms, however they
are defined. The melodramatic plot line may thus serve to draw in the
reader, while the second level of plot, often overtly signalled in Ida's
interpretive commentaries (this is not a subtle novel in that sense), provides a moral or ideological coding of events for a society in the process
of change.

El volumen de la ausencia offers not only a highly colored view of the
war between the sexes but also a dramatized portrait of the conflicts
arising among three generations of women—mother and mother-in-law,
daughter, and granddaughter. Here, mother-love is consistently used for
emotional blackmail with no relief allowed the unwary. The mother's
abnegation is a perverse form of pleasure; the mother-in-law's selfishness is culpable; the daughter's willed and socially approved blindness is
shown to be as dangerous as her husband's self-absorption; and the
granddaughter's flouting of conventional expectations in her open affair
with an older, rich, married man leads to a wasteland beyond social
redemption.

Salisachs writes in one of her early articles: "En otras circunstancias se
ha venido disertando con acierto sobre la dignidad del libro como
relación social y como vínculo intelectual en la comunicación de los
seres humanos. La misión que me corresponde en estos momentos es
tratar el libro 'como objeto permanente'" [In other circumstances,
discussions have correctly noted the dignity of the book as social relationship and as an intellectual link in the communication among human
beings. The mission that falls to my lot in these times is to treat the book
as a "permanent object"] (Salisachs 1959, 13). In a world in which every
other relationship seems disarticulated, in which too many things seem to
float, the book—any book—serves, in Salisachs's optimistic view, as an
index of culture, authenticity, weight. She continues: "lo que verdadera-

mente produce escalofríos, es comprobar la cantidad de gente que vive ignorando la existencia del libro como objeto, sea cual sea su finalidad" [what is really frightening is to recognize the number of people who live in ignorance of the existence of the book as an object, regardless of its purpose] (14), and for this reason, "no me asusto demasiado cuando se me objeta que Fulanito y Menganito han comprado libros a metros o a tanto el kilo. El hecho es bueno como síntoma y como probabilidad de mejora" [I do not get too upset when someone tells me that So-and-So and Such-and-Such have purchased books by the meter or at so much per kilo. The fact is good both as a symptom and as a potential for improvement] (18). For Salisachs, the weight (kilos) or volume (meters) of books suggests the possibility, at least, of a weightier attraction. So too with *El volumen de la ausencia*, whose frothy plot and platitudinous philosophizing might merge to form a solid, useful object. Her intuition was not wrong: 55,000 copies in the first two years alone is no mean sales volume in the Hispanic world.

El volumen de la ausencia tells the story of Ida Sierra, a middle-aged married woman with three children whose only real talent—largely unexpressed—is housekeeping. She lives in an apartment in the Calle de Aribau with her husband, Daniel, formerly an enthusiastic soldier in Franco's army and currently a publicity agent and author of several appallingly bad novels. Also sharing the apartment are her wicked mother-in-law, Soledad; her saintly mother; her deceased youngest son's dog, Hipo; and, intermittently, her daughter, Andrea, and her oldest son, Rodolfo. The novel's generating pretext is provided by Hipo, the dog, who has contracted a rare disease and passed it on to Ida. The dog is cured. Ida, however, is not so lucky. After the definitive diagnosis of her disease—an inoperable brain tumor—and a prognosis of only four months to live, the novel's heroine decides to spend the day wandering the streets of Barcelona, pondering whether or not to leave her husband for her lover, a mediocre and opportunistic painter named Juan Arenal. As she reviews her life, the reader participates vicariously in the following sequence of revelations: her husband is having an affair with Ida's feminist best friend (who, in a drunken driving spree, has accidentally killed Ida's beloved younger son); her older son is having an affair with his friend Carlos and is involved in a distasteful police sweep of homosexuals; and her daughter, Andrea, is having an affair—all very modern and financially motivated—with Andrea's best friend's father, an affair that everyone seems to know about but Ida.

Unsurprisingly, the novel's plot, with its highly colored concatenation of soap-opera-like events, is often in open conflict with its substantive concerns. The deep questioning of accepted beliefs is implicit in the title, of course—the volume (in both senses) of the absence of people, spaces, and culture, the material presence of a city that in itself reflects a voluminous emotional absence: "¿Sabías tú que también las ausencias puede[n] tener volumen?" Ida asks her absent lover. "Un volumen cada vez más hinchado de ti" [Did you know that absences can also have volume? A volume ever more swollen with you] (Salisachs 1983, 213). As has been suggested, Salisachs overtly salutes Laforet's *Nada* by setting her own work, like Laforet's, in an apartment on the Calle de Aribau and by giving one of her young women the same name as Laforet's protagonist. More importantly, she recognizes *Nada* not only as the quintessential novel of "nothingness" but also as a novel that reflects Ida's (and Laforet's Andrea's) own activity, a kind of purposeless wandering in search of a meaning that has largely been preempted by an increasingly consumption-oriented society. John Kronik, playing off of Laforet's preferred metaphors, describes her novel as "una narración sobre la nada, una presencia que señala una ausencia, un texto ahogado" [a narration about nothingness, a presence that signals an absence, a drowned text] (Kronik 1981, 201). Each of these terms finds immediate resonance in Salisachs's tale. If Laforet's Andrea drowns in nothingness, Salisachs's heroine floats in absence. The phrase "Ida nada," playing as it does on "nada" as "nothing" and on "nada" as the third person of the verb "nadar" [to swim], compares the heroine's life to that of an aquarium fish and also signals her will-less floating through life and the undisturbed superficiality that characterizes human relations in polite society. Ida comments at one point that, even as the founding illusions are gradually being stripped away from her idea of the family, a protective flotation gear remains operative: "nada se había modificado en aquel lugar: desayunos, almuerzos, cenas . . . , recogiendo siempre comentarios insulsos que flotaban sobre los platos unos instantes (los suficientes para convencernos de que seguíamos siendo una familia normal)" [nothing had changed in that place: breakfasts, lunches, dinners . . . , continually picking up insipid commentaries that floated over the dishes for a few minutes (just long enough to convince us that we were still a normal family)] (Salisachs 1983, 195). Decent women like Ida pointedly ignore dangerous or disturbing undercurrents; conventional social arrangements discourage diving deeper into the morass of human sentiment. For Ida, that unprepared floater, to attempt such deep-sea exploration would be to risk drowning.

By antinomy, the metaphorical floating also suggests a certain weight, a specific gravity, a particular displacement of space. Thus, Ida describes, for example, the privileges of a deferred existence: "En el fondo . . . , vivir es sentirse esperado. Y esperar. Y ocupar horas, lugares, recuerdos"

[Essentially . . . , to live is to feel waited for. And to wait. And to fill up hours, places, memories] (24). The young girl waits for love. The house-wife waits for her husband to come home, for the baby to be born, for the children to animate the house with their games. The beloved waits (twelve years!) for her lover to return; the condemned woman waits patiently for death to overtake her. Accordingly, monotony, emptiness, boredom—the essence of waiting—make Ida's time seem to pass more quickly rather than more slowly: "No es verdad que el tiempo tarda en transcurrir cuando la vida no nos interesa. La propia monotonía y la falta de relieve lo despedaza; es decir, lo unifica, lo convierte en una dimen-sión sin metas ni puntos de partida" [It is not true that time passes more slowly when life does not interest us. The selfsame monotony and lack of highlights breaks it up; which is to say, unifies it, converts time into a dimension lacking either goals or points of departure] (39). The time of waiting becomes the uniform and undifferentiated memory of waiting, becomes the substantial volume of ordinary life—and in the superim-posed text of Ida's long walk through the city, recollected fragments of memory from this time of waiting provide a grid to structure a time-out for reflection, a privileged time that will initiate the new volume of the short/long wait for death.

In Salisachs's novel, the connotations of "volume" pertain as well to the more common forms of mass communication. This is a novel stuffed to overflowing with references to popular culture and particularly to the inescapable visual effects of modern life in a big city. The protagonist's husband works for Estela Publicidad, one of the advertising companies responsible for huge signs that deface the cityscape. In her wanderings through the city, Ida stops to ponder a street sign, concluding: "No deja de ser curioso el empeño humano de asentar ideologías a fuerza de modificar los letreros callejeros. Es como si también ellos fueran parte esencial de los anuncios puramente destinados a la promoción de los productos de consumo" [It is a curious feature of human efforts that they establish ideologies by changing street signs. It is as if these too were an essential part of the advertisements purely destined for the promotion of consumer goods] (193). These consumer items become ever more distanced from any potential use: "Ver la tienda de artesanía toledana ofreciendo navajitas, pisapapeles y un sinfín de cosas inservibles que los turistas compran porque la filigrana es un arte que España heredó de los moros" [Look at the Toledo handicraft store, full of knives, paper-weights, and an infinite number of useless objects that tourists buy because filigree work is an art that Spain inherited from the Moors] (271). Nevertheless, a superfluity of useless commodities embellishes this novel, in which they paradoxically carry a double charge. The artifacts remind the reader of a Spanish culture produced for the tourist trade, for foreign consumption, while on another level such items also serve as a crucial defining element of the romantic fictions that Salisachs plays against, fictions where meticulously designated knickknacks such as these function as stock elements in a class-marked drama.

In the wake of such studied estrangements of objects from their uses, people are disarticulated—"Daniel había conseguido ser únicamente un periódico sostenido por dos manos, un par de ojos mirando el televisor y un silencio sorbiendo sopa" [Daniel had managed to become only a newspaper held up by two hands, a pair of eyes watching the television, and a silence slurping soup] (218)—or are obscenely multiplied, as when Ida passes by rank upon rank of televisions on display, each tuned to the same station, each projecting the same image. The implications of this increasingly displaced commercial reproduction of bodies and stereotypical cultural markers are political as well as social: "'Queremos jugar la baza de la democracia, pero no sabemos utilizarla', piensa Ida. [']Basta contemplar ese desfile de monotelevisores para comprenderlo[']" ["We want to learn the trick of democracy, but we don't know how to use it," Ida thinks. (")It is enough to contemplate that parade of monotelevisions to understand that(")] (167). The silent banks of television images blink at passersby; Ida's running commentaries provide the sound track for this moving documentary of contemporary mores. Michael Walsh writes of postmodern imagery that "there is no question of a reality which is coded or constructed or mediated or even textually contained; reality has instead disappeared, has abdicated, has been swallowed up by simulacra, by images" (Walsh 1991, 305–6). [4] All these popular/commercial representations banish "literary" or high-cultural concerns, filling that absence with a ceaseless renarrativization of banal and empty forms—something Salisachs clearly expects her readers to deplore. [5]

It is important that Salisachs articulates her most stringent critique of banal commercialism from the point of view of a middle-class woman, whereas her example of the uncritical consumer is the fragmented character/caricature of the man of the house. In this reversal of the traditional gendering of consumers, Salisachs encodes a moderate feminist impulse. Meaghan Morris has written persuasively about the pitfalls of the common identification of mass culture with women, or with a particularly stimagized sort of feminine sensibility: "There are many versions of a 'distraction' model [6] available in cultural studies today: there are housewives phasing in and out of TV or flipping through magazines in laundromats as well as pop intellectuals playing with quotes. . . . The rush of associations runs irresistibly toward a figure of mass culture not as woman but, more specifically, as bimbo" (Morris 1990, 23–24). Linda

Christian-Smith specifies the implications of this model for romance fiction's construction of ideal womanhood: "Shopping is a major form of consumption for white women and girls; it is also a mechanism for rein-forcing these girls' positions within traditional femininity. Shopping . . . is the activity through which women pass on their accumulated domestic knowledge" (Christian-Smith 1990, 68). This knowledge, which defines the modality of becoming a romance heroine, also, by extension, defines the romance novel's version of successful womanhood for the society at large.

If consumerism, or flitting restlessly from one banal representation to another, is associated with the bimbo, Morris argues, the contemplative mode and, in mass culture studies, the contemplation of distraction are "assumed to be the prerogative of male intellectual audiences" (Morris 1990, 24). Thus, tradition requires a masculinist institutional practice of knowledge to deal with the banal and to set it into an aesthetic or ideo-logical framework. Morris and Salisachs, from their very different perspectives, uncover the workings of that particular myth. Morris does so in her deconstruction of misogynistic traces in such thinkers as Bau-drillard. Salisachs achieves a similar end in presenting her critique of banal consumerism from a woman's perspective, in reasserting the value of the written object over the transient semifictions of television, bill-boards, and tourist displays, all of which Salisachs ambivalently codes for both masculine (high fiction) and feminine (low fiction) readings in her middlebrow text.

If (the) volume—"el objeto permanente"—is one of Salisachs's abid-ing concerns, another is the status of absence, which she figures not only as the absence of specific people whose lack is felt as an open wound (the lover Juan, the son Jacobo) but also as the absence of soul in the places that define a life and in the cultural markers that define a spiritual-ity. For Ida, who prides herself on her housekeeping talents, the estrangement from what should be her personally defined space, her apartment in the Calle de Aribau, is a singular anguish. As a young, newly married woman, Ida is not permitted to participate in such impor-tant decisions as where she and her husband will live or how her new home is to be decorated. Her opinions are shunted aside as the unformed tastes of a seventeen-year-old child, while her husband, with the assis-tance of his mother, chooses their apartment and furnishes it.

Ida accepts her husband's orders at first but in later years comes to realize that without the imprint of her personality the apartment can never be truly hers. Daniel refuses her request for change, with the result that Ida retreats ever further from the abusively indifferent, united front of husband and mother-in-law until "poco a poco fui perdiendo aquellos impetuosos deseos de renovación" [little by little I began to lose those impetuous desires to renovate] (Salisachs 1983, 21). The first definitive subordination of her desires at the hands of her mother-in-law, abetted by her new husband, sets the tone for Ida's marriage. She cannot feel "at home" in her home, and her need to imprint her own soul on her apartment gradually gives way to a defeated acceptance of her insignificance. She lives at odds with her apartment and its contents during all the years of her marriage, absently present, inattentive to family disturbances, unaccounted for in family councils, gone or "ida" in the most basic sense of the word.

Salisachs recounts that one of the most disturbing characteristics of her childhood was a systematic effort to avoid eating. Her mother resorts to ineffective threats of leaving, but when the menace of her absence becomes a frightening reality, it precipitates a trauma of mingled loss and guilt:

> —Si no comes me iré— decía mi madre.
> Y se cubría la cara fingiendo sollozos.
> Ni siquiera ante aquella perspectiva claudicaba. Por eso, cuando contra toda previsión un día se fue de verdad, tuve la impresión de que la culpa era mía.
> Empecé a notar su ausencia cuando el piano del salón dejó de sonar:
> —Mamá ya no toca el piano. . . .
> ¿Dónde está mamá?
> Nadie contestaba. Nadie parecía escuchar la pregunta.
> Alguna vez me dijeron:
> —No tardará en regresar.
> Pero el regreso jamás se producía. (Salisachs 1981, 49)

> ["If you don't eat, I will leave," my mother said, and she covered her face, pretending to sob.
> I would not give in even to that pressure. Thus, when one day, contrary to all expectations, she really left, I had the impression that it was my fault.
> I began to notice her absence when the piano in the living room stopped playing.
> "Mother doesn't play the piano anymore. . . . Where is mother?"
> No one answered. No one seemed to hear the question.
> Once they told me, "She'll be back soon."
> But she never did come back.]

The child's mourning for the lost mother takes the perverse form of eating even less: obscurely, so as to compel the mother's return, even if only in the form of a reiterated threat to leave. The child, starving herself for attention, almost gone from the mother, already gone. The reader of *El volumen de la ausencia* sees the other side of this family drama, the mother's side. Ida, who feels the barrier of the ugly apartment between herself and her family, is always already absent from her children. They tend to treat her alternatively as an innocent who must be protected from the real world or as a willfully blind and irresponsible woman who refuses to abandon comfortable illusions for an ugly reality. Ida intermittently tries to understand and to mend the differences between herself and her older children, only to discover/uncover ugly facets of their lives that compel her to retreat once again from these emotional starvelings, these products of an unloving relationship between an unanchored woman and a self-indulgent man.

Just as Ida floats and wavers, so does contemporary society experience a conceptual shift as the enduring Falangist image of woman comes into conflict with the realities of a modernized, post-Franco Spain. The stereotypical hypertraditionality of Ida's family hints at the first level of Salisachs's critique of the "Sección Femenina." The Salisachs of 1957 has already sketched the characterizations she will later deploy in 1983: the domineering mother-in-law, the saintly mother, the abusive husband. In *Adán-helicóptero*, Salisachs offers the parodic outline of the evil mother-in-law; with *El volumen de la ausencia*'s Soledad Pérez de la Sierra, she fills in the details. Soledad is proud, unyielding, incapable of admitting to any mistakes. Her illustrious genealogy presents a recurrent point of reference, though the war has erased the family fortune. Ida comments interlinearly: "Todo en la vida de esa mujer ha ido apoyándose en pedestales de cartón" [Everything in that woman's life has been propped up on cardboard pedestals] (Salisachs 1983, 55). According to the mother-in-law's own tales, Soledad was a rich orphan of good family, heartlessly disinherited by evil lawyers, later rescued by a good man, also of good family. Then came the war, the martyrdom of her beloved husband (vilely assassinated by the Communists), the loss of the family fortune, the subsequent necessity for her son to enter into the job market early. His efforts were promptly rewarded with the recognition that such energy and talent deserved. Soledad, although often "sola (solita)" [all alone] in the world, has one great accomplishment: never, not even in the most difficult times for her family, has she lowered herself to work. "No le importaba que la considerasen una inútil," comments Ida. "La inutilidad femenina era, para mi suegra, una suerte de afirmación jerárquica" [She did not concern herself about being considered useless. Female uselessness was, for my mother-in-law, a kind of hierarchical affirmation] (57).

Ida's own mother, again in good stereotypical form, could not be more different. In contrast with Soledad, she never talks about the past, never brags. Neither does she feel rancor: "jamás se quejaba. Era como un recipiente sin fondo donde lo que entraba para herirla, se perdía en olvidos" [she never complained. She was like the bottomless bucket into which whatever hurtful thing fell was lost in forgetfulness] (58–59). She devotes herself wholly to her daughter's family; she is the silent, self-sacrificing angel of the house who makes all in her passage comfortable and disappears to her sewing machine so as not to disturb anyone by her presence. "Su máxima ambición," says Ida, "consistía en no ser ambiciosa" [Her main ambition consisted in not being ambitious]; her particular heroic enterprise was, in her mother's own words, to ignore unpleasantness: "No hay como fingir que no se perciben. Todo se arregla haciéndose el ciego" [There is nothing like pretending that one does not see. Everything works out when one acts blind] (200–201)—that is, the best way to deal with an uncomfortable fact is to ignore its existence. For Ida, this model of self-annihilation is the inaccessible epitome of the perfect woman, the unstated reproach to Ida's own selfish moments.

The juxtaposition of these two women of the older generation, so perfectly counterbalanced—complete selfishness and perfect selflessness; the one disruptive, the other self-effacing; one parasitic, the other all-nourishing—suggests a straightforward critique of the roles women are traditionally taught to play. Between them the two older women represent the opposing poles of a single prototype, the ideal woman of the Falangist women's section. Ida clearly condemns the manipulative mother-in-law, the woman who has turned uselessness into an art and an opportunity for mischief. Implicit in this configuration of opposites is Salisachs's awareness of a pervasive value change in which society at large tolerates the working wife and actively supports any condemnation of the upper-class, bourgeois woman as an unproductive charge on society. What is surprising is that her heroine also feels some discomfort with the practiced pieties of her hardworking (though equally home-bound) mother. Although Ida states again and again that her mother's saintliness is the model of what womanhood should be, she uneasily suspects at times that her mother's blindness, so like her own, partakes less of Christian charity than of something more mundane, such as a wish to insulate herself from the bother of learning uncomfortable truths. Likewise, the mother's insistent self-effacement (her absence) subtly forces recognition of her omnipresence. At one point Ida comments: "Una vez más, mi madre se replegaba en aquellos segundos planos que lograban hacer de ella la persona insignificante más importante del mundo" [Once again, my mother slipped back into that secondary role that made of her the most important insignificant person in the world]

(260). Ida's mother is as manipulative as Daniel's, and to greater effect. This half-articulated recognition of masked egotism represents a crucial reevaluation of the effect of enforced repression on human interactions.

Daniel is the proto-arche-stereotypical husband. As the teacher in "la escuela internacional masculina" reminds his students, "El egoísmo ... es una de las características que más debe destacar el hombre. ... Sin él se corre el riesgo de afeminarse" [Selfishness ... is one of the most outstanding qualities for a man. ... Without it, he runs the risk of effeminacy] (Salisachs 1957, 127–28). Daniel is at no such risk. He is variously characterized as a hypocrite, a pretentious, if impotent, failure at any intellectual enterprise, a boot-licking minor functionary, a temperamental dictator who requires constant ego-stroking, an insecure and abusive spouse who elevates himself in his own estimation by denigrating his wife's abilities. He is always marvelously contained in an impermeable shell of egotism. Ida's feminist friend, Marta, calls him a "[f]ósil franquista pasado por las teorías de Carlos Marx. Ceños crónicos porque eso de sonreír es cosa de fachas. Marido de 'ida' sin vuelta" [Falangist fossil overlaid with Karl Marx's theories. A chronic scowl because smiling is for wimps. Husband of "ida" without a return ticket] (Salisachs 1983, 45).

This character's major delusion is that he imagines himself to be a great but misunderstood novelist. His first, mercifully ignored, novel was published only as a favor to a friend (this helpful friend of the publisher, ironically, is Ida's lover). Daniel naturally feels that his novel failed to win any important literary prizes because of his refusal to compromise his art, to prostitute himself for the literary mafia. Despite his supposed disdain, however, in his second book, also published through the good offices of Juan Arenal, Daniel decides to conform to the current literary fads, with even more nefarious results: "Nada era realmente genuino en el libro de Daniel. Todo quedó en un texto paranoico donde la magia de García Márquez se unía a la salvaje mítica de Caballero Bonald, a las rebeldías sistemáticas de Scorza y a las audacias literarias de Rulfo" [Nothing was really genuine in Daniel's book. It all came down to a paranoid text in which García Márquez's magic was tied to Caballero Bonald's mythic savage, to Scorza's systematic rebellions and Rulfo's literary audacities] (199). This time he does get reviewed, but the few pages devoted to the novel are scorchingly negative. As Tania Modleski reminds us, in literature as in life, "women have always had to 'read' men." In popular romances, the heroine typically "probes for the secret underlying the masculine enigma, while the reader outwits the heroine in coming up with the 'correct' interpretation of the puzzling actions and attitudes of the man" (Modleski 1982, 34). In contrast with Modleski's observation about the romantic hero who must be read by a clever, loving woman, Salisachs draws in *El volumen de la ausencia* a portrait of a dark and brooding man who is unworthy of reading, whose enigma, like his novels, derives only from a chaotic compilation of regurgitated—and wholly incomprehensible—commonplaces. He is at every level the personification of modern banality. At last Ida's much-tried patience runs out, and she refuses to buttress her husband's fragile masculinity any longer, refuses to waste her intellectual energies on puzzling him out, refuses to give his mediocre fictions the sympathetic reading he demands as his natural right and her obligation.

This declaration of independence is timely, for by this point in the novel Ida is on the verge of learning about her husband's long-standing affair with her only female friend, the outspoken feminist Marta Echave. Marta's role in the novel is also stereotypically delineated: she is the portrait of the feminist as fraud, the perfect counterpart for Ida's fraudulent, pseudointellectual husband, a woman who manipulates rehearsed novelty for seductive effect, "captando la atención de [los] invitados a fuerza de repetir sus consabidos lugares comunes sobre 'el feminismo inteligente', 'las realizaciones personales' y la 'imperiosa necesidad de la juventud de espíritu'" [capturing the attention of the guests by repeating well-known clichés about "intelligent feminism," "personal fulfillment," and the "imperative need for the youthful spirit"] (Salisachs 1983, 131). The bitter critic of contemporary mores, feminist or not, would already have suspected that such a woman's only use for friendship is the betrayal of a friend. This lack of close and supportive relationships between women holds not only in the satirical world of *Adán-helicóptero*, in the parodic aspects of *El volumen de la ausencia*, nor even in the more darkly shaded moments of the interactions between Ena and Andrea in *Nada*, but also more generally for popular fiction written for women. Jean Franco has noted that "significantly missing from mass literature is any form of female solidarity," and she suggests that this absence fulfills a specific function in service of the status quo: "it reinforces the serialization of women, which is the very factor that makes their exploitation as reproducers of the labor force and as cheap labor so viable even in corporate society" (Franco 1986, 266). Ida, like the heroines of the romances and soap operas she emulates and rejects, is a woman alone and hence vulnerable in both the social and the sexual marketplaces. She has a saintly mother, a repulsive mother-in-law, an alienated daughter, and a so-called "friend" who not only betrays her friendship through an affair with her husband but also kills her son. In Marta and in Daniel, Salisachs refines her critique of the contemporary social structures that license such hypocrisy.

Marta, in any case, has gone far beyond permissible boundaries. The social changes that allow women to enter the marketplace also set implicit limits on the degree of access. Marta is beautiful, charming, and exceptionally talented; as one coworker admits, "se ha convertido en la dueña absoluta de la empresa. Allí ya nada se hace y se dice sin saber cuál es la opinión de Marta Echave" [she has become the absolute owner of the business. Nothing can be said or done there without finding out Marta Echave's opinion] (Salisachs 1983, 44). She is too successful for comfort in the business world; everything in the novel points to a tacit agreement between Ida and her middlebrow reader on this point. Marta drinks too much, smokes too much, associates with other women's husbands too much. Despite her dazzling success, norms of the serial romance dictate that somehow she must be made to conform to the sedu- lously cultivated judgment of the essential wrongness, the pitifulness, of the unmarried career woman. Her fatal flaw is common to all soap opera villainesses who dare too greatly, who blur too completely the boundaries on which traditional notions of gender distinctions are propped. She is morally bankrupt, a fraud, a traitor, and (lightly hinted at) a nympho- maniac as well.

Ida, the would-be typical housewife, is far more circumspect both in her love affair and in her entry into the labor market. Her expanded role as critic of the old forms and model of the new requires considerable discretion. As Franco notes in her study of Latin American and U.S. romance, new plots are needed when considerations of salaried labor are involved in the story line (Franco 1986, 251). In her modern demiro- mance, Salisachs must steer a delicate course between depicting a job that is too subservient and hence unworthy of her heroine (waitressing or clerking come to mind) and a job that would show her as too ambitious or domineering (Marta Echave's CEO role is the counterexample). Work is necessary for this modern heroine. That work must be meaningful enough so that she can develop independence and a sense of self-worth, but it must not be too compelling. To this extent, Salisachs would implic- itly concur with those critics who have made the association between the "distraction model" and women's lives.

Despite her alienation from the domestic sphere, Ida realizes that housewifery is her true career and her gallery work only a hobby. Her failure to make her mark in the first realm is a crucial character flaw, while the very indefinition of her salaried labor suggests its primary function as a plot device. The "Silhouette Books" offer apposite guide- lines for depicting the modern unmarried heroine: "In spite of her fragile appearance, [she] is independent, high-spirited and not too subservient. ... Often she is starting a career, leaving college, unhappy with her present job. . . . Though she wants to work, and plans to after marriage (in some business with her husband), her home and children will always come first" (qtd. in Cohn 1988, 93). Ida Sierra's part-time job in the art gallery offers an elegant solution to this difficult problem of the working mother. Like the model for women's paid work offered in the Silhouette guidelines and normally followed in formula romances, Ida's job emphasizes the helping and caring dimensions of the service-sector roles most typical of romance heroines. The job is not overly demanding, involves an extension of traditional domestic tasks, represents a professional dead end, allows Ida to demonstrate her artistic sensibilities (in contrast to her husband's lack of aesthetic sense and Marta's overdeveloped urge for mastery), and also provides the occasion for getting to know her future lover, Juan Arenal, a painter whose exhibition in the gallery receives mixed, if generally favorable, reviews from art critics (no overreaching liaison with genius). It is impossible to measure the exact degree of delicate parody here; but other factors indicate that Ida's floating inefficiency implies some complicity with her own subjugation. At the same time, the author is careful to maintain a balance between the counterposing images of the self-sacrificing and distracted housewife and the egoistic and driven professional woman.

Ida habitually floats between the two shores of spicy melodrama and rejected reality. Eventually, however, she must come to some hard realizations about herself, even against her mother's training and her own impulses. A pretense of blindness has worked for her in the past. Just as Salisachs recalls of her younger self in *Derribos*, "Hay que fingirse crédula, nenita[,] porque de lo contrario los Reyes Magos jamás te dejarán sus juguetes. . . . o se admite sin chistar todo lo que 'no es' para obtener el premio de tu ficción, o se acepta la verdad con la derrota" [You have to pretend to believe, little girl, because otherwise the Wise Men will never leave you toys. . . . You either go along, without saying a word, with everything that "is not" in order to win the prize for your fiction, or you accept truth with defeat] (Salisachs 1981, 126). So too Ida: "Pensé que debía fingir. Aparentar que yo 'no sabía'" [I thought that I ought to pretend. To make believe that I "didn't know"] (Salisachs 1983, 265). But the pretense is no longer forgiving; the Three Wise Men no longer bring the desired toys even to the resolutely infantile.

Ida is forced to confront reality precisely through the melodramatic actions of her children. Rodolfo, the elder son, and his friend, Carlos, both have highly developed artistic sensibilities and speak authoritatively on matters ranging from human relationships to political issues to abstract philosophical concepts. They are endowed with an old-fashioned courtesy and gentlemanliness that make them always attentive to their companions. There is, however, a dissonance in this portrait of the perfect gentleman, a disharmony already signalled by their sensitivity—traditionally a feminizing trait, as Salisachs reminds the reader—and Ida is the one person who seems not to have guessed their secret. She learns the truth only after it has become public knowledge in the scandal sheets. While Ida is as circumspect and self-censuring in her revelations to her absent lover as the press is to its reading public, her coworker, Mónica, is more straightforward in her assessment. According to Mónica's version of the story, a depraved group of sexually obsessed, drug-addicted perverts, Luis Robledo and "sus chicos," have been thrown into jail. Among the group of jailed youths are Ida's son, Rodolfo, and his friend, Carlos, who feel for each other, it seems, "una de esas imposiciones afectivas que a veces duran toda la vida" [one of those affective commitments that sometimes last a lifetime] (252).

The safe world of Ida's ideal nuclear family crumbles even further when, in a strange turn of events, the whole family appeals for salvation to Ernesto Carihuela, the daughter's lover. The oddity of Ernesto Carihuela's adoption by the family goes beyond their urgent need for his advice and his influence in ameliorating the potential scandal that could result from an open revelation of Rodolfo's sexual preferences. Andrea, the beautiful, willful daughter, has (like her namesake in Laforet's novel) cultivated the friendship of the richest girl in school with the entirely pragmatic objective of finding and seducing the richest possible man to support her intended lifestyle (a rather cynical rewriting of *Nada*). That the most available candidate is her friend's father does not deter her in the least. Through his seduction she finds the means to negotiate a place in society for herself, and—in an enormous blow to conventionalism—Andrea's father, Daniel, opportunistically supports his daughter in this endeavor. Ida, like her mother, perhaps prefers to know nothing of the matter, and when she does discover her daughter's affair she must distinguish her own illicit affair from Andrea's: "'Son dos casos distintos.' . . . Probablemente Andrea se había unido a un hombre sólo por su dinero. En cambio, yo me estaba uniendo a ti sólo por amor. Era necesario desglosar los dos casos; llegar a la conclusión de que únicamente mi hija estaba pisando terreno falso" [They are two different cases. . . . Probably Andrea had gotten together with a man just for his money. In contrast, I attached myself to you only for love. It was essential to separate the two cases, to reach the conclusion that only my daughter was on shaky ground] (162). At question, then, for Ida are not Andrea's actions but Andrea's motivations.

Such distinctions are consonant with the tradition of the popular romance, which would comprehend a woman who gives herself for love and would even reward her with the upwardly mobile marriage of her dreams—the "payoff" for virtue. No one is so universally execrated, however, as the woman who forthrightly uses her body to achieve monetary goals; romance heroines must *seek nothing*. By contrast, Carihuela's wife soon demonstrates that contemporary society is less forgiving than popular fiction when she evenhandedly condemns both women. As far as respectable society is concerned, it is like mother, like daughter. Carihuela's wife arrives at the apartment door and with a gesture of repugnance informs Ida that she is "tan puta como su hija" [as whorish as your daughter] (179).

Ida has to come to terms with the knowledge that her own reading of her family is not an innocent one and reflects neither naïveté nor Christian forgiveness but rather a complicitous exploitation and radical reshaping of the family text. In order to reread the banal sensationalism of her life, she has to accept certain facts. Some realizations, such as her son's homosexuality, her daughter's financially motivated affair with a rich man, and her husband's use of the family apartment to conduct an affair with her exfriend Marta, impinge less immediately upon her writing of the text of her own life and motivations. Considerably more significant are the rereading and rewriting of her life in terms of a shifting sense of her woman's role in a changing society. She learns that she is not guiltless of her own subordinate status, that she has been vegetating her entire life, finding refuge in a prolonged childhood. If she has not known how to escape from her unhappy marriage, it is because *she* has made no real attempt to resolve her complaints. Her lifelong enslavement to others is a form of egotism. Her affair with a married artist is tainted. Her motive of "love" is as fraudulent as her daughter's excuse of economic gain or as Marta's feminist pronouncements, and she has used her young son Jacobo as a lover-substitute, investing the child with too much psychological weight in her determination to maintain her pedestrian life. After Jacobo's death, her perpetual rehearsal of the never-achieved reunion with her lover defers the resolution of pressing complications at home, allowing her to maintain the illusion that she is floating blamelessly above the surface of events.

The cumulative effect of these revelations is, at first, devastating: "Me sentía igual que una reclusa a la que se le despoja de todo. Olvidada. Desprendida de sus derechos de mujer. Expulsada de aquel nuevo sistema de vida que lentamente iba derrotando al antiguo, e incapacitada para formar parte de él, aun cuando todo en mí estaba reclamando ser admitido de nuevo" [I felt like a recluse who had been dispossessed of everything. Forgotten. Deprived of her rights as a woman. Expelled from the new system of life that had slowly been defeating the old system and incapacitated to become part of it, even as everything in me was demand-ing readmittance] (189). Finally, however, she feels a sense of liberation, of freedom to be herself: "Nada más que ella misma" [Nothing more than herself] (182). In the wandering through the city, in the review of the long series of errors that has marked her progress towards some signifi-cant closure, the real, the true, the profound uncover themselves at last. In reconstructing the story of herself, Ida Sierra effectively achieves her own liberation and an unexpected moral empowerment.

Perhaps this conclusion seems a little too pat, a little too contrived, a little too faithful to the new myth of the modern woman's coming to consciousness. Salisachs envisions the story of the self, after all, as a long monologue directed towards the absent lover, and this very other-directedness affects the nature of the final revelation. Then again, the implicit equation of naming with knowing and liberation seems too programmatically facile, at least in terms of a typical literary-critical reading. Certainly, it is difficult to imagine how Ida's hard-won truth about herself will survive her return to the miserable Aribau apartment or her husband's compulsive television watching, much less what form Ida's new acceptance of her own agency might take. If the novel's social and political agenda remain unclear, however, what is useful and impor-tant is its investigation of society's control mechanisms and of the nuances of male/female relationships. Salisachs reminds her middlebrow readers that such banalities as a bank of television screens or a wall plas-tered with advertisements for beauty products are regulatory mechanisms and that these mechanisms are capable of generating a perplexing degree of satisfaction with their traditional roles in a large proportion of the population.

Morse, in her theorizing about the ontology of everyday distraction, finds that "older concepts of liberation in everyday life based on 'escape attempts' and figurative practices are no longer viable. . . . Indeed older notions of the public realm and of paramount reality have been largely undermined, and a return to a pretelevisual world of politics, the street, and the marketplace is unlikely." She further notes that "recognizing the extent and scope of an attenuated fiction effect in everyday life—an effect now largely unappreciated or considered trivial and hence subject to little vigilance—might already be a step toward bringing distraction within a controlled psychic economy of disavowal" (Morse 1990, 213). Salisachs's middlebrow novel, more clearly and straightforwardly than many works of high culture, recognizes the power of fiction effects such as those described by Morse and suggests how difficult and how neces-sary it has become for her readers to understand their functioning. In *El volumen de la ausencia*, the melodramatic events that motor the plot will pull the reader into the fiction. At the same time, its obvious soap opera qualities, along with the emphatic repetition of images signalling the banalization of culture, offer a permanent dissonance—not an escape from fiction, or even from semifictional effects, but rather a controlled disavowal of distraction from within.

Notes

1. The main question Alborg asks himself is why this woman, who has a talent for theoretical abstraction, wastes her time on so many badly written "realist" novels. He suspects that "Mercedes Salisachs quizá ha sentido la preocupación de que ella no transitaba por estos predios que constituyen la 'gloria' de otros muchos, y ha querido satisfacerles o emularles" [Mercedes Salisachas has perhaps felt concerned that she was not traveling on the path that leads many others to "glory" and so has wanted to satisfy or emulate them] (Alborg 1962, 400), that is, she wastes what talent she does have trying to imitate current fads. Curiously, this type of faddist-influenced writer is one of the objects of Salisachs's satire in *El volumen de la ausencia*.

2. See the introduction to my *Talking Back* (Castillo 1992) for a discussion of this issue in relation to modern Latin American fiction by women.

3. Woman readers are traditionally taught to insert themselves into literary discourse as pseudo-men, a process Fetterley identified several years ago and called "immasculation" in her book on American fiction, *The Resisting Reader* (1978).

4. In this passage, Walsh is commenting on Baudrillard's recent work. I have taken the citation out of context, since it seems so appropriate to Salisachs's critique of consumer culture.

5. Salisachs's warning about the impact of commercialism and modern media representations is especially powerful given her status as an insider. She is a graduate of the Escuela de Comercio with a degree as a "perito mercantil," and she has worked for almost forty years with Spanish radio and television companies.

6. Margaret Morse provides a concise definition of the "distraction" model: "freeways, malls, and television are the locus of an attenuated *fiction effect*, that is, a partial loss of touch with the here and now, dubbed here as *distraction*" (Morse 1990, 193).

Works Cited

Alborg, Juan Luis. 1962. *Hora actual de la novela española*. Vol. 2. Madrid: Taurus.

Aparicio López, Teófilo. 1979. *Veinte novelistas españoles contemporáneos*. Valladolid: Estudio Agustiniano.

Armstrong, Nancy. 1987. "The Rise of Domestic Women." In *The Ideology of Conduct: Essays in Literature and the History of Sexuality*. Ed. Nancy Armstrong and Leonard Tennenhouse, 96–141. New York: Methuen.

Cabrera Infante, Guillermo. 1975. "Una inocente pornógrafa: manes y desmanes de Corín Tellado." In *O*, 39–60. Barcelona: Seix Barral.

Castillo, Debra A. 1992. *Talking Back: Toward a Latin American Feminist Literary Criticism*. Ithaca, N.Y.: Cornell University Press.

Christian-Smith, Linda K. 1990. *Becoming a Woman through Romance*. New York: Routledge.

Cohn, Jan. 1988. *Romance and the Erotics of Property*. Durham, N.C.: Duke University Press.

Fetterley, Judith. 1978. *The Resisting Reader: A Feminist Approach to American Fiction*. Bloomington: Indiana University Press.

Franco, Jean. 1986. "Plotting Women: Popular Narratives for Women in the United States and in Latin America." In *Reinventing the Americas: Comparative Studies of Literature of the United States and Spanish America*. Ed. Bell Gale Chevigny and Gari Laguardia, 249–68. Cambridge: Cambridge University Press.

Kojève, Alexandre. 1969. *Introduction to the Reading of Hegel*. Trans. James H. Nichols, Jr. Ithaca, N.Y.: Cornell University Press.

Kronik, John W. 1981. "*Nada* y el texto asfixiado: proyección de una estética." *Revista Iberoamericana* 47: 195–202.

Laforet, Carmen. [1945] 1980. *Nada*. 2nd ed. Barcelona: Destinolibro.

Modleski, Tania. 1982. *Loving with a Vengeance: Mass-Produced Fantasies for Women*. New York: Methuen.

Morris, Meaghan. 1990. "Banality in Cultural Studies." In *Logics of Television: Essays in Cultural Criticism*. Ed. Patricia Mellencamp, 14–43. Bloomington: Indiana University Press.

Morse, Margaret. 1990. "An Ontology of Everyday Distraction: The Freeway, the Mall, and Television." In *Logics of Television: Essays in Cultural Criticism*. Ed. Patricia Mellencamp, 193–221. Bloomington: Indiana University Press.

Radway, Janice. 1988. "The Book-Of-The-Month Club and the General Reader: On the Uses of 'Serious' Fiction." *Critical Inquiry* 14: 516–38.

Salisachs, Mercedes. 1957. *Adán-helicóptero*. Barcelona: AHR.

———. 1959. "Un objeto permanente." In *Tres conferencias sobre libros*, 13–21. Barcelona: Amigos de la Cultura y del Libro.

———. 1981. *Derribos: crónicas íntimas de un tiempo saldado*. Barcelona: Argos Vergara.

———. 1983. *El volumen de la ausencia*. Barcelona: Planeta.

Sieburth, Stephanie. 1994. *Inventing High and Low: Literature, Mass Culture, and Uneven Modernity in Spain*. Durham, N.C.: Duke University Press.

Simpson, David. 1994. "Feminisms and Feminizations in the Postmodern." In *Feminism and Postmodernism*. Ed. Margaret Ferguson and Jennifer Wicke, 53–68. Durham, N.C.: Duke University Press.

Stevens, Wallace. 1972. "The Snow Man." In *The Palm at the End of the Mind*. Ed. Holly Stevens, 54. New York: Vintage.

Walsh, Michael. 1991. "The Perfect Alibi of Images." In *Image and Ideology in Modern/Postmodern Discourse*. Ed. David B. Downing and Susan Bazargan, 299–307. Albany: State University of New York Press.

Wicke, Jennifer. 1988. *Advertising Fictions: Literature, Advertisement, and Social Reading*. New York: Columbia University Press.

Splitting the Reference: Postmodern Fiction and the Idea of History in Francoist Spain

DAVID K. HERZBERGER

Texts are always infected with meanings derived or appropriated from other texts. The critical procedures that draw forth these meanings, however, rarely ensure hermeneutic certitude. Roland Barthes has suggested, for example, that all intertextual linking forms an amorphous "mirage of citations" that resist the firm grasp of readers trying to pin them down (qtd. in Culler 1981, 102). Studies of source and influence may locate points of origin of a particular piece of writing or identify transtextual references (what Michael Riffaterre [1984] refers to as the obligatory intertextuality of reading), but texts generally gain meaning from the plurality of texts associated with them by a reader's experience and desire for sense-making. In critical practice, therefore, intertextual study assumes the form of specific impositions: new meanings are revealed, historical filiations discerned, and structural similarities laid bare among works that the reader chooses to summon forth (what might be termed the "reasoned aleatory" nature of intertextuality). As Jonathan Culler notes, intertextuality "casts its net . . . to include anonymous discursive practices, codes whose origins are lost, that make possible the signifying practices of later texts" (Culler 1981, 103).

Culler's emphasis on discursive practices that enable future significa-tion offers in brief the principal virtue of intertextual study: it limns the aperture for a diversity of textual relations. This diversity is crucial for two reasons: 1) it suggests the breakdown of traditional generic distinc-tions and therefore encourages the intersection of texts previously denied congruity or even juxtaposition (a sort of intertextual *ostranenie*); and 2) it disaffirms origin as a determinant of critical study, thereby disrupting signifying practices that assume the integrity of a metadiscourse within which resides a given meaning known as Truth. Both of these aspects of intertextuality are pertinent to the critical study I wish to undertake here: the relationship between historiography in Francoist Spain and post-modern fiction. In a general way, intertextuality shows how the propping of two discourses against each other urges a realignment of potential meanings. In the specific context of my study, intertextuality reveals how the association of two apparently disparate discourses compels the dehis-cence of monologism and of the coincident structures of myth.

The linking of the discursive practices of fiction and historiography should not be viewed as either natural or inevitable (as may be the case, for example, with intertextual scrutiny within a given genre). Indeed, there is a strong tradition of disciplinary isolation. The writing of history is most often based on long-held realist assumptions that the events of past time are both recoverable and representable and that language (narration) serves as an adequate vehicle for conveying the truth about such events. In contrast, postmodern fiction strains against the central premises of historiographic discourse: it generally denies the very possi-bility of historical truth and eschews the concepts of presence, centered-ness, and linear succession upon which the metadiscourse of historiogra-phy is founded.

The title of my essay suggests the tension between postmodern fiction and historiography, yet its (intended) ambiguity also hints at possible resolution. On the one hand, "splitting the reference" points to a perma-nent disciplinary division of methods and intentions and places history on one side of the discursive fissure, split from fiction, which lies on (and *as*) the other. On the other hand, the title suggests that splitting references is a way of undoing difference between historiography and postmodern fiction. Restrictive *textual* codes founded upon genre are repudiated, then recreated into *intertextual* codes that shape new congruences of meaning. The challenge is not to lay one discourse beside another asymptotically, as has often occurred with fiction and history, but rather to proceed in a way that compels one text to converge with the other. The confluence of diverse texts is a crucial determinant of poststructuralist thinking in general, and it bears forcefully upon history and the novel in particular. As E. L. Doctorow writes, "There's no more fiction or nonfiction now, there's only narrative" (qtd. in Lowenthal 1985, 227).

The leveling of generic differences into the broad field of narrative and the coincidence among intertextual relations thereby established create several problems. One of these has to do with intertextuality, another with textuality. First, if we propose that a text gains primary meaning by association with additional (and in this case antithetical) texts, how can the nature of that association be defined? Second, if the critical paradigms that seek to create meaning are grounded in the text, how is it possible to relate meaning to life without resorting to the special pleadings of subjectivity? The filiations of historiography and fiction are especially thorny in this regard, since one form of narrative owes its existence to the desire of a subject to convey the sense of what has really happened in life, while the other gains primary authority from its sublation of such a possibility. It is not feasible to account for the full range of intertextual contingencies that link historiography and postmodern fiction in a general sense, or even, for that matter, to identify these connections completely in Francoist Spain. I shall address the issue with the aim of drawing forth three of its most critical aspects: 1) the nature of Francoist historiography and its intertextual base; 2) the postmodern premises of fiction that militate against this historiography during the final years of the Franco regime; and 3) the depthless and ultimately suffocating nature of intertextuality if we embrace the postmodern assertion that narrative has no *representational* connection with life.

The weight of coercion often lies at the root of historiography for totalitarian regimes, which seek to create what Henry Steele Commager (1967) describes as necessary to the sustenance of any political state: a usable past. Under Franco, the state uses the past to underpin its existence as the fulfillment of Spain's historical destiny and to give moral legitimacy to its claim of authority in the present. This appropriation of history, however, is not carried out in order to dispute collective knowledge about Spain's past (the so-called "facts" of history) but rather to establish a normative set of strategies that define a particular *concept* of historiography. The consequences of this intentionality are twofold: Francoist historians assert and subsequently sustain their dominion over time and narration, so that history systematically emerges as myth; and historians of the Regime draw forth meaning from history that stands resolutely as the equal of truth. In this way they create a powerful master discourse for history, supported by the certitudes of myth, from which no deviations seem possible.

The government's historiographic claims upon truth are buttressed by a reflection theory of narration that locates the critical iconic structures of history within the world. That is to say, the story that historians tell about the past must be told because it is already embedded in events as they unfold in time. Yet the insistence by Francoist historians that they reflect the given story of Spain is only half the story. For in fact these writers draw upon a palimpsest of sign systems from other discourses inherent in their disciplinary tradition. The iconic voice of myth that lies at the center of their historiography speaks less as a necessary consequence of natural processes than as a contrivance of intertextual ones. Francoist historiography is therefore ultimately sustained through relationships established with previous discursive practices and the meanings that have been associated with them. This intertextual dependency serves to strengthen the idea of a master discourse from which all meaning originates because the Regime's urgency to make the past its own inevitably makes other voices alien.

Although many examples of the intertextual foundations of Francoist historiography illustrate the point, the discursive paradigms of Marcelino Menéndez Pelayo resonate with greatest authority in the Regime's mythmaking design. I am not suggesting that Menéndez Pelayo represents the point of origin of Francoist historiography. Yet the way in which his thinking draws forth the past informs the dictatorship's writing of history and is embedded in its ideological goals. Certainly, there is ample evidence that historians of the Franco years revered the Spanish scholar. In 1956 the review *Arbor* published a special issue honoring the centenary of his birth, and its editors offered a concerted plan to exalt his work as the paragon of accuracy and truth.[1] But Menéndez Pelayo's views of history had already been appropriated by the Regime several years earlier. Florentino Pérez Embid writes in *Arbor* in 1949:

> *Arbor* ha proclamado este mismo año su fundamental fidelidad a la concepción española de Menéndez Pelayo. . . . Don Marcelino . . . representa para nosotros una concepción permanente de la existencia española. . . . [P]ara buscar una unidad superior en el campo de la cultura, partimos de la concepción española que don Marcelino construyó con materiales definitivos a la altura de su tiempo. . . . [A]nte la ruina de los principios de la modernidad y de sus imitaciones españolas, buscamos . . . la vitalidad histórica de aquel maravilloso plano de España que don Marcelino tenía en la cabeza. (Pérez Embid 1949, 153)

> [*Arbor* this year has proclaimed its fundamental adherence to Menéndez Pelayo's conception of Spain. . . . Don Marcelino . . . represents for us a permanent conception of Spanish existence. . . . In order to seek a superior unity within the field of culture, we use as point of departure the concept of Spain that Don Marcelino constructed with the definitive data available in his time. . . . Confronted with the ruination of the principles of modernity and its Spanish imitations, we seek the historical vitality of that marvelous scheme of Spain that Don Marcelino had in mind.][2]

Pérez Embid integrates Menéndez Pelayo's ideas within the master discourse of the Regime and recreates the Spanish author as precursor by incorporating into his discourse the topoi of fascist rhetoric. Expressions such as "permanent conception of Spanish existence," "superior unity," or "historical vitality" reveal how one narration uses another and dramatically changes the meaning of both.

One additional example related to Menéndez Pelayo will illustrate the point fully. In 1949, in a stinging rebuke of Pedro Laín Entralgo's mildly dissident work *España como problema* [*Spain As a Problem*], the Franco apologist Rafael Calvo Serer insists upon the crucial impingement of the Spanish past upon the constitutive elements of Francoist Spain. He quotes Menéndez Pelayo's *Ensayo de crítica filosófica* [*Essay in Philosophical Criticism*] to authenticate his position:

> Pueblo que no sabe su historia es pueblo condenado a irrevocable muerte; puede producir brillantes individualidades aisladas, rasgos de pasión, de ingenio y hasta de genio, y serán como relámpagos que acrecentarán más y más la lobreguez de la noche. (Calvo Serer 1949, 165)

> [A nation that does not know its history is a nation irrevocably condemned to death. It may produce brilliant, isolated individualities, moments of passion, of creativity and even of genius, but these will be like bolts of lightning that accentuate the darkness of the night.]

Calvo Serer's use of Menéndez Pelayo's words alerts us to several important matters. To begin with, the Menéndez Pelayo intertext is clearly locatable and therefore becomes obligatory. Menéndez Pelayo's writing and his views of orthodoxy and authenticity now infuse Calvo Serer's text with meaning. In most instances, quoted intertextual connections make the original meaning more amorphous by relocating it in a new discursive context; in this case, precisely the opposite occurs. Calvo Serer does not coopt Menéndez Pelayo's words in order to create tension and deferral but to evoke a signifying force that limits the past to a single meaning through the sanctification of myth. Menéndez Pelayo's well-known assertion that "[e]l genio español es eminentemente católico: la heterodoxia entre nosotros, accidente y ráfaga pasajera" [the Spanish character is eminently Catholic: heterodoxy among us (is) accidental, a passing gust of wind] (Menéndez Pelayo 1947–48, 62), closely parallels the intellectual program of the Regime, which declares with the self-endowed authority of its perceived mission: "tenemos que mantener ahora a todo trance la homogeneidad lograda en 1939" [we must maintain now at all cost the homogeneity achieved in 1939] (Calvo Serer 1949, 167).

More significantly, Calvo Serer had already appropriated Menéndez Pelayo's thinking two years earlier (without attribution) but with a decisive twist that conceptually narrows Franco's entire historiographic

enterprise: "Pueblo que desconoce *el sentido de su historia* está conde-
nado a irremediable muerte, ya que sus esfuerzos sólo son positivos y
fecundos si están en la línea de la tradición nacional; la fidelidad a la
propia historia es condición necesaria para una cultura creadora" [A
people not familiar with *the meaning of their history* is condemned to
inevitable death, since their efforts can only be productive if they follow
the line of national tradition. Loyalty to one's own history is the necessary condition for a creative culture] (Calvo Serrer 1947, 334; emphasis
mine). As Calvo Serer draws upon Menéndez Pelayo to structure a
perception of history that slices away all impurities from discourse on the
past and as he coopts the aphorism on the value of knowing the past in
the present, he also introduces a critical semantic change. By adding the
word "meaning"—the meaning of history—to Menéndez Pelayo's valuation of the past, Calvo Serer edges closer to a fuller grasp of the writerly
component of history. There is both a truism and a paradox in his
position, however. It appears that history is no longer merely a question
of knowing the past. Calvo Serer seems to say that history is not the past
as such but the cognitive and discursive forces that sweep the past into
the present. These forces take root in the authority of narration and thus
move the strategies of historiographic composition to the fore. Moreover,
this new emphasis on writing suggests the full range of aporias inherent
in all discourses that seek to represent the real. The paradox of Calvo's
position surfaces in his refusal to allow the process of writing to give
history any meaning not already inscribed in the discursive orthodoxy. In
other words, he opens history to the contingent nature of meaning, but,
since his project is to sanctify what is permanent and essential, he also
closes off history from the very provisionality that his historiographic
posture implies and that intertextuality demands. Meaning results here
from a crucial intertextual linking with Menéndez Pelayo, but this linking
is intended to tighten the structures of closure further rather than to celebrate the ambiguous (and therefore troublesome) contingencies suggested
by the intersection of texts.

In the context of narrating the past, the pragmatics of intertextuality
requires any narrative that sets out to recover or reinvent the past in
Francoist Spain to stand immediately in *some* relation to the constituent
texts of the Regime. These texts become the end of all other such narratives. And while the dictatorship seeks to diminish the vulnerability of its
authority through the creation of its metadiscourse, it cannot, in the end,
impede the flow of counterdiscourses without the total suppression of
writing itself. Any number of dissenting discourses circulate between the
1950s and the 1970s (social realism and the novel of memory are among
the most prominent), but more recent postmodern fiction offers perhaps

the most strident and derisive dissidence. It attacks Francoist historiography at the root of its authority—the mythic hegemony of language and its single-voiced discourse—and undermines the capacity of history to have presence in the present.

Postmodern fictions are of course hard to pin down—the term "postmodern" itself is charged with diverse meanings and ambiguities.[3] Such fictions are particularly troublesome when history is involved, since on the face of it they assert that history is a narrative discourse whose referent can only be other discourses. This insistence on the discursive core of history and fiction makes Spanish postmodern narrative a powerful source of intertextual dissidence in the face of Francoist historiography. It discredits the concept of a master discourse capable of conveying the truth about the past and also undermines in a specific way the myths of history created and sustained by the state.

Postmodern fiction's insistent self-referentiality causes mimetic adequacy, which lies at the center of realistic traditions and historiographic assumptions about the representation of the real, to be displaced by a more aleatory dispersion of words into malleable forms and structures. It also redefines the so-called reality represented by a text as a mere juxtaposition of linguistic constructs shaped and reshaped through the play of signifiers incapable of drawing into presence anything but their own strategies of composition. The absence of the real compels the collapse of generic differences (one genre is no longer able to reproduce life more fully than any other, since life is not presented but invented through language). The traditionally differentiated discourses of history and fiction thus bleed into each other and form an undifferentiated field of narration. Two aspects of this collapsed polarity are pertinent to my study: first, the intertextual connections that reveal how postmodern fiction undermines the core assumptions of Francoist historiography; and second, the more amorphous concern of how this intertextual subversion relates to life (history) in postmodern texts that propose to refer to nothing other than themselves.

The postmodern novels of Gonzalo Torrente Ballester—such as *Fragmentos de apocalipsis* [*Fragments of Apocalypse*] (1977), *La isla de los jacintos cortados* [*The Island of Cut Hyacinths*] (1980), *La rosa de los vientos* [*The Rose of the Winds*] (1985)—are central to both of these concerns, for they purposefully establish intertextual connections between fiction and history and compel the vital dislodging of myth.[4] These novels reach into history by laying bare the conceptual frame of narrating the past, and they challenge any discourse that asserts itself as self-centered and single-voiced. For example, in *Fragmentos de apocalipsis,* Torrente Ballester does not call forth Spanish history per se as the referent of his work—the novel attempts to tell the fantastic story of the town of Villasanta and its inhabitants—but he does raise questions about the nature of narration as a sense-giving component of temporal cognitions. Most importantly, Torrente Ballester strives to sustain in this novel the idea of history as a question. He conveys, above all, the impossibility of creating a metanarrative capable of integrating the aporias of history into an enduring truth.

Torrente Ballester opposes the discursive narrowness of Francoist historians in several important ways. Rather than condense heterological voices into a hypostatic oneness (as does the Regime), he sustains difference and nuance. In *La rosa de los vientos,* he shows how the past always remains open to the oxymoronic imperative of what might be termed "disparate repetitions." As the narrator of the novel suggests, "me parece que la historia de mi destronamiento voy a tener que contarla varias veces, aunque confío en que de un modo distinto cada una de ellas; quiero decir, las mismas cosas con distintas palabras y desde puntos de vista variados" [I think that I will have to tell the story of my ruination several times, even though I trust that I will tell it differently each time; I mean by this, the same things with different words and from several points of view] (Torrente Ballester 1985, 26). Instead of preserving and legitimating history through the elimination of troublesome contingency, as do historians of the Regime, Torrente Ballester's narrator celebrates different voices and diverse narrations. This practice stands in marked contrast to the Francoist insistence on maintaining "fidelidad al sentido de nuestra historia" [loyalty to the meaning of our history] (Pérez Embid 1949, 153) and ignores the admonition that "no puede vacilarse en la repulsa de aquellos elementos que se hagan a sí mismos inasimilables para la tradición unitaria nacional y ortodoxa" [one cannot hesitate to reject those elements that make themselves unassimilable within the national and orthodox unifying tradition] (Calvo Serer, qtd. in Díaz 1974, 72).

In his speeches on the certitudes of history, Franco often underscored one of the overriding myths of the Spanish past—that the history of his nation was forged by accumulated deeds of heroism. In August of 1947, for example, he proclaimed: "Todo lo grande que existe en España no ha sido obra de la casualidad: ha sido obra de hidalgos, de santos y de héroes, fruto de grandes empeños, de minorías selectas, de hombres elegidos" [Everything great that exists in Spain has not been the work of chance: it has been the work of nobles, of saints, and of heroes, the fruit of great deeds, of select minorities, and of chosen men] (Franco 1949, 96). In contrast, Torrente Ballester reminds the reader of *La isla de los jacintos cortados* that the "truth" of heroism is not located in the world, merely to be extracted by the perceptive historian. It is, rather, only one of potentially multiple meanings constructed through the act of narrating: "La historia la hacen los héroes, y los héroes son, a fin de cuentas, nada más que nombre y facha, que palabra y retrato" [History is made by heroes, and heroes are, in the end, nothing more than names and appearances, words and representations] (Torrente Ballester 1990, 255). Torrente Ballester's assertion of the preeminence of the word in the construction of history speaks forcefully against the conceptions of the past summoned forth by the Regime. His intention, of course, is not to show that heroism is a fraud or that it should be excluded from our understanding of the past but that it is a conceit shaped and defined by the contingencies of narration.

Torrente Ballester further intensifies his assault on the metanarrative conception of history by using multiple voices that create and disperse disunity rather than harmony. The very idea of a single self as a source of meaning is precluded. Kathleen Higgins has shown how the postmodern novelist constructs a self "who is somewhere else, someone who was someone else the last time, someone who will be someone else the next time" (Higgins 1990, 192). This disintegration of a unified voice informs much of the recent fiction of Torrente Ballester but is perhaps most acutely pertinent to the narration of *Fragmentos de apocalipsis*. The narrator's recurrent insistence that he is made only of words (that he will create "[u]n conjunto de palabras en el que estaré yo mismo, hecho palabra también" [a mass of words in which I myself will be found, also made of words] [Torrente Ballester 1980, 132]) is a playful and parodic effort to dislodge the tyranny of monologism. More importantly for historiography, it shows that the desire to pin matters down and proclaim finality is a fatal illusion. Torrente Ballester does not set out to create a dialectic of self and other, with truth rooted in the former and deceit in the latter (as does Francoist historiography). His purpose is to show the dynamism between self and other—how they intersect, separate, and divide into new selves and new others as the narrative spins loose from representation and proclaims the triumph of the word. In contrast to the authority of logocentrism, where naming something is equivalent to creating it, naming for the narrator of *Fragmentos de apocalipsis* is only equivalent to naming: "No te olvides de que eres un conjunto de palabras, lo mismo da tú que yo, si te desdoblas somos tú y yo, pero puedes también, a voluntad, ser tú o yo, sin otros límites que los gramaticales" [Don't forget that you are a mass of words, you and I are both the same, if you divide yourself into two, we are you and I, but you can also, through willpower, be you or I, with no limitations other than grammatical ones] (16). The whole of *Fragmentos de apocalipsis* in fact embodies

this idea, from the narrator's belief that he may exist only in a text written by someone else to the denial of any system of meaning external to
discourse: "sólo por la literatura se justifican los hechos literarios" [only
through literature are literary facts justified] (275). Taken to its larger
conclusion, this assertion suggests the separation of life from discursive
practice in favor of Torrente's "mass of words." It also offends against
the belief that discourse is able to assert truth about anything outside itself. As Torrente Ballester writes in *Fragmentos de apocalipsis*, "La literatura . . . no es mentira ni verdad, no es más que eso, literatura"
[Literature . . . is neither false nor true, it is only what it is, literature]
(380).

Francoist historians frequently sought to buttress the foundations of
myth in their writings with binary oppositions. These oppositions represented Spanish history as a series of inclusions (Christianity, nobility,
heroism) and exclusions (Judaism, Islam, secularism). Instead of creating
the dialectic in order to produce harmonious synthesis, however, Francoist historiography operated through negation in order to endow the past
with sameness. In other words, official discourse disallowed one side of
the dialectic (the excluded) after it had been evoked and tainted with
difference. This process created what Thomas Docherty in another context has called a "scenario of deterrence," in which mythic discourse denies a trajectory of choices and alternatives for history (Docherty 1990,
174).

Two examples from postmodern fiction in Spain reveal how this
"scenario" can be undone. In Torrente Ballester's *Fragmentos de apocalipsis,* dialecticity as a structure of organization is repudiated. As the
narrator/novelist considers the introduction to the novel that he is writing,
he outlines a Manichean world defined by good and bad, order and
chaos, framed within a heroic struggle. The narrator contemplates the
efficacy of his oppositions but quickly dismisses them as exclusionary.
He is able to do so for several reasons, but two gain prominence. First,
the oppositions are linguistic constructs and, therefore, like everything
else in the novel, bear no mimetic value in relation to the world outside
the text. In other words, the world is not naturally organized into a series
of dialectics that are then reflected in literature. To the contrary, the
author has constructed the dialectic as a narrative strategy whose purpose
is to shape the text's structure as well as the reader's cognition. Hence,
the author is able to disallow the opposition by using the same inventive
authority with which he created it. More importantly, the proposed oppositions parallel Francoist historiography in their failure to achieve
synthesis. Yet synthesis remains unachieved here for reasons of inclusion
rather than exclusion. The whole of *Fragmentos de apocalipsis* demands

that meaning *not* be constituted through resolution of diversity and contradiction; it proposes instead the sustaining richness of tensions and randomness, which cannot be reduced to a single narrative or a single story. Rather than advance meaning with a double face (one aspect of which is stripped away as inauthentic, as in Francoist historiography), the novel proposes multiple faces that resist the totalitarian imposition of sameness in order to operate within the reversals and oscillations of difference.

Camilo José Cela's *San Camilo, 1936* offers a similar sublation of dialecticity. As a whole, the novel reveals an overriding concern with the meaning of history and stands dramatically opposed to the mythic historiography of the Regime. Cela makes the crucial thematic point through the voice of wisdom in the novel, the protagonist's Uncle Jerónimo:

> [L]uchemos cipote en ristre contra los mitos que atenazan al hombre, las banderas los himnos las condecoraciones los números las insignias el matrimonio los platos regionales el registro civil, tú y yo tenemos el deber de luchar contra los artificios que adulteran al hombre, que dan color de muerte a su existencia y sequedad de esparto a su conciencia. (Cela 1981, 304)

> [(L)et us fight with couched pricks against the myths that oppress man, the flags the hymns the medals the numbers the insignia the institution of marriage the regional cuisine the public records office, you and I are obliged to fight against the artifices that adulterate man, that give his existence the color of death and his conscience the dryness of straw.] (Cela 1991, 288)

Throughout the work, however, Cela calls forth binary oppositions to create a discursive process that distends beyond dialectics. He presents the traditional dialectic of Rightists and Leftists, Nationalists and Republicans, within the political sphere of prewar Spain but then compels the oppositions to break away from alterity and synthesis. In *San Camilo,* there is no aberration in the "other" side of difference, as in Francoist historiography. The focus on history and politics in the novel urges an unending process of inquiry that can never reach its destination. This is so not because such an inquiry is groundless but because there is no single ground that rises above all others and provides a totalizing base of support. As David Carroll writes concerning the postmodern problem of historical foundations, there is "no ground of all grounds" (Carroll 1987, 70). In *San Camilo,* this means the continual expulsion of metanarrative possibilities and the sustained displacement of one locus of meaning with another.

The breakdown of binary oppositions occurs both thematically and formally in *San Camilo*. The following passage, offered as a series of undecidable options for the main character, exemplifies the process:

> Sí, tú te encaras con el problema una y otra vez y sigues sin poder resolverlo, es probable que tenga una solución pero tú la ignoras. Llamar a las cosas por su nombre, no llamar a las cosas por su nombre, renegar de todo lo humano y todo lo divino, no renegar de todo lo humano y todo lo divino, acostarse con esta mujer que huele a sebo y a agua de colonia, no acostarse con esta mujer que huele a sebo y a agua de colonia, . . . pasear por el parque y por los solares donde las parejas cometen sus inevitables cochinadas, no pasear por el parque ni por los solares donde las parejas cometen sus deleitosas e inevitables cochinadas que acabarán acarreándoles debilidad . . . [etc.]. (Cela 1981, 14)

> [Yes, you face the problem again and again and you still can't solve it, it probably has a solution but you don't know what it is. To call things by their name, not to call things by their name, to swear off all things human and divine, not to swear off all things human and divine, to go to bed with this woman who smells of grease and cologne, not to go to bed with this woman who smells of grease and cologne, . . . to take a walk through the park and the vacant lots where couples do their inevitable dirty business, not to take a walk through the park or the vacant lots where couples do their enjoyable and inevitable dirty business that will eventually make them weak. . . .] (Cela 1991, 4)

Throughout *San Camilo,* Cela shows an acute awareness of the false dialectic operating in Francoist historiography (false in the sense that it is created only to disallow the Other), and he presents a catena of oppositions without privileging one side of a proposition over any other. In this way his novel embodies the postmodern tendency to heterogeneity and diversity. Coupled with his recurrent emphasis on the problems of history, Cela deterritorializes the past and urges that history be written, as Docherty has suggested, "always with the tongues of others in one's ear" (Docherty 1990, 174). The dialogic interplay of other discourses and competing texts creates a multiplicity of voices that inoculate the past against darkness. Cela is aware that his own heterological discourse is susceptible to exhaustion and will be superseded ("la costumbre es despótica y peligrosa, más despótica y peligrosa que el vicio" [Cela 1981, 150] [habit is despotic and dangerous, more despotic and dangerous than vice] [Cela 1991, 138]). He thus allows the voices of difference to remain different in *San Camilo* and advances his discourse as a paroxysm of radical possibilities whose profusion undoes the monologism of the Francoist past.

It is not surprising that postmodern fiction opposes a historiography based on the realist premises of mimetic adequacy and truth, nor is it unexpected that postmodern fiction in Spain stands against Francoist historiography. I am not suggesting that the postmodern novel uses Francoist history as a negative point of departure for all that it wishes to assert but that its relationship with historiography exemplifies how narrations are able to assimilate and deflect opposing signifying processes. My main concern is to note the obtrusion of dissent in postmodern fiction through writing at the level of text and the full exposure of dissent through intertextual connections. Yet a nagging problem remains in this scheme, one that stems from the supererogatory diffuseness of postmodern fiction and its compulsion to disunity. The problem is this: if narrative consists only of words, which in turn are able to engender largely unbounded meaning through the endless play of signs and structures within the discourse at hand as well as through other discourses implied or imposed, then how and at what point (if it does so at all) does narration relate to life? This problem is especially pertinent (and troublesome) to my explorations into the way in which postmodern discourse, whose assertions of meaning are largely self-directed, undermines and transforms the meaning of a historiographic discourse that makes truth claims on the real. One could legitimately suggest that the claims of historiography are acutely naive. At its most useful, one could further argue, historiography displays a seriousness of purpose and achieves a closeness to truth, although it must be recognized that other historical discourses equally serious in purpose will foster other truths and even opposing ones. Always in such instances, there exists an implied contract between writer and reader that (in the absence of propagandistic intent or political repression) binds the discourse of history to the representation of past life as it has authentically been lived.

Postmodern thinking makes no such promises and, in fact, celebrates all that stands in opposition to them. It appears, therefore, that we are left with an unresolved dialectic between an ingenuous referential premise and a radical nonreferential one; a belief that life (and, more concretely, history) unfolds naturally in a discourse fully able to represent it and an assertion that language, like a prisoner, can be freed from representation and direct itself to its own textual and intertextual devices. Such thinking has destructive consequences for history, for it suggests that the past embodied by language is defined only through its absence. As David Bennett puts it (drawing upon Fredric Jameson): "History has [now] become 'depthless'; the past as referent has been effaced, time has been textualized, leaving only representations, texts, pseudo-events, images without originals" (Bennett 1990, 262).

To leave the matter here is neither to offer a satisfactory solution to the dialectic nor to provide a discursive paradigm that fulfills the human need to make sense of history. If we sustain meaning only as text, as narration, and encourage the constant interplay of texts with other texts in an endless array of intertextual diversity, we must ask the critical question, Are we left in the end only with process perceived as product? To theorize the heterogeneous is tantamount to opening discourse intentionally to alterity, to perturbations that one text causes when it invades another and changes it forever. But is the recognition of alterity and heterogeneity limited solely to narration? Do intertextual configurations of meaning, especially those that relate to history and postmodern fiction, remain exclusively as text, or do they assert themselves as modes of knowledge in the world we inhabit?

The overriding *value* of literary meaning seems to demand that texts assert themselves in the world. The critical conjunction of text and world entails a form of split referentiality that draws forth the crossing point between the metonymic and metaphoric conceptions of discourse. To reconcile these two conceptions is to seek unity between the transitive and intransitive functions of language, which must coexist for the production of meaning to occur. The postmodern renunciation of metonymy presents an obstacle to reconciliation, especially in the case of Francoist historiography, which makes overt assumptions of authentic representation. At the same time, the postmodern effort to disentangle life and literature (the desire to dismember Orpheus, as Ihab Hassan [1982] has put it) is countered by intertextual strategies that coerce meaning through the language of other texts. What must be discerned here is that this language, because it relates to other words and opens to the world, because it is in the world and conveys public knowledge, is already (and always) meaningful. As Gerald Bruns explains in another context (on Heidegger), the meaning of words "is always 'present at hand,' already a part of man's world as the speech of being, the *Logos*" (Bruns 1974, 234). The discourse of Francoist historiography is "already a part of man's world" for postmodernism in two crucial ways: it bears the imprint of the institutional authority that engenders it, and its metonymic assertiveness, set forth as truth, indicates the homogeneity of the social space that surrounds it.

Postmodern fiction works at every turn to undermine this social space and its linguistic embodiment. In doing so, postmodernism breaks free of hermeticism and absence and proclaims its beingness in the world. This assertion of ontological standing occurs through the systematic functioning of split referentiality and its fostering of the (uneasy) alliance between literature and life (history). The intertextual linking of postmodern fiction and Francoist historiography promotes the creation of new congruences from formerly perceived incongruences. Such is the case, for example, when the diffuseness of postmodern dialogism is laid beside the constrictions of Francoist monologism. The two modes can then be perceived together in the context of temporal aporias to which both refer. The meaning of these new congruences is bound up with existing meanings attached to history and to postmodernism, both of whose discourses create a world and are in the world that they create. In other words, the intertextual filiations between postmodern fiction and Francoist historiography compel us to perceive similarity in difference not only *in language* (that is, the coalescence of discourses that appear antithetical prior to juxtaposition) but *in reality* as well, since they determine and constitute the processes by which we give meaning to the past and allow it to affect our lives. As Hayden White points out, writing is "both determined by external social processes and . . . 'socially determining' in the (idealized?) forms that it gives to those contents" (White 1980, 366). Split referentiality thus sustains the tension between the social and literary poles of discourse (more concretely, the historical and self-referential) but at the same time demands a paradigmatic deviance from each side of the opposition that compels proximity in spite of distance. The split leads to a point between the metaphoric and metonymic poles of discourse, the precise location of which depends on the particular juxtapositions of texts that are made. There is never a moment in intertextual scrutiny when the movement of the point can be halted, for the very nature of postmodern discourse precludes stasis.

The intertextual linking of Spanish postmodern fiction with Francoist historiography reveals a desire for destruction but not for nihilism. The intertextual demands of postmodernism destroy the view of history already established and advance a counterview that is a new way of *looking* at things as well as a new *order* of things. Within this new order, the historical desire of postmodernism—the desire for historical change—lays bare the tension between closure (the eschatological determinant of Francoist historiography) and transformation (the stereoscopic necessity of split referentiality fostered by intertextual juxtapositions). If a society's sense of history reveals how it wishes to define itself through time, postmodern fiction in Spain becomes a form of inquiry by means of which the diversity of the past is made possible. Herein lies the redemptive potential of the postmodern, nourished by intertextuality to reveal not only how the literary and the historiographic relate to each other but how both relate to our modes of understanding the world.

Notes

1. The thrust of this homage number (34, no. 127–28) is that Menéndez Pelayo was a great Catholic historian who identified the essence of the Spanish past and that his methodology was grounded in science and reason, which enabled him to discover the "truth" of history. Especially forceful in presenting this perspective is Vicente Palacio Atard.

2. All translations, except those from Cela's *San Camilo, 1936*, are my own.

3. It is not my intention to enter the debate over whether postmodernism "really exists," whether it is a chronological or conceptual term, or whether it can be defined with reasonable accuracy. My purpose is to show how intertextual meanings associated with specific postmodern texts in Spain militate against the texts of Francoist historiography.

4. These texts were published after Franco's death in 1975, but their intertextual referent (perhaps "obligatory" in Riffaterre's sense) continues to be the traditions of historiography under Francoism. Torrente Ballester's ideas on history were developed fully during the years of the Franco regime, and he frequently posited historiographic norms that controverted those espoused by the state.

Works Cited

Bennett, David. 1990. "Postmodernism and Vision: Ways of Seeing (at) the End of History." In *History and Post-War Writing*. Ed. Theo D'haen and Hans Bertens, 259–79. Amsterdam: Rodopi.

Bruns, Gerald. 1974. *Modern Poetry and the Idea of Language*. New Haven: Yale University Press.

Calvo Serer, Rafael. 1947. "Una nueva generación española." *Arbor* 8.24: 333–48.

———. 1949. "España, sin problema." *Arbor* 14.45–46: 160–73.

Carroll, David. 1987. "Narrative, Heterogeneity, and the Question of the Political: Bakhtin and Lyotard." In *The Aims of Representation*. Ed. Murray Krieger, 69–106. New York: Columbia University Press.

Cela, Camilo José. 1981. *San Camilo, 1936*. 14th ed. Barcelona: Noguer.

———. 1991. *San Camilo, 1936*. Trans. J. H. R. Polt. Durham, N.C.: Duke University Press.

Commager, Henry Steele. 1967. *The Search for a Usable Past and Other Essays*. New York: Knopf.

Culler, Jonathan. 1981. *The Pursuit of Signs*. Ithaca, N.Y.: Cornell University Press.

Díaz, Elías. 1974. *Pensamiento español 1939–1973*. Madrid: Cuadernos para el Diálogo.

Docherty, Thomas. 1990. *After Theory*. London: Routledge.

Franco, Francisco. 1949. *Franco ha dicho*. Madrid: Voz.

Hassan, Ihab. 1982. *The Dismemberment of Orpheus*. Madison: University of Wisconsin Press.

Higgins, Kathleen. 1990. "Nietzsche and Postmodern Subjectivity." In *Nietzsche as Postmodernist*. Ed. Clayton Koelb, 189–215. Albany: State University of New York Press.

Laín Entralgo, Pedro. 1948. *España como problema*. Madrid: Seminario de Problemas Hispanoamericanos.

Lowenthal, David. 1985. *The Past Is a Foreign Country*. Cambridge: Cambridge University Press.

Menéndez y Pelayo, Marcelino. 1947–48. *Historia de los heterodoxos españoles*. Vol. 35, *Obras completas*. Madrid: CSIC.

Palacio Atard, Vicente. 1956. "Menéndez y Pelayo, historiador actual." *Arbor* 34.127–28: 427–45.

Pérez Embid, Florentino. 1949. "Ante la nueva actualidad del 'Problema de España.'" *Arbor* 14.45–46: 149–59.

Riffaterre, Michael. 1984. "Production du texte: l'intertexte du *Lys dans la vallée*." *Texte* 2: 23–33.

Torrente Ballester, Gonzalo. 1980. *Fragmentos de apocalipsis*. Barcelona: Destino.

———. 1985. *La rosa de los vientos*. Barcelona: Destino.

———. 1990. *La isla de los jacintos cortados*. 4th ed. Barcelona: Destino.

White, Hayden. 1980. "Literature and Social Action: Reflections on the Reflection Theory of Literary Art." *New Literary History* 9: 363–80.

Intertextuality and the Reappropriation of History in Contemporary Spanish Fiction and Film

GONZALO NAVAJAS

Representation has been a central issue in debates about fiction, particularly since the last century and the emergence of realism with novelists like Galdós, Balzac, and Dickens. Even in recent times, when authors of fiction apparently view with disdain or indifference the aims of verisimilitude and the objective reproduction of reality, the issue of representation still hovers on the horizon of fictional discourse. The terms and intensity of the debate have changed, but the mimetic dimension that Aristotle first recognized has not vanished from the study of the novel (see, e.g., Chatman 1990, 6–21; Martin 1986, 57–75). In addition to the question of mimesis, fiction's axiological orientation has also materialized as a vital critical concern, since mimesis and ethics are inevitably intertwined. Realistic representation aims at criticizing and eliminating the negative aspects of social reality, and it suggests moral alternatives to social situations corrupted by degraded values. European modernism mounted a thorough assault on the classical premises of fiction and, with the innovations of Unamuno, Proust, and Joyce, seemed to have put an end once and for all to the representational controversy. Yet, the issue resurfaces with the Sartrean novel, with the documentary novel, and with the *nouveau roman*, among others.

The concept of intertextuality offers a fresh approach to the topic. Intertextuality changes the premises of the debate because it shifts the discussion away from the relationship between the outside and the inside of fiction to fiction's internal network (Plett 1991, 3–8). Viewed from this inward perspective, the mimetic influence that has conditioned Western fiction has apparently been circumvented altogether, and the objective referential components of the traditional novel are no longer acknowledged to be pertinent. Intertextuality could well be the instrument that has settled the aesthetic debate, since one of its fundamental components—the objective referent—becomes virtually dispensable, just as the eclosion of ironic and antinomic thought, typical of the deconstructive enterprises of de Man and Derrida, seems to abolish metaphysical and historical resolution (cf. McGowan 1991, 29; Vattimo 1993, 158–84). Intertextuality could conceivably bring about the absolute autonomy of fiction.

Nevertheless, intertextuality theory has been only partially successful in its aims. On the one hand, its premises have contributed to redefining the terms of the critical dialogue by reorganizing the conceptual priorities that traditionally dominated it. The primacy of objectivity has been replaced by a perception of the text as self-generating and self-developing. On the other hand, the intertextual enterprise has not managed to free fiction entirely from external dependence. Axiology and ethics, which would be excluded from a strictly self-referential text, continue to be integral aspects of fiction. Most recently, the postmodernist movement has attempted to eliminate the ethical in aesthetics through the dissolving influence of irony and paradox, but fiction cannot elude an axiological orientation, and it creates *malgré elle* ethical structures that link it to a nontextual environment. [1]

The phenomenon of intertextuality is not specific to the postmodern epoch, for European modernism already anticipates the intertextual enterprise. The separation between postmodernism and modernism, for which certain sectors of the current critical discourse have argued, rests on the need to establish an unequivocal demarcation between the present and the past (Gaggi 1989, 17–21; Hassan 1993, 152; Portoghesi 1993, 312). In fact, as Habermas has pointed out, postmodernity has many connections with the modernist episteme, and it is self-deluding to deny them (Habermas 1987, 341). European modernism anticipates the self-sufficiency of intertextuality with its advocacy of formal innovation for its own sake and its frequent recourse to such intraliterary references as mythology. James Joyce's *Ulysses* and Ramón Pérez de Ayala's *Tigre Juan* and *El curandero de su honra* [*The Healer of His Honor*] exemplify modernist fiction's penchant for self-containment. In the plastic arts, the reactions of Picasso and Braque against impressionism's affinities with nature are another example of modernism's inward turn. Ortega y Gasset, in *The Dehumanization of Art*, characterizes the new aesthetic mode as a shift from humanism to formalism.

Intertextual referentiality is more difficult to achieve in fictional and cinematographic narratives than in other art forms because it must deal with structures that depend on verisimilitude. The plot (or what structuralism disparagingly called the "anecdote") is a burden that narrative cannot fully evade. Poetry and music adapt with greater ease to the self-referential demands of twentieth-century aesthetics. Even in such extreme cases of self-referentiality in fiction as Robbe-Grillet's *La Jalousie*, the novel retains an active orientation toward the nontextual through an omnipresent *regard*. An objectifying story is decidedly apparent in that novel although in indirect and unconventional ways. Yet, despite their only partially successful attempts at avoiding the referential, both modern and postmodern fiction make an effort to distance themselves from representation through such varied procedures as the interior monologue, texts within texts, and, frequently, intertextual reference. Contemporary Spanish narrative offers vivid illustrations of the dialectics of fiction because of the specific circumstances of Spanish politics and culture. The basis of the aesthetic debate in Spain has been an unambiguous conflict between opposing concepts of the fictional. To clarify the process I propose to divide the development of the contemporary Spanish novel into two phases: the mimetic and the intradialogic.

The Mimetic Phase

The mimetic phase spans the first two decades of the Franco dictatorship, a period in which fiction strives to perform an instructional function that disciplines such as history cannot fulfill because of the restraints imposed upon them by a dictatorial establishment. Art assumes the moral imperative of exposing the authentic nature of a reality that was masked by the dictatorship's repressive measures. Fiction therefore attempts to replace official history with a new and more reliable version. Once it has accepted this challenge, fiction's repertoire of options narrows because it has placed itself in the delimiting position of disclosing truths that otherwise would be silenced. Mimetic fiction informs about the world; it questions and revises the ideological imprint of a dominant hierarchy. It projects the text as a neutral, transparent medium that conveys without deformation the contents of a political and social environment falsified by official mandate. Some of the novels of Armando López Salinas, Antonio Ferres, Juan García Hortelano, and Juan Goytisolo exemplify this view of fiction in which the epistemological and formal approaches to reality are classical and conventional despite the author's self-proclaimed intention of creating a revolutionary and innovative art.[2]

In a period when manifest reality is being systematically falsified, suspicion is the most likely response. Fiction has the task of restoring a

truth conspicuously missing from official history, and therefore subjectivity in literature becomes an interference that compromises fiction's
corrective and instructional functions. The ostensibly objective neutrality
of Rafael Sánchez Ferlosio's *El Jarama*, for instance, represents an
external reality that appears stable and easily apprehensible because the
distorting ideological parameters seem to have been eliminated. Yet in
this representational work nonreferential elements are also evident,
especially in the form of intraliterary and filmic allusions. Through such
strictly aesthetic devices, even texts that deny the artificiality of the
literary practice are determined by the general cultural context.[3] This
kind of narrative is highly mediated by its literary forebears as well. The
intertextual vehicles are various, and they are often associated with a
concept of fiction in which social criticism prevails over other aims. The
authors from the past that are most often alluded to in this connection are
Galdós, Blasco Ibáñez, and in particular Baroja. I will focus on the latter
to exemplify the mimetic handling of the interliterary allusion.

Rather than encompassing Baroja's entire production, the mimetic
phase is represented by those of his works that project a critical vision of
Spain's history, culture, or social condition. Novels such as *Aurora roja*
[*Red Dawn*] or *Mala hierba* [*Weeds*] act on the fictional unconscious of
narrative with their bitterly negative description of Spanish society. They
serve as models of Spain's contemporary plight, which the mimetic novel
examines and transforms through art. In the early decades of the twentieth century, Baroja, like Blasco Ibáñez and Valle-Inclán, was able to
address openly what the later fiction of the 1940s and 1950s could refer
to only timidly. The intertextual reference in Baroja's two novels magni-
fies the dismal conditions of the present, since the state of the nation not
only fails to show improvement but is, in fact, regressive.

Aurora roja presents social rebellion openly, and the narrative is
unrestricted in its opposition to the status quo. One character, *El Libertario*, alludes longingly to the days of street agitation in Paris during the
Dreyfus trial. His narration captures a revolutionary spirit intent on
destroying the institutions of the ruling groups that restrain the
dispossessed:

> Los manifestantes se pusieron a cantar *La Marsellesa* como locos, cargaron
> sobre los guardias y los arrollaron. . . . Al pasar junto a mí, iba la bandera roja
> desplegada, y la llevaba mi paisano el andaluz, que marchaba en medio de
> una turba de exaltados. . . . Desde alguna distancia, *La Marsellesa*, cantada
> por miles de personas, resonaba como una tempestad, y yo veía por encima
> de la multitud ondear la bandera roja, que brillaba, soberbia y triunfante,
> como una entraña sangrienta. (Baroja 1974, 166)

[The demonstrators started singing *La Marseillaise* as if they were mad; they charged against the guards and ran over them. . . . When they passed by me, the red flag was flying unfurled, carried by my compatriot the Andalusian, who was marching in the middle of the exultant crowd. . . . In the distance, *La Marseillaise*, sung by thousands of people, resounded like a storm, and I could see the red flag above the throng of people, shining, magnificent and triumphant, like a bloody piece of gut.] (All translations are mine.)

El Libertario's words reveal the substratum that underlies the consciousness of many characters in the social novels of the early postwar period who fervently oppose the country's situation but cannot manifest that opposition openly. *El Libertario* and other fictional characters akin to him are able to express that opposition, and so he becomes the emblem of defiance that the social novel has attempted to create. *El Libertario*'s companions deride his naive ideas, however, for Baroja's characters partake of the author's deep skepticism about all collective cultural and ideological enterprises.[4]

The writers of the mimetic phase during the early Franco years cannot indulge in such skepticism openly, since for them the literary word is to be read literally and without irony. They must take advantage of the few resources that are at their disposal under the cloud of censorship in order to convey a message with a specific purpose. Thus, in López Salinas's *La mina,* the flamboyant emblems of social rebellion (the *Marseillaise*, the red flag) openly displayed in Baroja become veiled references to a unified front against the oppressing forces: "Con un tantín así de unión— López mostraba la primera falange del dedo índice—nos duraban menos que un pastel a la puerta de un colegio" [With just a mite of unity— López pointed to the tip of his index finger—they (the oppressors) would last less time than a cake at a school entrance] (López Salinas 1970, 99). The confident rebelliousness of Baroja's character becomes a much more subdued suggestiveness as López confronts those who oppose changes in the miners' working conditions. The attitudes of the prior text (*Aurora roja*) and *La mina* are similar—opposition to the status quo—but the treatment of those attitudes differs in accordance with divergent sociopolitical situations.

One consequence of reconstituting the earlier intertext is the mythification of emblematic heroic figures. In Baroja, such figures are disqualified or diminished in stature either for having a bad conscience (they are impostors) or for lacking aptitude for action (they have a utopian view of reality). In the later social novel, those same figures are idealized, and their qualities become extraordinarily magnified. In a characteristically paradoxical move, the mimetic text, while intent on the faithful representation of a fixed external reality, actually idealizes and enhances that reality, thereby diminishing or canceling the representational impulse. Whereas Baroja's narrator often views critically some of the ideologically determined myths of his time, later novels reinforce those myths and elevate them to a level of absolute signification. Baroja's artists and workers, conventionally conceived as antagonists of the prevailing order, are usually unmasked as partaking of the same flaws that afflict that order's members. In this respect, Baroja's novels deconstruct the falsified components of the opposition. In *Aurora roja,* artists are "una gente mezquina e indelicada, una colección de intrigantuelos, llenos de ansias de cruces y de medallas . . . , con todas las malas pasiones de los demás burgueses" [mean and insensitive people, a bunch of cheap conspirators, full of desire for crosses and medals . . . , with all the vices of the rest of the bourgeois], while workers lack "el sentimiento del valor, de la dignidad y de la gratitud" [any notion of bravery, dignity, and gratitude] (Baroja 1974, 107, 108).

In the mimetic novel, economic and social marginalization are guarantees of purity. Rather than being depicted in a particular character, marginalization assumes the shape of a social collectivity endowed with superior attributes. The anonymous entity that the faceless mass of the dispossessed comprises (miners, laborers, fishermen) is destined to realize the goal of destroying the entrenched structure. The conclusion to Juan Goytisolo's *La resaca* [*The Undertow*] is an example of this abstract transfiguration of an objective phenomenon. Its effect is to present a unified counterreality that is hostile to a totalized system. Goytisolo's novel ends appropriately with Antonio Machado's lines on a new Spain: "Una España implacable y redentora, / España que alborea / con un hacha en la mano vengadora, / España de la rabia y de la idea" [An implacable and redeeming Spain / that awakens / with an ax in its vindictive hand, / Spain of rage and of ideas] (Goytisolo 1958, 275).[5] Although the text purportedly depicts the dire conditions of Barcelona's marginalized population, Goytisolo is more interested in foregrounding the Machado citation as an incitement to an uprising of the Spanish people. A fiction that attempts to remain entirely unmediated by the literary is thus ultimately compelled by a prior literary text to impose a subjective and engaged perspective on an objective reality that resists accepting it.

The Spanish cinema that parallels the mimetic fiction of the early postwar period is equally characterized by its idealization of objective reality and its utopian ethics despite a generally declared adherence to neutrality. The cinema of Luis Buñuel is the dominant intertextual referent for subsequent Spanish mimetic filmmakers. In *Tierra sin pan* [*Land without Bread*] (1932), Buñuel sets the guidelines at the beginning of his career for the cinema of representational social denunciation. That film has remained important in the history of cinematography because it lends dignity and value through art to the utterly dispossessed. The Spanish region of Las Hurdes and its people, forsaken by officialdom for centuries, becomes the focus of a work of art in a medium essentially directed at the masses. Buñuel's film proves the aptness of Walter Benjamin's prediction that the cinema, with its extensive capacity for reproducing reality, would change the aesthetic and axiological hierarchies of the modern world (Benjamin 1978, 224).[6] According to Buñuel, the function of film would be to reverse the established historical premises by quoting history against itself in order to unmask its ideological purport, its arbitrary exclusions and distortions. Buñuel achieves that reversal in *Land without Bread*, but one film's accomplishments cannot be repeated indefinitely, and a strong documentary component imposes restrictions that must eventually be overcome. *Los olvidados* [*The Forgotten Ones*], released almost twenty years later, in 1950, represents a noticeable development in Buñuel's treatment of the dispossessed. In *Los olvidados*, rural Las Hurdes becomes the abandoned outskirts of Mexico City, on which Buñuel focuses the film, disregarding other areas of the city. Subjective and nonrepresentational components now play a more significant role because history is reversed through the emergence of the unconscious. The external reality of the forsaken people becomes internalized in specific individuals and is presented through their convoluted and illogical mental processes.

Carlos Saura and Víctor Erice are among Buñuel's principal heirs in postwar filmmaking (see Higginbotham 1988, 77). Like the writers of the same period, Saura wants to reconstruct the history of Spain and to use the traces of the past as the working material with which to redefine history. To accomplish this reconstruction, Saura creates iconic figures that guide the process of rewriting time. In an early film, *La caza* [*The Hunt*], he alludes to the violence of Spanish history by creating an asphyxiating environment of random and senseless destruction. Subsequently, Saura redesigns the past through the creation of a new historical conscience to replace the traditional account of events forcibly imposed on Spain's collective consciousness. *El jardín de las delicias* [*The Garden of Delights*] reveals the outright dishonesty of the beneficiaries of the Franco regime by uncovering the true nature of a business family whose power derives from the corruption of the period, a corruption that the centrally controlled media conceal with impunity. The film's unmasking process culminates in the concluding scene where all the members of the family become as physically crippled as the paterfamilias and, like him,

are bound to wheelchairs. Their final silence and immobility are suggestive of the entire country's intellectual and moral paralysis.

In later works, such as *Bodas de sangre* [*Blood Wedding*], *El amor
brujo* [*Love, the Magician*], and *Carmen*, the reelaboration of the past
extends to all of Spanish history. The previous stark critique of the postwar period mellows or vanishes altogether as Saura comes to accept
some of the cultural values that Spain has represented in the Western
tradition and that the Spanish liberal mind has rejected since the Enlightenment. Saura differs from that liberal orientation, however. He perceives a worthy distinctiveness in the Andalusian South, whose
exoticism, marginality, and singularity contrast markedly with the
predictable uniformity of our age's electronic culture. Saura's
reappropriation of conventional Spanish attitudes resembles Unamuno's
reconstruction of Don Quixote as the defender of Spain's spiritual
excellence against European positivism at the turn of the century. Like
Unamuno, Saura reevaluates established notions about the Spanish *Geist*
and reverses them to show their insufficiencies. Marginality, as revealed
for instance in the atavistic habits of gypsies and bullfighters in *El amor
brujo* or *Carmen*, proves to have hidden and invaluable qualities that are
in need of reappraisal. In this trilogy, the self-reflectivity of Saura's films
reaches its height, for the main referent is cinema itself or other mediated
cultural constructs. Individual figures become, as in Unamuno's texts,
merely the embodiments of ideal concepts of culture.

In *El espíritu de la colmena* [*The Spirit of the Beehive*], Víctor Erice
exposes the contemporary Spanish situation through the eyes of a privileged viewer, a child unbound by the limitations that distort the perception of the adults who surround her. She is able to contemplate the world
from an unexpected vantage point that allows her to reverse the meaning
of events and to reveal the nature of the events' protagonists. From her
perspective, Frankenstein can become a "good monster," a persecuted
man, an emblem of repressed opposition to the regime. That "monster"
achieves dignity when, disregarding her family's concern, the youngster
provides him with assistance. Clearly, Erice's direct quotation of Boris
Karloff's Frankenstein and his reproduction of scenes from the original
black-and-white version are fundamental to his aim of improving a grim
cultural reality.

The foregoing examples lead to the conclusion that, even in fiction
and film with a mimetic orientation, intertextual reference transforms the
text into an artifice that is self-referential and linked to other artificial
constructs.

The Intradialogic Phase

Despite a prolonged delay in adjusting to the contemporary European cultural environment, Spanish art reaches a full-fledged intertextual phase that explicitly renounces the tenets of mimeticism. The aesthetic goals of European modernism were short-lived in Spain because of the violent rupture that the Civil War and the subsequent exile and internal repression of intellectuals produced in the country's cultural environment. Those conditions forced Spain into stagnation and inspired a primitive, often crude, representationalism in art. When the antirepresentational movement finally erupted at the end of the 1960s and in the early 1970s, it did so with special intensity.

Spanish fiction and film of the intradialogic phase are not characterized by one-to-one correspondences between aesthetic objects and their well-defined referents but by multiple sources in complex webs of signifying relations. The origins of the chains of signification are indefinite, and the terms of the relationships are unstable and in constant flux. Furthermore, this phase sees the elimination of the hierarchical priorities characteristic of representational art. The individual subject and specific qualities of the text prevail over canonical norms and restrictions. In accordance with the model created by Bakhtin and expanded by postmodernist aesthetics, the intradialogic phase produces an exchange among diverse aesthetic principles, which leads to the breakdown of well-established barriers and the equalization of texts of different and often opposing kinds (Bakhtin 1981, 348).

A significant change takes place with the revision of the emblematic character, or *Übermensch*. The fiction of the past had favored this exceptional character as the counterforce to the debased world that art was intent on destroying. Remnants of the emblematic paragon persist, but now that heroic figure is questioned and is portrayed as an unreliable subject worthy of suspicion rather than admiration. The new mode engages in an active exchange with the *Übermenschen* of the past in order to show their inconsistencies, and at the same time it creates counterfigures that undermine their premises. The resulting intertextual dialogue is wholly ironic. Representatives of the absolute values of other times become indeterminate subjects whose ambiguity typifies the epistemological and axiological uncertainty of the changed cultural environment.

Postmodern tendencies towards indeterminacy and the blurring of values and goals are reflected in the flawed *Übermenschen*, who are modeled after the transcendent subjects of the past but have fallen from grace and lack the fundamental attributes that their models displayed with assurance. Like his Nietzschean counterpart, the intradialogic *Übermensch* is beyond conventional restraints and is detached from the principles of the dominant hierarchy; but, unlike his Nietzschean model, his opposition to transcendental axiology is almost accidental. He has none of the sense of mission that ennobles Nietzsche's hero and transforms him into an exceptional figure. The fallen *Übermensch* inherits Nietzsche's drive towards ontological destruction, but he has lost the Nietzschean option of self-affirmation (Nietzsche 1979, 328).

Antonio Muñoz Molina's *Beltenebros* and *El invierno en Lisboa* [*Winter in Lisbon*] offer good illustrations of characters in whom heroism has been deprived of a promising objective. Darman in *Beltenebros* is a legendary figure in the clandestine struggle against Franco's dictatorship. His companions in the dangerous political life of the opposition admire him, and he serves as inspiration for all the members of the political organization to which he belongs. Yet he is not respected for his superior vision nor for his skills as a moral or intellectual leader. His prime quality is that of being a reliable servant of the revolution. With Darman, the revolutionary discourse of a significant segment of European political and literary thought during the first half of the twentieth century becomes a meaningless hodgepodge of grandiose ideologizing. The objectives of the revolutionary project (the elimination of political and social inequities and the building of a new world) have lost the significance that they perhaps held for him in the past. He has become a simulacrum of the revolutionary model (Malraux, Sartre) that advocated dedication to a cause as a means of redeeming intolerable existential or social conditions. In Muñoz Molina's characters, as well as in other literary creations of the postmodern era, the initial premises may remain, but only in a passive and degraded manner devoid of fervor.

Darman's main attribute is to be an efficient assassin in the service of his organization. He accomplishes his goal of eliminating Walter, a supposed traitor to the party, without showing hesitation or questioning the need for his action. For Luque, his young companion in the secret activities in Madrid, he incarnates the militant who has succeeded in removing all emotional constraints from his life. In his world, truth is equated with deception, and loyalty with betrayal. The mist that at times envelops *Beltenebros* communicates the duplicity and ambiguity of this reality. Darman displays the extraordinary qualities of classical heroic figures but not the capacity to focus those qualities on an enterprise of excellence.[7] And yet the classical reference is not entirely misapplied. His progression from indetermination and duplicity to the well-defined purpose of redeeming himself and Rebeca Osorio is characteristic of the axiological reversals that in spite of itself postmodern fiction often produces.

Beltenebros follows the format of the political novel transformed by Hollywood's *cinéma noir* of the 1950s. Darman has as intertextual analogues not only the figure of the clandestine, persecuted member of the opposition but in particular the self-torturing, antiheroic characters of black-and-white films based on novels by Dashiell Hammett and Raymond Chandler and acted by Humphrey Bogart and Robert Mitchum. Other Muñoz Molina figures are also fallen *Übermenschen*. In *El invierno en Lisboa*, Billy Swann, a jazz musician who replicates Charlie Parker, achieves greatness in his art but at the expense of self-destruction. The imprecision of Billy Swann's musical performances and his inconsequential life illustrate the indefiniteness of the new axiology.

The detective story frequently provides a structural framework in the intradialogic phase, since it is especially suited to one of the new fiction's goals, the introduction of popular forms into high art (see Jameson 1983, 114; 1991, 9). The adoption of the detective genre is not total, however. Intradialogic fictions do not seek to imitate but rather to transmute previous forms. The main components of the detective story—a violent criminal act, the search for the agent of the crime, the discovery and resolution by the investigator—are modified in significant ways. Nonetheless, the central purpose of the form is preserved, that is, the creation of an enigma that engages the reader's attention until the end. In its exchanges with the detective story form, intradialogic fiction chooses those aspects that make its assertions more accessible to a wide audience. Contrary to the view that postmodern art is intrinsically egalitarian, it in fact assimilates and stylizes popular devices.

Juan Benet's *El aire de un crimen* [*The Air of a Crime*] illustrates a similar mixture of high and low art. It combines the violent criminal act typical of the detective genre with the selective and stylized techniques that are the trademarks of Benet's fiction. In this novel, which is in some respects atypical of his work, Benet does not abandon his goal of creating an intensely personal fiction, but he does include conventional elements within it. The general intent of Benet's writing—to create a nonmimetic, irreproducible, fictional environment with uncommon attributes—is not forsaken but is revised to produce a variant of his characteristic style.

The goal of disguising an objective or a truth under the formal cover of the detective story is achieved in various ways by other novelists of this phase, for example by Manuel Vázquez Montalbán, in whose novels the critical presentation of society, a predominant aim of the social novel of the 1950s and 1960s, is readapted to conform to the current political scene. The heroic figures of the past, the downtrodden people of the urban wasteland and of the forlorn countryside (workers, peasants, miners) have ceased to appear in the text. In their place, Vázquez Montalbán creates the unusual figure of detective Carvalho, who with deceptive unpretentiousness exposes the inanities of current Spanish and European culture. Instead of mounting epic confrontations between irreconcilable social and political forces that jolt the foundations of history, Carvalho and those around him are concerned only with the immediate gratification of their individual needs without any consideration for the common welfare.

In women's fiction, the format of the detective story produces quite different results from those of the male authors considered thus far. Soledad Puértolas's *Queda la noche* [*The Night Remains*] introduces a variant of the spy story, but only as a secondary plot, interpolated as a novel within a novel that functions as a counterpoint to the process of Aurora's successful self-realization. In a different way, Adelaida García Morales's *La lógica del vampiro* [*The Vampire's Logic*] incorporates the elements of the search for and the unveiling of the culprit. The consequence of the search is the discovery of an improved and newly configured female self. Aurora in *Queda la noche* and Elvira in *La lógica del vampiro* are both feminine reworkings of the *Übermensch*, but now the fallen male figure becomes an assertive female who has overcome her insufficiencies and has created a new feminine psyche. The malady of modernity is the unreliability of human reason and the impossibility of replacing that reason with legitimate alternatives. The ontological uncertainty of many characters in contemporary fiction is still unresolved, but it is viewed from a more confident perspective in the fiction of the contemporary women writers in Spain.

Several of filmmaker Pedro Almodóvar's feminine characters take up the role of the woman who assumes the burden of male history in order to dismiss it and reshape it. The protagonists of *¿Qué he hecho yo para merecer esto?* [*What Have I Done to Deserve This?*] and *Mujeres al borde de un ataque de nervios* [*Women on the Verge of a Nervous Breakdown*] are examples of the assumption of history by female figures who have abandoned the apocalyptic vision of post-Nietzschean thought and have transformed the study of the human condition and human relations. In a similar vein, Bigas Luna's *Jamón, jamón* presents the female psyche as capable of undoing the mythical constructions (built, for instance, around phallus infatuation) that have traditionally determined the male-dominated Spanish culture.

The reconstruction of the present is not the only trend in current narrative and cinematic aesthetics. Another is the reassimilation of the past as an evasion of the subject's inability to find a cultural and emotional *Heimat,* or home. Jameson and Vattimo, building on Heidegger's notion of an ontological *Heimat,* have alluded to the cultural orphanage created by the postmodern episteme (Jameson 1983, 115; Vattimo 1988, 25). Modern Spain is exemplary in this regard because of the discouraging outcome of the undoing of Franco's regime. Instead of experiencing a complete reversal of its social and economic structures, the country had to settle for a less dramatic change that did not conform to the Utopian project of many who expected a radical transformation. Yet a nostalgic perception of time endures. The past is not dead but still active, since it has conditioned the evolution of the present. Today's writer or filmmaker cannot accept the present but at the same time feels powerless to change it and therefore opts for a renewed exploration of the past.

Vázquez Montalbán's *El pianista* illustrates the tendency to contrast Spain's past struggles against an oppressive political structure with the insufficiencies of the present. In order to foreground a bygone epoch, *El pianista* is organized into three temporal segments in reverse chronological sequence, from present to past. The first segment opens in present-day Spain with the characters lamenting their country's cultural mediocrity, the preponderance of trivial values, and the absence of noble pursuits. The characters reminisce about the heroic days of the struggle against the dictatorship and dream of an escape to Manhattan, the center of a vibrant culture. The present appears as a wasteland in which the possibility of realizing collective dreams has vanished. In the retrospective segments of the novel, the protagonist Rosell decides to abandon his promising career as a pianist in Paris and returns to Spain to join the armed forces fighting against Franco's troops. His act of self-denial contrasts with the self-centered aims of today's Spaniards, who are concerned only with their narrow, personal interests. The Spanish Civil War is nostalgically superimposed on a present that lacks value in itself. The past, although it cannot be reenacted, can at least serve as a point of reference for revealing the present debasement.

Montserrat Roig likewise quotes the past as an inspiration for the present in *La voz melodiosa* [*The Melodious Voice*], where Esperdenya parallels *El pianista*'s protagonist in his devotion to suprasubjective goals in the face of his companions' general indifference. His past context is the clandestine life of struggle against the dictatorship, a time when the individual subject could perceive himself as capable of determining history. That heroic time is portrayed as the uncovering of a lost memory of magnificent acts for the sake of humanity. The novel is thus a historical enterprise that takes up a portion of unrecorded oral knowledge and transcribes it for the future in written form. Similarly, Eduardo Mendoza in *La ciudad de los prodigios* [*The City of Marvels*] regards the collective conscience of Barcelona, icon of a national community, as a repository of the extraordinary attributes that the present fails to yield. The remembrance of that past is therefore an instrument for awakening the present to its own inadequacies.

Carlos Saura has made the recovery of the political and social past a focus of his films. During the years in which his work was subjected to censorship, he had a twofold purpose: the reassumption of historical events in a more thorough and plural fashion and the reinterpretation of those events from a dissenting perspective. *El jardín de las delicias, La prima Angélica* [*Cousin Angelica*], and *Cría cuervos* [*Cria*] adopt narrative perspectives that through irony and indirection reshape the story of the victors in the Spanish Civil War. The events leading to the conflagration in *El jardín de las delicias* are reviewed as a social struggle provoked by the intolerance of the leading forces in the country, especially the Catholic hierarchy. At the same time, don Antonio, the all-powerful paterfamilias, unexpectedly uncovers the corruption of his family and his business and in this way exposes the false moral and political premises that gave legitimacy to the regime and its followers. In *Cría cuervos,* a child is the observer of the historical past because her innocence can overcome the distorted vision that her military father imposes on her and the other female members of his family. The family unit in those films is a condensed replica of the collective Spanish family, and in each case a critical distance is established through a privileged member who becomes a vehicle for condemnation.

Once the repressive authoritarianism diminishes or disappears, Saura shifts the focus of his reconsideration of Spanish history, but a reconstructive approach to the past is still his favored procedure. In *Bodas de sangre*, *Carmen*, and *El amor brujo*, produced under an open political system, the earlier ironic and critical view becomes identified with figures who have played a secondary role in Spanish history. The camera's function is to retake that past, which had been appropriated by either traditional or foreign views of Spain, and to recast it. Saura is not interested in extolling the "eternal" values of the country or the unique nature of its customs; he wants, rather, to reinsert those values into the mainstream of current art, to renew the past by exploring its aesthetic possibilities.

Saura's cinema and that of directors such as Erice and Borau continues to be strongly linked to a past that determines its ideological orientation and formal structures. Almodóvar is the filmmaker who has broken most decisively with the onerous connection to history. Ideological authoritarianism has lost its grip on Almodóvar, so he devotes himself to more urgent and immediate issues. Saura's commitment to abstract and ethical principles is absent in the younger director, and the example of Buñuel, which in various intertextual forms guides or affects the orientation of nearly all early postwar Spanish filmmaking, disappears in him as well (see Smith 1992, 163–203). But this erasure of history does not eliminate the nostalgic perspective. Almodóvar is also intertextually determined, but his focus is on the trivial rather than on the prominent landmarks of history. He is suspicious of the rhetorical traps that falsify those landmarks. Instead of the work of the great directors, his main referents are the B-series films of Hollywood, which target wide audiences and are devoid of profound aesthetic aspirations. That cinema seems to Almodóvar more genuinely connected to the popular psyche than are the intellectual films of other Spanish and European directors. Like Fassbinder and Wim Wenders, Almodóvar relishes the popular, but he disregards the critical unconscious that underlies their cinematography. The melodramatic structure and tone of his films resemble soap opera narrative. *Tacones lejanos* [*High Heels*], unabashedly immersed in the world of commercial music, confirms that the ideological attachments of the past have become irrelevant, since they do not reflect the visual and electronic culture of the last two decades of the twentieth century.

It is not surprising that irony and parody are essential instruments for the repossession of history. Both rhetorical modes can evoke a prior text or source while at the same time allowing a significant distance from them. Both forms produce an indefinite deferral of meaning that seems to preclude all closure. Irony and parody point critically to other referents without proposing other options. In this manner they produce the open texts that characterize postmodern aesthetics.[8] Juan Goytisolo's novels are among those that make extensive use of a second degree of signification. The principles and language of the official order are disqualified by the appropriation of those very principles and language and by the exposure of their false premises and inconsistencies. The alternative to that order, however, is the complete rejection of any assertive position, and that rejection makes negation an absolute principle not very different from the principles Goytisolo attacks.

In other authors, the dissemination of signification does not end in absolute negation but rather prolongs itself inconclusively (cf. Habermas 1992). Therefore, irony seems never to be able to evolve into an assertive statement. Juan José Millás's *El desorden de tu nombre* [*The Disorder of Your Name*] is illustrative in this respect. It reveals that there is no direct key to the understanding of a circular text, since it seems to be rewriting itself in a perpetual referral to internal components and figures. Such a text appears unable to generate any ethical propositions. Yet irony does cease in some postmodernist texts, in those that propose unifying categories where the continual intertextual dissemination stops. For instance, several of Almodóvar's films conclude in all-encompassing metaphors of synthesis in which irony dissolves and conflicting elements of reality are reconciled. His *Átame* [*Tie Me Up, Tie Me Down*] ultimately reaffirms the Spanish family unit as the natural shelter from a disturbed urban civilization where no stable accommodation can be found. Vázquez Montalbán's *El pianista* proposes a final exaltation of the utopian revolutionary ideal as the only noble position in a corrupt world. Even a subcultural novel of popular eroticism or pornography like Almudena Grandes's *Las edades de Lulú* [*The Ages of Lulú*] concludes with the possibility of reconfiguring the affective life through the reunion of Lulú with her abusive friend/husband.

Contradictory affirmations are indicative of the paradoxes of the intradialogic phase. Despite its central impulse toward indirect reference and the uninterrupted deferral of signification, in the end the texts of this phase are oriented toward an integrative horizon—a goal which, despite poststructuralist and postmodernist critique, has not been entirely excluded from the aesthetic object and which shapes it in a subdued, indirect, yet unequivocal way. The ethical and axiological dimension, explicitly advocated in the mimetic phase, resurfaces in the intradialogic texts, thus proving that the exploration of representation has not ended but continues to shape itself in unexpected reconfigurations of the past.

Notes

1. I discuss the paradoxical nature of postmodernist aesthetics in greater detail in "Una estética para después del posmodernismo" (Navajas 1993). Norris (1985, 223) shows that it is not possible to evade the concepts and orientation of the philosophical tradition, even in movements like deconstruction and postmodernism, which are built on the opposition to and destruction of that tradition.

2. Juan Goytisolo writes *Problemas de la novela* in 1959 with the apparent intention of setting the new rules of fiction for the future (see Goytisolo 1959, 19).

3. Richard Rorty (1982, 99) and Hayden White (1978, 39) provide the theoretical premises for the cultural underpinnings of narrations that in principle seem free of subjective distortions.

4. Elsewhere I discuss Baroja's antisystematic position in relation to modern philosophy (Navajas 1990, 104).

5. Antonio Machado was a common referent for the social novel because his work combined a critical stance regarding traditional Spain with a capacity for transcendental vision.

6. With his emphasis on the democratic attributes of the new art, however, Benjamin did not foresee the trivialization that the visual media would later bring to cultural discourse.

7. On the epigonic character of Muñoz Molina's fiction and the "paranoic rhetoric" practiced by his figures, see Pope (1992, 112–17).

8. For a critical view of the complex epistemological and aesthetic ramifications of the often misinterpreted concept of postmodernism, see Connor (1989, 115); Hutcheon (1993, 262); Lipovetsky (1983, 117–23); Navajas (1994).

Works Cited

Bakhtin, Mikhail. 1981. *The Dialogic Imagination*. Ed. Michael Holquist. Trans. Caryl Emerson and Michael Holquist. Austin: University of Texas Press.

Baroja, Pío. 1974. *Aurora roja*. Madrid: Caro Raggio.

Benet, Juan. 1980. *El aire de un crimen*. Barcelona: Planeta.

Benjamin, Walter. 1978. "The Work of Art in the Age of Mechanical Reproduction." In *Illuminations*. Ed. Hannah Arendt. Trans. Harry Zohn, 217–51. New York: Schocken Books.

Chatman, Seymour. 1990. *Coming to Terms*. Ithaca, N.Y.: Cornell University Press.

Connor, Steven. 1989. *Postmodernist Culture*. Oxford: Blackwell.

Gaggi, Silvio. 1989. *Modern/Postmodern*. Philadelphia: University of Pennsylvania Press.

García Morales, Adelaida. 1989. *La lógica del vampiro*. Barcelona: Anagrama.

Goytisolo, Juan. 1958. *La resaca*. Paris: Club del Libro Español.

———. 1959. *Problemas de la novela*. Barcelona: Seix Barral.

Grandes, Almudena. 1989. *Las edades de Lulú*. Barcelona: Tusquets.

Habermas, Jürgen. 1987. "The Normative Content of Modernity." In *The Philosophical Discourse of Modernity*. Trans. Frederick Lawrence, 336–67. Cambridge, Mass.: MIT Press.

———. 1992. *Postmetaphysical Thinking*. Trans. William Mark Hohengarten. Cambridge, Mass.: MIT Press.

Hassan, Ihab. 1993. "Toward a Concept of Postmodernism." In *Postmodernism*. Ed. Thomas Docherty, 146–56. New York: Columbia University Press.

Higginbotham, Virginia. 1988. *Spanish Film Under Franco*. Austin: University of Texas Press.

Hutcheon, Linda. 1993. "Beginning to Theorize Postmodernism." In *A Postmodern Reader*. Ed. Joseph Natoli and Linda Hutcheon, 243–72. Albany: State University of New York Press.

Jameson, Fredric. 1983. "Postmodernism and Consumer Society." In *The Anti-Aesthetic*. Ed. Hal Foster, 111–25. Port Townsend, Wash.: Bay Press.

———. 1991. *Postmodernism*. Durham, N.C.: Duke University Press.

Lipovetsky, Gilles. 1983. *L'Ère du vide*. Paris: Gallimard.

López Salinas, Armando. 1970. *La mina*. Barcelona: Destino.

Martin, Wallace. 1986. *Recent Theories of Narrative*. Ithaca, N.Y.: Cornell University Press.

McGowan, John. 1991. *Postmodernism and Its Critics*. Ithaca, N.Y.: Cornell University Press.

Mendoza, Eduardo. 1986. *La ciudad de los prodigios*. Barcelona: Seix Barral.

Millás, Juan José. 1988. *El desorden de tu nombre*. Madrid: Alfaguara.

Muñoz Molina, Antonio. 1987. *El invierno en Lisboa*. Barcelona: Seix Barral.

——. 1989. *Beltenebros*. Barcelona: Seix Barral.

Navajas, Gonzalo. 1990. *Pío Baroja: el escritor y la crítica*. Barcelona: Teide.

——. 1993. "Una estética para después del posmodernismo." *Revista de Occidente* 143: 105–30.

——. 1994. "Posmodernidad/posmodernismo. Crítica de un paradigma." *Insula* 570–71: 22–26.

Nietzsche, Friedrich. 1979. *Thus Spoke Zarathustra*. Trans. Walter Kaufmann. New York: Penguin.

Norris, Christopher. 1985. *The Contest of Faculties*. London: Methuen.

Ortega y Gasset, José. [1925] 1970. *La deshumanización del arte*. Madrid: Revista de Occidente.

Plett, Heinrich, ed. 1991. *Intertextuality*. Berlin: Walter de Gruyter.

Pope, Randolph. 1992. "Postmodernismo en España: el caso de Antonio Muñoz Molina." *España Contemporánea* 5: 111–19.

Portoghesi, Paolo. 1993. "Postmodern." In *Postmodernism*. Ed. Thomas Docherty, 308–16. New York: Columbia University Press.

Puértolas, Soledad. 1989. *Queda la noche*. Barcelona: Planeta.

Roig, Montserrat. 1987. *La voz melodiosa*. Barcelona: Plaza y Janés.

Rorty, Richard. 1982. *Consequences of Pragmatism*. Minneapolis: University of Minnesota Press.

Sánchez Ferlosio, Rafael. 1956. *El Jarama*. Barcelona: Destino.

Smith, Paul Julian. 1992. *Laws of Desire*. Oxford: Clarendon Press.

Vattimo, Gianni. 1988. *The End of Modernity*. Trans. Jon R. Snyder. Baltimore: Johns Hopkins University Press.

——. 1993. *The Adventure of Difference*. Trans. Cyprian Blamires. Baltimore: Johns Hopkins University Press.

Vázquez Montalbán, Manuel. 1985. *El pianista*. Barcelona: Seix Barral.

White, Hayden. 1978. *Tropics of Discourse*. Baltimore: Johns Hopkins University Press.

The Discursive Field of *Tiempo de silencio*

ROBERT C. SPIRES

Critics have long recognized the contribution of Luis Martín-Santos's *Tiempo de silencio* [*Time of Silence*] to the renovation of postwar Spanish fiction, and I do not want to add yet another explanation of how Martín-Santos's modern classic helps define Spanish literary history. I propose, therefore, to examine the novel in a much broader context by analyzing it as a case study of global discursive practices. To attempt my version of *épistémocritique* and at the same time respect the parameters of this volume, I must beg the indulgence of my readers as I expand intertextuality from a structuralist to an epistemic concept, from a comparison of artistic works to a dialogue between literary and nonliterary texts.

In an effort to link intertextuality with discourse, I will examine *Tiempo de silencio* as a register rather than a mirror of a discursive field that extends well beyond the Spanish borders and whose components encompass the history, politics, religion, and science of the 1950s and 1960s. This intertextual project will be grounded on Foucault's thesis that discourse is an interdisciplinary phenomenon involving statements, objects, concepts, attitudes, and events (Foucault 1972, 21–39). Whereas a structuralist tends to view the work of fiction as a clockwork of detachable parts, I propose to argue that the text itself forms part of a vast field of nondetachable and dispersed events whose interconnections cross disciplines and national borders and point backward as well as forward, upward as well as downward. "Field" has become a popular metaphor for conveying the idea of a dispersion of discursive events or an intertextuality that goes beyond literary texts. In the scientific community, a field signals a nonlinear interconnected network of energy and matter (Hayles 1984, 15–27). Although my project examines *Tiempo de silencio* as an integral part of the global discursive network emerging after World War II, its point of departure is Francoist Spain.

A prominent scholar has argued convincingly that the Franco regime attempted to mythologize and thereby atemporalize Spanish history so that the nation would appear morally superior to other countries (Herzberger 1995). Spain's glorious past, the regime would have people believe, is written in stone and not subject to reinterpretation. Coinciding with this official campaign is a novelistic movement generally labeled neorealism. According to the same critic, the novelists of this movement set out to subvert the government efforts not by directly challenging the official historical view (which censorship would have made difficult, if not impossible) but by virtually eliminating history from their fiction. These neo- or social realists dedicate themselves to a fictional documentation of the social and moral decadence of the present, thereby undermining the official myth that Spain's present is directly linked to its glorious past.[1]

Perhaps because they were intent on disarming the Francoist version of history, the Spanish neorealists practiced a highly mimetic art that many readers consider excessively provincial, static, and uncommitted. The emphasis of these novelists on scenic descriptions echoes the earlier twentieth-century aesthetic of Henry James, Percy Lubbock, and others who advocated "showing" over "telling," that is, the virtual exclusion of narrative commentary from what Lubbock defined as "the craft of fiction." Serving as the principal spokesperson for a counterstylistics, Wayne Booth responded to those who would equate novelistic art with mimeticism by calling for a return to a "rhetoric of fiction." Booth's rhetoric refers to the writers' license to indulge in editorial intrusion, linguistic experimentation, or any kind of verbal excess. By the 1950s, North American, South American, and European writers were already breaking away from the restraints of an aesthetic based predominantly on showing. Yet in Spain, in part as a reaction against government censorship, that decade marked the zenith of mimetic fiction. Much more than their nineteenth-century predecessors, the twentieth-century Spanish neorealists transformed their narrators into cameras, thereby limiting considerably the expressive arsenal at the novelists' disposal.[2] Neorealism was not devoid of broad themes, but the thematic projection depended almost exclusively on metaphorical transformations. That self-imposed limitation on the "craft of fiction" prevailed throughout most of the 1940s and 1950s in Spain, but by the 1960s the forces for social and novelistic change began to manifest themselves.

The beginning of the 1960s signals a new era. In the middle and late 1950s, Franco appointed members of the Catholic lay organization Opus Dei to key positions in his government, and by 1960 the more progressive economic philosophies of that organization had begun to show effects.[3] Yet those liberating influences coincided with the culmination of the regime's program to consolidate its power, and as a result *Tiempo de silencio* arrived on the scene when Spain was experiencing a type of sociopolitical schizophrenia.[4]

In view of the Spanish context of the early 1960s, most observers agree that *Tiempo de silencio* represents a challenge to the new, privileged role of technology and science championed by the Opus Dei. The novel undermines the goals of that program by an excessive and hence parodic employment of technical and scientific terminology, neologisms, and foreign words.[5] While the "progressive philosophy" of Opus Dei may well inform *Tiempo de silencio*, Martín-Santos's novel also addresses science and technology in more universal terms. It dismantles much of the foundation of Western thought and tradition by calling into question syllogistic logic, systems of power and authority, paternalistic hierarchies, and the accepted definitions of centrality/marginality.

The plot of Martín-Santos's novel centers on Pedro, a young medical scientist who dreams of winning the Nobel Prize by detecting the virus that causes cancer. The project is threatened when the supply of imported laboratory mice runs out and there are no funds to buy more. He discovers that Muecas, a trash collector, has stolen some of the mice and is reproducing them in his shack. Hoping to bargain for the rights to some of the offspring, Pedro visits Muecas in the slum area where he lives with his wife and two daughters. They fail to reach an accord on that occasion, and later Muecas appears at Pedro's boarding house in the early hours of the morning and begs the young doctor to help one of the daughters, Florita, who Pedro later discovers is suffering the miscarriage of a pregnancy caused by Muecas himself. Pedro agrees to help, inspired by the possibility that the girl has been infected by the mice and may provide the key to the virus for which he has been searching. He arrives too late, for Florita is already dead. That unhappy turn of events does not deter him from performing a surgical intervention, and when the police are informed, they arrest Pedro as the person responsible for the young woman's death. The victim's mother then confesses that her husband is to blame, and the young scientist is given his freedom. He is dismissed, however, from the laboratory where he works, and shortly thereafter his fiancee is murdered by Florita's boyfriend, who believes Pedro was responsible for the pregnancy. The novel ends as Pedro heads for a remote village where he plans to set up a modest medical practice.

In the early part of *Tiempo de silencio*, the reader is introduced to the slum area of Madrid where Muecas and his family live. As the narrator adjusts his lens, the focus falls first on the city proper, then widens to project the nation-state, and finally pans to the extrageopolitical region of world poverty and hunger: "la vecina ciudad aún no destruida por la bomba ... el Estado no destruido por la bomba ... , y el país del hambre —ése sí— era radicalmente indestructible por la bomba" [the neighboring city still not destroyed by the bomb ... the State not destroyed by the bomb ... and the land of hunger—that for sure—was radically indestructible by the bomb] (Martín-Santos 1987, 70).[6] This passage, which ironically underscores the power of the atomic bomb to eradicate everything but poverty, also points to a dramatic change in attitude toward scientific/technological progress. Although science and technology were satirized and ridiculed in much of the literature of the 1920s and 1930s (see Cano Ballesta 1981), nothing so concrete as the atomic bomb could then be cited as proof of the betrayal of the social utopia these disciplines were supposed to create. With the global projection of the photographs of Hiroshima and Nagasaki, however, utopia suddenly became Armageddon, and a new discursive field emerged.[7] The bomb hastened a growing conviction that the time had come to question the authority behind basic social, religious, and political assumptions: perhaps people should begin to contemplate alternative ways of thinking and being.

Many now argue that since the nineteenth century science/technology and capitalism have been inexorably united in the Western world (see, among others, Jameson 1991 and Lyotard 1989). The social philosophy of Opus Dei, with its thesis that scientific/technological progress will pave the road to economic development for Spain, stresses such a union. Yet, *Tiempo de silencio* points to progress as an exacerbation of poverty, for juxtaposed with the signifiers of supposed progress are scenes of demonstrable squalor from life in the *chabolas,* or slums, of Madrid. The problem is further complicated by the young scientist-protagonist's lack of adequate funds to maintain a supply of laboratory animals for his study of a cancer-causing virus. Scientific research is, therefore, also a casualty of national poverty. It is not a question of science eradicating economic needs, as the technocrats claim, nor of a simple polarity between technology and penury. Technology and totalitarianism, progress and poverty, power and paternalism are all linked, although not in a linear, syllogistic pattern. The connections run in all directions, each cause also constituting an effect.

A more subtle undermining of linear, syllogistic representation takes place on a syntactical level. A direct challenge to linearity occurs in the very first words of the novel as Pedro, who is working with his assistant Amador in a science laboratory, narrates: "Sonaba el teléfono y he oído el timbre. He cogido el aparato. No me he enterado bien. He dejado el teléfono" [The phone was ringing and I heard the sound. I grabbed the device. I didn't understand very well. I put the phone down] (Martín-Santos 1987, 7). Acting as both speaker and focalizer, Pedro employs a verbal construction that is discordantly unorthodox; it is more paratactic (based on caesuras) than syntactic (based on linking words). Listeners depend on the logic of speech acts to span the gaps. The logical sequence in this case would be "the phone rings and I answer it." But the speaker unnecessarily fills in the gaps and provides an excess of information, thus paradoxically producing a sensation of cacophonous fragmentation or noise:[8] "He dicho: 'Amador'. Ha venido con sus gruesos labios y ha cogido el teléfono. . . . Está hablando por teléfono. . . . Habla despacio, mira, me ve" [I said: "Amador." He came over with his fat lips and took the phone. . . . He is talking on the phone. . . . He speaks slowly, he looks, he sees me] (Martín-Santos 1987, 7). In communication theory, "noise" is the term used to indicate the part of a message that is lost in transmission. In addition to mechanical or audio interference, noise may result from too much or too little information or from information that is too surprising or too predictable. Excess in any form could be cited as one of the principal producers of noise. In the passages just cited, Pedro nullifies the readers' inclination to form logical connections, to anticipate deductively the effect of a given cause, and leaves them with the sensation of a world of detached parts, separated into individual slides like those observed through his microscope. Apparently, Pedro tries to live in a Newtonian universe of perfect succession; but by unwittingly exaggerating the Newtonian paradigm, he effects a reorientation of cognitive processes. Pedro's paratactic syntax, a reflection of his efforts to reason and understand the world around him, negates the readers' dependence on the familiar linearity of cause and effect. Contiguity replaces continuity as the key to logic.

Following this initial section of the novel, in which Pedro as speaker subverts linear reasoning by carrying it to an extreme, an extradiegetic narrator intervenes to demonstrate nonlinear relationships involving power hierarchies. Convention represents such alliances in the form of a vertical line, with the source at the top and a diminution of power at each descending step: at the top the politically and economically powerful, at the bottom the politically and economically powerless. Martín-Santos modifies that perpendicular paradigm in three fundamental ways. Rather than a single vertical line, the author suggests a horizontal dispersal of short but interconnected lines. Whereas power is usually thought to flow downward, here there is a capillary effect, or an upward and downward movement. Furthermore, if politics and economics are generally considered the outward trappings of power structures, the textual strategy in this instance posits paternalism as their hidden but essential foundation. This

revisionist view of power hierarchies emerges when the narrative focus
turns to the infrastructure of the slums, specifically to Muecas, his wife,
and their two daughters.

Muecas has stolen the laboratory mice (ironically, imported from
Illinois) with the hope of selling them back to the young scientist for his
cancer research. Although as a slum dweller Muecas subsists at the very
bottom of the macrosocioeconomic order, possession of the Illinois mice
bestows on him a privileged social status within the slum world:

> Gentleman-farmer Muecasthone visitaba sus criaderos por la mañana donde
> sus yeguas de vientre de raza selecta, refinada por sapientísimos cruces
> endogámicos, daban el codiciado fruto purasangre. Emitía órdenes con gruñi-
> dos breves que personal especializado comprendía sin esfuerzo y cumpli-
> mentaba en el ipso facto. (Martín-Santos 1987, 67)

> [Gentleman-farmer Muecasthone visited during the morning the breeding
> stables where his select breeding mares, thanks to a refining process of highly
> sophisticated endogamic crossings, produced prized pureblood offspring. He
> issued orders by means of brief grunts, which a highly specialized staff easily
> understood and carried out in an ipso facto.]

This passage parodically echoes English feudalism and colonialism and
suggests, rather than a single hierarchical line descending from above
(the British throne) to below (the Madrid slums), an infinite number of
lines running horizontally and vertically. Neither hierarchy nor poverty
knows geographical boundaries. Indeed, a few pages later another
metaphor underscores the similarity between power structures that occur
at points totally removed in time, space, culture, and social level:

> Príncipe negro y dignatario Muecas paseaba su chistera gris perla y su
> chaleco rojo con una pluma de gallo macho en el ojal orgullosamente, entre
> los negritos de barriga prominente y entre las pobres negras de oscilantes
> caderas que apenas para taparrabos tenían. (71)

> [The Negro prince and dignitary Muecas paraded proudly, in pearl-grey top
> hat and red vest with a rooster feather in the lapel, among the pot-bellied
> pygmies and their poor women with swinging hips who hardly had a g-string
> to cover themselves.]

Muecas serves as the focal point in a discursive field that comprehends
the family structures of a contemporary Madrid slum, a colonial English
manor, and a sempiternal African tribe. The interconnections for this
field are multi- rather than unidirectional.

Despite the cultural, geographical, and generational differences among the contexts of the two previous examples, Muecas reveals the common denominator by beating his wife and daughters each night and "haciendo así otra vez evidente su naturaleza de señor" [thus reaffirming his seigniorial status] (72). Although writing from within a dictatorship where power seemed to flow vertically from the top down, Martín-Santos challenges that unidirectional concept. The textual strategy signals that dictatorships are merely larger and more dramatic examples of a vast, horizontal network anchored by the family unit. The family (citizens, vassals, or tribal members) grants the power that the father (executive, lord, or chieftain) exercises over it. Franco often referred to Spanish citizens as his children and began many of his public addresses with the salutation "Hijos míos" [My children]. The dictator's use of the word "children" when referring to the people may well serve as an unconscious indicator that the system he helped to create also created him. *Tiempo de silencio* points to the conclusion that paternalistic attitudes are the source of democratic as well as totalitarian political and economic structures.[9]

Just as the novel points to the conclusion that political hierarchies are founded on paternalistic principles, so does it imply that the patriarchal right and obligation of the state is to control and punish its subjects. Society must discipline itself, and to that end the state must classify and segregate its citizens:

> que el hombre nunca está perdido porque para eso está la ciudad (para que el hombre no esté nunca perdido), que el hombre puede sufrir o morir pero no perderse en esta ciudad, cada uno de cuyos rincones es un recogeperdidos perfeccionado, donde el hombre no puede perderse aunque lo quiera porque mil, diez mil, cien mil pares de ojos lo clasifican y disponen, lo reconocen y abrazan, lo identifican y salvan, le permiten encontrarse cuando más perdido se creía en su lugar natural: en la cárcel, en el orfelinato, en la comisaría, en el manicomio, en el quirófano de urgencia, que el hombre —aquí— ya no es de pueblo. (Martín-Santos 1987, 19)

> [for a man is never lost because that is what the city is for (so that a man will never become lost), for a man can suffer or die but not be lost in this city— each of whose nooks and crannies is a perfect lost-and-found souls department—where a man cannot become lost even if he tries because a thousand, ten thousand, a hundred thousand pairs of eyes classify and catalogue him, recognize and embrace him, identify and save him, thereby allowing him to find himself when he feels most lost in his natural setting: in jail, in an orphanage, in the police station, in the insane asylum, in the emergency room, because a man—here in this place—no longer forms a part of the pueblo.]

Some thirteen years after *Tiempo de silencio* appeared, Foucault published *Discipline and Punish*, in which he argues that the contemporary disciplining state tries to act as a gigantic panopticon and devotes much of its efforts to classifying its citizens. With the emphasis in this passage on "State apparatuses" (Althusser 1971, 135–41) for finding, identifying, classifying, and segregating its citizens, Martín-Santos anticipates Foucault. The state is intent on developing classificatory systems whose primary purpose, the narrator states (and Foucault no doubt would echo), is to account for every citizen. When at the end of the passage the narrator employs the word "pueblo," he contrasts it with the repetition of "ciudad" at the beginning—"pueblo," *populus*, connotes humans, while "ciudad," *civitas*, connotes institutions—thereby adding dehumanization to his implicit definition of the disciplining state.

As the previous example indicates, the state uses its institutions—prisons, jails, orphanages, hospitals, asylums—to force threatening nonconformists into physical isolation. Difference must be punished, in more severe cases erased, and the offenders ostracized or eliminated. The punishment depends on the degree to which society feels menaced by the offenders. This concept of social polarization defines centers and margins arbitrarily (nonconformity as opposed to disobedience, peccadillo as opposed to crime, eccentricity as opposed to insanity). The capriciousness of the system emerges when Pedro, out for a Saturday night on the town and walking along the Calle de Cervantes in the old section of the city, begins to contemplate some of the implications of *Don Quijote* and its creator: "¿Qué significa que quien sabía que la locura no es sino la nada, el hueco, lo vacío, afirmara que solamente en la locura reposa el ser-moral del hombre?" [What does it signify that the person who knew that insanity merely means nothingness, empty space, a vacuum, should have affirmed that only in insanity does man's moral being reside?] (Martín-Santos 1987, 75). This association of madness with morality underscores the difference between social and medical definitions of insanity, between being and nonbeing. And, whereas Don Quijote often passes as a comically eccentric character intent on righting imagined wrongs, Pedro finds something tragically serious in the Cervantine farce:

Lo que Cervantes está gritando a voces es que su loco no estaba realmente loco, sino que hacía lo que hacía para poder reírse del cura y del barbero, ya que si se hubiera reído de ellos sin haberse mostrado previamente loco, no se lo habrían tolerado y hubieran tomado sus medidas montando, por ejemplo, su pequeña inquisición local, su pequeño potro de tormento y su pequeña obra caritativa para el socorro de los pobres de la parroquia. Y el loco, manifiesto como no-loco, hubiera tenido en lugar de jaula de palo, su buena camisa de fuerza de lino reforzado con panoplias y sus veintidós sesiones de electroshockterapia. (76)

[What Cervantes is shrilly shouting is that his madman was not really mad but rather that he was doing what he was doing so that he could laugh at the priest and the barber, for if he had laughed at them without having previously demonstrated his madness, it would not have been tolerated and they would have taken measures, such as creating their own little local inquisition, their little torture chamber, and their little charitable society for helping the poor of the parish. And the madman, clearly not a madman, would have had, in place of a portable cage, his nice straitjacket and his twenty-two sessions of elec- troshock therapy.]

The lesson of Pedro's meditations is all too clear. Society tolerates insane people much more readily than it does the sane who are guilty of subver- sive behavior. Indeed, in Cervantes' days the insane asylum was a fairly recent institution. Previously, the mentally ill were tolerated in society. For Martín-Santos, however, the issue is not unique to seventeenth- century Spain, since the word "electroshockterapia" extends the discur- sive field to modern times. As Foucault was to argue, the primary motive for creating insane asylums was not to cure the mentally ill but to control and discipline social nonconformity—that is, to curb any behavior that the disciplining society labels "public nuisance." Thus, madness is defined as much by sociopolitical ideology as by medical abnormality. The terms "sane" and "insane," in fact, are not common in modern medi- cal terminology. They have been appropriated by an inquisitional discourse devoted to order and obedience.

As Pedro's ruminations on Cervantes' legacy near their end, he decides that Don Miguel had no recourse but to base his farce on contra- dictions in order not to go insane himself. Insanity renders ethical behav- ior possible and serves as the ultimate threat for those who fail to act ethically. Or, to reverse the equation, the reward for ethical behavior is sanity, yet sanity impedes one from acting ethically. This paradox some- what resembles a "Strange Loop" in logic, as when on one side of a paper is written, "the statement on the other side is true," and on the reverse is written, "the statement on the other side is false" (qtd. in Hayles 1984, 34). Each statement cancels the other, and therefore the question of truth and falsehood is undecidable. The center of authority and truth, the sense of unity provided by belief in such a center, is shat- tered. Of course, if there is no center or if the traditional center proves to be a myth, there are no margins. This expression of what is popularly labeled "situational ethics" indicates that ethical behavior cannot be reduced to the binarisms good and bad, right and wrong, virtue and sin.

Human beings probably will always need to rely on opposites to determine moral conduct, but the definitions of those opposites are, or,
according to the novel, should be, dependent on context. The reference to
Cervantes and his masterpiece challenges the validity of fixed centers
and margins, of stability and unity, of absolute moral and ethical
authority.

In addition to making arbitrary the distinction between sane and
insane, prevailing practice draws an equally arbitrary separation between
the self and the other. In the opening laboratory scene, *Tiempo de
silencio* disputes the social myth of clearly differentiated selves. The
telephone rings and, as Amador answers it, that neatly binary division
also seems to break down:

> "No hay más." "Ya no hay más." ¡Se acabaron los ratones! El retrato del
> hombre de la barba, frente a mí, que lo vio todo y que libró al pueblo ibero de
> su inferioridad nativa ante la ciencia, escrutador e inmóvil, presidiendo la
> falta de cobayas. Su sonrisa comprensiva y liberadora de la inferioridad
> explica —comprende— la falta de créditos. (Martín-Santos 1987, 7)

> ["There are no more." "There aren't any more." The mice are gone! Facing
> me, the portrait of the bearded man who saw it all and who freed the Iberian
> people from their innate inferiority in science, scrutinizing and immobile as
> he presides over the lack of specimens. His comprehending and inferiority-
> liberating smile explains—comprehends—the lack of funding.]

The bearded man of the picture is Santiago Ramón y Cajal, who as of
1962 was the only Spanish scientist to have won the Nobel Prize. Under
the influence of Opus Dei, the regime incorporated him into its discursive
campaign by hanging his picture in virtually every science laboratory.
Apparently, the idea was to make him the "object of desire" for the new
scientific generation. Since Pedro is the narrator and focalizer of this
scene, it seems reasonable to assume that the telephone message concerning the lack of mice for the experiments triggers a mental bifurcation in
which he projects himself into the picture on the wall. Before the call, the
nature of Pedro's narration and his perspective on the events indicate that
he advocates a scientific approach to reality. The picture almost certainly
represents his ideal "other." After hearing the telephone message,
however, Pedro assumes the perspective of the photo on the wall and
views himself as a failed and alienated "other." In this scene, Pedro is
simultaneously the focalizing subject and the focalized object. As
focalizing subject, he is the ambitious young scientist who aspires to
become another Ramón y Cajal and win the Nobel Prize. As the
focalized object (that is, the Pedro under observation by his bifurcated

Ramón y Cajal self), he is subjected to the judgment of a sociopolitical system that encourages vainglorious dreams but refuses to provide the economic support to make the dreams even remotely possible. Rather than a unified self, the text posits two Pedros, one of whom views the other with condescending scorn in his futile attempts to achieve scientific glory. In effect, by referring to himself in the third person, he has negated his own being. As Benveniste has observed, "the 'third person' is not a 'person'; it is really the verbal form whose function is to express the *nonperson*" (Benveniste 1971, 198). The passage suggests, therefore, that Pedro-the-aspiring-Nobel-Prize-winner is not a person at all. He is a product of the regime's official discursive campaign to champion science and technology, which in turn is the product of what Lyotard has labeled Western society's scientific master discourse.

Whereas in the early part of the novel Pedro transforms himself into a nonperson by virtue of his third-person self-focalization, he begins to refer to himself in the second person as the events unfold. Benveniste explains that the first two persons are on a totally different plane from that of the third nonperson: "'I' and 'you' are reversible: the one whom 'I' defines by 'you' thinks of himself as 'I' and can be inverted into 'I,' and 'I' becomes a 'you'" (199). The novel offers an example of this reversible self-focalization as Pedro contemplates his fate in the jail cell where he has been confined. He was arrested for his role in the fatal miscarriage of Muecas's daughter, Florita. The police charged him with practicing medicine illegally when he responded to Muecas's pleas to help Florita, who, as noted, had died before Pedro arrived. The young medical student had just returned from a drunken Saturday night on the town when Muecas awakened him, and Pedro responds to the solicitation with entirely self-serving motives.

The incarcerated Pedro undergoes a crisis of identity while staring at a stain on the wall that he imagines to be a siren: "Desde aquí, tumbado, la sirena puede mirarme. Estás bien, estás bien. No te puede pasar nada porque tú no has hecho nada. . . . Está claro que tú no has hecho nada" [From here, if I lie down, the siren can look at me. You are fine, you are fine. Nothing can happen to you because you have not done anything. . . . It is clear that you have not done anything] (Martín-Santos 1987, 216). The object with which he identifies in this case is not an icon sponsored by the state but a spot on the wall that he anthropomorphizes into a young woman. That change is fundamental. The Ramón y Cajal photograph is a visual sign on the laboratory wall for an official ideological purpose; the stain on the jail wall that Pedro gradually transforms into the dead Florita's image suggests the power of human values that transcend governmental discursive policies. That transcendence helps explain the narrative switch from the third nonperson in the initial section of the novel to the second person in the middle.

Human values notwithstanding, the switch to the second person indicates Pedro's attempt to deny responsibility for his actions and motives. He soon discovers, however, that "you" and "I" are reversible, as Benveniste has explained: "Tú no la mataste. Estaba muerta. No estaba muerta. Tú la mataste. ¿Por qué dices tú? —Yo" [You didn't kill her. She was dead. She wasn't dead. You killed her. Why do you say you?—I]. The fusion of past and present, you and I, is in turn erased: "No pensar. No pensar. No pensar. . . . No pensar tanto" [Don't think. Don't think. Don't think. . . . Don't think so much] (217). The negatives along with the Spanish infinitives convey a denial of everything, a retreat into nonresponsibility, nonidentity, and nonbeing. But the spot on the wall refuses to disappear, and the anthropomorphism intensifies:

> va tomando forma semihumana y . . . acompaña porque llega un momento en que toma expresión, va llegando un momento en que toma forma y llega por fin un momento en que efectivamente mira y clava sobre ti —la sirena mal dibujada— sus grandes, húmedos ojos de muchacha y mira y parece que acompaña. (217–18)

> [it is taking on a semihuman form and . . . it stays by your side because the time comes when it takes on an expression, the time finally comes when it assumes a form and it looks and fixes on you—this poorly drawn siren—its large, teary child's eyes and it looks and it seems to stay by your side.]

Pedro's bifurcated self will not let him ignore the victim ("que acompaña") nor the circumstances: "¿Por qué tuviste que hacerlo borracho, completamente borracho?" [Why did you have to do it drunk, completely drunk?] (216). Finally, the struggle between accepting and denying guilt, between bifurcation and unification of self, culminates in a momentary, first-person acceptance of responsibility: "Tú no la mataste. Estaba muerta. Yo la maté. ¿Por qué? ¿Por qué? Tú no la mataste. Estaba muerta. Yo no la maté. Ya estaba muerta. Yo no fui" [You didn't kill her. She was dead. I killed her. Why? Why? You didn't kill her. She was dead. I didn't kill her. She was already dead. It wasn't I] (220). Not only is the fusion of self by means of the first-person verb form tentative, but the confession of guilt is misguided and finally denied. The only guilt Pedro seems to recognize is his intoxicated state when he operated on the poor young girl. But then, since she was already dead, his drunkenness is not an issue, and he is not guilty of anything. Never does his other self confront him with his motives. The sense of psychic unity ("Yo no fui") is false, and the section ends appropriately with the word "Imbécil" (221), an apparent self-indictment, though lacking any verbal markers to specify who is the speaking subject and who the indicted object.

At the end of the novel, Pedro has decided to transfer to a village and blend into the social order that now totally subjects him. Any hint of unity of self is destroyed by the emergence of a new voice with biblical overtones: "Podrás cazar perdices, podrás cazar perdices muy gordas cuando los sembrados estén ya . . . podrás jugar al ajedrez en el casino. . . . Estarás así un tiempo esperando en silencio, sin hablar mal de nadie" [You will be able to hunt partridges, very fat partridges when the fields are sown . . . you will be able to play chess in the casino. . . . You will spend a time waiting in silence, without speaking badly of anyone] (293). This reiteration of future imperatives echoes the biblical phrase "Thou shalt," which in turn underscores the cosmic implications of Pedro's moral decay. Rather than a true speaking and acting subject, he is the conduit for a discourse of which he is really the object. The imperatives suggest that Pedro must assume responsibility for allowing his socially imposed ambitions to transform him into a product of society. The novel implies that, in an emerging consumer society fueled by science and technology and controlled by a panoptic and paternal system, the individual must nevertheless find a means for making ethical choices.

If Pedro emerges as the tragic product of a scientific imperative that is willing to sacrifice morality for comfort and conformity, *Tiempo de silencio* offers one character who refuses to make that ethical compromise. She is Muecas's wife, Ricarda, a woman whose physical description connotes both a subhuman status and religious avocation (61). Since Ricarda witnessed Pedro's intervention in her daughter's miscarriage, she tells the police that the young man is innocent, and he thereby gains his freedom. As the narrator begins to penetrate Ricarda's consciousness, the grieving mother seems incapable of dealing with the sophisticated medical and legal nuances of the case:

No saber nada. No saber que la tierra es redonda. No saber que el sol está inmóvil, aunque parece que sube y baja. No saber que son tres Personas distintas. No saber lo que es la luz eléctrica. No saber por qué caen las piedras hacia la tierra. No saber leer la hora. No saber que el espermatozoide y el óvulo son dos células individuales que fusionan sus núcleos. No saber nada. No saber alternar con las personas, no saber decir: "Cuánto bueno por aquí", no saber decir: "Buenos días tenga usted, señor doctor". Y sin embargo, haberle dicho: "Usted hizo todo lo que pudo". (248)

[To be totally ignorant. To be ignorant of the roundness of the earth. To be ignorant of the sun's immobility, because it seems to rise and fall. To be ignorant of the three distinct persons of the verb. To be ignorant of what an

electric light is. To be ignorant of why rocks fall toward the earth. To be
ignorant of how to tell time. To be ignorant of the fusion of the nucleus of the
two individual cells named the sperm and the ovum. To be ignorant of everything. To be ignorant of how to interact socially with people, to be ignorant of
how to say: "How nice things are here," to be ignorant of how to say: "May
you have a nice day, Doctor." And yet, to have said: "You did everything you
could."]

The repetition of the words "no saber" reinforces the implicit protest
against the dehumanizing effect of making scientific and technological
knowledge the foundation of our modern worldview. Language
contributes to that effect as it obfuscates rather than expresses human
sentiments.

Ricarda represents a precivilized and almost presymbolic (or prelin-
guistic) stage of development. She does not understand scientific explanations of human life nor possess the linguistic sophistication for effec-
tive social interaction, but she somehow manages to say and do the right
thing: "'Él no fue'. No por amor a la verdad, ni por amor a la decencia, ni
porque pensara que al hablar así cumplía con su deber, . . . sin ser capaz
nunca de llegar a hablar propiamente, sino sólo a emitir gemidos y
algunas palabras aproximadamente interpretables" ["It wasn't him." Not
for love of the truth or decency, nor because she thought that by speaking
this way she fulfilled her duty, . . . without ever becoming capable of
speaking adequately, only able to emit groans and a few words that were
barely interpretable] (248–49). Ricarda negates science, logic, social
discipline, and paternal authority with her act of righting the wrong done
to Pedro. She even defies the laws of the symbolic order with her use of
words that are only "barely interpretable." But somehow her primitive
"Él no fue" is sufficient to negate the lies, political maneuvering,
bureaucratic red tape, and legal complexities of a civilized Western
society. How, then, do we explain this marginalized being's need to say
and do the right thing when, according to the narrator, she has no ethical
motive? Perhaps the relationship between ethics and marginality can be
explained by reference to the earlier section on *Don Quijote*, whose hero
can express his sense of ethics only by being "ex-céntrico." Martín-
Santos carries the Cervantine model one step further by offering a female
character who does not inhabit the margin by choice but because of the
pressures of society, yet who, like Don Quijote, expresses from the
margin a sense of ethics that those in the center seem incapable of
duplicating.

Pedro ardently aspires to reach that center. Although he is innocent of
the crime with which he is charged, he is guilty of offering his help in the

vainglorious hope of winning the Nobel Prize. In his ruminations on Cervantes, he addresses the problem of ethical behavior, and briefly in the jail cell he approaches recognition of his own moral responsibility. Finally, however, Pedro opts for the comfortable role of passivity, and he apparently will incur divine punishment. There is little evidence that his actions, in or out of the laboratory, are motivated by human compassion or moral awareness. As he reveals in the opening scene of the novel, he seems to serve as a register of irrational rationality and the dehumanization wrought by the modern nation-state. The juxtaposition of Pedro, the socially integrated character, with the socially marginalized Ricarda allows the focus to fall on their respective expressions of ethics. In his efforts to reach the center, Pedro becomes enslaved by unethical behavior, while the margin allows Ricarda the freedom to act ethically.

The strategy of presenting Muecas's wife, the pariah, as the moral heroine of the novel can also be seen as a challenge to logocentrism. The novel denies the possibility of reifying a code of ethics or of centralizing its area of operation. The definition and location of ethical codes lies somewhere between the signifier and the signified, in the silent zone where meaning must be created by context rather than by custom or decree. Standing in judgment on the choices made or avoided by each individual is the discursive practice labeled Christianity, which transcends the practices of the Franco regime, the Industrial Revolution, and the scientific episteme that comprehends Newton, Galileo, Ptolemy, and finally Plato and Aristotle. Thus, the intertextuality of *Tiempo de silencio* does not merely involve thematic, stylistic, and structural similarities between this novel and others, but it appropriates the very discursive practices from which texts emerge.

Franco's death thirteen years after publication of Martín-Santos's novel and the Spanish elections of 1977 can be seen as two key forces for change within a network of similar sociopolitical events in Eastern Europe and Latin America. The move away from political centrality and totalitarianism that the intertextual complexities of *Tiempo de silencio* adumbrate is later expressed in the Spanish elections and ultimately in the changes in dictatorial regimes all over the globe. But the interconnections do not stop there. The global breakdown of geopolitical centers and the shift to ethnic margins have correlations in the physical and social sciences as well as the arts. Each of these centrifugal movements belongs to a larger web of allusive interrelationships. Like the textual strategies of *Tiempo de silencio*, each forms part of a nonlinear discursive field in which speaking subjects are also subjects of other speakers, in which hegemony cedes to heterogeneity, and in which power, paternalism, and the panopticon become one. Martín-Santos's experiments with nonlinear relationships convert intertextual reverberations into multitextual polyvalence by creating horizontal as well as vertical hierarchies that extend beyond geographical, cultural, and temporal divisions. *Tiempo de silencio* thus ushers into the Spain of 1962 a discursive field whose borders extend at least to our world today.

Notes

1. In addition to Herzberger's article and book, see Pope (1987–88). These studies, along with Jones's (1985), provide more detailed discussions of the term "neorealism" (sometimes called "social realism") and identify the principal novels assigned to that category. The standard overviews of the novel of this period are by Sobejano (1970) and Soldevila Durante (1980). My own *La novela española de posguerra* (Spires 1978) offers analytical studies of some of the key novels of the postwar period.

2. Fernando Morán (1971) was perhaps the first critic to point out some of the limitations of this extreme adherence to mimetic representation.

3. Opus Dei was founded by the priest José María Escrivá de Balaguer in 1928. Escrivá, who like Franco died in 1975, was selected for beatification by Pope John Paul II on 17 May 1992. During the Spanish Civil War, the Opus Dei founder supported Franco and the Nationalists. Although Escrivá and his followers were religious conservatives opposed to the reforms of Vatican II, they qualify as fiscal liberals by virtue of their commitment to scientific and technological innovation as a means of making Spain competitive in the international marketplace.

4. There are several bibliographical sources for studies of *Tiempo de silencio;* the titles of the articles and books in most cases serve as accurate indexes of their approach. See, for example, the essays and Gorrochategui's bibliography in the special issue of *Cuadernos Universitarios* (1990). Compitello (1989) and Sherzer (1989) offer additional critical references, as do Dolgin (1991), Jerez-Farrán (1988), and Knickerbocker (1994).

5. For Pérez Firmat (1981), Martín-Santos's novel is built around verbal excess. In that respect, *Tiempo de silencio* differs from Rafael Sánchez Ferlosio's *El Jarama,* Jesús Fernández Santos's *Los bravos* [*The Brave*], Ignacio Aldecoa's *El fulgor y la sangre* [*Splendor and Blood*], and Juan García Hortelano's *Nuevas amistades* [*New Friendships*], four prototypical neorealist works in which the narrator's basic function is that of a recording camera rather than a speaking voice.

6. All translations are my own.

7. Michel Foucault discusses the importance of the atomic bomb in transforming discursive practices. He argues that the bomb marked a change from the "universal" intellectual (the writer) to the "specific" intellectual or scientist (he cites Robert Oppenheimer as the prime example) and that, with the development of the bomb, "for the first time the intellectual was hounded by political powers, no longer on account of a general discourse which he conducted, but because of the knowledge at his disposal: it was at this level that he constituted a political threat" (Foucault 1980, 128).

8. For more on this concept, see Campbell (1982), Hayles (1984, 1990), and Paulson (1988).

9. Stephen Hart, in his analysis of the novel, coins the neologism "phallocracy" to describe the Francoist political regime (Hart 1992, 46), a term that applies not only to postwar Spain but perhaps to modern political systems in general.

Works Cited

Althusser, Louis. 1971. "Ideology and Ideological State Apparatuses (Notes towards an Investigation)." In *Lenin and Philosophy and Other Essays*. Trans. Ben Brewster, 123–73. London: NLB.

Benveniste, Émile. 1971. *Problems in General Linguistics*. Trans. Mary Elizabeth Meek. Coral Gables: University of Miami Press.

Booth, Wayne C. 1961. *The Rhetoric of Fiction*. Chicago: University of Chicago Press.

Campbell, Jeremy. 1982. *Grammatical Man: Information, Entropy, Language, and Life*. New York: Simon and Schuster.

Cano Ballesta, Juan. 1981. *Literatura y tecnología (las letras españolas ante la revolución industrial 1900–1933)*. Madrid: Orígenes.

Compitello, Malcolm. 1989. "Luis Martín-Santos: A Bibliography." *Letras Peninsulares* 2: 249–69.

Dolgin, Stacy. 1991. "*Tiempo de silencio*: desmitificación de la psique española." In *La novela desmitificadora española (1961–1982)*, 71–95. Barcelona: Anthropos.

Foucault, Michel. 1972. *The Archaeology of Knowledge and the Discourse on Language*. Trans. A. M. Sheridan Smith. New York: Pantheon.

———. 1977. *Discipline and Punish: The Birth of the Prison*. Trans. Alan Sheridan. London: Penguin.

———. 1980. *Power/Knowledge: Selected Interviews and Other Writings 1972–1977*. Trans. Colin Gordon et al. New York: Pantheon.

Gorrochategui Gorrochategui, Pedro. 1990. "Una bibliografía global: Luis Martín-Santos." *Cuadernos Universitarios* 8: 195–234.

Hart, Stephen M. 1992. *The Other Scene: Psychoanalytic Readings in Modern Spanish and Latin-American Literature*. Boulder: SSSAS.

Hayles, N. Katherine. 1984. *The Cosmic Web: Scientific Field Models and Literary Strategies in the Twentieth Century*. Ithaca, N.Y.: Cornell University Press.

———. 1990. *Chaos Bound: Orderly Disorder in Contemporary Literature and Science*. Ithaca, N.Y.: Cornell University Press.

Herzberger, David K. 1991. "Narrating the Past: History and the Novel of Memory in Postwar Spain." *PMLA* 106: 34–45.

———. 1995. *Narrating the Past: Fiction and Historiography in Postwar Spain*. Durham, N.C.: Duke University Press.

James, Henry. 1914. *Notes on Novelists with Some Other Notes*. New York: Scribners.

Jameson, Fredric. 1991. *Postmodernism, or, The Cultural Logic of Late Capitalism*. Durham, N.C.: Duke University Press.

Jerez-Farrán, Carlos. 1988. "'Ansiedad de influencia' versus intertextualidad autoconsciente en *Tiempo de silencio* de Martín-Santos." *Symposium* 41: 119–32.

Jones, Margaret E. W. 1985. *The Contemporary Spanish Novel, 1939–1975*. Boston: Twayne.

Knickerbocker, Dale F. 1994. "*Tiempo de silencio* and the Narration of the Abject." *Anales de la Literatura Española Contemporánea* 19: 11–31.

Lubbock, Percy. 1957. *The Craft of Fiction*. London: Viking Press.

Lyotard, Jean-François. 1989. *The Postmodern Condition: A Report on Knowledge*. Trans. Geoff Bennington and Brian Massumi. Minneapolis: University of Minnesota Press.

Martín-Santos, Luis. 1987. *Tiempo de silencio*. 27th ed. Barcelona: Seix Barral.

Morán, Fernando. 1971. *Explicación de una limitación: la novela realista de los años cincuenta en España*. Madrid: Taurus.

Paulson, William R. 1988. *The Noise of Culture: Literary Texts in a World of Information*. Ithaca, N.Y.: Cornell University Press.

Pérez Firmat, Gustavo. 1981. "Repetition and Excess in *Tiempo de silencio*." *PMLA* 96: 194–209.

Pope, Randolph. 1987–88. "Historia y novela en la posguerra española." *Siglo XX/Twentieth Century* 5: 16–24.

Sherzer, William. 1989. "An Appraisal of Recent Criticism on *Tiempo de silencio*." *Letras Peninsulares* 2: 233–47.

Sobejano, Gonzalo. 1970. *Novela española de nuestro tiempo*. Madrid: Prensa Española.

Soldevila Durante, Ignacio. 1980. *La novela desde 1936*. Madrid: Alhambra.

Spires, Robert C. 1978. *La novela española de posguerra: creación artística y experiencia personal*. Madrid: CUPSA.

Nested Intertexts in Galdós's *Gerona*

DIANE F. UREY

Benito Pérez Galdós's First Series of *Episodios nacionales* consists of ten historical novels written between 1873 and 1875. They challenge readers to confront the complex interaction of their perceiving selves with the literary, historical, and material worlds they perceive. The novels comprise the fictional autobiography of the young orphan Gabriel Araceli, who writes his life and his history of Spain between 1805 and 1813, and they constitute a self-conscious exposition of their own textual practice. Through the device of an ancient narrator looking back on himself after nearly seventy years, the series foregrounds the act of writing and suggests the vast range of interpretations that the reader of his or her own life, inside or outside the text, may compose. Like all of Galdós's novels, the *Episodios* acknowledge the constant interplay of many texts, codes, and values in discourse. The interchange among different systems of signs throughout the series undermines conventional hierarchies of writer and text, truth and illusion, fiction and history.

Gabriel recounts his experiences from the Battle of Trafalgar through Spain's War of Independence against Napoleon. His chief objective is to attain an honorable, socially viable identity that will make him worthy of the noble Inés. His endeavor recalls that of Spain's first picaresque hero of the eponymous *Lazarillo de Tormes*. Instead of pointing to Lazarillo as his precursor, however, Gabriel first names Lazarillo's most parodic successor, Don Pablos of Quevedo's *Buscón*. In the opening lines of *Trafalgar* (1873), Gabriel writes: "Doy principio . . . a mi historia como Pablos, el buscón de Segovia; afortunadamente, Dios ha querido que en esto sólo nos parezcamos" [I begin . . . my story like Pablos, the scavenger rogue from Segovia; fortunately, God has willed that this be the only similarity between us] (Pérez Galdós 1979, 181).[1] Galdós's choice of the protagonist of the *Buscón* over Lazarillo as the chief external point of comparison for Gabriel suggests how other intertextual relationships might be viewed in the First Series: they are always more complicated and ambiguous than they initially appear and often conceal parody and satire within presumably straightforward representations. The *Buscón* is filled with difficult, baroque word play and is a vehement satire on society. With that allusion at its opening, *Trafalgar* alerts the reader to its own language games and to the critique of society they conceal. Through the mediation of the *Buscón*, *Trafalgar* calls up the text that Quevedo imitates and parodies, the *Lazarillo*, and with it the other prior texts, against which that anonymous novel was written. The first in the receding succession of texts nested within Galdós's *Episodios nacionales* can never be identified, since the reader is in fact confronted with an ever-expanding series of intertextual allusions.

Julia Kristeva offers one of the earliest definitions of intertextuality when she writes of "an insight first introduced into literary theory by Bakhtin: any text is constructed as a mosaic of quotations; any text is the absorption and transformation of another. The notion of 'intertextuality' replaces that of intersubjectivity" (Kristeva 1986, 37).[2] She later refines the term as the "transposition of one (or several) sign-system(s) into another." Further, "if one grants that every signifying practice is a field of transpositions of various signifying systems (an intertextuality) . . . its 'place' of enunciation and its denoted 'object' are never single, complete, and identical to themselves, but always plural, shattered" (111). The *Episodios* include named external works—specific "extratexts"—in addition to extratextual resonances and echoes. They contain internal stories within stories and interpolated tales, or "intratexts," and a mosaic of phrases and single words that resonate overtly or obliquely through the many different sign systems comprising the narratives. Intertextuality invites analysis from many points of view: cultural, linguistic, historical, cognitive, and political, as well as from the literary perspective that is the focus here. Galdós's First Series functions like a kaleidoscope, an oscillating spectrum of other texts transforming themselves before the reader's eyes. Individual words always suggest more than a literal or immediate meaning; they migrate through the different stories and discourses of Galdós's novels like chameleons in constant metamorphosis. The prismatic intertextuality of the *Episodios* broadens the reading experience and foregrounds the novels' metafictional artistry and their variegated critique of society and individual conduct.

Gabriel is much like the first-person autobiographer of the *Lazarillo* who attempts to persuade "Vuestra merced" [Your Mercy], the unknown recipient of his memoirs, of his personal honor. The aim of each protagonist is to create a socially acceptable persona, as Ricardo Gullón has demonstrated. Gabriel portrays himself as deserving the high social and military positions he eventually obtains. Yet, while depicting his meritorious behavior, Gabriel often undermines his credibility by revealing either his self-interested motives (see Bly 1984) or by exposing the games of social fiction he plays to achieve his ends. Gabriel's narrative appears transparent and naive, but it is, like the picaresque novel, profoundly deceptive. One of the main functions of the *Episodios'* evocation of the picaresque is to underline the self-contradiction of autobiography.

The autobiographical mode of the First Series places in relief the linguistic, temporal, and interpretive conventions by which readers customarily approach historical novels. In autobiography, whether fictional or not, the textual referent is always the self being written. This inescapable paradox subverts the genre's pretense that there is a distinct, real subject behind or beneath the words of the text. Both Gabriels, the writing self and the written self, the old narrator and the young character, are within the text. The artful projection of self and past in the *Episodios* takes on character in the act of being written and sustains the illusion of a subject moving through time, alive. Yet the coincidence of apparently opposing temporal and perceptual modes and fields prohibits the terms or poles in each opposition from being original or authoritative. Consequently, there are no authentic or definitive times or perspectives in the texts, no reliable representations. The impossibility of autobiography, which Cervantes' picaresque character Ginés de Pasamonte affirmed almost three centuries before in *Don Quijote*, suggests the vanity of pursuing historical truth. *Don Quijote*, with its interplay of authors, historians, narrators, and translators, constantly reiterates this point. It would seem, therefore, that the labels "fictional autobiography" and "historical novel" are tautological and empty, as are the fundamental premises of any representative endeavor.

Gabriel's fictional autobiography inscribes and reinscribes its readers and its writer, just as the historical novel creates and contains the past it pursues outside of discourse. Gabriel's role as historian coincides with his literary self-creation. One of the lengthiest and most openly metafictional articulations of his dual function occurs at the beginning of *Gerona* (1874), the seventh *Episodio* of the First Series. As the only novel not narrated from Gabriel's own experiences, *Gerona* occupies a unique position in the series, for it places the primary narrator, Gabriel, another step away from the historical events he portrays. The novel seems to create a hiatus in the serial development of Gabriel's self-narrated character, yet the usurping narrator of the siege of Gerona, Andrés Marijuán, serves as a foil to and critique of Gabriel. The autobiography therefore continues to develop by proxy. The illusory separation between primary and secondary narrators, the mark that distinguishes *Gerona* from the other nine *Episodios*, constitutes an intriguing and multitiered reinscription of the "hybrid genre" of the *Episodios nacionales*.[3]

The nesting of texts in *Gerona*'s opening pages foreshadows the interior design of the novel and announces its overt self-consciousness about truth in writing. Like the other novels of the First Series, *Gerona* recalls texts written earlier and anticipates many written later in the nineteenth and early twentieth centuries, including Galdós's own last three series of *Episodios nacionales* (1898–1912). Galdós rewrites, writes within, and writes in advance of texts published before and after the 1870s. He weaves works from different epochs and languages into the fabric of the First Series—Spanish masterpieces, Ovid, Homer, Shakespeare, Rousseau. A self-consciously Cervantine pseudoautobiography, *Gerona* is told by a starving participant in the siege, and it is rewritten, with the aid of a madman's diary, by an octogenarian intent on reliving his youth. Andrés Marijuán is Gabriel's companion and fellow picaro from a previous *Episodio, Bailén*. He recounts his experiences in Gerona to Gabriel after the two meet at an inn near Bailén. Their units, now in defeat, retrace the course of their earlier journey to the first European victory over Napoleon. Gabriel is torn between his desire to continue the story of *Cádiz* and his reunion with Inés, and his "patriotic duty" to relate Andrés's tale. He concludes that his love story, the central fictional plot of the series, must give way to Andrés's account of the "maravillosas hazañas" [extraordinary feats] of Gerona.

The use of phrases like "maravillosas hazañas" or "nunca vista defensa" [astonishing defense] (Pérez Galdós 1979, 784), the circumstance of old friends meeting at the inn, the self-conscious delay of the main action, the presence of interpolated stories, and the quixotic nature of the characters all indicate that the Cervantine voice pervades *Gerona*. Gabriel's trick of suspending his narration while another story is told recalls the first part of *Don Quijote*. In chapter 8 of Cervantes' novel, the action stops with the swords of Don Quijote and his challenger poised for battle, while the "segundo autor" [second author], or narrator, laments that the "autor," who now becomes a character, claims to have come to the end of the manuscript he possesses. In chapter 9, the second author retraces his steps to the discovery of the missing manuscript, which is written in Arabic. After finding someone to translate it into Castilian, the second author can finally proceed with the true history of Don Quijote's adventures.[4] The First Series's shift in chronological course and logical discourse is suspenseful not only for Gabriel, who is eager to reach Cádiz, but for the reader, who must wait the length of an entire novel for further news of the romance. The ensuing discussion of why and how Andrés's story is told serves the function of a prologue in the novel.

Gabriel's prologue-like introduction to *Gerona*, his "fore word," is another feature of this novel that is unique among the volumes of the First Series. It raises a number of questions concerning literary conventions, writing about writing, authorship, and historical truth. Like Cervantes' playful dialogue about reading and writing in general and prologues in particular in the prologue to *Don Quijote* (Cervantes 1971, 1:19–25), *Gerona*'s prologue provides its readers with insights into how to read the *Episodios*. Gabriel Araceli's apology for altering Marijuán's style, like Cervantes' for his inability to write a prologue, is another sign of *Gerona*'s metafictional stance. The apology exemplifies what Derrida has shown to be primary functions of the preface or prologue: a desire to control how the book is read, a narcissistic absorption of the body of the text into the prologue, much like the absorption of the son into the father. The preface and book are already within each other, indistinctly (Derrida 1981, esp. 44–49). In this way does Gabriel attempt to appropriate and control Marijuán's history. His justification for revising the text may revise the reader's impressions of Gabriel as a narrator, and so might Marijuán's discourse. Since the autobiographical self exists only as it is written, the gap between Gabriel's and Andrés's texts, like that between prologue and book, is illusory. Each ostensibly separate section of *Gerona* encompasses and is part of the other. Gabriel's remarks cannot be set off from Andrés's story like a picture frame or a book cover, themselves debatable distinctions. *Gerona*, in its turn, reinscribes the other *Episodios* while being inscribed within the sequence of the First Series.

Despite his resolution to tell Andrés's story, Gabriel pauses to visit the now abandoned Rumblar palace near the army encampment. In the familiar mansion, Gabriel seeks some sign of his beloved Inés, María de Rumblar's niece. His thoughts about Inés's physical absence, set against her presence in his memory, exemplify how he imagines his past as present before his eyes, a process described in detail at the beginning of the First Series.[5] His nocturnal musings contain a critique of historical discourse in general, of the *Episodios*, and of the narrators and readers who try to recapture the past through words:

> [U]na dulce, inexplicable claridad llenaba mi alma durante aquella muda y solitaria exploración. No hubo mueble que no me dijese alguna cosa, y mi imaginación iba poblando de seres conocidos las desiertas salas. La alfombra conservaba a mis ojos una huella indefinible, más bien pensada que vista; . . . y en los espejos creí ver, no la huella ni la sombra, porque estas voces no son

propias, sino una nada; mejor dicho, un vacío dejado allí por la imagen que había desaparecido. (Pérez Galdós 1979, 756)

[A sweet, inexplicable clarity filled my soul during that silent and solitary exploration. There was not a single piece of furniture that did not say something to me, and my imagination populated the deserted salons with people I knew. The carpet seemed to me to retain an indefinable imprint, more imagined than seen; . . . and in the mirrors I thought I saw not an impression or a shadow, because these terms do not quite fit, but a void; to put it more clearly, an emptiness left there by an image that had disappeared.]

The past is perceived in the same way that objects speak. The mind populates the void—here the dark and silent room—with figures, sounds, and meanings. Gabriel's efforts to find the right words to describe the indescribable—his sense of a trace of the presence of an absent image and of events that time has left behind—underline the impossibility of representing the past or of recreating life. Yet, for Gabriel, "[e]l silencio de aquel lugar no me parecía el silencio propio de los lugares donde no hay nadie, sino aquel que se produce en los intervalos elocuentes de un diálogo cuando, hecha la pregunta, el interlocutor medita lo que va a responder" [the silence of that place did not seem like the kind one finds in deserted places but rather the kind that is produced during the eloquent lulls in a dialogue when, the question having been asked, the interlocutor thinks about how to respond] (756). Silence speaks more eloquently than words, since words cannot express the inexpressible. The interplay of silence and words in the scene has a substantive analogy in Marijuán's account of the besieged Gerona. Not only is the past gone but so is the food that sustains the lives of the people. They lose the ability to use language before insanity, death, or the city's eventual surrender puts them out of their misery. Marijuán's portrayal of the interchange between silence and food demythifies Gabriel's own demythification of historical discourse and goes a step farther than Gabriel in exposing the "lack of substance" behind words.

Gabriel begins the game of narratorial one-upsmanship with Marijuán when he seeks to establish his authority as the master narrator and historian. Yet he frequently subverts his self-aggrandizing efforts. He condescendingly explains that he has revised and corrected Andresillo's uncultured language for inclusion in his own history, maintaining that only in this way is he able to retell it. For convention's sake, Gabriel makes the narrative uniform, a stylistic alteration he mentions again at the conclusion to Marijuán's "leyenda," or legend, as he dubs it (833). His defense of the changes he makes unmasks the bias that "uniformity of style" produces clarity, since clarity is not the same as truth.

Besides emphasizing the artificiality of that approach to style, the passage characterizes both Gabriel and Marijuán. Gabriel is more educated than Marijuán, and more rhetorically versed. His use of the diminutive, Andresillo, reinforces the hierarchy he would establish between them. However, Gabriel modifies not only Marijuán's unschooled discourse but his own, telling the reader not to be surprised to find

> en las páginas que siguen observaciones, frases y palabras impropias de un muchacho sencillo y rústico. Tampoco yo me hubiera expresado así en aquellos tiempos; pero téngase presente que, en la época en que hablo, cuento algo más de ochenta años, vida suficiente, a mi juicio, para aprender alguna cosa, adquiriendo asimismo un poco de lustre en el modo de decir. (757)

> [in the pages that follow remarks, sentences, and words that would not be appropriate for a simple and rustic young man to use. I would not have expressed myself in this way at that time either; but keep in mind that, as I now speak, I am more than eighty years old, a sufficiently long life, in my opinion, to learn a thing or two, acquiring in the process a bit of polish in my manner of speaking.]

This is the sole instance in the First Series where Gabriel comments on the difference between his present writing style and his former mode of expression. While readers will never hear Marijuán's story in the original, neither will they observe Gabriel's real life or Spain at the turn of the century. The original is already rewritten, in accordance with the sometimes covert, yet inevitable nested design of the First Series. Gabriel's words insinuate further that, as he refines and edits Marijuán's youthful language and his own, he may revise his history and his autobiography to give his life a bit more polish too.

Gabriel places Gerona in the larger and ostensibly more significant (con)text of Spain. He writes that, by the winter of 1809–10, Spain's formidable enemy surrounded and besieged the country. The events of the period are like a one-act epic satire in which petty intriguers and insignificant "generales pigmeos" [pygmy generals] vie for position and control. [6] Only the *pueblo*, retaining "cierta inocencia salvaje" [a certain savage innocence]—a phrase of oxymoronic irony—keeps the national sentiment alive. Thus, "España, hambrienta, desnuda y comida de pulgas, podía continuar la lucha" [Spain, hungry, naked, and flea bitten, could continue the struggle] (Pérez Galdós 1979, 753–54).

Gabriel's words are an even more accurate description of Gerona, the city-at-siege, than of Spain, and especially of the Geronese children. By defining the part, Gerona, in terms of the whole, Spain, Gabriel attempts to delimit and contain—surround—Andrés's text. His efforts to minimize

the uniqueness and importance of protracted combat and thus the power
of Marijuán's discourse fail in significant ways. Since all texts are intertexts and therefore open-ended, Gabriel's cannot delimit either Marijuán's or his own writing. In addition, the contents or "denoted 'object'"
(Kristeva 1986, 111) of Marijuán's story powerfully overshadow
Gabriel's remarks about Spain. Gabriel may claim the whole story of
Spain's war and misery, but Marijuán's narration of the brutal siege and
blockade and the ravages of hunger are anything but trivial. They constitute Galdós's most vivid condemnation of war in the First Series and
arguably in all of the forty-six *Episodios nacionales*.

Andrés demonstrates his defiance with a self-assured humility that
thwarts Gabriel's superior attitude. He believes he may be the only
soldier in Spain who does not hope to become a general. Gabriel, in
contrast, self-mockingly reveals in the last lines of the series that after the
war he has continued to rise in rank to that of general because of his
powerful mother-in-law. He becomes one of those pygmy generals he
portrays so disdainfully. Moreover, the petty intriguers vying for command fittingly describe Gabriel, as he vies for, but does not necessarily
achieve, the dominant narratorial position. Gabriel further incriminates
himself in another way. When referring to the conspirators that take over
Sevilla in the absence of the Junta Central, he says: "a este y a otros
hoyos de nuestra historia les echaría tierra, mucha tierra" [I would bury
this and other pockmarks on our history very deeply] (Pérez Galdós
1979, 757). Even if he could censor or, better yet, eat his words, fame has
already made them public. He compounds his false logic when he says
that the conspirators have left no visible mark on history: "Su pequeñez
les hace desaparecer en las perspectivas de lo pasado, y sus nombres sin
eco no despiertan admiración ni encono" [Their insignificance makes
them disappear from view, and their names, without echo, elicit neither
admiration nor rancor] (757). The statement is a critique of writing
history, of the relation of historical discourse to the past, and of the
historian's choice of subject matter. Gabriel's commentary questions the
integrity and motives of the historian who, like him, claims he would
bury, swallow, or hide part of Spain's past. His decision to write about it
is another example of his rivalry with other "historians." What Gabriel or
any historian chooses to include or exclude from the text, and what
Gabriel or any reader believes he or she knows of the past from history
books, may or may not name the people or portray the events of that
time. The names of the petty and the infamous leave not a trace, but so it
may be with the honorable, too, and with whole peoples and nations.
History is not objective or ethical about what it records, and one never
knows the entire story.

Gabriel's prefatory philosophizing seems almost ludicrous compared to Andrés's depiction of an anguished city, blockaded and besieged to the point of physical, moral, and linguistic starvation. During the third French siege of Gerona, more than forty thousand French troops struggled from May through December of 1809 against fewer than six thousand starving Spaniards. Having killed twenty thousand French soldiers, the citizens of Gerona only capitulated when their leader, General Mariano Álvarez de Castro, fell gravely ill. This siege, considered by most Spaniards to be the noblest in Gerona's history, was only the fourth of the twenty-five attempted that would eventually result in the city's capture. The other successful conquests were by Charlemagne in 785, the Moors in 795, and the French in 1694. During the War of Independence, Gerona had held off the first two French attacks before finally succumbing to the third. The inner resources—selves, texts—that the soldiers and citizens of Gerona call upon to sustain their impossible defense are founded on a complete lack of sustenance, signified expressly by the absence of food. And with their increasing hunger comes their progressive inability to speak. The correlation between Gerona's hunger and the lack of food is like the relation of Galdós's historical novel to the past or like Gabriel's search for Inés's image in the mirror. The people of Gerona, history, and Gabriel are all sustained by an emptiness left by the trace of an image that has disappeared.

Gabriel sets his prologue to *Gerona* in the middle of the War of Independence (1810) and after Gerona surrenders. Andrés's account, along with its many interpolated tales, focuses on the latter part of the siege. Beginning in medias res is a common trait of classical depictions of the siege and fall of Troy, like those of Homer, Aeschylus, Euripides, Virgil, and others, all of which begin near the end of the ten-year Trojan War and narrate by repeated retrocession. Similarly, Cervantes initiates his historical drama *El cerco de Numancia* [*The Siege of Numancia*] near the end of sixty-two years of Roman war against the Celtiberian city. These extratextual subtexts, along with *Gerona*'s diverse intratexts, are woven into the fabric of the novel and expose its metafictional strategies. They underline ways in which lives and realities are created in language, and they reinforce the *Episodio*'s dominant themes: the waste of war, the nature of heroism, the savage within, hunger, and death.

The idea that Gabriel rather cynically introduces in the prologue—that even the most heroic individuals and celebrated events fade into insignificance and oblivion over time—is carried throughout *Gerona*. The theme is likewise central to the *Iliad*, a text that resonates eloquently in the novel even though it is not named. Bernard Knox writes of Homer's somber view of war:

[A]ll the human struggles, the death of heroes, the fall of cities, are only of
passing interest, to be forgotten as they are replaced by similar events played
out by different actors. Troy will fall now, but so someday will the cities of
its conquerors. And the great wars that brought glory and death to the heroes
will not even be allowed to leave a mark on the landscape. (Knox 1990, 37–
38)

The *Iliad* opens with the deaths of many valiant warriors, "their bodies
carrion, / feasts for the dogs and birds" (Homer 1990, 1.4–5). It ends with
Hector's death and Achilles' brutal treatment of his body, the funerals of
Patroclus and Hector, and Achilles' prophesied death (bks. 23 and 24).
For Homer, war is patently a "criminal and barbarous waste of lives and
energy" (Michalopoulos 1966, 137). The death knell tolls ceaselessly in
Gerona as well.

Marijuán's shocking account begins with the funeral of his friend
Mongat, the father of Siseta and her three brothers, Badoret, Manalet,
and Gasparó. Mongat died from wounds received in the second French
offensive against Gerona, and his funeral marks the initiation of the third
and final siege. After the funeral, Marijuán vows to marry Siseta and
"adopt" her young brothers. The brothers become storytellers in the
novel too, but their first statement requires no words. The orphans turn
their eyes to Siseta with an eloquent question. Andrés, understanding that
mute interrogation, asks Siseta if there is anything left to eat in the house,
and there is not (Pérez Galdós 1979, 759). The central characters' lives
together begin with a funeral and the ever-present threat of death, if not
from war, then from hunger. Marijuán's narration ends with the death of
more than ten thousand citizens and soldiers in Gerona and with the impending assassination of General Álvarez at the hands of the treacherous
French.

An impression of tragic, wanton destruction permeates *Gerona*. In the
epilogue, another untitled and apparently separate narrative fragment
designed to control and contain Marijuán's discourse, Gabriel expounds
on Marijuán's harrowing tale. He writes of the extent of the humiliations
and crimes that Napoleon's forces committed against the remaining
citizens and soldiers of Gerona and of their gross breaches of the terms of
surrender. The magnitude of the French atrocities is incomprehensible to
the incredulous Spanish victims, to Andrés, to Gabriel, and to the aston-
ished and dumbfounded historian who has no words to describe them
(834). Knox writes of the "sense of waste" at the conclusion to the *Iliad*,
"which is not adequately balanced even by the greatness of the heroic
figures and the action" (Knox 1990, 63). In both *Gerona* and the *Iliad,*
ephemeral glory and valor recede before the degradation and ultimate
futility of war.

In contrast to Gabriel's words in the epilogue, his prefatory abstractions seem more certain of their sufficiency for their object and, in retrospect, quite shallow. Before the event, he can summarize the treacherous rivalry between factions in Sevilla as "lo más denigrante que he visto en mi vida" [the most contemptible event I have seen in my life] (Pérez Galdós 1979, 757). For him there is no emotion more violent than the one that causes him to hate his countryman more ferociously than the foreign invader. Gabriel has not yet heard of Andrés's immensely more appalling experiences in Gerona. There, hunger, not politics, the absence of substance, not the excess of words, demeans the actions of some to a level far below that of the "reptiles" in Sevilla, who savagely invade their neighbors' homes. A few people, like Andrés's neighbor, the learned physician Pablo Nomdedéu, turn into animals, the patriotic cause virtually forgotten in their primitive struggle for survival. The characters not only eat cats, rats, and even more filthy and loathsome creatures that Andrés refuses to name (811), they nearly eat each other. Moreover, they literally as well as figuratively eat words.[7] The most bitter war portrayed in *Gerona* is waged between human beings and the beasts that may be hidden within them. Each person carries another self within, another text, nested inside an outer, civilized frame. These texts can complement or violently contradict each other.

As the people of Gerona begin to starve, Andrés observes that, while dying in battle may be noble, even pleasant, dying of starvation is far more horrifying. Although during combat "la vista del compañero anima; en el hambre, el semejante estorba . . . se aborrece al prójimo porque la salvación, . . . sea pedazo de pan, debe repartirse entre muchos" [the sight of a companion lifts the spirits; but with hunger, another person is an obstacle . . . one hates one's neighbor because salvation, . . . even if it is a piece of bread, must be shared among many] (784).

The starving, wretched, and desperate soldiers may be called selflessly heroic, but this is an empty phrase since conditions have destroyed all remnants of the familiar human or humane self. Andrés, like the other soldiers, continues to fight on Gerona's walls, now a mere specter of a man:

> Estaba ciego y no veía nada ni a nadie. Mi cuerpo desfallecido apenas podía sostenerse. . . . [H]ice fuego, me batí con desesperación contra los franceses . . . , gritaba como los demás y me movía como los demás. Era la rueda de una máquina. . . . Lo mismo era para mí morir que vivir. Este es el heroísmo. (807)

> [I was blind and could not see anything or anyone. My enfeebled body could hardly hold itself up. . . . I fired, I fought desperately against the French . . . , I

yelled like everyone else, and I moved like everyone else. I was the wheel of
a machine. . . . It was all the same to me if I died or lived. This is heroism.]

Heroism, brutality, hunger, and death are also central to Cervantes'
Numancia. The final siege of Numancia that ended in 133 B.C. is the
most celebrated in Spanish history. It symbolizes for Spaniards their
fierce independence, honor, and courage. Cervantes' version of the
legend echoes with silent power through *Gerona*. Numancia's struggle
finally ends because the Romans blockade the town, letting hunger win
the war (Casalduero 1966, 277). Escipión, or Scipio, admits this is the
only way to triumph over a population that has already defeated two
Roman generals (Cervantes 1970, act 1, ll. 321–24). Similarly, after the
entire city rallies to Gerona's defense on 19 September 1809, the cowardly French opt to let hunger do their work: "conocían la imposibilidad
de abrir las puertas de Gerona por la fuerza de las armas, y se detuvieron
en su línea de bloqueo con intención de matarnos de hambre" [they knew
it was impossible to open the gates of Gerona by force, so they formed a
blockade with the intention of killing us by starvation] (Pérez Galdós
1979, 784).

Neither Numancia's leader nor Gerona's will surrender his city,
believing that death is preferable. When Numancia's Teógenes asks his
people to burn the city, they ultimately agree. As the fire consumes
everything of personal and general value, the men kill their families and
then themselves. Álvarez perseveres in his command that Gerona will not
admit defeat while he is alive, even though the population is rapidly
succumbing to a disease spreading as quickly as starvation. The city does
surrender, however, when Álvarez is too overcome with fever and delirium to control those who must take command. Although the thousand
remaining soldiers and most of the citizens remain loyal to Álvarez and
refuse to consider capitulation, a clamoring minority, among them
Nomdedéu, have their way. Yet, in order to go to the French encampment to sign the pact, the negotiators must disguise their true motives for
leaving the city from the armed phantoms who continue to patrol its
walls. The Numantines, for their part, follow Teógenes to their death,
with only one brief exception. When Scipio enters Numancia, a frightened boy remains; he too upholds the city's honor, however, by jumping
from a tower to his death rather than becoming the Romans' only prize.

History's veneration of Numancia is augmented by Cervantes' self-
reflexive prediction of it. Teógenes says:

> Sólo se ha de mirar que el enemigo
> no alcance de nosotros triunfo o gloria;

antes ha de servir él de testigo
que apruebe y eternice nuestra historia;
   y si todos venís en lo que digo,
mil siglos durará nuestra memoria,
y es que no quede cosa aquí en Numancia
de do el contrario pueda hacer ganancia.
                                   —Cervantes 1970, act 3, ll. 1418–25

[We only need to make sure that the enemy does not gain any victory or glory from us; rather he must serve as a witness that proves and eternalizes our history; and if you all do what I say, the memory of us will last a thousand centuries, and let it be that in Numancia there remain nothing that can be of value to the enemy.]

Cervantes and Galdós recognize the authority of discourse in creating the history of people and events. It determines whether and how they are remembered. Just as Teógenes and the Numantines declare that they are the true victors of the siege, so do the heroes of Gerona. Such claims of victory in defeat devalue the outcomes and thus the causes of war, and both texts finally ask whether the sacrifices it demands, however admirable, are worth the cost in human life.[8]

The major difference between *Numancia* and *Gerona* is the starving citizens' attitude towards one another. Cervantes' characters, although terrified too, are for the most part altruistic, sharing what little food they have. The men kill their families to save them from becoming Roman slaves. In contrast, Nomdedéu—and at least a few other characters in *Gerona*, one surmises—displays almost inconceivable extremes of selfishness and savagery. Álvarez, unlike Teógenes, seems heedless of the suffering of his men. He gives the second line of defense orders to shoot anyone in the first line who tries to retreat (Pérez Galdós 1979, 774, 807). The soldiers are more fearful of him than of the entire French army, yet they proudly emulate his fervent patriotism and bravery in battle, even when he is no longer in command.

Álvarez's apparent lack of human kindness suggests Achilles and the Homeric text more than Cervantes' Teógenes. Achilles will not allow his troops to rest, eat, or drink, so intent is he on killing Hector. When Odysseus pleads with him to let the men rest and eat before returning to battle, Achilles ends his furious reply with these words: "You talk of food? / I have no taste for food—what I really crave / is slaughter and blood and the choking groans of men!" (Homer 1990, 19:253–55). Achilles' ire moves him to consider cannibalism. When Hector asks for an honorable burial rather than having his corpse eaten by animals,

Achilles answers: "Beg no more, you fawning dog . . . ! / Would to god
my rage, my fury would drive me now / to hack your flesh away and eat
you raw" (22:407–9). Álvarez's anger with Nomdedéu's pleading for an
end to the siege earns him the reply: *"Veo que sólo usted es aquí
cobarde. Bien: cuando ya no haya víveres, nos comeremos a usted y a
los de su ralea"* [*I see that you are the only coward here. So, when there
is no food left, we will eat you and the others of your ilk*] (Pérez Galdós
1979, 790), a ruthless yet fitting response to one who threatens to eat
Siseta (796, 816–18). Achilles is virtually inhuman, a war machine; at
times, Álvarez's resemblance to him is remarkable.

The Trojan chief Hector, while a more sympathetic figure than
Achilles, is as single-minded as the other leaders. Álvarez evokes Hector
too, chiefly through his relentless patriotism.[9] Gabriel, echoing voices in
Gerona, considers Álvarez to be the century's most patriotic Spaniard.
When one of Hector's men, Polydamas, having seen a bad omen, persists
in arguing that they retreat from the impending battle, Hector responds in
words that anticipate Álvarez's to Nomdedéu or to any soldier who
would flee the line of defense:

> . . . Enough, Polydamas!
> Your pleading repels me now—
> you must have something better than this to say.
> . . .
>
> Fight for your country—that is the best, the only omen!
> You, why are you so afraid of war and slaughter?
> Even if all the rest of us drop and die around you,
> grappling for the ships, you'd run no risk of death:
> you lack the heart to last it out in combat—coward!
> But if you hold back from the bloody foray here
> or turn some other soldier back from battle,
> . . .
>
> at one quick stroke my spear will beat you down,
> you'll breathe your last!
> —Homer 1990, 12:267–69, 281–89

Carried to such extremes, the unyielding patriotism of Hector and the
ruthless courage of Achilles are murderous and as potentially suicidal as
Teógenes' straightforward directive to Numancia. Álvarez is a mosaic of
his famous predecessors. When the Geronese express pride in their
astonishing defense of the city on 19 September, Álvarez tells them that
their feat surpassed those of antiquity's most heroic figures. Yet Nomde-

déu, in a moment of clarity, observes that, while the day was glorious, it exacted a tremendous toll (Pérez Galdós 1979, 777).

Neither Cervantes nor Homer nor Galdós spares the reader the gruesome facts of war. In spite of *La Numancia*'s idealization of the collective suicide, it graphically depicts the physical and psychological torments of hunger, fear, and death. Of the *Iliad* Knox writes:

> There is no attempt to gloss over the harsh realities of the work of killing . . . and no attempt, either, to sentimentalize the pain and degradation of violent death. Men die in the *Iliad* in agony; they drop, screaming, to their knees, reaching out to beloved companions, gasping . . . , clawing . . . ; they die roaring . . . , bellowing, . . . moaning. (Knox 1990, 26)

Gerona details the mass slaughter of Spanish soldiers and the rampant death from starvation and fever throughout the city. Soldiers climb mindlessly over the bodies of their dead or dying companions. Terrified young children, like the toddler Gasparó, witness scenes of heinous brutality and ghastly deaths. Some formerly civilized adults display a feral, egotistical savagery on a par with that of Achilles in his cruelest fury. Nomdedéu mercilessly attempts to murder Andrés for scraps of food. He takes on the behavior and appearance of the lowly animals he hunts. His face contorts inhumanly; he ceases to speak; his only sounds are like the muffled snarls of his prey. Nomdedéu's loss of human speech marks his transformation into an inarticulate beast, the emergence of his inner, other, darker text. He seems cognizant of his change, but like Achilles, he is not remorseful. He later tells Andrés almost nonchalantly that in such circumstances man is not master of himself because the "pícaro instinto de conservación hace que el hombre se convierta en fierecita" [tricky instinct for survival makes a man turn into a little hellcat] (Pérez Galdós 1979, 790). Unlike almost all of the Numantines who consider the common good, Nomdedéu thinks only of himself. No picaro, not even Quevedo's Don Pablos, approaches his level of degradation.

After Gerona's surrender, Marijuán searches for Siseta, whose brothers have hidden her, fearing that Nomdedéu would eat her as he threatened. Andrés walks through the streets strewn with the dead in various stages of decomposition and with thousands more sick and dying. As Montesinos realized, Galdós hated this war (Montesinos 1968, 102); Dendle writes that even heroism "becomes suspect" in Galdós's world (Dendle 1986, 135). In its aversion to war and its suspicion of heroes, *Gerona* echoes other literary accounts of the Trojan War besides Homer's. Aeschylus's *Agamemnon*, for instance, is specifically mentioned in Galdós's novel. The Greek tragedy portrays war as complete disaster, without glory, and exposes the egotistical motives of many of its champions. Euripides' *Trojan Women* describes the misery of the inhabitants of Troy and the malevolence of its conquerors. Book 2 of Virgil's *Aeneid* also relates the horrors of the fall of Troy. Its narrator, Aeneas, affects reluctance to recall such tragic events, but he agrees to do so for his audience's sake (Virgil 1975, 2:1–13). This feigned disinclination to relate painful memories is a topos that characterizes Gabriel's self-conscious posture throughout the First Series. Carroll Johnson cites a number of other parallels between the *Aeneid* and *La Numancia*, all of which transfer to *Gerona*, just as *Trafalgar* summons the *Lazarillo* and a multitude of other texts through the mediation of the *Buscón*. Like that extratextual series of associations at the beginning of the first *Episodio*, this exchange of signs among the *Aeneid*, *La Numancia*, and *Gerona* reveals the metafictional strategies of Galdós's novel and restates its major themes.

In similar fashion, *Gerona*'s intratextual relationships underline its metafictionality and reiterate its principal arguments. The stories told by others to Marijuán create the illusion of a comprehensive vision of events. They fill the inevitable gaps in Marijuán's eye-witness history. Particularly important are Badoret's and Manalet's accounts of street scenes, the armies of rats, and Nomdedéu's treatment of Siseta and Gasparó. They are indeed innocent savages. The children's stories of their experiences make Gabriel's statement in the prologue about the Spanish *pueblo* seem banal (Pérez Galdós 1979, 574). The narratives of Manalet and Badoret bear the same relationship to Andrés's story that Andrés's does to Gabriel's. Their texts often subtly demythify Andrés's version, much as Marijuán's interpolated tale—the siege of Gerona—sometimes discredits Gabriel's narration of Spain's War of Independence.

Of all the narrators in *Gerona*, the most noteworthy storyteller is Nomdedéu. Andrés's first conversation with him and Nomdedéu's dying confession bracket the main action that Andrés narrates and are further metadiscursive commentaries on story- and history-telling. The name Nomdedéu suggests a creator figure (Tsuchiya 1990, 127), and the character's roles as prolific writer and indefatigable conversationalist enhance this image. The benevolence implied by the "Name of God" is absent from his character, however. Even after Nomdedéu's death, Andrés refers to him with the epithet "el buen médico" [the good doctor], and the effect is quite different from that of the Cid's epithet, "el que en buena hora nació" [he that was born under a favorable sign], or of Don Quijote's "el de la triste figura" [he of the sad countenance]. While the latter designations are, in their own ways, complimentary and representative, the former becomes increasingly ironic. At one point, after the most ferocious battle between them in the novel, Andrés refers to Nomdedéu as "ese espejo de los médicos" [that model of all physicians] (Pérez Galdós 1979, 810). The insistence on Nomdedéu's "goodness" provokes revulsion in the reader, who has witnessed Nomdedéu's physical and psychological transformation.

The analogies between the intrepid teller of tales, Don Quijote, and Nomdedéu, who might as well be a Doctor of Conversation, are ubiquitous in Andrés's portrayal of him. Andrés always derives from Nomdedéu "alguna enseñanza provechosa" [some helpful bit of wisdom] (760), much as Sancho does from his master. His physical appearance, living arrangements, book collection, apparent insanity, and dying confession superficially parallel *Don Quijote*'s characterization and plot, but his inner self, his hidden text, is quite unlike that of Cervantes' knight: it is egotistical, debased, and murderous. Even as he expires, Nomdedéu, in a long-winded death scene, evades the truth about what he attempted to do to Siseta and selfishly asks his daughter to die with him.

The first conversation between the two neighbors provides insight into how Andrés views his own narration and those of others. The history he recounts to Nomdedéu during this scene emphasizes the importance of intratextual as well as extratextual nesting to the structure of the novel and to the creation of narrative indeterminacy. Andrés tells Nomdedéu what he has heard about a French batallion's night in a Catalan village. The soldiers demanded provisions of pork for the next morning, so the mayor ordered the villagers to slaughter their hogs ("porchs") at midnight. The people understood the mayor's covert meaning—the derisive "swine" alluded to the French—and each killed his sleeping French guest. The mayor's play on words indicates that different sign systems can intersect at any point in the novel, including at a single word. Each term is an intertext and cannot be taken to refer univocally either to a represented reality or to its own discourse. Nomdedéu and Andrés speculate on whether the story is true, and Marijuán replies: "Séalo o no . . . , con estos y otros cuentos se anima la gente" [Whether it is or not . . . , these and other stories lift people's spirits] (761). The purpose of the first interpolated story in Andrés's history is to give pleasure and encouragement; its truthfulness is not relevant. In Andrés's eyes at least, this is the chief aim of narrative. The anecdote of the "porchs" comments on the possibility of truth in history, on the interpretive process, on the endless series of narrative voices revising other voices in the novel, on the effects of stories or histories on their readers and on themselves as polyvalent signifying practices. The tale emphasizes further the equivocal correspondence between words and things and the uncertainties, often dangers, of interpreting discourse at face value. This first story, then, nested within Andrés's narration within Gabriel's history and told to a Cervantine listener by a picaresque narrator, underlines once again how histories are created and interpreted and reinscribes the process and content of the novel.

Nomdedéu is the author of several different types of discourse or scripture, among them notes, letters, and diaries. From the beginning, it is clear that he is no stranger to fiction. He holds written conversations with the deaf and invalid Josefina: "La escritura servía a hija y padre de medio de comunicación" [Writing served as the means of communication between father and daughter] (761). To calm her, he replies to her anxious inquiries about the war with lies about imminent peace and present plenty in the city. When his own written words do not have the desired effect on Josefina, he places in her hands the words of Cervantes, "la primera parte del *Quijote*, el cual abrió ella por donde lo tenía marcado, comenzando a leer tranquilamente" [the first part of the *Quijote*, which she opened where she had it marked, calmly beginning to read] (762). She obviously prefers a fiction that acknowledges its own game to one that insists on being taken for truth.

In a more structured format, Nomdedéu composes letters to Josefina every night. This epistolary account of events in Gerona is idealized and optimistic, the opposite of the personal diary he keeps. His *diario* is a purportedly accurate and thus quite pessimistic record, which he bequeaths to Marijuán on his deathbed. Marijuán gives it to Gabriel as a wedding present, and Gabriel uses it as a powerful aid when writing this part of his history of the War of Independence. He incorporates Nomdedéu's written account along with his uniformly styled revisions of Andrés's narration into his own historical autobiography. The veracity of Nomdedéu's diary is questionable, however, given his perverse psychology and his skill at lying. Andrés's account is already suspect, as has been shown, since he believes that the purpose of any story is to inspire, regardless of its truth. Gabriel's history is dependent on the words of Andrés and Nomdedéu and includes his own self-serving tamperings with the truth. This series of stories written from stories within other stories whose narrators' interest in truth is at best ambivalent could well be no more than the ravings of an "egotistical madman" (Rodríguez 1967, 65).

Nomdedéu's fallacious letters to Josefina function no differently from his bleakly objective diary, or from Marijuán's story to Gabriel, or Gabriel's revised and uniformly styled history, or Galdós's *Gerona*, or even from official histories of the siege. They all have equal value and serve the same purpose as long as their readers believe they represent truth. The overlapping narratives and the interpolated stories in *Gerona* foreground the ineluctability of intertextuality as well as its equivocating nature. Even the conclusion to the *Episodio* reiterates this disorienting principle. In the epilogue, Gabriel, Marijuán, and the other soldiers who have heard Marijuán's tale speculate on how the French murdered Álvarez. Each one has a different version, but no version represents the truth.

Through its fabric of extra- and intratextual discourses, *Gerona*'s grim story reverberates in the lives and the literature before and after 1874. Perhaps more than any of its literary predecessors, *Gerona* offers a unilateral condemnation of war, and its harrowing vision is the more ghastly for its ceaselessly duplicitous intertextual resonances. All the words of *Gerona* are potentially lies, like Nomdedéu's letters to Josefina. Truth is elusive, as with Andrés's story of the "porchs" or the versions of Álvarez's death, and the beginning of a chain of intertextual connections can never be found: *Trafalgar* refers to the *Buscón*, which evokes the *Lazarillo*, which rewrites other texts, and so on. The origin of all the memoirs, letters, tales, and histories within the *Episodios*, and of the intertextual allusions outside of them, is like the trace of an image that only might have been reflected in a mirror long ago. However celebrated, all battles come to the same dead end. Their victors and vanquished, the brave and the cowardly, eventually disappear from memory. Only by chance will they leave a mark of what might have been on a page of a history book that may eventually be eaten by rats.

Galdós's *Episodio* illustrates that its truth and its origin are impossible to define and that the point is moot anyway as long as the reader is entertained or instructed. The value of the text lies in its effect on the reader, or so says Andrés, who can receive worthy advice even from a vicious madman. Since each reader is a text as well, no two readings could be the same. Yet, whether called fiction or history, truth or delusion, *Gerona* offers its readers lessons in how to read themselves and others. Its inevitable and interminable intertextuality makes the reader's search for meanings, genres, sources, narrative voices, and authors just one more signifying practice, one more system of signs, woven into the discursive texture of *Gerona*.

Notes

1. All translations are mine.

2. Kristeva's first remarks on intertextuality were published in *Sēmeiōtikē* in 1969 and translated as *Desire and Language* in 1980 (Moi 1986, 34). Her early work on Bakhtin

was the basis for her later development of intertextuality in her 1974 doctoral thesis, translated ten years later as *Revolution in Poetic Language* (89).

3. Gilman uses this phrase in his comments on the *Episodios* (Gilman 1981, 55). See Urey (1989, 6–11) on classifying the *Episodios* as fiction or history.

4. See Ruth El Saffar's brilliant study of these chapters and of the effect of *Don Quijote*'s multitiered narration on the novel's readers (El Saffar 1975, 38–44, 114–39).

5. I discuss this passage in a forthcoming volume on the First Series, *Galdós and the New Reader.*

6. Triviños dedicates a book to detailing why the First Series is not an epic. According to his definition, an epic must present war in positive terms, as he claims the *Iliad* does (Triviños 1987, 110). His lengthiest discussion of *Gerona*, which he considers the least epic of the first *Episodios*, is on pp. 120–48.

7. The symbolism of the rats has been discussed by critics like Ribas (1974), Triviños (1987), and Ullman (1993). The house of the Canónigo, who is the foremost antiquarian in upper Cataluña, according to Andrés, is devastated by rats, starving children, and bombs, a clear image of war's destruction of civilization. Rare manuscripts, irreplaceable works of art, ancient artifacts, and precious religious relics are lost. What is not eaten or otherwise ruined is irretrievably scattered: "materia caótica de la Historia, que ningún sabio podía ya reunir ni ordenar" [the chaotic stuff of history, which not even the most learned scholar could gather up or put in order now] (Pérez Galdós 1979, 796–97).

8. Considerable critical debate exists over whether these works exalt or condemn war. See Alberti (1979), Dendle (1986), and Schraibman (1976) on *Gerona*; Avalle-Arce (1962), Edwards (1981), Johnson (1981), Stroud (1981), and Whitby (1962) on *La Numancia*.

9. The reader sees at the end of Marijuán's narration that, like Hector, Álvarez is fiercely patriotic yet also compassionate. As Álvarez and his men, now prisoners of war, march toward France, his only concern is for them even though the French continually torture him while he suffers a potentially fatal fever.

Works Cited

Alberti, Rafael. 1979. "Un episodio nacional: *Gerona.*" In *Benito Pérez Galdós.* Ed. Douglass M. Rogers. 2nd ed. El Escritor y la Crítica, 367–78. Madrid: Taurus.

Avalle-Arce, Juan Bautista. 1962. "Poesía, historia, imperialismo: *La Numancia.*" *Anuario de Letras* (Mexico) 2: 55–75.

Bly, Peter A. 1984. "For Self or Country? Conflicting Lessons in the First Series of the *Episodios nacionales.*" *Kentucky Romance Quarterly* 31: 117–24.

Casalduero, Joaquín. 1966. *Sentido y forma del teatro de Cervantes.* Madrid: Gredos.

Cervantes Saavedra, Miguel de. 1970. *El cerco de la Numancia.* In *Obras completas.* Ed. Ángel Valbuena Prat, 169–206. 16th ed. Madrid: Aguilar.

———. 1971. *Don Quijote de la Mancha.* Ed. Martín de Riquer. 2 vols. Barcelona: Editorial Juventud.

Dendle, Brian J. 1986. *Galdós: The Early Historical Novels.* Columbia: University of Missouri Press.

Derrida, Jacques. 1981. "Outwork, Hors d'oeuvre, Extratext, Foreplay, Bookend, Facing, Prefacing." In *Dissemination*. Trans. Barbara Johnson, 1–59. Chicago: University of Chicago Press.

Edwards, Gwynne. 1981. "La estructura de *Numancia* y el desarrollo de su ambiente trágico." In *Cervantes: su obra y su mundo. Actas del I Congreso Internacional sobre Cervantes*, 293–301. Madrid: EDI-6.

El Saffar, Ruth. 1975. *Distance and Control in "Don Quixote": A Study in Narrative Technique*. North Carolina Studies in the Romance Languages and Literatures, no. 147. Chapel Hill: University of North Carolina.

Gilman, Stephen. 1981. *Galdós and the Art of the European Novel: 1867–1887*. Princeton: Princeton University Press.

Gullón, Ricardo. 1979. "'Los Episodios': la primera serie." In *Benito Pérez Galdós*. Ed. Douglass M. Rogers. 2nd ed. El Escritor y la Crítica, 403–26. Madrid: Taurus.

Homer. 1990. *The Iliad*. Ed. Bernard Knox. Trans. Robert Fagles. New York: Penguin.

Johnson, Carroll B. 1981. "*La Numancia* y la estructura de la ambigüedad cervantina." In *Cervantes: su obra y su mundo. Actas del I Congreso Internacional sobre Cervantes*, 309–16. Madrid: EDI-6.

Knox, Bernard. 1990. Introduction to *The Iliad*, by Homer. Ed. Bernard Knox. Trans. Robert Fagles. New York: Penguin.

Kristeva, Julia. 1986. *The Kristeva Reader*. Ed. Toril Moi. New York: Columbia University Press.

Michalopoulos, Andre. 1966. *Homer*. New York: Twayne.

Moi, Toril. 1986. Introduction and editorial comments to *The Kristeva Reader*, by Julia Kristeva. Ed. Toril Moi, 1–22. New York: Columbia University Press.

Montesinos, José F. 1968. *Galdós*. Vol. 1. Madrid: Castalia.

Pérez Galdós, Benito. 1979. *Episodios nacionales*. Ed. Federico Carlos Sainz de Robles. 4th repr. Vol. 1. Madrid: Aguilar.

Ribas, José A. 1974. "El episodio nacional *Gerona*, visto por un gerundense." *Anales Galdosianos* 9: 151–65.

Rodríguez, Alfred. 1967. *An Introduction to the "Episodios Nacionales" of Galdós*. New York: Las Américas.

Schraibman, José. 1976. "Espacio histórico/espacio literario en *Gerona*." *The American Hispanist* 2.12: 4–7.

Stroud, Matthew D. 1981. "*La Numancia* como auto secular." In *Cervantes: su obra y su mundo. Actas del I Congreso Internacional sobre Cervantes*, 303–7. Madrid: EDI-6.

Triviños, Gilberto. 1987. *Benito Pérez Galdós en la jaula de la epopeya*. Barcelona: Ediciones del Mall.

Tsuchiya, Akiko. 1990. *Images of the Sign: Semiotic Consciousness in the Novels of Benito Pérez Galdós*. Columbia: University of Missouri Press.

Ullman, Pierre L. 1993. "Las ratas de *Gerona* y la polisemia quinaria." In *A Sesquicentennial Tribute to Galdós 1843–1993*. Ed. Linda M. Willem, 222–33. Newark, Del.: Juan de la Cuesta.

Urey, Diane F. 1989. *The Novel Histories of Galdós*. Princeton: Princeton University Press.

———. Forthcoming. *Galdós and the New Reader*. Durham, N.C.: Duke University Press.

Virgil. 1975. *The Aeneid: An Epic Poem of Rome.* Trans. L. R. Lind. Bloomington: Indiana University Press.

Whitby, William. 1962. "The Sacrifice Theme in Cervantes' 'Numancia.'" *Hispania* 45: 205–10.

The Female Body under Surveillance: Galdós's *La desheredada*

AKIKO TSUCHIYA

Critical dialogue on the body in the past decade has led to a reevaluation and questioning of the traditional notion of the body as an ahistorical, biological given. Literary and cultural critics are defining the body as a social and discursive construct, bound up with systems of "representation, cultural production, and socioeconomic exchange" (Grosz 1994, 19). Claiming that "deployments of power are directly connected to the body," Michel Foucault theorizes the ways in which the body has been produced in the service of power relations in Western culture (Foucault 1980, 151).[1] According to Foucault, the rise of bourgeois capitalism and industrialization in Europe at the turn of the nineteenth century was accompanied by a proliferation of social institutions and measures that made it possible to keep the body and sexuality under surveillance (126).

In Spain, the Restoration period represented the culmination of a disciplinary society that had been in the process of formation since the late eighteenth century. It was during this time that the number of jails, penitentiaries, and insane asylums multiplied significantly, civil registers were expanded, and an increasing number of legislative measures were passed to put a tighter control on vagrancy and other forms of social disorder (Trinidad Fernández 1982, 166–67). These institutionalized expedients for social control led to a more panoptic society in which bodies subjected to the omniscient Eye of power automatically became reduced to "cogs of a machine" (Foucault 1979, 169).

Although Foucault does not engage directly with issues of gender and its relationship to power, feminist theorists have taken his analysis of body politics in nineteenth-century Europe as a point of departure for exposing the ways in which masculinist structures, institutions, and discourses have rendered the *female* body the most frequent target of disciplinary practices.[2] The "hysterization" of the female body, through which the woman's body came to be seen as inherently pathological and biologically determined, served the purpose of safeguarding the family institution and of controlling populations (Foucault 1980, 146–47; Martin 1988, 10–11). Such a notion of the female body as it was represented in medical, scientific, and legal discourses functioned to control women's access to the public sphere and to rationalize their exclusion from it.[3] Alicia Andreu, Bridget Aldaraca, and Catherine Jagoe, among others, have examined the ways in which a wide range of cultural discourses of nineteenth-century Spain—from conduct literature to medical texts—served to revise, to circumscribe, and to control general perceptions of the female body.[4] The dissemination of the Victorian image of the desexualized "Angel of the House" in conduct manuals, the pathologizing of female desire in medical/psychiatric texts, and the regulation of prostitution through registers and health inspections are all manifestations of the highly biased nature of gender politics in nineteenth-century Spain.

Bodies are central to the novels of Benito Pérez Galdós, which explore the relationship between social institutions, cultural production, and literary representation by establishing a link between corporeality and textuality. Galdós's fiction often sets the deviant female body against the disciplinary forces of a society interested in "organizing and policing deviance" (Brooks 1984, 158–61): numerous female bodies are the targets of institutions, measures, and practices that seek to guarantee their docility. The bodies of such female characters as Fortunata, Mauricia la Dura, Rosalía de Bringas, Tristana, Ándara, Isidora Rufete, and others are subjected not only to physical and psychological enclosure within specific institutions but also to a "permanent, exhaustive, omnipresent surveillance," which ensures the automatic functioning of power (Foucault 1979, 214).

The male gaze, which typically "projects its fantasy onto the female figure" and turns it into a spectacle (Mulvey 1989, 19), can be seen as but one manifestation of the generalized panoptic gaze of the bourgeois patriarchal culture as a whole. Many of Galdós's female characters, who believe themselves to be struggling against society's "faceless gaze," are in fact resisting the Eye of power that is bound up with bourgeois male hegemony. Prostitution, dismemberment, disease, or death are fates that the male Galdosian narrator often reserves for these women. Isidora Rufete, the protagonist of *La desheredada*, is exemplary in this regard: in her struggle to mobilize resistance to power, her body becomes a contested site where discourses of desire and discipline vie for control.

In presenting Isidora's journey down the path to poverty and degradation, the narrator rarely turns away from a view of her body, whether to observe that it is beautifully adorned or that it is physically debased through disease, violence, and prostitution. If the novel documents the female protagonist's struggle to transcend poverty through her imagination, the narrator, bound by classist and patriarchal values, condemns such an aspiration as a dangerous fantasy kindled by the uncritical consumption of popular literature. As Jagoe has noted, the exercise of the imagination to escape reality, especially by a woman, is seen as an unforgivable sin that violates the "rules of nature" (Jagoe 1993, 237). What happens in the novel is yet another example of the way patriarchal societies have justified the oppression of women as the natural order of things "by connecting women more closely than men to the body" (Grosz 1994, 14). This "coding of femininity with corporeality" (ibid.) is evident in the narrator's repeated attempts to tie and to reduce the female protagonist to her body by interpreting her fantasies as manifestations of a physiological/neurological disorder. Her "neuralgias de cabeza" [neuralgia of the brain], her "segunda vida encajada en la vida fisiológica" [second life encased in physiological life], her "gran excitación cerebral" [great cerebral agitation], her "nervios" [nerves] are, for him, "Violación de los órdenes de la Naturaleza" [Violation of the laws of Nature] (Pérez Galdós 1980, 59, 258, 259; all translations are my own). The identification of the female body with disorder and disease is clear.

While Galdós's novels abound in male characters whose quixotism is the object of sympathy and even of romantic exaltation (Maxi Rubín, Alejandro Miquis, Nazarín, Pepe Rey, the Count of Albrit, to name some of the more obvious ones), the female protagonist of *La desheredada* is relentlessly punished for her uncontrolled imagination (Jagoe 1993, 238–40). Not unlike the narrator of Leopoldo Alas's *La Regenta*, the narrator of *La desheredada* is a voyeur who tries to force the reader to participate in the spectacle of Isidora's progressive degeneration (in society's eyes) from delusional hysteric to criminal to prostitute. Her moral downfall, as the narrator sees it, is a by-product of her alienation from her body. Throughout the novel, he is highly critical of her obsession with her image, that is, of her desire to produce simulacra of social, economic, and, by extension, moral value that do not correspond to the "true" value of her body. If we accept the lesson of the narrator's story, the cult of appearances is a symptom of the desire to be what one really is not and should never aspire to be, both socially and economically. It is apparent that women are especially prone to such (dis)simulation or *cursilería*, above all in the adornment of their bodies. This attitude becomes evident as the narrator follows Isidora and Miquis on their walk through Madrid's business district. As he calls attention to Isidora's "deseo oculto de mirarse en los cristales" [hidden desire to look at herself in the shop windows], he adds: "es costumbre de las mujeres, y aun en los hombres, echarse una ojeada en las vitrinas, para ver si van tan bien como suponen o pretenden" [it is a habit of women, and even of men, to glance at themselves in the showcases to see if they really look as good as they think they do] (Pérez Galdós 1980, 62).

The epitome of Isidora's delusion, according to the narrator, is her belief in the fiction of her noble birth, generated by her reading of popular novels.[5] It is significant that she looks closely at her mirror image immediately before visiting the marchioness's palace in hopes of being recognized as her disinherited granddaughter. The image that Isidora has created for herself as the marchioness's granddaughter and that she takes to be superior to that of other common beauties seems so authentic (that is, reflective of her true class origin) that even the marchioness, at one point, discerns nobility and honor in her physiognomy (Fernández Cifuentes 1988, 301). Yet the narrator once again negates the image as a sign of value by exposing Isidora's delusion: the external signs of beauty fail to correspond to the truth of moral character, in the same way that her adornments fail to correspond to her real class origin. When she is rejected by the Marquesa de Aransis, Isidora tries to recuperate the value of the sign by seeing in her own reflection in the shop windows a truly noble body luxuriously adorned.

In a society caught in a process of political and cultural transformation, however, the question of what is real and what is a simulacrum becomes difficult to answer with certainty.[6] Isidora's nonrecognition by the Marquesa de Aransis is the first blow to her fantasy of upward social mobility, and it coincides, significantly, with King Amadeo's abdication and the declaration of the Republic. After she leaves the marchioness's palace, Isidora steps out into the streets and joins a turbulent crowd outfitted for the upcoming Carnival celebration. Amidst the masks and disguises of the Carnival, an occasion when the transgression of social order and hierarchies is permitted, the people of Madrid hail the new Republic, in which class distinctions are to disappear and everybody is purportedly equal. As Isidora's body becomes one of many in the multitude, her identity is cast into doubt not only because she is no longer what she thought she was but because the very notion of a representational system capable of positing a stable identity has been questioned.[7] Baudrillard has shown that, in capitalist societies, representation itself is a simulacrum, so that any attempt to separate the true from the false, the real from the artificial, turns meaningless. It is a society in which fallen aristocrats and the petty bourgeois alike engage in conspicuous consumption to disguise their lack of economic and symbolic capital.[8] Even the Republic, rather than truly representing the principles of democracy and equality, is no more than a meaningless concept, an empty sign to fill the void left by the failure of the *ancien régime*. In the narrator's words, quite simply, "La República entraba para cubrir la vacante del Trono" [The Republic entered to fill the void left by the Throne] (Pérez Galdós 1980, 231).

At the same time, according to Baudrillard, "When the real is no longer what it used to be, nostalgia assumes its full meaning. There is a proliferation of myths of origin and signs of reality; of second-hand truth, objectivity and authenticity" (Baudrillard 1988, 171).[9] This nostalgia is precisely what Isidora is experiencing. At the end of part 1, when her fiction (representation) and hence her identity have been divested of meaning, her desire to recuperate the myth of her noble origin is redoubled: "Antes morir que abandonar sus sagrados derechos. '¡Las leyes!—pensó—. ¿Para qué son las leyes?' ... Sí; ella confundiría el necio orgullo de su abuela; ella subiría por sus propias fuerzas, con la espada de la ley en la mano, a las alturas que le pertenecían" [She would rather die than abandon her sacred rights. "Laws!" she thought. "What are laws for?" ... Yes; she would confound her grandmother's foolish pride; she would rise by her own strength, with the sword of the law in her hand, to the heights that belonged to her] (Pérez Galdós 1980, 231). At this point, rather than returning home a failure to live with her useless godfather José Relimpio, Isidora finds her lover, Joaquín Pez, and escapes with him into the crowd. What seems to be Isidora's moral suicide from society's point of view is really a calculated attempt to recover her value as a woman with agency over her body and her destiny. She runs away with Joaquín not as a gesture of defeat after having suffered the loss of her illusions but as an opportunity to renew her fantasies of a romantic and comfortable life with the man of her dreams. She exchanges her body for this fantasy, yet she believes that she is doing so for the sake of honorable love. In a previous encounter, Isidora has rejected Joaquín's sexual advances, inspired by feelings of pride, honor, and dignity. Needless to say, Isidora remains willfully ignorant of the dissipated and shallow character concealed behind her lover's flashy and seductive exterior. The pursuit of appearances, and of what is elusive, is the essence of the romance that she has written for herself.

When Isidora disappears into the crowd at the end of part 1, the narrator loses sight of and control over her. Elizabeth Wilson, in her fascinating study of the relationship between urban life, the control of disorder, and women, shows how the crowd since the nineteenth century "was increasingly invested with female characteristics," particularly with disruptive sexuality and prostitution. As an example, Wilson refers to another theorist of the crowd, Gustave Le Bon, who evokes the image of a devouring female monster, the Sphinx at the center of the city, as a metaphor for the disruption that characterized nineteenth-century urban life. Women have become an "irruption in the city" that threatens the bourgeois patriarchal order (Wilson 1991, 7–9). In *La desheredada*, the female protagonist turns into just such a disrupting Sphinx who evades the control of the narrator and the disciplinary hand of a series of other masculine figures. Significantly, the narrative thread breaks off precisely at the moment when Isidora melts into the crowd. Moreover, Isidora's rebellion coincides with a moment of social and political upheaval. The narrator explicitly links this political chaos with female disorder by equating the moral outrage over Juan Prim's assassination, "la página más deshonrosa de la historia contemporánea" [the most dishonorable page of contemporary history] (Pérez Galdós 1980, 233), with the act that will bring dishonor to the protagonist.[10]

When the narrative resumes two years later in the second part of the novel, Isidora has literally given birth to a monster, a macrocephalic child whom his father, Joaquín, refuses to recognize. For her friend Augusto Miquis, who is the voice of bourgeois (masculine) reason and discipline, the biological monster is a product of (feminine) moral depravity.[11] As the discord and disturbances in the protagonist's life increase, the child Riquín's deformed head takes on monstrous proportions. Isidora is the antithesis of the "ángel del hogar": neither submissive nor selfless nor asexual, she represents a threat to the bourgeois ideal of female virtue and domesticity.[12] As a poor, single woman with a child born out of wedlock, she has neither a husband nor a father who can support her in bourgeois decency. By opting for a life that evades bourgeois discipline, she scandalizes society, much in the same way that her brother Mariano's delinquency incites society's anger rather than its pity. The unruly household that Isidora sets up in the Calle de la Hortaleza is antithetical to the narrator's image of the "verdadero hogar doméstico" [truly domestic home] (Pérez Galdós 1980, 247) and represents yet another defiance of the bourgeois domestic ideal. The narrator characterizes the house by its "gran falta de orden y simetría" [great lack of order and symmetry]: objects of true value obtained from liquidation sales are mixed and confused with cheap imitations to the point that what is real and what is fake become indistinguishable.[13] The fact that much of the furniture comes from liquidation sales anticipates the fate of Isidora's own possessions upon the dissolution of her relationship with Joaquín soon afterward.

As the gap that separates Isidora's fantasy world from her actual economic condition grows increasingly wider in the second part of the novel, she redoubles her struggle to elude "the gaze, the control and the interventions" of a bourgeois disciplinary machine that seeks to regulate her desire and transform her into a docile body.[14] Upon learning of Isidora's whereabouts in a chance encounter with Augusto Miquis, the narrator renews his surveillance of her by presenting a chronicle of her life during the months in which she has remained out of his sight (chap. 19). In the following chapter, entitled "Liquidación," the narrator rebukes the female protagonist, whom he condescendingly calls "Isidorita," for her moral and economic disorder, linking her "apetitos de lujo" [appetite for luxury] to her illegitimate sexual activity (Aldaraca 1991, 96–97). As Jagoe has shown, the nineteenth-century rhetoric that exaggerates women's insatiability as consumers conceals a deeply ingrained cultural anxiety about controlling female desire (Jagoe 1994, 90). The narrator's admonition to Isidora, then, reflects the patriarchal bourgeois fear of a female desire that cannot be contained.[15] Her rather inept protector through her trials and tribulations, José Relimpio, reproduces the narrator's rhetoric. When she breaks up with Joaquín and is forced to pawn all of her possessions, Relimpio urges her to embrace "una vida de orden, economía y trabajo" [a life of order, economy, and work] as the only way of saving her honor (Pérez Galdós 1980, 269). The life that he proposes to her is tied to the machine, literally and metaphorically: to labor in front of the sewing machine is to submit oneself to the capitalist machinery of production, exchanging labor honorably for capital. Isidora first idealizes the life of the laborer, imagining herself fabricating flowers and lace, but she soon rejects the idea of her subjection to the machine, opting instead for purchasing her freedom with the only capital she has left: her body.

Isidora transforms herself into a commodity, but as Fernández Cifuentes has shown, she is not an ordinary commodity: she is a luxury, a fetish. She inspires awe and fascination in those around her: José Relimpio contemplates her beauty "como el salvaje contempla el fetiche" [as a savage contemplates a fetish object] (Fernández Cifuentes 1988, 300); Joaquín perceives her as a "signo de elevación sobre el nivel común" [sign of something above the common level] (Pérez Galdós 1980, 304); even the "rationalist" Miquis cannot help being seduced by the aura that surrounds her. As a fetish, she exercises fascination because she is a *sign* of beauty, an artifact, which veils the real work of the body and tries to be "sufficient unto itself" (Baudrillard 1988, 94).[16] This fetishized beauty becomes the object of desire for a series of masculine figures who compete to read, to name, and to transform her. Isidora consciously exercises her choice to place herself under the protection of these men, who are willing to provide her, at least temporarily, with the means for basic sustenance and even for the consumption of luxury goods in exchange for the use of her body. Although these men vary in social position, economic means, and even in their personal attitudes toward her, what they have in common is a desire to demystify her by subjecting her to discipline, whether it is through physical punishment, surveillance, or an insistence on work and regimentation.

Once Isidora decides to abandon the orderly life that she has temporarily embraced and converts herself into a commodity, her body literally becomes the object of the male gaze.[17] One day, when she enters the church, a place where the elegantly dressed bourgeoisie goes to look at others and to be seen, she notices a pair of eyes staring at her with persistence. The narrator does not immediately reveal the man's identity but refers to him as "el señor mirón" [Mr. Peeping Tom] or "aquel señor de los ojos irreverentes" [the gentleman with the irreverent eyes] (Pérez Galdós 1980, 277), thus calling attention to his power as the controller of the look. Later, the narrator discloses, first through a dialogue between Mariano and José Relimpio and later through Isidora's own words, the identity and character of this man, the millionaire politician Sánchez Botín, who has offered to take Isidora as his mistress. Once Isidora becomes his lover, he adorns her body with beautiful clothing in order to transform her into his own fetish object. He places her under his constant vigilance by confining her to the enclosed space of his home and by limiting her vision. When they go to the theater, she says: "le veo atisbándome desde las butacas y observando si miro o no miro. . . . Si me ve asomada al balcón, ya se le figura no sé qué" [I see him spying on me from his seat, watching if I'm looking or not. . . . If he sees me leaning out of the balcony, who knows what he imagines] (311). Isidora herself cannot become the gazing subject, nor is she permitted to draw the gaze actively to herself. In the church scene, she remains invisible and forgotten in a dark corner of the chapel until Botín seeks her out with his gaze and discovers her. The sexual dynamic of the gaze reveals the woman's inability to participate in the power that is invested in the male looker. At the end of her relationship with Botín, Isidora is transformed yet again into a spectacle for the male gaze, as her lover forces her to undress in front of him and reduces her to a "despojada imagen" [stripped image] (323), thus demanding that she return to him all of the signs of wealth and nobility that he bestowed upon her.[18] Here the narrator occupies the position of a voyeur who willingly participates in the disciplining and punishment of the woman through her objectification.[19] Yet Isidora refuses to remain a passive object of masculine sexual pleasure and contemplation. Not only does she continue her affair with Joaquín,

thereby resisting Botín's attempt to control her sexuality, but, in reaction
to her lover's anger, she raises the exchange value of her body so that it
is beyond his reach: "Su dinero de usted no basta a pagarme. . . . Valgo
yo infinitamente más" [Your money is not enough to buy me. . . . I'm
worth infinitely more] (322). The image of Isidora's body in her under-
garments, about to disappear beyond the reach of the masculine eye,
leaves Botín face-to-face with a lack that he can no longer disavow with
the ownership of a reassuring fetish object.[20] It is he who is unable to
overcome the force of his desire and who, in the end, begs his mistress to
return to him.

Botín is only one of a series of Isidora's protectors who subject her
body to discipline and surveillance. José Relimpio's son Melchor, with
whom she takes refuge after leaving Botín, also gazes upon her as a
fetish object to be bought and possessed. When Melchor first sets his
eyes on her, "no quitaba del rostro de Isidora sus ojos, y parecía
pasmado, fascinado por religiosa o mitológica visión" [he couldn't take
his eyes off Isidora's face, and he seemed smitten and fascinated by some
religious or mythological vision] (Pérez Galdós 1980, 330). Melchor, like
the other masculine figures in the novel, transforms her into an emblematic sign of beauty by adorning her body with elegant clothing: "Volvió a
ver lucir su belleza dentro de un marco de percales finos, de cintas de
seda, de flores contrahechas, de menudos velos, y a recrearse con su
hermosa imagen delante del espejo" [She showed off her beauty once
more, framed by fine percales made of silk ribbons, artificial flowers, and
tiny veils, and took pleasure again in her beautiful image in the mirror]
(339). The narrator makes it evident that the alluring adornment is no
more than an image that veils the real labor of the body, which has been
put to use as a sexual commodity. The price Isidora must pay to maintain
this image becomes clear when Melchor insists on accompanying the
elegantly garbed beauty to El Escorial, as if to put her on display as his
possession. This situation too comes to an end when Melchor goes
bankrupt and moves to Barcelona, leaving the "stripped image" of
Isidora behind.

When Isidora again finds herself destitute, the petty bourgeois lithographer Juan Bou is eager to take on the role of her next protector. While
he proposes to legitimize their relationship by marriage, it is clear that he
too sees her beauty as a commodity to be bought and owned. What he offers in exchange is a respectable and orderly bourgeois life. When she
rejects his offer of marriage, affirming, as she did on abandoning Botín,
that she was worth infinitely more than he, his concealed misogyny rises
to the surface: "El demonio le hizo a ella la hermosura, y a mí, los ojos.
. . . La mujer es una traba social, una forma del oscurantismo, y si el

hombre no tuviera que nacer de ella, debería ser suprimida" [The devil gave her the beauty and me the eyes. . . . Woman is a social obstacle, a form of obscurantism, and if man didn't have to be born of her, she should be eliminated] (353). Isidora arouses her suitor's anger and undoubtedly his anxiety by displaying an image of her body yet refusing him the power to gain ownership, control, and mastery of that image. As his words to Mariano reveal, Bou envisions her at first as an angel capable of being domesticated in the bourgeois home, but he soon becomes dismayed upon finding a soul full of appetites who threatens to devour what little capital he has. Later, when she continues to reject his offer of marriage, even after having prostituted herself with him, he becomes enraged at her unwillingness to grant him the exclusive ownership of a commodity that he believes he has purchased: "La saqué de la miseria, la vestí, la calcé, le di regalo, comodidades, cuanto pudiera apetecer. Ella abría la boca, y yo abría el bolsillo y *palante* siempre. Pues mira el pago" [I lifted her out of misery, I gave her clothes, shoes, gifts, all the good things in life, whatever she wanted. She opened her mouth, and I opened my pocketbook, always without fail. And look at what I get in return] (419).

Although the figure of the Catalan lithographer is an obvious parody on one level, it is also evident that the narrator contrasts the exemplarity of Bou's orderly life of hard work and bourgeois respectability with Isidora's disorderly habits of excessive consumption and sexual promiscuity.[21] The narrator's attitude toward women emerges in his diatribe against Bou's first wife, whom he also characterizes as a vampire, "una hembra disipadora, antojadiza, levantada de cascos" [a spendthrift, a whimsical and frivolous female] (Pérez Galdós 1980, 282), responsible for the lithographer's financial ruin. He thus reiterates the cultural unease about uncontrolled female desire and its potential threat to masculine wealth and, by extension, to the very foundation of patriarchal capitalist economy (Jagoe 1994, 90). Ironically, despite Bou's purported identification with the disenfranchised working class, he perpetuates the same capitalist machinery of production that his rhetoric so violently opposes. His printing shop nearly becomes a prison for the downtrodden Mariano, who is put to the monotonous task of mechanical reproduction so integral to capitalist industry.[22] In Bou's shop, Mariano virtually turns into a machine: "por momentos se suponía también compuesto de piezas de hierro que marchaban a su objeto con la precisión fatal de la Mecánica" [at times he also imagined himself to be made of iron parts which moved toward their object with infallible mechanical precision] (Pérez Galdós 1980, 286). Under the omnipresent eye of power, symbolized by the lithographer's rotating eye (288), Mariano is reduced to a mere cog in society's machinery of power.[23]

It is hardly surprising that marriage to Bou is the solution that the doctor, Augusto Miquis, advances for Isidora's problems when, in hunger and desperation, she seeks his assistance. As the voice of science and "reason," Miquis is cast as the narrator's spokesperson, whose role it is to discipline the female protagonist.[24] The power relationship between the two characters is apparent from the beginning. Miquis obviously enjoys the privileges of his position, education, and knowledge, all of which have been denied to Isidora. Furthermore, from the moment she enters his office with the poignant entreaty, "Dame de comer y no me toques" [Give me something to eat and don't touch me] (Pérez Galdós 1980, 356), he is aware of his power to deprive her entirely of her increasingly fragile command of her body. At the same time, the astonishment and fear that Isidora's body continues to inspire in him reveal his own unease in the presence of uncontrolled female desire. By viewing Isidora's desire as a physiological disorder, a cancer, a disease that needs to be contained, Miquis reproduces the nineteenth-century discourses that pathologize the feminine (Aldaraca 1991, 100–108). Fearing contamination by Isidora's moral infirmity, Miquis summons the detached objectivity of the scientist in an effort to overcome his irrational desire for her. The cure that he prescribes requires her utter subjection, first to the machine (the same sewing machine that has enslaved Relimpio's daughters for life) and then to a man whose wish is to remake her into a bourgeois Angel of the House. In his ironic yet patronizing mode, Miquis recommends patience and modesty, essential characteristics of the bourgeois feminine ideal, and advises Isidora to "bordar unas zapatillas al señor Juan Bou" [embroider slippers for Mr. Juan Bou] (Pérez Galdós 1980, 368). Throughout the novel, the physician rarely allows her to escape his vigilance and control. His efforts to discipline Isidora parallel the role of the novel's narrator, who, in the guise of reason, sets out to teach the protagonist a moral lesson about the dangers of uncontrolled imagination.[25]

Miquis's attitude toward Isidora's moral affliction recalls the tenets of nineteenth-century literary naturalism, which was in vogue at the time of La desheredada's publication. The medicine that Miquis prescribes for Isidora's cure, like the "experimental medicine" on which Émile Zola bases his theory of naturalism, is undeniably tied to questions of power, control, and morality (Zola 1964, 31). According to Zola, the role of the novelist, like that of the physician/scientist, is to master, direct, reduce, and dominate human and social phenomena, thus permitting him the regulation of morality: "to be the master of good and evil, to regulate life, to regulate society . . . to give justice a solid foundation by solving through experiment the questions of criminality" (25–26). In Galdós's novel, the male physician seeks to contain what he perceives as a threat to masculine bourgeois morality by proposing to cure the female protagonist of her moral illness scientifically. Zola evokes the image of the machine to represent the goal of the experimental novelist: "Here is our role as intelligent beings: to penetrate to the wherefore of things, to become superior to these things, and to reduce them to a condition of *subservient machinery*" (25; emphasis mine). This is precisely the attitude of the Galdosian narrator, who, through Miquis, seeks to transform Isidora into an obedient and well-disciplined body-machine, a productive member of bourgeois society (cf. Foucault 1979, 153). The narrator's discourse increasingly pathologizes the protagonist, and, by referring to her as "nuestra enferma" [our sick woman] (Pérez Galdós 1980, 369), he reveals his identification with Miquis's attitude toward her.

Ultimately, Isidora resists society's disciplinary attempts, disobeying Miquis's recipe for moral cure and opting instead to pursue the course of desire. For her, dressing up in beautiful clothes is clearly an act of defiance and empowerment and a way of reaffirming her identity. In an emblematic scene, Isidora's passion for clothes leads her to Madame Eponina's dress shop, where she tries on an expensive evening gown and contemplates her image admiringly in the mirror. Not only does she assert her sexuality by expressing autoerotic gratification with that image, but she also imagines that she is displaying her body for others' viewing pleasure: "Isidora encontraba mundos de poesía en aquella reproducción de sí misma. ¡Qué diría la sociedad si pudiera gozar de tal imagen! ¡Cómo la admirarían, y con qué entusiasmo habían de celebrarla las lenguas de la fama! ¡Qué hombros, qué cuello, qué . . . todo!" [Isidora discovered a poetic world in that reproduction of herself. What would society say if it could enjoy such an image! How they would admire it, and with what enthusiasm words of fame would celebrate it! What shoulders, what a neck, what a . . . everything!] (369). By artistically (re)producing her body through self-adornment, precisely at a moment when everyone else seeks to subject it to discipline, Isidora reaffirms its intrinsic value. Miquis, who walks into the shop at this moment, becomes enraptured—and nearly seduced—by the beautiful image that Isidora has constructed for society's gaze. When Miquis, with great effort, recovers his moral equilibrium and reminds her of the regimen to which she must be submitted, Isidora responds by rejecting his prescription and reaffirming her fantasies. In a final act of defiance, she offers to sell her body to

Miquis, thus threatening to break down his role as the disciplining hand. Yet, rather than viewing her body as ordinary merchandise to be handed over to the male consumer, she sees it, once again, as a luxury commodity worth the price of her lover's honor. When Miquis refuses the offer, she abandons Emilia's home, where she has begun to embrace an honorable life dedicated to sewing, and rejoins the now destitute Joaquín Pez. Although she remains constant in her love for him and even sells her body to save his honor, she continues to assert her personal independence and sexual freedom, affirming that she will never marry: "viviré soltera, riéndome del mundo" [I'll live the life of an unmarried woman, laughing at the world] (390). Her unbounded desire continues to find expression in her obsession with clothes, as she heads for the fabric stores in the Calle del Carmen.

Despite Isidora's resistance to masculine discipline, she is never completely able to escape the omnipresent Eye of power that maintains her under constant vigilance. She continues to be pursued by a society that refuses to pardon her crime of imagination, which has kindled her desire to transcend her social and economic circumstances. Isidora's imprisonment in the Modelo prison is a metaphor for enclosure in a society where the exercise of control is virtually automatic.[26] It is Miquis who gives the metaphor expression: "La vida toda es cárcel, sólo que en unas partes hay rejas y en otras no" [All of life is a prison, it's just that in some places there are bars and in others there aren't] (Pérez Galdós 1980, 405). In this prison, we see Isidora's transformation into a hysterical body, as the identity she has constructed for herself gradually destabilizes under the force of reality. According to the narrator, the nervous disorder that Isidora suffers soon after imprisonment leaves her in a state similar to somnambulism. Later, when forced to confront the failure of her lawsuit, she is overcome by a fit of delirium whose symptoms are incoherent speech and exaggerated screaming and shouting.

In many cultural discourses, as Janet Beizer shows, the woman and the hysteric have been regarded as virtually interchangeable. The hysteric, like the woman, is associated with "disorder, duplicity, and alterity"; she is seen as a "forger of fictions and a lover of lies" (Beizer 1994, 18–19).[27] The narrator of Galdós's novel, through the perspective of other male characters, presents Isidora in precisely this way. There are mocking references to her self-transformation into a novelesque type, to her pretty role, to her theatrical representation, and to her "comedia" [play] (Pérez Galdós 1980, 403, 415, 431, 434). Her "hysteria" consists precisely in her refusal to give up the fiction of her noble birth: "Soy noble, soy noble" [I'm noble, I'm noble], she exclaims in her fit of delirium. "No me quitaréis mi nobleza, porque es mi esencia, y yo no puedo ser sin ella" [You will not take my nobility away from me, because it's my essence, and I can't exist without it] (440). If the discourses of hysteria and, by extension, women, have been defined as elusive and resistant to circumscription, the function of masculine discourse is to impose order on these intractable forces and to contain them (Beizer 1994, 9, 17). This appears to be the project of Galdós's narrator, who, along with other male characters in the novel (including Miquis, Bou, and the notary, Muñoz Nones), seeks to reduce Isidora to the object of masculine discourse by attempting her moral and aesthetic reformation.[28] Yet Isidora is a hysteric who escapes the constraints of disciplinary society and as such comes to embody the cultural anxieties of an epoch that is "experienced as anchorless and uncentered: a moment of crisis related to the razing of political and social structures and, more significantly, the demolishing of a symbolic system" (Beizer 1994, 8).

After Isidora leaves the Modelo prison, she becomes the mistress of the degenerate gambler Frasquito Surupa (alias Gaitica) in a final, desperate attempt to pursue a life of comfort and high style. Those who come in contact with her during her three months with Gaitica are quick to note her degeneration from a woman who is elegantly dressed to a being in a state of physical disintegration: she is pallid from disease, her voice has become hoarse, and her clothes are now in tatters (Pérez Galdós 1980, 460). Miquis, who makes one last effort to rescue her, is once again quick to pronounce judgment on the protagonist by attributing her physical decline to moral decay. The narrator, who now refers to her unambiguously as "una mala mujer" [a bad woman] (461), appears to share Miquis's viewpoint. Isidora's body has suffered devaluation through use and abuse and is no longer a valuable commodity with which she can bargain for a life of luxury. Patriarchal society has reduced her to nothing more than a victim, having forced her to exchange her body and honor for a life of deprivation and physical abuse. The disfiguring scar on her face, inflicted by Gaitica's knife, becomes symbolic of the moral degradation to which Isidora has descended in society's view, and of the impossibility of effacing its mark. As Brooks shows in his analysis of the prostitute's role in the nineteenth-century French serial novel, bourgeois morality dictates that "bodily experience of certain markings is indeed ineffaceable" (Brooks 1984, 150). The woman, then, is ultimately and inescapably tied to her body, which becomes a *sign* of her sin or crime.

With the declarations, "yo no existo" [I don't exist] and "Ya no soy Isidora" [I'm no longer Isidora] (Pérez Galdós 1980, 465, 477), the female protagonist continues to defy society's attempts to name her and to fix her identity. Her disordered body together with her inscrutable silence resist conscription into social discourse. In the final chapter of the novel, Miquis finds Isidora not only in physical disarray but also in a state of absolute silence that baffles his medical expertise. Yet again, Miquis and, by extension, society link the woman to hysteria through her undefinability, her instability. In an emblematic scene at the end of the novel, Isidora once more scrutinizes the image of her body in the mirror. She finds not "una vana imagen" [an empty image] in the mirror but a body whose value is capable of being recuperated: "Todavía soy guapa . . . , y cuando me reponga seré guapísima. Valgo mucho, y valdré muchísimo más" [I'm still beautiful . . . , and when I recover I'll be doubly beautiful. I'm worth a lot, and I'll be worth a lot more] (475). Isidora's attempt to reclaim herself through a reaffirmation of her beautiful image might not seem fundamentally different from her mystification by the male characters who have imposed their gaze on her. It could be argued that in the end she remains alienated from the real work of her body by reinserting herself into a network of capitalist value relations. Yet it must be remembered that Isidora's story is told to the end from the viewpoint of a male narrator who persistently negates the protagonist's desire to recuperate the value of her body as a means of self-realization. From Isidora's perspective, the reaffirmation of her boundless beauty and its infinite value, in spite of the violence done to it, places her body somehow beyond the reach of the society that continues to impose its disciplining hand on her. It is therefore logical that, when facing the mirror at this moment, Isidora asserts her independence from a socially determined identity and chooses finally to embrace the life of the anonymous prostitute.

Isidora's disappearance into the streets at the conclusion of the novel reflects the moment at the end of the first part when she escapes into the crowd with Joaquín Pez. If the reader accepts the narrator's viewpoint, this second disappearance permits the restoration of the patriarchal bourgeois order that she has disrupted through her failure to accept her place in society: "La presa fue devorada, y poco después, en la superficie social, todo estaba tranquilo" [The prey was devoured, and soon afterward, all was tranquil on the social surface] (480). At the same time, as Elizabeth Wilson has noted, the city also has the potential to emancipate the woman from the constraints of bourgeois discipline and domesticity and to permit her to gain certain freedoms (Wilson 1991, 10, 56). Isidora recognizes the relative freedom that the anonymity of the prostitute's life permits and, for this reason, consciously chooses the forbidden path. This is not to imply that the prostitute is guaranteed freedom from social surveillance in any absolute sense or that a brighter future necessarily awaits Isidora beyond the final pages of the novel. Still, by refusing to be pinned down, to be drawn irrevocably into masculine discourse, she writes her own ending to the story with her body.

Ultimately, *La desheredada*, like all of Galdós's novels, eludes an unambiguous ideological closure despite the heavy-handed moralizing in the final section. Given the irony of the narrator's voice throughout the novel, his position cannot necessarily be identified with that of Galdós himself. Yet, regardless of the mitigating irony of the narrator's words, he in fact realizes the near devastation of the female protagonist through the tale he tells. If we trust the tale rather than the teller, it becomes clear that the male narrator's irony conceals an anxiety about female desire and its potential to transgress bourgeois patriarchal constructions of the woman's body. This is not to claim that Galdós's novel serves as a repository of an unequivocal ideology that can be equated in any simplistic way with the author's conscious intention. The narrator's is but one voice among many that proclaim their competing ideologies in the textual field. Although Isidora is a constant object of moral condemnation by the narrator and by the other masculine characters, the force of her resisting body—as physical presence and aesthetic image—counteracts all attempts to control, contain, and annihilate her. The textual body, mirroring the protagonist's own body as text, becomes a cultural battlefield where conflicts between the dominant discourses of bourgeois patriarchy and the oppositional force of the protagonist's imagination are dramatized. Isidora is a contested site where readers can either recreate the gender- and class-inflected assumptions that inform the narrator's reading of her story or resist those assumptions and rewrite the ending.

Notes

1. Thomas Laqueur, in his groundbreaking work *Making Sex*, similarly shows how knowledge and interpretation of the body from ancient Greece onward is "inevitably about the social order that it represents and legitimates" (Laqueur 1990, 11). Grosz (1994, 149) notes: "The body is indeed the privileged object of power's operations": it is a site where desire is regulated and machine-like docility is generated.

2. By "disciplinary practices," Foucault means a wide range of power operations and techniques that serve to achieve social control through the production of "subjected and practised bodies, 'docile' bodies" (Foucault 1979, 138). Although the imposition of discipline can and often does occur within formal institutional structures (such as churches, schools, prisons, etc.) and through specific individuals in positions of authority, what is more important for Foucault is the spread of disciplinary practices that takes place beyond the boundaries of enclosed institutions, in anonymous but omnipresent "centres of observation disseminated throughout society" (211–12). Cf. Bartky (1988, 75) and the other essays in Diamond and Quinby (1988), especially those by Diamond and Quinby, Martin, and Bordo; see also Hunt (1992) and Stanton (1992).

3. In her study of female delinquency in nineteenth-century Paris, Shapiro (1992) shows that the medicalization of discourses on the woman is ultimately about the masculine desire to contain the female sex. For the Spanish context, see Aldaraca (1989) and Jagoe (1994, 13–41).

4. Other important book-length studies on the body in Hispanic literature include Smith's *The Body Hispanic* (1989) and Read's *Visions in Exile* (1990). Gold (1993) explores the recurrent metaphors of the body in *Fortunata y Jacinta* and the body's relationship to contemporary economic, social, and cultural forces. See also Charnon-Deutsch (1990) on the representations of women in nineteenth-century Spain.

5. For a foundational study of Isidora's relationship to popular literature, see Andreu (1982, 111–30). Bauer (1989, 49–50) argues that the novel challenges Isidora's "escapism"—her "delusions of grandeur" and belief in class privilege—through a parody of the conventions of the popular novel. I depart from these critics in their tendency to participate in the narrator's condemnation of Isidora as an uncritical consumer of popular literature. Jagoe (1993, 238), in contrast, questions the narrator's perspective, identifying his condemnation of mass culture with the "phallocentric and classbound" political agenda of the novel, as does Sieburth (1994, 45), who problematizes the narrator's discourse and his reflections on the role of art in the modern age as a product of his class, gender, and cultural capital.

6. Sieburth (1994, 27–31) presents a useful summary of the social, political, and cultural changes that provide the backdrop for *La desheredada*. Galdós himself was highly aware of the impact of these changes on the literary and cultural scene of nineteenth-century Spain, as his speech before the Spanish Royal Academy reveals (Pérez Galdós 1972).

7. Fernández Cifuentes notes: "Given texts, given signs cannot appear in this context as either entirely meaningful and reliable or entirely meaningless and inapplicable; they seem instead to exist in a state of transition, where they are not so much a source of disbelief as they are a source of 'doubt' and 'disturbance'" (Fernández Cifuentes 1988, 300).

8. I adopt from Bourdieu (1993, 7) the term "symbolic capital," which refers to diverse manifestations of capital, such as formal education, linguistic competence, and accumulated prestige, that are not reducible to economic capital but that, nevertheless, act as signs of one's socioeconomic standing.

9. For a discussion of the narrator's nostalgia in *La desheredada*, see Sieburth (1994, 39–40).

10. In her study of *La de Bringas*, Delgado (1995) convincingly demonstrates the link between feminine disorder and political chaos in the cultural imagination of the late nineteenth century.

11. In her reading of *La Regenta*, Valis (1992) examines the cultural implications of the identification between the female body and the metaphor of the monster in nineteenth-century naturalist discourse.

12. For an analysis of the ideology that gave rise to the image of the "ángel del hogar," see Aldaraca (1991, 5–87) and Jagoe (1994, 13–31).

13. Sieburth (1994, 27–49) presents an incisive analysis of this "eclipse of authenticity" in the context of social and cultural transformations in nineteenth-century Spain, referring specifically to the advent of industrialization and consumer capitalism. For Sieburth, the confusion between what is ostensibly real and what is "cursi" is a product of

the "society of the spectacle," in which members of each stratum of society create their identities based on the gaze of the Other.

14. I adopt here the words of Diamond and Quinby (1988, 14), who, in a different context, provide an account of how "woman, as a category of meaning, and women have been subject to the gaze, the interventions, and the control" of experts who have discursively constructed women's bodies and identities according to phallocentrically defined notions of truths and universals.

15. Such cultural anxiety, of course, is not unique to Spain, as Brooks's study of nineteenth-century French narrative reveals. In reference to Zola's *Nana*, Brooks (1984, 145) demonstrates that the author's obsession with unveiling the female body is based on "the need to seduce and master women" but also on the realization that the power of female eroticism will ultimately remain resistant to man's desire for control and mastery.

16. Elsewhere I have explored the phenomenon of fetishism in *La de Bringas* in similar terms (Tsuchiya 1993).

17. For a discussion of the male gaze, a concept that originally derives from psychoanalysis and has been applied extensively in feminist film theory, see Lacan (1977, 67–119), de Lauretis (1984), and Mulvey (1989).

18. I owe this observation to Elena Delgado.

19. Although it could be argued that the narrator directs himself to an *implied* reader who shares his voyeuristic attitude toward the female protagonist, the *actual* reader of the novel, whether female or male, can choose either to partake in the narrator's ideological vision or to resist it consciously.

20. In her by now classic essay on the relationship between gender and the gaze in cinema, Mulvey (1989, 21) analyzes the man's role as the bearer of the look in precisely these terms.

21. According to Aldaraca (1991, 100–108), the diatribes against luxury in prescriptive literature (e.g., conduct manuals) in Spain emphasized a direct relationship between conspicuous consumption and uncontrolled sexual desire.

22. Mariano's transformation into a machine and his resulting self-alienation can be seen as effects of the advent of mass production at the turn of the century. See Benjamin's famous essay (1969) for a critique of the waning of authenticity, that is, of the "aura" of the work of art in the age of mechanical reproduction. For a more detailed discussion of the relationship between mass production and the role of art in *La desheredada*, see Sieburth (1994, 91–99).

23. See Castillo (1988) for an analysis of Mariano's relationship to the machine.

24. The relationship between reason and the body has been explored by Malcolm Read, for whom reason is predicated on the denial of the body, which he identifies with the feminine as defined by Kristeva's psychoanalytically based notion of the semiotic (Read 1990, x, 85–107).

25. See Sieburth (1993, 37–39) for another view of Miquis's disciplinary role in the novel.

26. Trinidad Fernández (1982, 166–81) has undertaken a fascinating study, viewed from a Foucauldian perspective, of the penitentiary system in Restoration Madrid and, in particular, of the disciplinary role of the "cárceles modelos" that proliferated during that period.

27. Aldaraca (1989, 402–11) examines the medical discourses on female hysteria in nineteenth-century Spain.

28. I do not claim to equate all of these male characters in their *conscious* attitudes to Isidora and in their views of their relationship with her. Some of her protectors are more sympathetic toward her, while others, obviously, are less so. Some, like Gaitica, see her strictly as a commodity to be bought, or a body to be exploited, while others, like Miquis (and Bou, up to a point), view themselves more ingenuously as her saviors, offering her the possiblity of a better life. In the end, the position of economic privilege occupied by these men (vis-à-vis Isidora) allows them to submit her to a relationship of dominance and submission and to discipline her as they see fit in conformity with bourgeois patriarchal notions of the woman's place in society.

Works Cited

Aldaraca, Bridget A. 1989. "The Medical Construction of the Feminine Subject in Nineteenth-Century Spain." In *Cultural and Historical Grounding for Hispanic and Luso-Brazilian Feminist Criticism*. Ed. Hernán Vidal, 395–413. Minneapolis: Institute for the Study of Ideologies and Literature.

———. 1991. *El ángel del hogar: Galdós and the Ideology of Domesticity in Spain*. North Carolina Studies in the Romance Languages and Literatures, no. 239. Chapel Hill: University of North Carolina.

Andreu, Alicia G. 1982. *Galdós y la literatura popular*. Madrid: Sociedad General Española de Librería.

Bartky, Sandra Lee. 1988. "Foucault, Femininity, and the Modernization of Patriarchal Power." In *Feminism and Foucault: Reflections on Resistance*. Ed. Irene Diamond and Lee Quinby, 61–86. Boston: Northeastern University Press.

Baudrillard, Jean. 1988. *Selected Writings*. Ed. Mark Poster. Stanford: Stanford University Press.

Bauer, Beth Wietelmann. 1989. "Isidora's Anagnorisis: Reading, Plot, and Identity in *La desheredada*." *Anales Galdosianos* 24: 43–52.

Beizer, Janet. 1994. *Ventriloquized Bodies: Narrative of Hysteria in Nineteenth-Century France*. Ithaca: Cornell University Press.

Benjamin, Walter. 1969. "The Work of Art in the Age of Mechanical Reproduction." In *Illuminations*. Ed. Hannah Arendt. Trans. Harry Zohn, 217–51. New York: Schocken Books.

Bordo, Susan. 1988. "Anorexia Nervosa: Psychopathology as the Crystallization of Culture." In *Feminism and Foucault: Reflections on Resistance*. Ed. Irene Diamond and Lee Quinby, 87–117. Boston: Northeastern University Press.

Bourdieu, Pierre. 1993. *The Field of Cultural Production*. New York: Columbia University Press.

Brooks, Peter. 1984. "The Mark of the Beast: Prostitution, Serialization, and Narrative." In *Reading for the Plot: Design and Intention in Narrative*, 143–70. New York: Vintage Books.

Castillo, Debra. 1988. "*La desheredada*: The Institution and the Machine." *Modern Language Studies* 18: 60–72.

Charnon-Deutsch, Lou. 1990. *Gender and Representation: Women in Spanish Realist Fiction*. Philadelphia: John Benjamins.

De Lauretis, Teresa. 1984. "Desire in Narrative." In *Alice Doesn't: Feminism, Semiotics, Cinema*, 103–57. Bloomington: Indiana University Press.

Delgado, Elena. 1995. "'Más estragos que las revoluciones': detallando lo femenino en *La de Bringas.*" *Revista Hispánica Moderna* 48: 31–42.

Diamond, Irene, and Lee Quinby, eds. 1988. *Feminism and Foucault: Reflections on Resistance*. Boston: Northeastern University Press.

Fernández Cifuentes, Luis. 1988. "Signs for Sale in the City of Galdós." *MLN* 103: 289–311.

Foucault, Michel. 1979. *Discipline and Punish: The Birth of the Prison*. Trans. Alan Sheridan. New York: Vintage Books.

———. 1980. *The History of Sexuality*. Vol. 1, *An Introduction*. Trans. Robert Hurley. New York: Vintage Books.

Gold, Hazel. 1993. "Therapeutic Figures: The Body and Its Metaphors in *Fortunata y Jacinta.*" In *A Sesquicentennial Tribute to Galdós 1843–1993*. Ed. Linda Willem, 72–87. Newark, Del.: Juan de la Cuesta.

Grosz, Elizabeth. 1994. *Volatile Bodies: Toward a Corporeal Feminism*. Bloomington: Indiana University Press.

Hunt, Lynn. 1992. "Foucault's Subject in the *History of Sexuality.*" In *Discourses of Sexuality: From Aristotle to AIDS*. Ed. Domna C. Stanton, 78–93. Ann Arbor: University of Michigan Press.

Jagoe, Catherine. 1993. "Disinheriting the Feminine: Galdós and the Rise of the Realist Novel in Spain." *Revista de Estudios Hispánicos* 27: 225–48.

———. 1994. *Ambiguous Angels: Gender in the Novels of Galdós*. Berkeley: University of California Press.

Lacan, Jacques. 1977. *The Four Fundamental Concepts of Psycho-Analysis*. Trans. Alan Sheridan. New York: Norton.

Laqueur, Thomas S. 1990. *Making Sex: Body and Gender from the Greeks to Freud*. Cambridge, Mass.: Harvard University Press.

Martin, Biddy. 1988. "Feminism, Criticism, and Foucault." In *Feminism and Foucault: Reflections on Resistance*. Ed. Irene Diamond and Lee Quinby, 3–19. Boston: Northeastern University Press.

Mulvey, Laura. 1989. *Visual and Other Pleasures*. Bloomington: Indiana University Press.

Pérez Galdós, Benito. 1972. "La sociedad presente como materia novelable." In *Ensayos de crítica literaria*. Ed. Laureano Bonet, 173–82. Barcelona: Ediciones Península.

———. 1980. *La desheredada*. Madrid: Alianza.

Read, Malcolm K. 1990. *Visions in Exile: The Body in Spanish Literature and Linguistics: 1500–1800*. Philadelphia: John Benjamins.

Shapiro, Ann-Louise. 1992. "Disordered Bodies/Disorderly Acts: Medical Discourse and the Female Criminal in Nineteenth-Century Paris." In *Gendered Domains: Rethinking Public and Private in Women's History*. Ed. Dorothy O. Helly and Susan M. Reverby, 123–34. Ithaca, N.Y.: Cornell University Press.

Sieburth, Stephanie. 1993. "Enlightenment, Mass Culture, and Madness: The Dialectic of Modernity in *La desheredada.*" In *A Sesquicentennial Tribute to Galdós 1843–1993*. Ed. Linda Willem, 27–40. Newark, Del.: Juan de la Cuesta.

————. 1994. *Inventing High and Low: Literature, Mass Culture, and Uneven Modernity in Spain*. Durham, N.C.: Duke University Press.

Smith, Paul Julian. 1989. *The Body Hispanic: Gender and Sexuality in Spanish and Spanish American Literature*. New York: Oxford University Press.

Stanton, Domna C. 1992. "Introduction: The Subject of Sexuality." In *Discourses of Sexuality: From Aristotle to AIDS*. Ed. Domna C. Stanton, 1–46. Ann Arbor: University of Michigan Press.

Trinidad Fernández, Pedro. 1982. "La reforma de las cárceles en el siglo XIX: las cárceles de Madrid." *Estudios de Historia Social* 22–23: 69–187.

Tsuchiya, Akiko. 1993. "The Construction of the Female Body in Galdós's *La de Bringas*." *Romance Quarterly* 40: 35–47.

Valis, Noël. 1992. "On Monstrous Birth: Leopoldo Alas's *La Regenta*." In *Naturalism in the European Novel: New Critical Perspectives*. Ed. Brian Nelson, 191–209. New York: Oxford University Press.

Wilson, Elizabeth. 1991. *The Sphinx in the City: Urban Life, the Control of Disorder, and Women*. Berkeley: University of California Press.

Zola, Émile. 1964. *The Experimental Novel and Other Essays*. Trans. Belle M. Sherman. New York: Haskell House.

The Domestication of Don Juan
in Women Novelists of Modernist Spain

ROBERTA JOHNSON

Several studies of women and Spanish fiction have revealed a dual writing culture in nineteenth-century Spain that divided novelists roughly by gender and reading public.[1] The division deepened in the modernist[2] period when the intellectual (male) author, represented in literary histories by such figures as Ramón del Valle-Inclán, Miguel de Unamuno, Azorín, and Pío Baroja, began to speak directly to a growing literary (and also male) intelligentsia. The other writing culture, unrepresented in any history of literature, included Carmen de Burgos, Concha Espina, Sofía Casanova, and Blanca de los Ríos, whose fiction usually appeared in popular journalistic venues like *La Novela Corta*, *La Novela Semanal*, and *Los Contemporáneos*.[3] Unlike male-authored novels of the early decades of this century, which focused on philosophical issues and developed innovative narrative techniques that broke with the intellectual past, women's narratives were largely concerned with literary practices as they impinged on women's lives—that is, with the impact of literary representation on social customs and the influence of male editors on female literary production.

Perhaps because the female-authored novel of the modernist era does not relate to the Spanish literary tradition in the same way that the male novel does, critics and literary historians have preferred to ignore it. In works by Valle-Inclán, Unamuno, Baroja, and Azorín, there is evidence of a manifest need to supersede the realist/naturalist practices of their nineteenth-century precursors, Galdós and Clarín, while women novelists of the same period, not having been schooled in the positivist philosophy that underwrote realism, could comfortably rely on using realism's representational forms to address the social problems that concerned them.

Foremost among those concerns were women's intimate and communal spheres, which in male-authored novels had been insistently hidden from view or skewed to philosophical or masculine preoccupations. Yet, while male and female writing cultures remained fairly distinct in their themes, forms, publishing media, and readership, there was considerable interaction on an intertextual level.

One of the recurring intertexts in the female-authored fiction of the modernist period was the archetypal figure Don Juan, who often appeared filtered through his contemporary reincarnation, Ramón del Valle-Inclán's Marqués de Bradomín. Male writers of the period also turned to the Don Juan figure for literary inspiration—Valle-Inclán in the *Sonatas* and in many other works, Miguel de Unamuno in *Dos madres* and *El hermano Juan*, Azorín in *Don Juan* and *Doña Inés*, Ramón Pérez de Ayala in *Tigre Juan y El curandero de su honra*, and Benjamín Jarnés in *El convidado de papel*. The male writers tended to call directly on the classical figure of Tirso de Molina's *El burlador de Sevilla y convidado de piedra* or on José Zorrilla's *Don Juan Tenorio*, while the women writers almost invariably entered into a dialogue with Valle-Inclán's contemporary treatment of the figure.

The male seducer represented a serious threat to women's precarious position in a bourgeois milieu at a time when the "angel of the house" archetype was the preferred model for female behavior.[4] The woman who did not conform to the hallowed ideals of motherhood and purity had two options: prostitution or the convent. Employment in domestic service was often denied the woman who was viewed as licentious or "fallen,"[5] and since Valle-Inclán ironizes and parodies the male who leads the female into the realm of the forbidden, his invariable representation of women in romantic/*modernista*/decadentist terms haunted the female literary imagination in a particularly ominous way.

The Marqués de Bradomín, so often evoked in the narratives of Concha Espina, Carmen de Burgos, Blanca de los Ríos, and Sofía Casanova, differs from the classic Don Juans of Tirso de Molina and José Zorrilla in that he tells his own story, constructs his own persona. This modernist Don Juan is a writer of fictions, and his most important creation is himself.[6] While no less self-serving than the classic confessions of Saint Augustine and Rousseau, the Marqués's "confessions" shift the man-God or man-society relationship to new ground. Bradomín can imagine himself only in relation to a woman, a woman who adores him absolutely and unconditionally. María Rosario of Valle-Inclán's *Sonata de primavera* (1904) follows Ophelia into madness over the Marqués's Hamlet-like indifference; la Niña Chole of *Sonata de estío* (1903) defies a brutal father/husband for the Marqués's company; the tubercular Concha of

Sonata de otoño (1902) hastens her own death when she complies with the Marqués's sexual demands (he laments Concha's death as the loss of a personal idolater); and the Marqués's own daughter Maximina (*Sonata de invierno* [1905]) commits suicide rather than face her incestuous love for her father.

The Marqués's realization at the end of *Sonata de invierno* that he no longer appeals to women terrifies him. He is overcome with the sense of an existential loss of self:

> [C]uando se tiene un brazo de menos y la cabeza llena de canas, es preciso renunciar al donjuanismo. ¡Ay, yo sabía que los ojos aterciopelados y tristes que se habían abierto para mí como dos florecillas franciscanas en una luz de amanecer, serían los últimos que me mirasen con amor! Ya sólo me estaba bien enfrente de las mujeres la actitud de un ídolo roto, indiferente y frío. (Valle-Inclán 1989, 185)

> [When one has an arm missing and a head full of grey hair, one must renounce Don Juanism. Ah, I knew that those sad velvet eyes that had opened up to me like two Franciscan flowerlets in the dawn light would be the last to look at me with love! Now the only appropriate attitude I could assume before women was that of a broken, indifferent, cold idol.] (All translations are my own.)

When María Antonieta, the one woman who still loves him, renounces him to care for her invalid husband, he turns to writing his memoirs. Bradomín thus keeps alive the self that thrives only in the presence of female adoration by recalling and inscribing his past conquests through literature. Significantly, it is a woman, the Marqués's aunt, who formulates what is apparently his favorite description of himself: "Eres el más admirable de los Don Juanes: Feo, católico y sentimental" [You are the most admirable of Don Juans: Ugly, Catholic, and sentimental] (185).

What distinguishes the female versions of the Don Juan-Bradomín figure from Valle-Inclán's is a notable absence of the kind of parody or irony Valle-Inclán employs to situate the Marqués in an ambiguous space where neither his ridiculous nor his sentimental side can predominate.[7] Irony cuts two ways, as Ross Chambers has pointed out; it can be subversive, "[turn] the tables on the discourse of power," but it can also be enlisted to affirm a conservative position: "those tables can always be turned again and ironic distance shown to be in complicity with what it opposes" (Chambers 1991, 101). While "irony judges," as Linda Hutcheon indicates, it can also reaffirm: "It is as potentially conservative a force as corrective, deriding laughter. Parody, which deploys irony in order to establish the critical distance necessary to its formal definition, also betrays a tendency toward conservatism, despite the fact that it has been hailed as the paradigm of aesthetic revolution and historical change" (Hutcheon 1985, 53, 67–68). Women novelists of the early twentieth century use irony sparingly, and primarily from an objective narrative standpoint, to judge and secure an ethical position. Valle-Inclán's first-person narrator harnesses the other side of irony—its wry smile, its indulgent wink—to license and legitimize by means of humor and narrator-reader complicity what is in effect deviant or morally unacceptable behavior. For just such reasons as this, Julia Kristeva denigrates parody (which Hutcheon considers the master genre of irony), because parodic literature fosters the principle of "*law anticipating* its own transgression" (Kristeva 1980, 71).

The ironic-parodic cast of the Marqués de Bradomín's narration of his licentious life softens the repulsive nature of his posturing, his egotism and self-aggrandizement. "Boys will be boys" is the interlinear message of the *Sonatas*. It is not surprising that Nietzsche, archenemy of the polarization of morality in terms of good and evil, should have sympathized with a wish to mask one's identity: "I could imagine that a human being who had to guard something precious and vulnerable might roll through life, rude and round as an old green wine cask with heavy hoops; the refinement of his shame would want it that way" (qtd. in Behler 1990, 96). As Ruth House Webber points out (1964, 135), the Marqués's *bagatela* echoes the devaluation of all values in Nietzsche, one of modernism's most pernicious purveyors of invective against women.

A number of novels authored by women during the years following publication of the *Sonatas* betray anxiety about Valle-Inclán's cavalier portrayal of the male "othering" of the female. Modernist women writers like Blanca de los Ríos, Sofía Casanova, Concha Espina, and Carmen de Burgos seem to have known, long before studies of the media's impact on society's behavior, that representation can be a powerful contribution to prolonging social ills or an ally in combatting them. Each found narrative recourses for unmasking and neutralizing Valle-Inclán's sympathetic portrayal of an amoral Don Juan figure, whose fatal attraction to women consistently spelled their gender's doom in the form of insanity, mutilation, or death. Like *Sonata de invierno*, Blanca de los Ríos's *Las hijas de don Juan* [*The Daughters of Don Juan*] (1909) casts the Don Juan figure in a paternal and obliquely incestuous role, only to reverse the *Sonata*'s designation of the Marqués as sentimental martyr. Sofía Casanova's *Princesa del amor hermoso* [*Princess of Beautiful Love*] (1910) posits a female version of Don Juan who eventually rejects the role of superficial seducer. In *La esfinge maragata* [*The Maragatan Sphinx*] (1914), Concha

Espina contrasts a literary and imaginative Don Juanesque male with the harsh realities of life in the Maragatan region. And in *La entrometida* [*The Busybody*] (1924), Carmen de Burgos converts the aristocratic Marqués de Bradomín into a middle-aged, middle-class aesthete who does not consummate his affairs with women.

Blanca de los Ríos, too, invents a domesticated and bourgeois Don Juan, but traces of romanticism remain beneath her protagonist's middle-class veneer. In an act of rebellion against bourgeois pretensions, he marries a working-class woman, named Concha like one of Bradomín's women. This Concha, instead of luxuriating at her medieval manor, where she has constructed an imaginary world of princesses and pages, "no conocía, ni aun de nombre, la estética" [did not know aesthetics even by name] (Ríos 1989, 72). She spends her days searching for bargains and her nights carping at her daughters and husband. The daughters fall into illness and prostitution, having been left unattended by a father who spends most of his time and his income on hedonistic pursuits and a mother who must ply the shops for inexpensive goods to cover the family's necessities.

For Blanca de los Ríos's narrator, the place of Don Juanism in contemporary society is self-evident: "Era, pues, don Juan una de las personalidades más típicas del Madrid de la Restauración" [Don Juan, then, was one of the most typical personalities of Madrid during the Restoration] (Ríos 1989, 70). Don Juan's legacy has a social as well as a literary dimension. In her version, de los Ríos weaves together several literary connections. Don Juan thus achieves the status of a late romantic who fuses the essentialism of Bécquer with the tragic theatricality of Echegaray and the patriotism of Galdós's first series of *Episodios nacionales*. Making the connection between literary and social discourse, the narrator reminds the reader that the appearance of Galdós's historical novels coincided with public recitations in high romantic style:

[P]or entonces, por los días en que los *Episodios* prendían fiebre en las almas entusiastas, y Rafael Calvo electrizaba a los concursos con su declamación candente y con sus fogosas recitaciones de los poemas de Núñez de Arce, amanecía la mocedad de don Juan inflamada en el romanticismo contagioso que era atmósfera del Madrid de aquellos años. (67–68)

[Around then, in the days when the *Episodios* were sparking fever in enthusiastic souls, and Rafael Calvo electrified literary gatherings with his candescent declamatory style and his fiery recitations of the poems of Núñez de Arce, Don Juan's manhood was dawning, inflamed with the contagious romanticism that was Madrid's atmosphere in those years.]

If de los Ríos's narrator employs a kind of irony in describing the modern bourgeois Don Juan, it is an objective irony that critiques a social situation, whereas the Marqués de Bradomín's ironic stance, deeply informed by romantic notions, positions him above social morality. The romantic literary legacy, with its emphasis on male subjectivity and the idealization of women, was a powerful ally in modernism's war on realism. Small wonder that women "modernists" found the legacy suspect.

Blanca de los Ríos also inscribes the romantic Don Juan figure into the social register: "don Juan era el histórico seductor *gallardo y calavera* que lo prostituyó todo, menos la estética y la arrogancia, y el prestigio de su romántica persona" [Don Juan was the historical seducer, *gallant and libertine*, who prostituted everything, except aesthetics and arrogance and the prestige of his romantic persona] (69). This is not Tirso's or Zorrilla's legendary hero or antihero but a run-of-the-mill representative of Restoration Spain. He is a literary and a social decadent. He prefers art to religion and is a devotee of *flamenquismo* (showy Spanish customs), but his decadence is archaic and does not achieve truly modern amorality: "quedábase en inmoral, no llegaba a ser *amoral* como los decadentistas actuales" [he remained in the realm of the immoral; he did not achieve the *amorality* of contemporary decadents] (70).

When faced with the choice between their mother's practical vulgarity and their father's tasteful disdain for contemporary reality, Don Juan's daughters, Dora and Lita, prefer the latter. In denying their natural gender connections to their mother, the daughters sow the seeds of their own moral destruction.[8] The process is hastened when Dora and Lita, often left home alone, discover some salacious letters to their father from a female friend. The girls assume more mature and more sexually defined identities almost overnight. Dora becomes intensely romantic and takes up religious practices inspired by Saint Teresa of Ávila, and her tubercular condition is said to date from that fateful day when she read Don Juan's letters. Lita, for her part, becomes more worldly, begins to attend *tertulias*, and engages in flirtations with men.

Interestingly, Don Juan, never a focalizer of the novel, disappears from the text after the first ten pages, when the daughters take center stage. He does not reappear until the novelette's final pages. He remains only as an invisible presence, a pernicious influence to be overcome. The daughters redirect their attention, if not their sympathies, to their mother, who, upon learning of their epistolary discovery, unburdens herself of her years of torture as the wife of the profligate, decadent Don Juan. The sisters form a bond like the biblical sisters of Lazarus, Martha and Mary: "Dora era, en fin, éter de misticismo; Lita, brasa de pasión; las dos juntas hubieran poseído el cielo y la tierra; ¿qué sería la una sin la otra, si la suerte desataba aquel nudo de contrapuesto gemelismo?" [Dora was, in the end, ether of mysticism; Lita, a hot coal of passion; the two together would have possessed heaven and earth; what would happen to one without the other if providence untied that knot of juxtaposed twinship?] (Ríos 1989, 90).

The daughters' uselessness is highlighted when Don Juan's intemperate ways bring economic ruin to the household: "Dos señoritas inútiles, ¿para qué sirven, vamos a ver? ¡Pues para pedir limosna, o . . . *para otra cosa peor!*" [Tell me; what are two useless young ladies good for? Well, for begging, or . . . *for something worse!*] (92). Concha expresses a modification of the prevailing belief that prostitution was attributable to innate female lasciviousness: "¡No, y como lo lleváis en la sangre, en algo malo acabaréis vosotras! ¡Ésa será la herencia que os deje ese grandísimo canalla!" [No, and since it is in your blood, you two will end badly! That will be your inheritance from that great scoundrel!] (ibid.).[9] The underlying cause of prostitution is left hanging between biological and social determinants; either their father's sexual licentiousness or his fiscal irresponsibility has driven the sisters to stray from traditional morality.

Literature in the form of a novelist—Paco Garba—is the final catalyst in Lita's progress towards prostitution: "degenerado por herencia, decadentista por oficio, . . . no era antiguo ni moderno, sino sencillamente detestable" [degenerate by inheritance, decadent by vocation, . . . he was neither ancient nor modern but simply detestable] (97–98). The narrator understands that fin-de-siècle literary trends like decadentism, which emphasizes sexual perversion, were extremely damaging to women.[10] Garba is a bad writer, but the upwardly mobile couple that promotes his fame is sufficiently uneducated to be incapable of distinguishing good art from bad. So Garba becomes a social success, and Lita, filled with romantic notions of love, succumbs to Garba's posturing: "—¡Lita, la fuga o mi muerte! . . . El romanticismo de aquella novelesca fuga, la inminencia de la dicha, el vértigo de la acción asieron de ella" ["Lita, either we flee or I shall die!" . . . The romanticism of that novelesque flight, the imminence of happiness, the dizzying action took hold of her] (107, 109). Garba's is the same romantic posture that buries all of the Marqués de Bradomín's women but that ironically "saves" the Marqués himself. In de los Ríos's novelette, the Don Juan figure who actually perpetrates female destruction is destroyed. Here, the father was the first cause, sowing the seeds of his own dishonor. Evoking Baudelaire, Don Juan, the father, seeks relief for the misery he has wrought on his family by taking morphine, and he finally dies of an overdose of drugs and alcohol when forced to witness Lita's degraded life.

De los Ríos symbolically kills off the Don Juan legacy with Lita's degradation: "en Lita acabó la estirpe de don Juan" [Don Juan's lineage ended with Lita] (125). There is no room for Don Juan and his progeny in a world that is more hospitable to women. De los Ríos's novelette, written in the melodramatic mode, has many of the marks of a moral allegory of that genre in which good is pitted against evil. The daughters are typecast, but these stereotypes combine with the Don Juan intertext to represent genuine social problems in the material world—parental neglect, Don Juanism, and prostitution. Rather than being presented as yet another self-reflection of the narcissistic Bradomín, this Don Juan is described objectively to prevent him from escaping into the ironic, self-indulgent position. Melodrama's capacity for oversimplifying good and evil appears to define a fixed moral attitude, while the kind of irony employed by Valle-Inclán in the *Sonatas* often leaves the moral message ambiguous.

Two years after *Las hijas de Don Juan* appeared in the series of *El Cuento Semanal*, Sofía Casanova published a less sociological and more psychological interpretation of the Don Juan figure in the same popular venue. Her novel *Princesa del amor hermoso*, however, is no less morally grounded than *Las hijas de Don Juan*. Challenging the legendary Don Juan with a contemporary female "Doña Juana," Casanova incorporates more direct allusions to Valle-Inclán's Marqués de Bradomín (note, for example, the Valle-Inclanesque "princesa" in the title). Laura, who has been betrayed by her fiancé, the philandering Fernando, decides to imitate his licentious behavior, but, in the end, she reassumes her socially responsible moral posture. Like *Sonata de otoño*, *Princesa del amor hermoso* begins with a long letter from a woman, Laura, to a Don Juan type, but Casanova reverses some of the details and roles of Valle-Inclán's original. The Marqués of the *Sonata* deliberately includes no more than a phrase of Concha's letter, while in Casanova's version Laura's entire communication is quoted. In the first of several defiant gestures toward *Sonata de otoño*, Casanova's narrator quotes only a fragment of Fernando's letter, which is nearly identical in length to Concha's fragment quoted by the Marqués.[11] In her letter, Laura breaks off with Fernando, referring to his "Don Juanesque fatuity." She also informs him that she will never marry, nor will she take up the religious life, traditionally the only other alternative for respectable women.

Laura effectively writes herself out of the Bradomín scenario for the woman as love object, refusing the role of the helpless female, dependent on the stronger male's attentions; but in the process she almost writes herself into the role of Bradomín, the superficial seducer: "voy a divertirme, a *flirtear*, a ver pasar junto a mí las emociones que inspiro y no comparto. Voy a coquetear, sí, a coquetear, que es jugar a los dados y las almas" [I am going to have a good time, to flirt, to watch pass before me the emotions that I inspire but do not share. I am going to be coquettish, yes, coquettish, which is to play dice with souls] (Casanova 1989, 160). When her tubercular cousin José Luis (a character feminized not only by his disease but by the intensity of his gaze and the redness of his lips) becomes obsessed with her, her first inclination is to use his infatuation to make Fernando jealous, but she finally rejects such ill use of another's affections.

As in *Las hijas de Don Juan*, life and literature are shown to be interdependent. Modern literature lacks common sense, according to one of Laura's female acquaintances; another prefers love duels in real life to those in literature. Laura herself is attracted to love in both life and literature, although she spurns the misogyny in Leopardi's love lyrics: "Es desesperante en esa poesía su desprecio a la mujer" [The scorn for women in that poetry is exasperating] (167). Literature's long tradition of casting women in the antithetical roles of evil schemers and idealized objects is perceptible throughout the novelette. Women are either "umbrías virgilianas" [Virgilian shades] or "bienaventurados geórgicos amores" [blissful Georgic loves], Lady Macbeths or Ophelias (Casanova 1989, 162, 165, 184). Contrary to the gender division in the traditional Don Juan story, the male José Luis's view of the world is wholly romantic, while Laura's is skeptical, even cynical at times.

Concha Espina incorporates a complication of the Don Juan figure into her long novel *La esfinge maragata*. Rather than inverting the male and female roles as Casanova does, Espina exaggerates the literary gender stereotypes. This exaggeration in the opening passages of the novel prepares the way for a new kind of female bildungsroman quite unlike the traditional romance plot of boy meets girl and, after overcoming numerous obstacles, boy marries girl. Florinda meets and falls in love with the poet Rogelio on a train as she travels from Galicia to the Maragatan region to live with relatives. Her widowed father has decided to go to America to save the foundering business of an ailing brother. Florinda's father and relatives pin their hopes of economic recovery on Florinda's marriage to a wealthy cousin. For much of the novel, she evades the marriage proposal because she is in love with Rogelio. In true Don Juanesque fashion, Rogelio eventually tires of Florinda, and when she realizes that the romantic idyll is over, she accepts the cousin's hand.

Rogelio has much in common with the Marqués de Bradomín, whose creator he reveres: "saluda con reverente pensamiento al peregrino autor de las *Sonatas*, al poeta de *Flor de santidad*, cuya musa galante y campesina trovó en estas silvestres espesuras páginas deleitosas" [with a reverent thought, he salutes the singular author of the *Sonatas* and the poet of *Flor de santidad*, whose gallant rural muse fashioned delightful pages in these wild thickets] (Espina 1989, 58). As a writer, Rogelio too exploits his relationships with women for their literary value, although Rogelio spins his fantasy a priori while the Marqués de Bradomín narrates his amorous exploits a posteriori. Like the Marqués de Bradomín (and in contrast to the traditional Don Juan), Rogelio genuinely believes himself to be in love at the moment of his infatuation with his love objects. And like the Marqués, he journeys into unfamiliar territory to meet his "princess." Whereas Valle-Inclán situates the Marqués's conquests in papal and princely Italy, exotic Mexico, the highly literatur- ized Brandeso Palace, and the royal camps of the Carlist wars, Espina heightens the discrepancy between literary portrayals of women and women's real lives by setting her novel in the Maragatan region of León, where the agricultural economy can no longer support its inhabitants. Most of the healthy men work abroad, leaving the women to tend the land, and life is a daily struggle to feed and shelter the children whom the men have fathered on their yearly visits.

Like Valle-Inclán's Concha, Espina's Florinda collaborates with her seducer in his romanticization of her. (When Rogelio first casts his gaze on Florinda asleep on the train, she is referred to as "la bella durmiente" [the sleeping beauty].) Florinda, too, harbors romantic pretensions. She tells Rogelio that the man her family has designated as her husband, a cousin who owns a grocery store, is not her ideal. She would prefer a sailor: "Parece que detrás de esa confesión ha volado muy lejos el alma de Florinda a perseguir por remotos mares la silueta romántica de algún velero audaz" [After that confession, it appears that Florinda's soul has flown far away in pursuit of the romantic silhouette of some daring sail- ing ship through remote seas] (65).

Throughout her education in the harsh realities of a life of work and privation, Florinda continues to cling to the romantic ideal of the male- female relationships she has read about in adventure novels and favorite books like Enrique Gil y Carrasco's *El señor de Bembibre*. Valle-Inclán parodies romanticism through the Marqués de Bradomín's clichéd language in order to place the Marqués in an ironic light.[12] Espina too evokes romanticism's emotive, idealistic language early in the novel only to have Florinda reject it later by dramatically shredding Rogelio's letters and casting them out among the snow flakes.

After the initial chapters, Rogelio's literary perspective disappears as Florinda enters the female world of Maragata, which is a lived rather than a written or writing culture. That Maragatan men do not write letters

to women is a recurrent motif, and when Maragatans do write, the effect
is deleterious. Marinela is actually frightened by Rogelio's use of
language: "—¡Salve, oh maragata, augusta *Señora del Páramo*, salve!—
Con lo cual la aludida [Marinela], escandalizada ante una oración nueva,
no escuchada jamás, tuvo al viajero por hereje o por loco" ["Hail, oh
Maragatan woman, august *Lady of the Plain*, hail!" Upon hearing this
new, unheard-of utterance, Marinela, to whom it alluded, took the trav-
eler for a heretic or a madman] (Espina 1989, 178). Rogelio is referred to
elsewhere as the modernist Quijote, and his association with *modernismo*
and its quixotic, often sacrilegious, portrayal of women is not gratuitous.

The people of Valdecruces call Florinda Mariflor, a name more in
keeping with her prosaic present. When she lives up to her last name,
Salvadores, it is not by acting as a spiritual *salvadora* [savior] in the
tradition of Zorrilla's Doña Inés but by becoming a material provider.
Rather than a pawn of divine intervention, she is a free agent who has
made a difficult personal choice. In the Valdecruces world inhabited
almost entirely by women, Florinda encounters a natural paradigm that
contrasts with the idyllic model of the romance: instead of a union with
an idealized male who idealizes her in return, she is offered the opportunity to establish genuine ties with her female relatives, especially through
her cousin Olalla.

The unflamboyant and singularly nonverbal Olalla stands in sharp
contrast to Rogelio, the fickle and untrustworthy male with a facility for
language. Olalla, who is capable of deep emotional ties and an unflag-
ging constancy, speaks through her physical presence. Unlike the tenuous
verbal understanding between Rogelio and Florinda, the pact between
Olalla and Florinda is sealed with a physical sign: "pero el impulso
cordial prevalece por debajo del vuelo de las almas, y un pacto de amor
se firma con el estallido de un largo beso" [but the cordial impulse
prevails beneath the flight of the souls, and a love pact is signed by the
sharp sound of a long kiss] (98).

As Rogelio disappears from Florinda's perceptual horizon, her
strengthening bonds with women are expressed in a series of avian
images. The dovecote, first introduced to Florinda by Olalla, becomes
her haven, an island of peace and solace in her harsh new world. When
Marinela's health and illusions fail, she too escapes to the dovecote,
which is situated in the light-filled upper story of an otherwise dark and
depressing house. A piece of down from a baby dove adheres to Olalla's
feminine form during the first excursion to the dovecote. This suggests a
number of metonymic links between Olalla, the doves, and her role as the
titular mother figure within the family: "Y *Mariflor,* al ver un instante
ambas cabecitas inocentes refugiadas con regalo en el seno de la moza,

recordó al punto aquella dulce caricia en que el pichón recién nacido perdiera un copo de pluma" [And *Mariflor,* upon seeing for an instant both innocent little heads taking happy refuge in the young woman's breast, immediately remembered that sweet caress in which the newborn pigeon lost a flake of a feather] (122).

The habits of the storks, who mate for life and return year after year to the same nest, are symbolically woven into the narrative at appropriate moments and are evoked most meaningfully during the wedding cere- mony of the priest Don Miguel's niece. When, at the end of the novel, Florinda, now Mariflor, announces that she will marry her wealthy cousin, the doves come to feed from her lap: "Volvióse hacia el carasol para abrir las vidrieras, tomó el centeno en su delantal y todo el bando de palomas acudió a saciarse en el regazo amigo, envolviendo la gentil figura con un manso rumor de vuelos y arrullos" [She turned toward the sun porch to open the windows, she took the grain in her apron, and the whole band of pigeons came to sate itself in the friendly lap, surrounding the elegant figure with the gentle noise of wings and cooing] (397).

Whereas the Marqués de Bradomín engages in a nostalgic retrospec- tive of his excursions into alternative worlds laden with potential for literary escapism, Florinda enters a foreign but all too realistic world of work, suffering, and privation. The Marqués employs the romantic language and tropes associated with Latin American *modernismo* to seduce women and to vindicate himself and his life; Espina's narrator uses those same linguistic styles to reveal the harm they can do to women. The Becquerian echoes of Rogelio's letter to the priest in which he indicates his loss of interest in Mariflor are a compelling reminder that men's romantic dreams of women cause pain in the real world. While the Marqués looks back mournfully to a "glorious" past in which he has seduced and directly or indirectly caused the death of more than one woman, Mariflor looks hopefully forward to a future of social responsibility.

In *La entrometida*, a novelette published in *La Novela Corta*, Carmen de Burgos domesticates Valle-Inclán's romantic-*modernista* version of Don Juan by converting him into a bourgeois aesthete whose power over women is more editorial than physical. It will be recalled that the Marqués de Bradomín, who is invoked on several occasions in the portrayal of Burgos's male focalizer Pérez Blanco, edits the voice of Concha and the other women out of the *Sonatas*. In *La entrometida,* Pérez Blanco's female writer escapes from him and publishes her own story. Pérez Blanco is a middle-aged bachelor, aficionado of good cook- ing and intimate dinners with a highly select group of young women, most of them married: "El no era un galanteador de oficio, ni un seductor, no era más que un *despelusador*, a cuyo contacto las mujeres, sin perder la castidad, perdían la inocencia" [He was not a professional lover, nor a seducer; he was only a hair-musser, in contact with whom women lost their innocence without losing their chastity] (Burgos 1924, n.p.). [13]

He enjoys a woman as he would a good book or a fine wine; his Don Juanism is limited to the vicarious activities of counselor and confidant, although he claims to have been much loved by women in his youth. The reader becomes wary of these claims, however, when to document his rakish past, Pérez Blanco tells stories that are almost identical to those of the Marqués de Bradomín: "el relato repetido de aquella noche en que la voluptuosidad avivada por la muerte de una mujer respetada, que en su último momento le revelaba su pasión, le hacía abrazar a la hermana de la difunta en el mismo lecho mortuorio" [the repeated story of that night in which voluptuousness enlivened by the death of a respected woman, who in her last moment revealed her passion, made him embrace the sister of the dead woman on the very death bed] (Burgos 1924, n.p.). Pérez Blanco also laments the loss of a fiancée, a widow who broke off their engagement because her daughters fell in love with him. Since the Marqués de Bradomín embroiders his libidinous history with literary tropes, Pérez Blanco's amorous memories are in effect twice-borrowed literature.

Pérez Blanco develops a special interest in Clarisa, a declared feminist who has spent time abroad and who plans to mobilize feminist activities in Spain. He undertakes a campaign to redirect Clarisa's life toward more feminine (that is, less public) pursuits and convinces her to dictate her life story to him and to include her most intimate feelings and thoughts. When she finds herself in financial difficulty and decides to publish her memoirs for money, Pérez Blanco abandons her. In Burgos's rewriting, the "Marqués de Bradomín," who is capable of occupying the space of four novels with his own very public memoirs, cannot abide a woman's similarly revealing her subjectivity. Perhaps he cannot even accept that women have a subjectivity. The end of the novelette finds Clarisa in England, where she has resumed her feminist activities, but she writes to Pérez Blanco that she is wavering between becoming a writer and taking up prostitution. Clarisa's equation of writing with prostitution, of publishing one's ideas or sentiments with defiling one's body, is significant. By publishing her memoirs, she forfeits her legitimate relationship with Pérez Blanco, the paternalistic male figure; his interpretation of her act renders it illegitimate and prostitutorial. Clarisa's apparent escape from the influence of a male editor on her work is left ambiguous. Prostitution, the primarily female profession occasioned by the pressures of male needs and male social forms, becomes a metaphor for the relationship between men and women in the literary as well as the carnal world.[14]

The difference in approach to the Don Juan theme between male and female writers of the modernist period is very marked. Male writers draw on aspects of the Don Juan archetype in Tirso de Molina's *El burlador de Sevilla* and Zorrilla's *Don Juan Tenorio* to fashion works that have little to do with the theological or moral purposes of the originals. The versions of the Don Juan figure in Unamuno's *Dos madres* and *El hermano Juan* empty Tirso de Molina's and Zorrilla's stories of their moral content and fill the shell with existential philosophizing. The Don Juan in both of Unamuno's works is engaged in the same struggle for identity as are most of his other characters. The female characters in these works are not Don Juan's sexual pawns but rather threatening figures who rob Don Juan of his selfhood. Azorín takes Zorrilla's contrasting pair—the diabolical Don Juan and the angelical Doña Inés—as a pretext for exploring the temporal relationship between history and eternity. Pérez de Ayala's *Tigre Juan y El curandero de su honra* complicates the Don Juan intertext with Calderonian overtones and an intensely ironic style that catches the reader up in its densely layered artfulness. Benjamín Jarnés gives Tirso's stone statue a vanguardist fillip by converting it into salacious photographs of women that circulate clandestinely in a seminary. In contrast to these masculine refurbishings of the primary Don Juan texts, the women writers focus almost exclusively on Valle-Inclán's Marqués de Bradomín, whose ambiguous morality their countertexts confront and undermine.

The cultural war of intertexts waged in novels by women like Blanca de los Ríos, Sofía Casanova, Concha Espina, and Carmen de Burgos emerged in Spain as full-blown, latent feminism in the late 1920s and 1930s. Yet, despite the important social legacy left by women's fiction of the first thirty years of the century, literary history has not been kind to narratives that in an intensely aesthetic age employed intertextuality for social commentary rather than for philosophical ruminations or ingenious mind games. The anxiety that women's fiction of the modernist period reveals about the values expressed in male literary forms was not unfounded. After all, the influence of male values on the formation of the subsequent literary canon left women writers and their concerns buried in oblivion.

Notes

1. See Andreu (1982), Bieder (1992, 1996), Blanco (1993), and Sieburth (1994).

2. I use "modernist" to refer to literature of the early twentieth century written by authors born in the 1860s and 1870s who began to write in the 1890s. The group that has traditionally been called the "Generation of '98" has never included women writers. That time frame is problematic for women, since many of them were involved with marriage and child-rearing in the 1890s and did not begin to write for publication until the end of the first decade of the twentieth century. As an alternative classification for the Generation of '98, "modernism" also presents problems for the inclusion of women writers, since modernism comes freighted with expectations of artistic innovation, philosophical overtones, and explorations of individual consciousnesses (usually male). Few of these expectations are fulfilled in the female literary production of the period. Nonetheless, "modernism" has at least the negative advantage of not conveying the sense of an all-male club as "Generation of '98" does.

3. See Bieder (1992) for a discussion of the relationship of women writers to the male canon of the modernist era.

4. Aldaraca (1991) studies the "ángel del hogar" archetype in Galdós.

5. López-Cordón Cortezo (1986) and Perinat and Marrades (1980) discuss the social constraints placed on women in late nineteenth- and early twentieth-century Spain.

6. For studies on aspects of the Marqués's self-construction, see Spires (1988, 35–47), Valis (1989), Loureiro (1993), and Epps (1993).

7. The complex narrative strategies in *Sonata de otoño* have given rise to a great deal of critical commentary. See especially Alberich (1965), Predmore (1988), Gulstad (1970–71), and Spires (1988).

8. Nancy Chodorow (1978) theorizes female psychological development in terms of women's continuing identification with the mother, which contrasts with a male psychology that is marked by separation from the mother. She postulates that women's ongoing maternal attachment prompts them to approach life as a series of relationships, while men's lives are defined by independence and detachment.

9. Sander Gilman (1985) discusses the common view in fin-de-siècle Vienna that prostitution was inherent in some women, who were led into the profession by their lascivious natures. It is not unlikely that such views were held in other European countries as well. There was a widespread tendency to overlook economic necessity and the role that highly restrictive sexual practices and lack of birth control measures for "honest women" (married and unmarried) played in creating a demand for paid sex.

10. For discussions of artistic representations of women in fin-de-siècle Europe, see Apter (1991), Dijkstra (1986), Pierrot (1981), and Showalter (1990). One must, however, be mindful that these studies do not address the particular Spanish context, and the tendencies they discuss are secondhand and diluted when they appear in Spain.

11. The Marqués de Bradomín's narration is singularly reluctant to give voice to women. The four *Sonatas* have many passages in which the Marqués interrupts women's attempts to tell their stories or in which women's conversation is relegated to background murmuring (noise). See Ciplijauskaité (1987) for a discussion of this phenomenon, although not specifically in reference to the *Sonatas*.

12. See Alberich (1965) on Bradomín's language as a parody of earlier literary styles.

13. Maryellen Bieder (1996) points out that the Pérez Blanco figure has certain characteristics in common with the novelist Pío Baroja: the headgear designed to cover baldness, the plaid robe and slippers. In addition, I note that the names bear Baroja's initials and that *La entrometida* could be a response to Baroja's *El mundo es ansí* [*So Goes the World*] (published twelve years earlier), in which a male narrator edits the intimate letters and diary of the female protagonist Sacha and in which feminists are subjected to a bashing. I am indebted to Maryellen Bieder for supplying me with a copy of *La entrometida*, which has not been republished since its 1924 appearance in *La Novela Corta*.

14. Judy Kirkpatrick skillfully analyzes the authorial-patriarchal relationship between Pérez Blanco and Clarisa. She concludes, however, that Clarisa "remains trapped within the male fiction" (Kirkpatrick 1992, 69), whereas I believe she has achieved a measure of autonomy.

Works Cited

Alberich, José. 1965. "Ambigüedad y humorismo en las *Sonatas* de Valle-Inclán." *Hispanic Review* 33: 360–82.

Aldaraca, Bridget A. 1991. *El ángel del hogar: Galdós and the Ideology of Domesticity in Spain.* North Carolina Studies in the Romance Languages and Literatures, no. 239. Chapel Hill: University of North Carolina.

Andreu, Alicia G. 1982. *Galdós y la literatura popular.* Madrid: Sociedad General Española de Librería.

Apter, Emily. 1991. *Feminizing the Fetish: Psychoanalysis and Narrative Obsession in Turn-of-the-Century France.* Ithaca, N.Y.: Cornell University Press.

Behler, Ernst. 1990. *Irony and the Discourse of Modernity.* Seattle: University of Washington Press.

Bieder, Maryellen. 1992. "Woman and the Twentieth-Century Spanish Literary Canon: The Lady Vanishes." *Anales de la Literatura Española Contemporánea* 17: 301–24.

———. 1996. "Self-Reflexive Fiction and the Discourses of Gender in Carmen de Burgos." In *Self-Conscious Art: A Tribute to John W. Kronik.* Ed. Susan L. Fischer, 73–89. Lewisburg: Bucknell University Press.

Blanco, Alda. 1993. "The Moral Imperative for Women Writers." *Indiana Journal of Hispanic Literatures* 2: 91–110.

Burgos, Carmen de. 1924. *La entrometida. La Novela Corta* 4.292.

Casanova, Sofía. 1989. *Princesa del amor hermoso.* In *Novelas breves de escritoras españolas (1900–1936).* Ed. Ángela Ena Bordonada, 151–94. Madrid: Castalia.

Chambers, Ross. 1991. *Room for Maneuver: Reading Oppositional Narrative.* Chicago: University of Chicago Press.

Chodorow, Nancy. 1978. *The Reproduction of Mothering: Psychoanalysis and the Sociology of Gender.* Berkeley: University of California Press.

Ciplijauskaité, Biruté. 1987. "La función del lenguaje en la configuración del personaje femenino valleinclanesco." In *Genio y virtuosismo de Valle-Inclán.* Ed. John P. Gabriele, 163–72. Madrid: Orígenes.

Dijkstra, Bram. 1986. *Idols of Perversity.* Oxford: Oxford University Press.

Epps, Brad. 1993. "Recalling the Self: Autobiography, Genealogy, and Death in *Sonata de otoño.*" *Journal of Interdisciplinary Literary Studies* 5: 147–79.

Espina, Concha. 1989. *La esfinge maragata*. Madrid: Castalia.

Gilman, Sander. 1985. *Difference and Pathology: Stereotypes of Sexuality, Race, and Madness*. Ithaca, N.Y.: Cornell University Press.

Gulstad, Daniel E. 1970–71. "Parody in Valle Inclán's *Sonata de otoño*." *Hispanic Review* 36: 21–31.

Hutcheon, Linda. 1985. *A Theory of Parody*. New York: Methuen.

Kirkpatrick, Judy. 1992. Redefining the Male Tradition: Novels by Early Twentieth-Century Spanish Women Writers." Ph.D. diss., Indiana University.

Kristeva, Julia. 1980. *Desire in Language*. Ed. Leon S. Roudiez. Trans. Thomas Gora, Alice Jardine, and Leon S. Roudiez. New York: Columbia University Press.

López-Cordón Cortezo, María Victoria, et al. 1986. *Mujer y sociedad en España 1700–1975*. 2nd ed. Madrid: Ministerio de Cultura. Instituto de la Mujer.

Loureiro, Ángel G. 1993. "La estética y la mirada de la muerte: *Sonata de otoño*." *Revista Hispánica Moderna* 46: 34–50.

Perinat, Adolfo, and María Isabel Marrades. 1980. *Mujer, prensa y sociedad en España. 1800–1939*. Madrid: Centro de Investigaciones Sociológicas.

Pierrot, Jean. 1981. *The Decadent Imagination 1800–1900*. Trans. Derek Coltman. Chicago: University of Chicago Press.

Predmore, Michael C. 1988. "Satire in the *Sonata de primavera*." *Hispanic Review* 56: 307–17.

Ríos, Blanca de los. 1989. *Las hijas de Don Juan*. In *Novelas breves de escritoras españolas (1900–1936)*. Ed. Ángela Ena Bordonada, 61–125. Madrid: Castalia.

Showalter, Elaine. 1990. *Sexual Anarchy: Gender and Culture at the Fin de Siècle*. New York: Viking.

Sieburth, Stephanie. 1994. *Inventing High and Low: Literature, Mass Culture, and Uneven Modernity in Spain*. Durham, N.C.: Duke University Press.

Spires, Robert C. 1988. *Transparent Simulacra*. Columbia: University of Missouri Press.

Valis, Noël M. 1989. "The Novel as Feminine Entrapment: Valle-Inclán's *Sonata de otoño*." *MLN* 104: 351–69.

Valle-Inclán, Ramón del. 1989. *Sonata de otoño. Sonata de invierno*. Ed. Leda Schiavo. Madrid: Espasa-Calpe.

Webber, Ruth House. 1964. "The *bagatela* of Ramón del Valle-Inclán." *Hispanic Review* 32: 135–41.

Memes: Intertextuality's Minimal Replicators

H. L. BOUDREAU

[T]he most elementary task of scholarship [is] the delimitation of the corpus and the *état présent* of the question.

—Paul de Man 1988

[T]he impossible attempt to achieve Apollonian reduction of Dionysiac materials.

—J. Hillis Miller 1989

[I]n all things the factor of greatest importance is the idea; once that is put forward, positive and negative evidence is bound to be discovered, and upon the data thus brought to light a structure can gradually arise that may rightly demand the assent of a schooled intelligence.

—W. A. Heidel 1933

Richard Dawkins, a zoologist, conceived, named, and defined the meme in "Memes: the New Replicators," which is the final, brief chapter of his 1976 book, *The Selfish Gene*. Dawkins posits cultural evolution as analogous to biological evolution and thus feels the need of a term to match biology's "gene." For this purpose, he invents the word "meme" to signify a unit of imitation. It is intended to sound like "gene" but also to suggest "memory" and the French word "même." "Examples of memes," writes Dawkins, "are tunes, ideas, catch phrases, clothes fashions, ways of making pots or of building arches. Just as genes propagate themselves in the gene pool by leaping from body to body via sperm or eggs, so memes propagate themselves in the meme pool by leaping from brain to brain via a process which, in the broad sense, can be called imitation" (Dawkins 1976, 206). Dawkins quotes a colleague who had read an earlier draft of the chapter: "When you plant a fertile meme in my mind you literally parasitize my brain, turning it into a vehicle for the meme's propagation in just the way that a virus may parasitize the genetic mechanism of a host cell" (207). Earlier in the book, a gene had been defined as "a unit which survives through a large number of successive individual bodies" (26). Obviously, the same could be said of a meme-unit as Dawkins later defines it. Deciding what constitutes a smallest unit, however, is a problem—and it will continue to be one for memologists. Dawkins pragmatically decides that it would simply be considered a unit of convenience sufficiently distinctive and memorable to be abstractable from a larger whole—the four-note phrase that begins Beethoven's Symphony No. 5, for example—although in another context the entire work might be called a meme (210). It seems to this nonscientific writer that the problem of constituting a unit exists in equal measure in the literature on genes. There may be a single gene for blue eyes but surely not for big feet, because that structure is too complex. Scientists are now apparently making rapid progress in this area. The media were recently (October 1995) filled with references to the fact that the body has been determined to contain more than eighty thousand genes, while individual organs have many hundreds.

Continuing with the gene/meme analogy, Dawkins says that successful memes must have what successful genes must have: longevity, fecundity, and copying fidelity, fecundity being more important than the longevity of particular copies (208). Apart from these useful distinguishing attributes, Dawkins provides only a few hints about how we might set about understanding and working with memes. He observes that some memes survive because of their psychological appeal (God, for example), that there are mutually assisting memes (God and hell, for example), and that "some memes, like some genes, achieve brilliant short-term success . . . [say, fads and styles] but do not last long in the meme pool" (207, 213, 209). Like other biologists, Dawkins maintains that "all life evolves by the differential survival of replicating entities," but, unlike his predecessors, he includes both genes and memes in that equation: "When we die there are two things we can leave behind us: genes and memes" (206, 214).

Having provided only a few undeveloped but important suggestions for understanding and working with memes, Dawkins concludes with a call to action: "We have the power to defy the selfish genes of our birth and, if necessary, the selfish memes of our indoctrination. . . . We are built as gene machines and cultured as meme machines, but we have the power to turn against our creators" (215). Thus ends the founding document of memology, one that has the possibility of achieving an importance comparable to that of Darwin's *On the Origin of Species* in the study of culture, the new evolution.

More than twenty years having passed since publication of *The Selfish*

Gene, what has been the fate, thus far, of the meme meme? The original reception of Dawkins's ideas was not notably positive—except by general readers—and most of the ink spilled had to do with the concept of the "selfish gene" (crudely put, a gene is "interested" in its own survival, not in that of its host) rather than with the "meme."[1] Dawkins was the inventor of the meme meme but not its propagator. In *The Extended Phenotype,* he draws back on his claims for the similarities of genes and memes and—unfortunately—says that the meme's "main value may lie not so much in helping us to understand human culture as in sharpening our perception of genetic natural selection" (Dawkins 1982, 112). In *The Blind Watchmaker* (1986), he repeats in brief and general terms the content of the last chapter of *The Selfish Gene* without even mentioning the word "meme." As Daniel Dennett points out, Dawkins had earlier written: "I do not know enough about the existing literature on human culture to make an authoritative contribution to it" (Dawkins 1982, 112). That, of course, is the problem of all interdisciplinary work, and literary and cultural critics will find themselves in the reverse predicament of not being scientists and knowing little of genetics.

Daniel Dennett is decidedly the most active and important of the advocates of the value of the meme. He is a philosopher but also, like Dawkins, an evolutionist, and he is by no means ignorant of scientific matters, as his *Darwin's Dangerous Idea* (1995) makes clear. In 1990–91, there was a resurgence of the idea of the meme involving a slow but growing acceptance among scientists. These were also the years of the two Dennett articles and his book *Consciousness Explained.*[2] Dennett's 1990 essay "The Evolution of Consciousness" is a capsule summary of his controversial book, which soon inspired a volume of commentary and critique (Dahlbom 1993). In that essay, Dennett describes how "[t]hree processes of evolution conspire to create consciousness":

1) *The evolution of species with genetic transmission.*

2) *The evolution of neural patterns.* Patterns of activity within individual brains, in processes of learning and training.

3) *The evolution of "memes."* Ideas available in the cultural environment, culturally transmitted and "implanted" in individual brains by social interactions. In each process the mechanism is classically Darwinian. (Dennett 1990a, 88)

Dennett's other 1990 article, "Memes and the Exploitation of Imagination," is his most direct reaction to the Dawkins stimulus. It was intended to reintroduce the meme to humanists, and the present essay is a response in that spirit. Versions of Dennett's article appeared in both of his subsequent books. For our purposes, the main points of the piece, some of them important extensions of Dawkins's ideas, are the following: 1) The brain is "a sort of dung-heap in which the larvae of other people's ideas renew themselves, before sending out copies . . . in an informational Diaspora." 2) "Units [memes] are the smallest elements that replicate themselves with reliability and fecundity." 3) "The first rule of memes, as it is for genes, is that replication is not necessarily for the good of anything; replicators flourish that are good at . . . replicating!" 4) Memes may be good (environmental awareness) or bad (anti-Semitism)—and everything in between—as well as general (music, for example) or particular (*The Marriage of Figaro*). 5) "A meme's existence depends on a physical embodiment, a vehicle in some medium" (images, books, oral expressions, for example), and these vehicles (paper, say, or the electronic media) will have spent "at least a brief, pupal stage in a remarkable sort of meme-nest: a human mind." 6) There are meme filters (factors that inhibit replication) and meme linkages (associations of one meme with another) that promote replication (Dennett 1990b, 128–32).

Dennett's rich, persuasive, and readable *Darwin's Dangerous Idea* contains—in addition to restatement of the above material—many further terms and perspectives for the study of the meme. These will inform the final section of this study where specific memes are examined. To put the argument simply, Dawkins is concerned with evolution and the parallel (analogical) nature of genes and memes. Dennett, in *Consciousness Explained*, is concerned with the functioning of the human mind, while in the Darwin book he makes a detailed case for the workings of evolution. Without entirely ignoring those large subjects, this essay will shift the emphasis to the processes of culture, beginning with an example of the extraordinary life of one ubiquitous meme.

A paper/print vehicle of that meme is Gustavo Adolfo Bécquer's 1863 *leyenda* "La promesa" ["The Promise"] (Benítez 1974, 271–83). The story concerns the seduction of Margarita, a lower-class girl, by a powerful Castilian count whose status is unknown to her. The setting is thirteenth-century Spain at the time of the reconquest of Seville from the Moors by Fernando el Santo. The disguised count gives her a ring and promises to return to restore her honor after assuring his own in battle. Since the promise was apparently false, the guilty count later has visions of a mysterious hand that appears before him and protects him on the field of battle. Finally, he overhears a minstrel tell his own and Margarita's story in a *romance*, or ballad, that reveals that the girl has been put to death by her brothers for the dishonor she has brought upon their family. But the hand in question, the hand with the ring finger, will not remain buried and rises above the grave. The count, remorseful, returns with a special papal dispensation and marries the girl posthumously, whereupon the hand, graced with the wedding band, sinks into the grave, never more to emerge.

The intertextual motif of the dead hand is the meme in question here, but despite its ubiquitousness, it has been overlooked by Bécquer's critics.[3] Yet, once readers become aware of the numerous texts (meme vehicles) of many kinds that contain it, they are sure to think of others. The sampling that follows is merely a beginning: Maupassant's "The Hand" and "The Withered Hand," LeFanu's "The Narrative of a Ghost of a Hand," Golding's "The Call of the Hand," Conan Doyle's "The Brown Hand," Harvey's "The Beast with Five Fingers" (movies have been made of a number of these), Martínez-Tolentino's "El amuleto," the French film *Les Mains d'Orlac*, Keats's chilling poem beginning "This living hand," the Brazilian story by Silveira de Queiroz "A mão direita," Valle-Inclán's "Comedia de ensueño," Wagner's *Twilight of the Gods* (Siegfried's dead hand in the last act), the movie *Body Parts*, Aleshkovsky's novel *The Hand*, Tom Lehrer's tender ballad "I Hold Your Hand in Mine" (it is a severed hand), a Calvin & Hobbes comic strip in which the father invents a bedtime story for his son called "The Dismembered Hand that Strangled People," and so on and on.[4] The really extraordinary thing about this meme in all of these instances—and also in others of a different type that will be taken up later—is that, as in Bécquer's case, it is invariably composed of the same three semes: life, death, and power.

The pervasiveness of this meme continues unabated today. Even the linguistic cliché "the dead hand of tradition," or "the dead hand of the past," or any of the other members of this popular linguistic paradigm contains all three semes. In the episode of the raising of Lazarus in the film *The Last Temptation of Christ*, Jesus entreats Lazarus to live again and then sits outside the dark hole that leads into the burial cave. After a long pause, Lazarus's dead and rotting hand flops out into the light to end the scene. We note that the power seme has moved metonymically to Jesus, but it is still in operation. Variations in one or another of the three semes keep the meme viable for further replication. During the 1991 Soviet crisis, there was a news report that showed a toppled statue of Lenin. The photographer shot it so that the huge, threatening hand filled the television screen. Once again, death and life are fused opposites, and power is the result. It should be noted that the upright statue had expressed no such threat; the meme was replicated by the photographer, in whose mind, as meme nest, as host, the meme had spent its pupal stage before moving to the electronic vehicle that transferred it to the viewer's mind. Similarly, a few years ago, the San Francisco Opera's presentation of Richard Strauss's *Elektra* used a palace courtyard set furnished only with a monstrous bench in the shape of a male human hand. The designer was obviously expressing the power of the dead-but-alive Agamemnon in that bench. The opera begins with a musical expression of the four syllables of his name and ends with that same sequence in altered form, the king's murder having been avenged.

Most American readers probably know W. W. Jacobs's horror story "The Monkey's Paw." The tale is a variation on the "dead-hand-with-strange-powers" meme, and readers who recognize it may realize that a lucky rabbit's foot is a further variation. Quite possibly, the lucky horse-shoe is still another, since in ancient times (for example, in fables or in Alfonso el Sabio's texts) horses, lions, and the like were said to have "manos" [hands] instead of front feet. Numerous hand amulets of this sort exist, like the Brazilian "figa" (a good luck charm in the form of a clenched hand) and the comparable Caribbean "mano de azabache" [black (jet) hand] or the Spanish (Galician) "furaman" [hand with hole].

There are many more examples. It is hardly possible to turn on the television, see a movie, or read the funny papers without finding further instances daily. Even one of our holidays, Halloween, has as its most popular artifact (the Halloween Trade Fair confirms it) a mechanical hand for frightening people. The following final example carries special appeal because of the transformation of the power seme into its opposite. There was a fad a few years ago for coffee table boxes—little coffins, actually—that were considered to be quite funny. If you opened them, a grisly hand reached up from inside and closed the lid again, the only act of power of which it was capable. Clearly, memes submit to parody as well as to other modes of transformation.

The foregoing examples of the dead hand in literature and in high and low culture make the case that this meme is constant, widespread in time and space, and still very much alive in all the meme vehicles. It is a true case of a minimal unit of cultural transmission, probably generated and sustained by an atavistic human fear. It does, however, like all good memes, often ride piggyback on others, or others link themselves temporarily to it. The Bécquer instance alone is combined with two other hand memes: woman as property (giving her hand in marriage) and woman as identified by white hands. The white hands meme has its own abundant life: "mano de nieve" [hand of snow] elsewhere in Bécquer, "manos blancas" in a Calderón title and in a famous episode of nine-teenth-century Spanish history ("Manos blancas no ofenden" [White hands do not offend]) (Holt 1967, 37), "mano candida" in the *Rigoletto* quartet, and pale hands in myriad poems and novels of the 1800s, although the occurrences are by no means limited to that period. The Valle-Inclán and Wagner examples given earlier also contain the "white hands" meme. Gerald Prince, coiner of the term "narratee," in the essay that invents and explains the term—indeed, in the very first example chosen to illustrate it—cites a phrase from Balzac calling the narratee "you with white hands." Prince does not recognize the intertext—that is, that "white hands" equal woman—and he proceeds to identify it as a reference to race, not gender (Prince 1988, 316). Unawareness of a meme can certainly trip us up. Prince's misreading, however, and the fact that no one seems to have noticed it in so influential and anthologized an essay, reveals incontrovertibly that that particular meme no longer replicates well.

Given that a thematologist would doubtless have called the hand meme a motif (as I did early on), a few words are in order about the possible relationship of memetics to the recent resurgence—if it can be called that—of thematics. Three large collections make the claim that thematics is back (Bremond et al., Sollors, Trommler). Their titles speak of return, reconsideration, and new approaches. Each volume begins with theoretical articles about the discipline, followed by case studies. The reader is not notably encouraged by these books to believe that thematics is back because, although the articles are of high quality, they contain so little that is new. The theoretical pieces rehearse the history of this type of criticism and spend the bulk of their space rearguing the intractable methodological problem that has always plagued thematics: the definition of terms, in particular the fundamental ones "motif" and "theme" and their distinctions. There is much exhortation to produce a firmer disciplinary basis but scant real progress in that direction. Thematics has, of course, returned in a nonspecific sense—that is, in the current rejection of formalism, theme being what is left over if study of form is frowned upon. The formalist movement in its new-critical heyday was responsible for the fall from favor of thematics because of the latter's concern for content rather than form, a content, moreover, that was seen as floating from work to work rather than being an element in a single "verbal icon."

The most surprising aspect of the "resurgence" of thematics is its failure to profit from the current hegemony of cultural studies. Thematology remains mired in the purely literary. Folklore aside (that has always been a part of the discipline), culture beyond the contents of literary works is still insufficiently addressed.[5] It is just possible that memology could provide an answer to this need for expansion into the broader realm of culture, and memology might also be able, though not without difficulty, to break through the terminological roadblock that thematics still confronts. Even the editor of one of the three thematics volumes calls his discipline a "terminological Babel" and a "minefield without adequate maps" (Sollors 1993, xxii–xxiii). The accumulated history of critical and literary movements suggests that it would be unusual for thematics to succeed in making a significant return without drastic change.

Jonathan Culler tells us that "theory is initially a reflection on whatever is taken as natural, a questioning of . . . assumptions" (Culler 1992, 226). This questioning has been a characteristic of every theoretical movement of the last thirty years, and memology will be no exception. It is as true of structuralism as it is of gender studies as it is of new historicism. The concern with the difference that lies beneath is usually accompanied by interdisciplinarity, a breeching of barriers that originated in structuralism's concern for all the "human sciences," a term that is again frequent in the titles of recent books on the new rhetorics. Feminism excepted, most of the many late-twentieth-century theoretical movements have held relatively brief sway in the United States: five years of effervescence, give or take. Things were different before. New criticism was dominant for some thirty years! But critical or literary dominance will eventually produce a reaction, and there is little doubt that the extrinsic focuses of most recent theory are reactions to that long, formalist hegemony. Instrumentalism is now the order of the day. The current brevity of the active lives of theories may complicate the lives of scholars, but it should never be read as a series of failures. On the contrary, no major theory of this period has failed to enrich our professional perspectives. None has failed to build on what came before; none has failed to effect change and to leave behind important legacies that will remain with us. "Deconstruction is compost," someone wrote recently (Parini 1995, 52). Perhaps, but compost fertilizes.

In addition to rapidly succeeding one another, all of the theories have evolved, often changing their names in the process. Could thematics do that? When structuralism's concern for static structures veered toward a concern for communication, it turned into or was replaced by semiotics. When intertextuality went sociocultural, it became discourse. When feminism became markedly more theoretical in nature, it was renamed gender studies—and of course new historicism has been rebaptized by Stephen Greenblatt, its founder, as cultural poetics because of a broadening and redefining of its purview. Most recently, the term "cultural studies" is in ascendance, and all new historicism can fit under that rubric, even though the reverse is not true. This is a time of dispersal, of the centripetal, of ethnicity, not of melting pots—of regionalism, of break-up. Indian artifacts are going back to the Native Americans and federal concerns back to the states. If culture can overtake literature, why not memes instead of themes?

Many theories tend to bleed into others or balloon into global ones, so there must be limits to any focus; otherwise, intertextuality becomes semiotics, which is as all-inclusive a concept as discourse. All three critical modalities are really the same thing, but a "thing" that may be entered at different levels of specificity. And without specific focus, one cannot get a handle on anything. The recent new rhetoric is a perfect example. If everything beyond a datum like $2 + 2 = 4$ is susceptible of rhetorical analysis, how do we carve out an object of study from so amorphous a mass? Everything is text if we want it to be. Everything, likewise, is ideology, everything is discourse, everything semiosis, and the entire contents of our minds consist of memes, the mind being where all culture lives. Memes are the stuff of our thought and our memory and become the stuffing of anything we create, be it a novel, a poem, a movie, a song, a TV program, a scholarly article, a world view, the way we raise our children, or our manner of understanding history. We can think only with the memes we have acquired and go on acquiring. All the memes in your individual pool are available for replication, and you will pass them on to others on any vehicle you care to use. Many of them you will replicate without knowing it, however, because memes are everything legendary or folkloric or mythic, traditional, clichéd, generic, formulaic, patterned, or proverbial—in a word, anything repeated or replicable. How then do we reduce this excessively broad field so that a methodology can be developed?

A methodology for memetics should include a taxonomy of types, a consideration of vehicles and meme motivation, a semantics, and a concern both for the life cycle of memes and for their interrelationships. All of these aspects of memetics emerge in the present treatment of individual memes, with the partial exception of the taxonomy, which turns out to be imposingly difficult to elaborate. This study's identification of several meme categories hardly begins to constitute a taxonomy. This is simply an early attempt at finding order in a new and dauntingly suggestive field of cultural study.[6]

The meme types that promise to yield less significant or less interesting results for the study of culture might for present purposes be bracketed off. Among these types are purely factual memes and those of individual personal experience. The latter would include such matters as what I/you bought at the grocery this morning. A meme of this sort is highly unlikely to replicate and is soon forgotten even by the person involved. Like everything else in the mind, it is a meme, but a short-lived one of nearly zero fecundity—unless, of course, the shopping list contains twenty-three cans of chocolate syrup and a single bottle of tabasco sauce. There is always the possibility that something so freakish would strike the funny bone of the checkout clerk and that that person would pass it on to others, thereby giving it a brief but active life as a ridiculous narrative about incomprehensible customers. But even that is unlikely; the trip-to-the-grocery meme has little hope of furthering our understanding of anything. It and others in the category of personal experience can safely be omitted from the cultural spectrum. Likewise with things of a purely factual and informational nature: how to raise chickens or Robert's Rules of Order, for instance, or the principles of geometry. If these immense and relatively inert meme categories are set aside, what remains is still intimidatingly vast, but it has a distinctly "cultural" feel to it—that is, it encompasses the material we associate with the life of the mind in its communication with the social and culturally inherited world around it. This material would include, among other ideas, the content of the arts, of mythology, of language, of belief, and of customs of every kind. Culture comes to us secondhand, and meme study immediately makes clear—if we ever doubted it—that culture is largely a tissue of lies upon which we have a peculiar, dependent relationship. We know that there are no such things as unicorns, but we also know that they are white. Not all memes are false in this sense, but the false ones are often the most intriguing. Their evident untruth seems not to impede their transmission in the least. Take, for example, the color of the rose in poetry, the rose meme's prime vehicle. "Roses are red," as the children's rhyme indicates. That roses are always red is in fact the default cultural assumption unless there is specification to the contrary. Hence the need for reiteration in Robert Burns's line "My love is like a red, red rose." Since "My love is like a rose" would already have carried the redness seme, to have written "like a red rose" would have been tautologically unpoetic. Therefore, the second "red" is a poetically essential intensifier. Yet, *The Rose Bible* tells us that in the garden, as opposed to the cultured mind, "Pink . . . is the most common color in all rosedom" (Reddell 1994, 19).

Types and Tokens

Many memes have the quality of standing behind their concrete exemplifications in the form of an abstraction or, as Daniel Dennett might call it, a "semantic property" (Dennett 1995, 356). Individual manifestations are the tokens of a type. (Biologists might prefer the parallel terms "genotype" and "phenotype.") We might think of the type as the recipe and the token as the resulting dish. This structure often obscures the relationship that each token has with its fellows and, more important, obscures the fact that it has any fellows. An evolutionist might consider this kind of meme a case of "replication with variation" (152). A structuralist perspective (always helpful when looking for relationships) would see this link between type and token as a paradigmatic one that invites substitution of items. The type of fascinating-fearful-mysterious beings, for instance, that has such a firm hold on human imagination would include as tokens the Loch Ness Monster, Bigfoot, the Abominable Snowman, and UFOs. They all satisfy the same human need and, despite much effort, never have been proven to exist. The mystery must live on. A million people a year go to (not) see the Loch Ness Monster, and there was a recent conference at MIT on UFOs. Yet there seems to be no social awareness of the meme, despite a Gary Larson cartoon that spoofs at least part of it: "Just as Dale entered the clearing and discovered standing together the Loch Ness Monster, Bigfoot and Jackie Onassis, his camera jammed." One of the major contributions of an awareness of memes as memes—a meme perspective, if you will—is that tokens become visible and thus identifiable. Most of the memes examined in this study have heretofore been largely invisible.

Another meme from among the many having this paradigmatic structure is that of the seer, a concept motivated by the search for knowledge unavailable in the realm of evidence. The tokens of this type are the blind, children, beggars, and the insane, all of whom have been thought to have privileged knowledge. There is a body of scholarship on this characteristic of each of these societal groups as seen in general culture, and literature is filled with examples. Surely no author has made greater use of this meme—including all four of its tokens—than Benito Pérez Galdós throughout his novelistic production. If a blind person is mentioned or appears in one of his novels (and there are many of them), whether the character is major or minor, the knowledge seme always accompanies that individual.

Language Memes

By virtue of definition and repetition, language memes are clichés but of a number of kinds, many more than can be illustrated here. Most prominent are set phrases without semantic burden that have become so routine that we could neither talk nor write without them: on the one hand, on the other hand, be that as it may, at the same time, in other

words, no simple feat, if anything, without a doubt, etc. Many others
contain a word that is used nowhere else, yet it feels completely natural
in its context: wrack and ruin, left in the lurch, to run amok. The extreme
cases are those that contain terms whose meanings are entirely unknown
to the user: beyond the pale, on the lam, by dint of, spick and span, in
fine fettle, a spate of, to put the kibosh on, to be in cahoots. These last are
examples of memes that have lost their referent and continue to exist
only by force of rote repetition. That lack of referent will eventually
finish them off. The death of the referent always ultimately dooms such
words and phrases, just as it can kill off more substantive memes. It is
part of the normal creation, life span, and death of such units. Some of
them, however, are granted a very long life because they have become
fixed on things or texts. Around the world there are hills and mountains
called "Sugarloaf" because of their resemblance to a common household
item of the past that no longer exists. Those names, that meme, will
remain indefinitely, but no new mountain, no new thing, will be given
that name. "[N]ovel artifacts can only arise from antecedent artifacts"
(Basalla 1988, vii–viii). It is as true in the world of technology as it is in
that of texts.[7] The computer's parents—who could doubt it?—are the
typewriter and the TV. The TV set orginally had a dial because it was
modelled on the radio. That dial has now disappeared, yet we still occasionally hear characters on the screen telling us, "Don't touch that dial!"
The loss of the referent, however, is rapidly doing away with the expression. Memes from one medium or technology move into the new one
until such time as the newcomer can develop its own. Television still
talks of "magazine" shows and the computer of "bulletin boards."
"[M]emes will propagate [only] as long as the environment is conducive
to growth" (Csikszentmihalyi 1990, 215).
    A particularly curious and unnoticed language meme is that of the
famous name that has been reduced, in terms of cultural usage, to a
single seme. "He's an Einstein, a Beau Brummel, a Don Juan, a Benedict
Arnold, a Scrooge, a Machiavelli, a Solomon; she's a Mrs. Malaprop." In
every case, the figure has been reduced to one value: intelligence, elegant
dress, rapacious sexuality, treason, parsimony, political duplicity,
wisdom, linguistic mayhem. The "rules" for these formations remain
quite opaque. How does one get on the list? Fame alone, no matter how
great, does not do the trick; Marx and Freud, otherwise considered
central cultural figures, have not been so honored, nor have supremely
popular cult figures like Marilyn or Elvis. How long does the meme last?
How soon can a name get into such distinguished company? Solomon is
ancient, Einstein is quite recent. Yet the latter's seat on the dais is very
secure. "He's no Einstein" is heard with some frequency. The only things

the list makes clear are that such names may be either fictional or real, positive or negative, and that they must be part of common knowledge, like any other cliché.

Horse Memes

If we set aside specific horses, animal husbandry, and our individual experience with horses, there remain at least two expansive memes based on perceived qualities of these animals. One of these memes, the horse as passion, is ancient, and the generating text is Plato's *Phaedrus*. The other is the horse as power, which arises out of the importance of the horse in modern (though not contemporary) agriculture and other practical endeavors. The horse as passion has found expression most frequently in the arts, while the horse as power dominates in everyday life, technology, and language. The first is epitomized by those "flaming" nineteenth-century paintings of horses that used to be seen on parlor walls. Gustavo Adolfo Bécquer, in his "Rima 5" of the 1860s, looks back directly to Plato for his image of the horses that pull the poet's chariot, emblems of inspiration (that is, passion) and form. In one of his *leyendas*, "El monte de las ánimas" [The Haunted Wood], the meme of untrammeled emotion appears again: "Una vez aguijoneada la imaginación, es un caballo que se desboca y al que no sirve tirarle de la rienda" [Once the imagination has felt the spur, it is a runaway horse that cannot be reined in] (Benítez 1974, 145). The same image lurks in a poetic line like Vicente Aleixandre's "Soy el caballo que enciende su crin contra el pelado / viento" [I am the horse that ignites its mane against the raw wind] (from "Destino") or in the sexualized horses of García Lorca's plays *El público*, *Bodas de sangre*, and *La casa de Bernarda Alba*. More recent examples still are Peter Shaffer's *Equus* (play and movie) as well as the film *Farinelli* or the still-used linguistic expression "unbridled passion."

The more modern horse meme arises out of the animal's role in everyday life and the loss of that role to technology. The first trains were called iron horses, the first automobiles horseless carriages, and those first cars, like other artifacts, required models and therefore carried along quaint aspects of their horse-drawn antecedents. Still today, horsepower is the only means and the only term by which a car's power (and that of many another motor or machine) is measured. This aspect of the meme shows no sign of decline; it has no substitute or synonym, and none is on the horizon. The horse's centrality to a culture now past could not be better illustrated. The cavalry still exists as a combat unit, but the horses have become tanks. In language, the meme is present and flourishing in dozens of picturesque expressions, such as to harness waterpower or the atom, to give free rein to something or, contrariwise, to rein something in, but also to take the bit in your teeth, to kick over the traces, to hold your horses, and so on, each expressing the energy of the horse. It could be that the two horse memes, the ancient and the modern, provide differ- ent versions of the same thing (passion/power). Both are of a cultural past, the first case because it expresses a romantic approach to the world, the second, because it conjures an image of daily life that no longer has a referent. The continued vitality of the two memes in language, metaphor, and technology expresses the unpredictability of the life of certain memes.

The Death Meme in Music

Among the most interesting of memes for the student of culture may be those that by their nature are free to appear in multiple vehicles. Others, however, are limited to a single medium. Extremely common film and television memes of today are "the corpse that will not die" and "the rafters (or girders) chase" and their variants. Both being visual memes, they are limited to the film medium but are so strong there that directors seem to be helpless in their thrall. In *Jurassic Park,* even the dinosaurs enter a building and pursue the human characters, while in the 1996 modernized filming of Shakespeare's *Richard III*, the final battle- field scene takes place up in the girders.

Another meme that is limited to a single vehicle is the death meme in music. Although it can appear only in music, it can, of course, show up in any medium where music is used. This meme has been little noticed, but its ubiquity must surely mean that at least any pianist or orchestra player is aware of it on one level or another. It is only a characteristic rhythm, but it is motivated by the hesitating steps of real-life coffin bearers. If there exists a funeral march that does not contain the meme, I have not been able to locate it. All Western culture seems to have adopted the Chopin funeral march (Piano Sonata No. 2, op. 35, third movement) as its official music at funerals. The particular rhythm that undergirds the funeral march is called by David Rosen an anapestic figure, but this is certainly an oversimplification (Rosen 1995, 26). The anapest's two shorts followed by a long can be, and often are, the very reverse. In fact, the musical death meme may have one of four forms: two or three shorts followed by a long, and a long followed by two or three shorts. The doubter need only listen carefully to the funeral march movement (the second) of Beethoven's *Eroica Symphony* or the first-movement march of Mahler's Fifth to hear all of these variations. These two symphonic movements are among the most brilliant extended usages of the death meme because in each case the rhythm both generates and becomes the melody; it does not remain merely an accompaniment. Julian Budden, who gives a few Verdi examples, warns that context and emphasis determine whether any such figure is in fact the death motif (his term), anapestic rhythms being found throughout music (Budden 1992, 189). We need look no further for examples to support Budden's view of the importance of context than to the opening figure of Beethoven's Fifth (three shorts and a long) or the first three notes of the final section of Rossini's overture to *William Tell* (two shorts and a long), not to mention TV's *Bonanza* theme (two shorts and a long). These last two are thought to echo horses galloping, and none of the three would ever be identified as the death meme, even though, without the determining context, all three are musically identical to that meme. Budden's "emphasis" surely must include instrumentation, since it would be difficult for a composer to express the seme of this figure on the piccolo or the triangle. This is to say that the seme is generated by an extramusical context, but also that it creates its own context with the sombre instrumentation that is normally used. There can be exceptions, however, as I learned while attending a performance of Verdi's *Requiem* and experiencing an epiphany of recognition in the anapestic, mounting trumpet calls of the "Tuba mirum" that herald the emptying of the graves and the last judgment. Bright trumpet sounds are atypical for this figure, but the context here imposed itself thrillingly.[8] The recent film *Carrington* also contains the death meme expressed effectively on an unlikely instrument, the solo violin. It is repeated many times in the last few minutes of the movie from the point at which the protagonist decides on suicide until the sound of the gunshot that kills her.

Some of the most striking examples of the meme are in opera or program music. In those contexts, the meme can announce or prefigure death. Examples are the soft drum beats that follow the last orchestral cataclysm of Tchaikovsky's *Romeo and Juliet Overture*; they tell the listener that the lovers are dead. In Verdi's *Otello*, act 3, Otello twice throws Desdemona to the floor, and on each occasion we hear a pair of the anapestic figures that prophecy her death at his hands in act 4. One of the most brilliant and expressive uses of the meme in opera is its attachment to the fate theme (as it is usually called) of Bizet's *Carmen*. The second section of the overture repeats that baleful melody a number of times, and on each occasion it is followed by two short notes (soft beats on the timpani), so that the prior final note of the melody becomes the long note of the anapestic death meme. The short, much reiterated "fate theme" is, of course, a well-known meme in its own right. What is under discussion here is its combination with the death meme in a parasitic—even symbiotic—relationship, each enhancing the expressive qualities of the other. This pairing happens in many places in the opera, one of the most inspired instances being the sassy accompaniment to Carmen's first entrance, when the fate melody is transposed into a fetching violin figure followed by the two shorts in the woodwinds. More prefiguring occurs in Don José's "Flower Song," which is a melodic development from the fate motif. The aria's final two plucked notes quietly remind us once again where events are leading. Then, at the end of the opera comes the ultimate metamorphosis of this material, when José, having just murdered Carmen, sings his last desperate line, one that grows out of and extends the fate theme. The final note is followed by the last two chords of the opera, which return the listener to the death meme first suggested in the overture. Bizet thus avoids the usual nineteenth-century cliché of opera and symphony, the sense of an ending produced by rhetorical emphasis rather than thematic content.

Nothing makes clearer the power of a meme nor the risks of not recognizing it than Beethoven's so-called *Moonlight Sonata* (op. 27, no. 2). This piece is never recorded, played, written about, or discussed without the sobriquet, yet it was not named by the composer but by a listener—and he was dead wrong. The adagio is a contemplation of death, as the thudding rhythm of the sombre death meme throughout should have told us long ago. This is an excellent illustration of the effect of a title meme linked to its work, where each replicates the other. A contrary example, that of a filtering meme, would be the case of a cheap, delicious fish called "cusk," which is said not to sell only because of its name.[9]

There can be no doubt that in the *Moonlight* case, the name is responsible for that sonata's extreme popularity relative to Beethoven's many other sonatas. Recordings often depict a moonlit night on their covers. Yet this mental image imposes an entirely false reading of the work, one that has never, it would seem, been unmasked. Moreover, the "unmasking" done here will be quite ineffective in wounding that false title meme. In the face of such a powerful and universally replicated unit, I do not have Richard Dawkins's faith that pernicious memes can be destroyed by evidence (Dawkins 1976, 212). If we had no information about what the title of Picasso's *Guernica* referred to, we would not find the Spanish Civil War in it, and if it were called *Corrida de toros*, we would find the bullfight in it and we would contextualize it with the painter's other bullfight paintings and sketches. Title memes, once estab-lished in culture, tend to stay put, riding piggyback on the work to which they are linked. In the case of the *Moonlight Sonata*, a later composer has supported, in a purely musical way, the views expressed above. Dmitri Shostakovich's final work, written just weeks before his death, is the Sonata for Viola and Piano, op. 147, whose last movement, an adagio, is a powerful meditation on death. It pointedly quotes the *Moonlight Sonata*'s adagio, including its rhythm of death.

In the movie *The Remains of the Day*, the old butler collapses on the patio (he will soon die), and the spectator immediately hears the death meme in the background music. I once heard it in a nature program on television when the lions made their kill. The TV episode of *NYPD Blue* of 30 April 1996, contained a startlingly foregrounded example. A divorced man's son had been killed, and the camera followed the father as he walked to his former wife's apartment. Upon his arrival—the camera idly focused on a corridor wall—the background music suddenly thundered out the three-note meme. Instantly, the apartment door opened and the father abruptly announced to his ex-wife, "He's dead." The figure is demonstrably available to composers of all kinds, whether it is employed consciously or the meme speaks through its own reiterating power—a power that allows its emotional seme to be felt, whether listeners are able to identify it or not. Death being a constant of life, the meme is as fertile today as it was a hundred years ago, and no change is in sight.

The Dead Hero

Among the memes examined in this essay, that of the dead hero is undoubtedly the most culturally significant and immediate one to contemporary Americans. It also best exemplifies the need for a memetic perspective because a very large and general phenomenon in mass psychology is passing completely unnoticed while individual tokens are being studied without awareness of the meme complex to which they belong. The meme in question has a long history and is growing stronger. It is always concerned with a hero of some kind, be it national (a king, a president) or cultural (Elvis "The King," Amelia Earhart). The hero's renown may have arisen from good power (Lincoln), evil power (Hitler), or simple cultural power (Marilyn Monroe). Public interest regularly focuses on the death of the cult figure in an attempt to restudy that death, dig up that body, resuscitate it, and deny its death, thereby keeping it alive.

The distant past also provides examples, and I am sure that historical study would unearth many more. Hispanists will remember the ballads of the Cid who, having been killed in battle, was propped up on his horse by his troops to convince the enemy that he was not dead and that his power could still win battles. Spain's Charles V, Holy Roman Emperor, is another example. Late in life, he abdicated and retired to a monastery, but even after his death there, rumor had it that he was still alive. The story survives in the Schiller play that Verdi used for his *Don Carlo*. At the end of the opera, Philip II is king, but his son, pursued by the Inquisition, is saved by the startling appearance of a "monk" who is identified as the long-dead emperor, his grandfather. When Verdi came to compose the final scene—and he did it with extraordinary effect—he had to ask his librettist, "What is going on here?" No one recognized the meme, and, to my knowledge, students of the opera still do not know the legend of Charles V that produced that ending.

One of the most striking aspects of most of these cases is that evidence never wins out over belief, *pace* Dawkins. The Lincoln assassination will be restudied again and again, as it already has been. He and John Wilkes Booth will be dug up again and again. Truth will always remain in doubt, and thus the hero will in that sense remain alive. President Zachary Taylor was exhumed in 1991 to determine if he had been poisoned, and Jesse James was dug up in 1995. Aviator Amelia Earhart is a hero especially amenable to manipulation because the body was never found, but the supposed wreckage of her plane has been found all over the world, and personal sightings have been frequent. For decades after Hitler's known death, he was frequently reported alive in South America. In that case too there were exhumations and reexaminations. There have been several recent studies of the "death and resurrection" of Captain James Cook in Hawaii in 1779 that relate his death and expected return to the myth of the return of the god after ritual killing and sacrifice (see Obeyesekere 1992). Readers will remember Joseph Campbell's *The Hero with a Thousand Faces*, but his book has a very different focus from that of meme study: "It is the purpose of the present book," he wrote, "to uncover some of the truths disguised for us under the figures of religion and mythology" (Campbell 1949, vii).

The remarkable prominence in recent American society of the multiple restudyings by various individuals and governmental commissions of the John F. Kennedy assassination is, of course, the paramount example of the meme in our time. The matter has cost the American taxpayer many millions of dollars, but no examination is ever accepted as accurate, and the most ridiculous conspiracy theories are entertained and brought to television, newspapers, books, and movies. "The recent release of 90,000 pages of secret documents has contributed little to what is known about the case, except, according to one commentator, to show that this is the most investigated crime in history" (Kirkpatrick 1995, 171). I myself have heard innumerable discussions of the Kennedy phenomenon and read an equally large number, yet not one treatment has posited mass psychological need as an explanation of its persistent recurrence. The case is never compared with others. The dead-hero meme is obviously extraordinarily powerful, but it lives in the unconscious. It is an excellent instance of the longevity, the fecundity, and the variability of a meme.

Another illustration of that meme's variability is the appearance in the 1990s of the preoccupation with MIAs, who now, with the public reevaluation of the Vietnam War, have become dead-but-alive war heroes. This preoccupation and reexamination, as in the Kennedy case, produced little evidence at the time and, indeed, after so many years, it seemed quite quixotic to have expected it to do so. H. Bruce Franklin's 1993 book on the subject is prime evidence of the hiddenness of the meme, even for those who are studying one of its tokens. Although the book is entitled *M.I.A. or Mythmaking in America*, its author never stumbles on the truth despite his focus on myth. He makes no comparisons and relates the myth only to political interests. There is even a section in the book called "Crucifixion and Resurrection," yet the meme, announcing itself loudly and crying to be let out, is not heard.

An epilogue to the discussion of this meme might be in order. Strangely enough, it can be related to the first meme studied in this essay, that of the dead hand. There, the hand was a free-floating unit, yet it may well be a variant of a larger meme complex: the Undead. One of its fellow tokens would be vampires, which have become culturally prominent in the last few years as a result of the contemporary loss of truth and the consequent return of the occult. The whole subject of the "unquiet grave" in poetry, folksong, and story is an aspect of the meme. The reader will recall that in the Bécquer vehicle the hand rises from the grave. Paul Barber's *Vampires, Burial, and Death* contains an entire chapter called "Hands Emerging from the Earth" (Barber 1988, 133–46). The term "unquiet grave" and the juxtaposition of the dead hand and the dead hero might lead us to wonder if there is not a curiously inverted emotional motivation behind the two death memes or meme complexes studied here. The one returns the dead we fear, the other the dead we desire.

Meme pools are individual and can only be populated by the memes of one's own cultural experience. No reader of this essay need be told that its author, given the examples he uses, lives in the United States, is a Hispanist, and has special interests in literary theory and music. Like anyone else's sampling of representative cultural memes, what has been presented here is the merest glance at a huge and fascinating subject. Its terminology is in flux, its perspective is that of an amateur in a new field,

it answers few questions. But, as Douglas Robinson puts it, "The joyful-
ness of infinite play, its laughter, lies in learning to start something we
cannot finish" (Robinson 1991, 194). Perhaps this endeavor may serve to
illustrate the risks and riches of a new approach to cultural study.

Scientists have been uncomfortable with the meme concept, but many
of the positions they have taken are easily refuted—at least by humanists.
Certainly John Searle's rejection of the gene/meme analogy on the basis
of his belief that "[b]iological evolution proceeds by brute, blind, natural
forces" while ideas develop as "a conscious process directed toward a
goal" cannot even withstand the evidence of this essay (Searle 1995, 57).
In a review of *Darwin's Dangerous Idea*, John Maynard Smith wrote:
"My uneasiness with the notion of memes arises because we do not know
the rules whereby they are transmitted. A science of population genetics
is possible because the laws of transmission—Mendel's laws—are
known. . . . [N]o comparable science of memetics is as yet possible"
(Smith 1995, 47). We shall have to work toward that goal, despite the
difficulties. It should be remembered that "Darwin had no proper *unit* of
heredity, and so his account of the process of natural selection was
plagued with entirely reasonable doubts about whether it would work"
(Dennett 1995, 20). The earlier complaint of scientists that a "meme"
was just a metaphor need not concern students of culture. Its pragmatic
utility is what matters. Nietzsche called truth itself "a mobile army of
metaphors" (Nietzsche 1968, 46). Moreover, literary theory has accomplished wonders with such metaphors as "the death of the author" and
mise en abyme. "Meme" can serve equally well because, as Dennett says,
"metaphors are the tools of thought. No one can think about consciousness without them" (Dennett 1991, 455). Stephen Jay Gould, with whom
Dennett disagrees about evolutionary matters, adds: "Has any truly
brilliant insight ever been won by pure deduction, and not by metaphor
or analogy?" (Gould 1996, 10).

These pages are a tentative response to Daniel Dennett's hope that the
meme might take root among humanists. I conclude with his words: "The
invasion of human brains by culture, in the form of memes, has created
human minds, which alone among animal minds can conceive of things
distant and future, and formulate alternative goals. The prospects for
elaborating a rigorous science of memetics are doubtful, but the concept
provides a valuable perspective from which to investigate the complex
relationship between cultural and genetic heritage. In particular, it is the
shaping of our minds by memes that gives us the autonomy to transcend
our selfish genes" (Dennett 1995, 369).[10]

Notes

1. See Midgely (1979), for example, and Dawkins's response (1981), an exchange in which she does not understand the concept and he does not even mention memes.

2. Mihaly Csikszentmihalyi's "Memes vs. Genes: Notes from the Culture Wars" (1990) was another especially useful article of those years.

3. In an appendix to Sebold's *Bécquer en sus narraciones fantásticas*, Armistead considers only the *romance* embedded in Bécquer's story. He finds details and antecedents in a number of traditional *romances* and considers nothing else, while Sebold himself claims that "[t]odo lo que no deriva de las fuentes señaladas por Armistead es creación de Bécquer" [whatever does not derive from the sources indicated by Armistead is Bécquer's creation] (Sebold 1989, 52).

4. It would be both impractical and hopelessly pedantic to give bibliographical data for each of the hundreds of meme tokens that appear in this essay. It is, however, appropriate to note that my collection of dead hands began with Noël Carroll's article (1987, 55–56).

5. A welcome and subtle exception is Werner Sollors's "The Bluish Tinge in the Halfmoons; or Fingernails as a Racial Sign: The Study of a Motif," in Bremond, Landry, and Pavel (1995, 69–88).

6. I should not fail to mention two studies of memes that I would identify as such despite their authors' presumed unfamiliarity with the neologism. These are Robert Pogue Harrison's *Forests: The Shadow of Civilization* (1992), a masterful study of the Dark Forest meme in human history (one I have myself studied with very different examples), and Geoffrey K. Pullum's "The Great Eskimo Vocabulary Hoax" (1989), which is about the myth, so beloved by linguists, that Eskimos have astounding numbers of words for "snow." Be it noted that Pullum's "unmasking" of this "alien loose on the ship" (his metaphor) has had little effect. Serious and popular examples of the meme still proliferate.

Aaron Lynch's *Thought Contagion* was published in October 1996, just after this volume had gone to press. Lynch's work, like mine, was generated by Dawkins's neologism, and it too attempts to develop the concept for cultural study. Timing has made it impossible for me to allude to Lynch's book in the body of this essay. Lynch's work and mine are entirely complementary, however, and duplication is minimal. We are writing for very different audiences.

7. George Basalla's *The Evolution of Technology* (1988) parallels the concern for evolution in the scholarship of Dawkins and Dennett but in the field of invention, from the wheel to the atomic power plant, seen as a continuous process. The concept of "intertext," whether or not the word itself is used, has been transforming many disciplines simultaneously.

8. Rosen's book (1995), which appeared after the experience referred to, mentions Verdi's anapestic figure and compares it to a like one in the *Requiem* of Hector Berlioz.

9. Dennett discusses a humorous example of this phenomenon in his "Memes and the Exploitation of Imagination" (1990b, 132).

10. The editors of this volume are old friends but also talented and supremely accomplished professionals who have the highest editorial standards. My gratitude to them is beyond expression, but I am able to promise them never again to hyphenate a compound word without a twinge of guilt. In the spirit of a collection of articles on the subject of

intertextuality, and as a gesture of appreciation, each of the contributors to this volume will find embedded in my essay a phrase taken without attribution from his or her own published work.

I should also like to thank the many friends who helped with the task of harvesting meme tokens, especially Jeanne Brownlow, Harlan Sturm, Angel Loureiro, Richard Hall, Jaime Martínez-Tolentino, Tamara Al-Kasey, and Timothy Boudreau. There is not as yet—and may never be—a methodology for capturing units of culture on the wing. Theodore Ziolkowski provided a practical guide for students of thematics in his *Varieties of Literary Thematics* (1983, 201–27). I cannot follow suit; there seems to be no way to "research" a meme. My collection method is simply to "read" broadly in all kinds of texts (not just written ones) and to keep a file of examples as each potentially significant meme—virginity, foundation plantings, heresy, tipping, paisley, the good death, sonata form, Roman numerals, "Stone walls do not a prison make," orchestral weeping, conspiracies, angels, dying during the sex act, O vs. zero in spoken numbers, hunting—shows itself and the multiplicity of tokens reveals the cultural contours (history, geography, semantics, motivation, etc.) of that meme and its part in the culture that creates our minds.

Works Cited

Armistead, Samuel G. 1989. "Sobre el 'Romance de la mano muerta.'" In *Bécquer en sus narraciones fantásticas*, by Russell P. Sebold, 211–16. Madrid: Taurus.

Barber, Paul. 1988. *Vampires, Burial, and Death: Folklore and Reality*. New Haven: Yale University Press.

Basalla, George. 1988. *The Evolution of Technology*. Cambridge: Cambridge University Press.

Benítez, Rubén, ed. 1974. *Leyendas, Apólogos y otros relatos*, by Gustavo Adolfo Bécquer. Barcelona: Labor.

Bremond, Claude, Joshua Landy, and Thomas Pavel, eds. 1995. *Thematics: New Approaches*. Albany: State University of New York Press.

Budden, Julian. 1992. *The Operas of Verdi*. Rev. ed. Vol. 2. Oxford: Clarendon Press.

Campbell, Joseph. 1949. *The Hero with a Thousand Faces*. Princeton: Princeton University Press.

Carroll, Noël. 1987. "The Nature of Horror." *Journal of Aesthetics and Art Criticism* 46: 51–59.

Csikszentmihalyi, Mihaly. 1990. "Memes vs. Genes: Notes from the Culture Wars." In *Speculations*. Ed. John Brockman, 209–26. New York: Prentice-Hall.

Culler, Jonathan. 1992. "Literary Theory." In *Introduction to Scholarship in Modern Languages and Literatures*. Ed. Joseph Gibaldi, 201–35. 2nd ed. New York: MLA.

Dahlbom, Bo, ed. 1993. *Dennett and His Critics*. London: Routledge.

Dawkins, Richard. 1976. *The Selfish Gene*. New York: Oxford University Press.

———. 1981. "In Defence of Selfish Genes." *Philosophy* 56: 556–73.

———. 1982. *The Extended Phenotype*. San Francisco: Freeman.

———. 1986. *The Blind Watchmaker*. New York: Norton.

de Man, Paul. 1988. "The Resistance to Theory." In *Modern Criticism and Theory*. Ed. David Lodge, 355–71. London: Longman.

Dennett, Daniel C. 1990a. "The Evolution of Consciousness." In *Speculations*. Ed. John Brockman, 85–108. New York: Prentice-Hall.

———. 1990b. "Memes and the Exploitation of Imagination." *Journal of Aesthetics and Art Criticism* 48: 127–35.

———. 1991. *Consciousness Explained*. Boston: Little, Brown.

———. 1995. *Darwin's Dangerous Idea*. New York: Simon and Schuster.

Franklin, H. Bruce. 1993. *M.I.A. or Mythmaking in America*. New Brunswick: Rutgers University Press.

Gould, Stephen J. 1996. "Why Darwin?" *New York Review,* 6 April, pp. 10–14.

Harrison, Robert Pogue. 1992. *Forests: The Shadow of Civilization*. Chicago: University of Chicago Press.

Heidel, William A. 1933. "A Suggestion Concerning Plato's Atlantis." *Proceedings of the American Academy of Arts and Sciences* 68: 206–39.

Holt, Edgar. 1967. *The Carlist Wars in Spain*. London: Putnam.

Kirkpatrick, Ken. 1995. "The Conspiracy of the Miscellaneous in *Foucault's Pendulum*." *Studies in Twentieth-Century Literature* 19: 171–84.

Lynch, Aaron. 1996. *Thought Contagion: How Belief Spreads Through Society*. New York: Basic Books.

Midgely, Mary. 1979. "Gene Juggling." *Philosophy* 54: 439–58.

Miller, J. Hillis. 1989. "The Figure in the Carpet." In *Modern Literary Theory: A Reader*. Ed. Philip Rice and Patricia Waugh, 172–85. London: Edward Arnold.

Nietzsche, Friedrich. 1968. *The Portable Nietzsche*. Trans. Walter Kaufmann. New York: Viking.

Obeyesekere, Gananath. 1992. "'British Cannibals': Contemplation of an Event in the Death and Resurrection of James Cook, Explorer." *Critical Inquiry* 18: 630–54.

Parini, Joe. 1995. "The Greening of the Humanities." *New York Times Magazine,* 29 October, pp. 52–53.

Prince, Gerald. 1988. "Introduction to the Study of the Narratee." In *Essentials of the Theory of Fiction*. Ed. Michael Hoffman and Patrick Murphy, 313–35. Durham, N.C.: Duke University Press.

Pullum, Geoffrey K. 1989. "The Great Eskimo Vocabulary Hoax." *Natural Language and Linguistic Theory* 7: 275–81.

Reddell, R. C. 1994. *The Rose Bible*. New York: Harmony.

Robinson, Douglas. 1991. *The Translator's Turn*. Baltimore: Johns Hopkins University Press.

Rosen, David. 1995. *Verdi: Requiem*. Cambridge: Cambridge University Press.

Searle, John R. 1995. "The Mystery of Consciousness: Part II." *New York Review,* 16 November, pp. 54–61.

Sebold, Russell P. 1989. *Bécquer en sus narraciones fantásticas*. Madrid: Taurus.

Smith, John Maynard. 1995. "Genes, Memes, and Minds." *New York Review,* 30 November, pp. 46–48.

Sollors, Werner, ed. 1993. *The Return of Thematic Criticism*. Cambridge, Mass.: Harvard University Press.

Trommler, Frank, ed. 1995. *Thematics Reconsidered*. Amsterdam: Rodopi.

Ziolkowski, Theodore. 1983. *Varieties of Literary Thematics*. Princeton: Princeton University Press.

Contributors

MARYELLEN BIEDER, after teaching at Syracuse University and the State University of New York at Albany, joined Indiana University at Bloomington, where she is Professor of Spanish. *Narrative Perspective in the Post-Civil War Novels of Francisco Ayala* is the product of her early work on the modern Spanish novel; more recently she has devoted her critical attention to nineteenth-century women writers, including in particular Emilia Pardo Bazán but also figures whom the literary canon has neglected.

HAROLD L. BOUDREAU is Professor Emeritus of Spanish at the University of Massachusetts, Amherst. He is coeditor of Camilo José Cela's *La familia de Pascual Duarte* and *Studies in Honor of Sumner M. Greenfield* and a member of several editorial boards He has written and lectured widely on the novels of Benito Pérez Galdós, on the modern Spanish novel, especially Ramón del Valle-Inclán and Miguel de Unamuno, on contemporary Spanish poetry, and on literary theory. He is the Spanish literature editor of the *Columbia Dictionary of Modern European Literature*.

DEBRA A. CASTILLO is Professor of Romance Studies and Comparative Literature at Cornell University, where she came from the University of Tulsa. In addition to articles on a wide array of subjects, she is the author of *The Translated World: A Postmodern Tour of Libraries in Literature* and *Talking Back: Toward a Latin American Feminist Criticism*. She recently translated Federico Campbell's *Tijuana: Stories on the Border*. A forthcoming book deals with the figure of the prostitute in Mexican literature.

HAZEL GOLD, Associate Professor of Spanish at Emory University, has also taught at Columbia and Northwestern. She has published widely in the field of nineteenth-century Spanish narrative, concentrating on the key writings of Benito Pérez Galdós and Leopoldo Alas. She is the current president of the International Galdós Association. Her book *The Reframing of Realism: Galdós and the Discourses of the Nineteenth-Century Spanish Novel* appeared in 1993.

DAVID K. HERZBERGER, winner of the William Riley Parker Prize for an outstanding article in *PMLA*, recently published *Narrating the Past: Fiction and Historiography in Postwar Spain*. He taught at Marquette University before moving to the University of Connecticut, where he is Professor of Spanish. He has concentrated his work on contemporary fiction in Spain and is the author of earlier studies on Juan Benet and Jesús Fernández Santos. He is also the cocompiler of a bibliography on post-Civil War fiction.

ROBERTA JOHNSON, who specializes in Spanish narrative and thought of the early twentieth century, is Professor of Spanish and Director of the Hall Center for the Humanities at the University of Kansas, Lawrence. Previously she taught at Scripps College. She has paid particular attention to the writings of Azorín and Gabriel Miró and has developed an interest in women's writing of the modernist period. Her books include the Twayne series volume on Carmen Laforet, *El ser y la palabra en Gabriel Miró, Crossfire: Philosophy and the Novel in Spain, 1900–1934*, and an annotated catalogue of the libraries of Azorín.

ANGEL G. LOUREIRO is Professor of Spanish at the University of Massachusetts, Amherst. The modern Spanish novel and autobiography stand out among his many interests. He has written or edited several books and a special issue of a journal, among them *Mentira y seducción: la trilogía fantástica de Torrente Ballester*, *La autobiografía y sus problemas teóricos*, and *El gran desafío: feminismos, autobiografía y sus problemas teóricos*.

GONZALO NAVAJAS, Professor of Spanish at the University of California, Irvine, has published extensively on subjects dealing with modern narrative, literary theory, cultural criticism, and film. His books, in addition to two novels, include *La novela de Juan Goytisolo, Mímesis y cultura en la ficción: teoría de la novela, Teoría y práctica de la novela española posmoderna, Unamuno desde la posmodernidad: antinomia y síntesis ontológica*, and *Más allá de la posmodernidad: estética de la nueva novela y cine españoles*.

RANDOLPH D. POPE is Professor of Romance Languages and of Comparative Literature at Washington University, St. Louis. He has also taught in Germany and at Dartmouth and Vassar Colleges and was Director of the Middlebury College Spanish Summer School for four years. His research interests include both Latin American and Peninsular literature and have regularly focused on autobiography. He is the author of *La autobiografía española hasta Torres Villarroel, Novela de emergencia: España, 1939–1954*, and *Understanding Juan Goytisolo*.

ROBERT C. SPIRES has taught at Ohio University and is now Professor of Spanish at the University of Kansas. His panoramic appraisal of twentieth-century Spanish fiction is grounded in modern critical theory and includes *La novela española de posguerra, Beyond the Metafictional Mode: Directions in the Modern Spanish Novel, Transparent Simulacra: Spanish Fiction 1902–1926*, and, most recently, *Post-Totalitarian Spanish Fiction* (University of Missouri Press, 1996), which includes a modified version of his essay in this volume.

AKIKO TSUCHIYA, Associate Professor in the Department of Romance Languages at Washington University, St. Louis, taught previously at Purdue Univesity. She is the author of *Images of the Sign: Semiotic Consciousness in the Novels of Benito Pérez Galdós* and, with the support of an NEH fellowship, is currently completing a book-length study on Spanish women writers of the post-Franco era.

DIANE F. UREY is Professor of Spanish at Illinois State University and former Chair of the Department of Foreign Languages. She has devoted most of her scholarly attention to Benito Pérez Galdós, to whose fiction she has brought fresh critical perspectives in articles and papers and in her *Galdós and the Irony of Language*. More recently, she has focused on Galdós's series of historical novels in *The Novel Histories of Galdós* and the forthcoming *Galdós and the New Reader*.

Index